AMERICAN
PUBLIC
POLICY
IN A
COMPARATIVE
CONTEXT

AMERICAN PUBLIC POLICY IN A COMPARATIVE CONTEXT

•A15042 786984

Howard M. Leichter
Linfield College

Harrell R. Rodgers, Jr.
University of Houston

McGRAW-HILL BOOK COMPANY

New York   St. Louis   San Francisco   Auckland   Bogotá
Hamburg   Johannesburg   London   Madrid   Mexico   Montreal   New Delhi
Panama   Paris   São Paulo   Singapore   Sydney   Tokyo   Toronto

This book was set in Optima by Monotype Composition Company, Inc. (ECU).
The editors were Christina Mediate and Barry Benjamin;
the production supervisor was Diane Renda.
The cover photograph and design were done by Infield, D'Astolfo Associates.
R. R. Donnelley & Sons Company was printer and binder.

AMERICAN PUBLIC POLICY IN A COMPARATIVE CONTEXT

1 2 3 4 5 6 7 8 9 0   DOCDOC   8 9 8 7 6 5 4

ISBN 0-07-037067-2

Library of Congress Cataloging in Publication Data

Leichter, Howard M.
    American public policy in a comparative context.

    Includes index.
    1. Policy sciences. 2. United States—Politics and
government. 3. Comparative government. I. Rodgers,
Harrell R. II. Title.
H97.L44 1984   361.6'1'0973   83-16242
ISBN 0-07-037067-2

To the memory of
Bertha and Hyman Leichter
and
James and Virginia Parsons

CONTENTS

PREFACE

This book grew out of two problems, as perceived by the authors, in the teaching and study of public policy in American colleges and universities. The first is the inadequate attention paid to, and understanding of, the public problems and policy responses of nations similar to our own. In Chapter 1 we suggest several reasons why a cross-national or comparative perspective on American public policy is intellectually and practically desirable. Without completely preempting that discussion, we would simply note here that all of the policy issues and attendant problems discussed in this book—i.e., crime, poverty, housing, education, health care, the economy, and women's rights—have been or are being confronted in other nations. It simply makes good sense for students of, citizens affected by, and those who make public policy in this country to be attentive to the successes and failures of other comparable nations in dealing with these issues so that we may all make more intelligent decisions.

The second problem we address in this book is the general neglect of divergent ideological perspectives on public policy issues. Most books and courses are either simply descriptive (e.g., "American welfare policy includes the following programs . . .") or are implicitly or explicitly biased in one ideological direction or another (e.g., "The United States should adopt national health insurance because it is the only decent thing to do"). There is a need and place for both of these approaches to the study of public policy. However, there is also a need for an approach which exposes students to the sincere and legitimate policy preferences of conservatives and liberals on these issues. We have written this book with the intention of providing a balanced treatment of both conservative and liberal perspectives on several critical issues, and allowing the reader to make up his or her own mind as to the preferability and efficacy of each.

Finally, it is with pleasure that we take this opportunity to acknowledge those people whose aid and support made this project possible. A number of talented and generous colleagues at the University of Houston and Linfield College read and critiqued one or more chapters. University of Houston Professors Paul DeGregori (Economics); William Nelson (Philosophy); Malcolm Goggin, Richard Hofstetter, and Alan Stone (all of Political Science); and Doug Cruikshank (Education) of Linfield College, offered sound professional advice with both patience and good humor. We hope that the final product reflects in some way their efforts and wisdom.

We would also like to thank the following colleagues who reviewed the manuscript for McGraw-Hill: Professors Jill Clark (University of Texas, Arlington), George C. Edwards, III (Texas A & M University), Virginia Gray (University of Minnesota), and Kathleen Kemp (Florida State University). The extraordinarily careful and constructive criticism offered by these very fine scholars significantly improved our final product. We hope they each understand that their advice sometimes conflicted, leaving us to search for a middle ground or arbitrate a complex issue. This is an uncomfortable but inevitable product of the review process. In the final analysis, the thought provoked by these conflicts helped produce a better volume.

The authors also were fortunate in having a number of very able people who mastered the simple mysteries of our computers and the complex mysteries of our handwriting to produce an electronic recording of the manuscript. To Maxine Leo, Gregory and Becky Taylor, and Lisa Sewell we owe a considerable thanks. Lynn Chmelir and Michael Engle provided very able and patient library assistance.

As always, our greatest debt is to our families. Elisabeth, Laurel, Alexandra, and Lynne each gave love, support, and assistance in her own beautiful and nourishing way. They know that we could not have completed this project without their special contribution.

Howard M. Leichter
Harrell R. Rodgers, Jr.

CHAPTER 1

PUBLIC POLICY IN A COMPARATIVE PERSPECTIVE

In July 1981 there was an interesting exchange of views over the issue of gun control between two U.S. congressmen, John Ashbrook and Peter Rodino, Jr. The remarks, which were introduced into the *Congressional Record,* are instructive not only for their content but because they serve to introduce the central concerns of this book.

Mr. Ashbrook, a conservative Republican from Ohio, began by noting that "those who want gun control are endlessly telling us about countries with strong gun control laws and few gun-related crimes. And they never mention Switzerland." The Ohio Republican went on to explain that Switzerland has the lowest number of gun-related crimes in Europe, yet "every adult male in Switzerland is not only allowed, but required to have a gun and know how to use it." Furthermore, "they may carry them wherever they want to, so long as they are not used for criminal purposes." What bothered Mr. Ashbrook was that "when the gun grabbers start praising strict weapons laws," they ignore Switzerland. Mr. Ashbrook felt that more emphasis should be placed upon the enforcement of existing laws rather than, as he sees it, the infringement of Constitutional rights.[1]

One week later Congressman Rodino, a liberal Democrat from New Jersey, who is an advocate and author of gun-control legislation, responded to the remarks of Mr. Ashbrook. Rodino was prompted by his colleague's remarks to look further into the Swiss case. The Swiss Embassy in Washington provided Rodino with a report entitled "Gun Control in Switzerland." Summarizing the report, the New Jersey Democrat noted:

It reveals, for instance, that military authorities keep an exact record of all military rifles and pistols kept in the homes of Swiss militia members. It also reveals that, although there is no national gun-control law, all the cantons (states) have restrictions and that there is an intercantonal "concordat" on controls to which all cantons are parties. This pact required licensing of all who sell firearms or ammunition and licensing of buyers, with restrictions on those who can be licensed. Dealers must keep detailed records of each sale.[2]

There are, in short, considerable restrictions on, and monitoring of, firearms in Switzerland.

It should be noted here that this exchange solved nothing: no new legislation resulted. Mr. Ashbrook continued until his death in 1982 to be a devoted opponent of gun-control legislation and Mr. Rodino an equally committed advocate of restricting the manufacture, sale, and purchase of handguns. The dialogue is useful, however, for it introduces two increasingly common features of the policy-making process of this and other nations. It would be useful at this point to briefly mention these features and then elaborate upon each.

The first is that public policy debates are increasingly characterized by disputes over the very fundamental issue of the appropriateness of governmental intervention. Clearly there are implicit in this debate two very different views of government. For Mr. Rodino, one answer to the problem of violent crime is for the government to restrict access to a main instrument of that type of crime. Mr. Ashbrook, on the other hand, like most conservatives, viewed such restrictions as unwarranted assertions of governmental authority, a further erosion of individual liberty, and something that will not work.

Who is right—Mr. Rodino or Mr. Ashbrook? We do not know. Our purpose in this book is not to supply simple answers to complex policy problems. Indeed, one of the points made in this book is that policy makers in this country, and elsewhere, confront problems for which there frequently are no self-evident truths. What there are, are different perceptions, based upon different political values and experiences, of what can and should be done about certain societal problems. One should not assume, of course, that government is responsible for dealing with all such problems. In fact, throughout the world, national debates have become less concerned with choosing among alternative public policy options and more concerned with the issue of whether government should act at all. The appropriate role of government, rather than the appropriate policy option, has become the focus of much political discourse.

The Ashbrook-Rodino exchange demonstrates a second increasingly common feature of policy making in this and other countries. It is quite common for policy makers to look to other nations for policy inspiration, guidance, and assistance. The reasons for this comparative approach to policy making are discussed below. The point that we wish to make at this juncture is that because the policy-making process often is comparative, both students of and citizens affected by public policy must enlarge their perspective to include an understanding of the policies of other nations.

This book then is intended to raise the level of consciousness and understanding of students to the worldwide debate over the appropriate role of government in society, as well as the appropriateness of specific policy solutions to certain public problems. We are suggesting that an understanding of the more general issue (i.e., "the role of government") and the more specific ones (e.g., "gun control") is best served by doing what policy makers in this country do—look at the experiences of other nations. We can now look at each of these features of the policy-making process—the debate over the appropriateness of governmental action and a comparative approach to policy making—in more detail.

IS GOVERNMENT THE PROBLEM OR THE SOLUTION?

On January 20, 1981, Ronald Reagan was sworn in as the fortieth President of the United States. In his Inaugural Address, President Reagan spoke of "an economic affliction of great proportions" which confronted the United States. However, unlike most of his predecessors over the past nearly one-half century, the President did not promise to bring the resources of the national government to bear on this crisis. Quite the contrary. "In this present crisis," he said, "government is not the solution to our problem; government is the problem." The President's remark goes to the heart of a debate that spans centuries and continents. What is the appropriate role of government? And what are the implications of governmental intervention? Some, like Ronald Reagan and Prime Minister Margaret Thatcher of Great Britain, echo the words of Ralph Waldo Emerson that "the less government there is, the better." Others, however, believe that the ultimate responsibility for the well-being of society and particularly its most vulnerable segments rests with government. While the issue goes back centuries, there have been few times in history when it has been so deliberately confronted in so many different countries and with such diverse results. In the late 1970s and early 1980s the people of Australia, Great Britain, Norway, and the United States looked to the political right, while those in France and Greece looked to the left for solutions to their nations' problems. What does all this mean? And should we as citizens of the United States care what others do? To answer the latter question first, we obviously feel that we should care. What other nations do, and how they do it, affects our lives just as what we do affects theirs. We will have more to say about this shortly.

What does it all mean? From a historical perspective it may represent yet another critical period in the development of the modern nation-state in which the relationship between the individual, society, and the state will undergo a fundamental investigation, and perhaps change, in various countries of the world. From the less profound, but no less important, perspective of individual U.S. citizens (or French citizens, or Greeks) it may represent important changes in their daily lives. In order to place both the historical and personal implications of the issue of what role government should play in society in perspective, we would like to do two things in this section. The first is to lead a brief guided tour through history to explain where we have come from in terms of the role of government in society. The second is to look at the political discourse which has sought to explain and justify different views of the role of government.

The Evolution of the Modern State[3]

The modern nation-state emerged in the course of the sixteenth to eighteenth centuries. It was during this time that the nation-state acquired the characteristic form of a centralized authority (or state), able to exercise reasonably consistent control over a relatively well-defined territory and population (or nation). In addition, it was during this period that many of the activities we now associate with state activity made their first appearance. In fact, it is with considerable surprise that many students discover that sixteenth- through eighteenth-century rulers issued edicts (i.e., public policy) concerning antipoverty and antipollution measures, consumer protection, minority rights, urban development, the military draft, and veterans' benefits.[4] In a great many respects the state intervened in society in as wide a range of areas 300 years ago as it does today. But let us be a bit more specific about this newly emerging political entity called the nation-state. Clearly, given the number of political units and length of time involved, great variation in state involvement occurred, so that a definitive characterization would be impossible. Nevertheless, certain general features are discernible.

To begin, the primary and preoccupying function of the early modern state (i.e., during the sixteenth and seventeenth centuries) was to provide the individual and society protection from external enemies and disruptive forces within society. This, in turn, would ensure the appropriate environment for developing a prosperous national economy. It was in fulfilling this primary state function that many of the activities engaged in by governments were undertaken and justified during the formative years of the modern nation-state. It is only a slight overstatement to suggest that most of the other state activities, in large part, were exercised in order to fulfill the national defense and public order obligations of state.

Perhaps the most obvious and important of these activities was the development of public taxation and finance systems. According to one authority, the modern state "arose in the 16th century and after, primarily out of the needs of the princes and monarchs of the European states to pay the expenses of war. . . . Taxes thus came to be levied, and a bureaucratic administrative system arose to collect, and then spend these monies."[5] The above comment applies equally to most of the traditional eighteenth century kingdoms of Asia where regional warfare and tax collection were the two main activities of state. Raising adequate revenues stretched the ingenuity of the ruler, the activities of the state, and the frequency with which public authority and private individuals came into contact. And it was a major source of popular discontent. Chroniclers of this period tell of frequent peasant revolts and urban riots over yet another levy to support yet another war. Taxpayers' revolts were not invented in California in the 1970s. A major political accusation of that time, as well as our own, was that the tax system was unfair and burdensome.

Another feature which our era shares with this earlier time was extensive and elaborate government regulations which affected virtually every facet of life. It was, in fact, in regulating socioeconomic behavior that the early state became most intimately involved with the largest number of people. To a considerable extent many of these regulations were intended to support the war-making and order-maintenance capacity of the state. Thus, for example, most states established policies regulating the production, storage, and distribution of food grains so that the state was guaranteed supplies to feed the military even during times of food shortages. In addition, traditional rulers "recognized very clearly the connection between hunger and peasant rebellions"[6] and used such food stores to prevent internal disorders during poor crop years.

But the regulatory policies of the traditional state were motivated by other than national defense and internal order concerns of the state. The prevailing paternalistic concept of monarchical rule dictated that rulers provide for the general well-being of their subjects. This concern led to the most incredibly detailed and wide-ranging regulations of economic activity including "minute rules concerning the quality of hops and malt in brewing, the size of buckets, the type of materials to be used in the manufacture of thread, leather, soap, glass, tobacco and a host of other products." Similarly, in seventeenth- and eighteenth-century France, there were laws "establishing minimal levels of salt consumption and prescribing the number of threads in the warp of a piece of fabric."[7]

State economic regulatory activity during this period was above all committed to the promotion and protection of newly developing national economies.[8] This tendency of the traditional state to intervene in the economic life of a society entailed grandiose efforts aimed at regulating the very nature of a nation's industries, its supply of precious metals and raw materials, and its international trade balance. In large measure, the laws described above specifying the quality and quantity of ingredients for various products (e.g., leather, thread, soap) were an attempt by the state to ensure the quality, hence salability and competitiveness, of exported goods. Collectively, these protectionist policies were part of an economic doctrine, later called "mercantilism" (or cameralism in Germany), which dominated much of Europe in the sixteenth through eighteenth centuries. Mercantilism again illustrates the length to which the early modern state intervened in the individual and collective life of the nation.

There is one final issue in which the early state became involved, and one which provides a useful reminder of the timelessness of certain social problems. We refer here to social welfare. The paternalistic concept of government, buttressed in Europe by the tenets of Christian morality, was well suited to the development of state-supported welfare or poor-relief programs during this period. By the seventeenth century, virtually every European state had some sort of centrally established public welfare program. As in other policy areas, there was considerable variation in control and operation among programs. Nevertheless, certain distinguishing and common philosophical assumptions and substantive elements could be found in most European welfare systems. The most noteworthy of these features deserve attention because in them we find some direct links to our own modern concept of welfare.

The first point to emphasize is that the motivation behind early welfare systems was not exclusively paternalistic or religious. In many instances, relief for the poor was an exercise of the state's police power. It was simply another instrument for dealing with the problem of maintaining law and order. Throughout this period, in Europe and elsewhere, landless peasants, persons uprooted by war, and returning and unemployed soldiers resorted to vagrancy, begging, stealing, and extortion to support themselves. In an effort to get these people off the streets, reduce crime, and keep them physically apart from the more respectable members of society, welfare or poor-relief systems were established.

A second common feature of early poor-relief systems was the legal distinction between categories or types of needy persons. The primary distinction was between those who were legitimately poor (e.g., the aged, insane, blind, or otherwise physically handicapped) and the able-bodied scoundrels, rogues, and professional beggars who refused honest work. From the very beginning welfare was deemed justified only in cases of severe disability.

A third feature of pre-nineteenth-century welfare systems was the assumption of local responsibility for the poor and needy. Although early welfare laws were centrally promulgated, they were typically financed and/ or administered by local governments. Such responsibility was rarely welcomed by local authorities, who were increasingly burdened by these financial obligations and who were therefore encouraging recipients to leave their jurisdiction. The dispute between local versus central responsibility for welfare programs, an issue of considerable current concern in the United States, has a long tradition.

The final noteworthy feature of these programs was that acceptance of public relief carried with it considerable social stigma, marking the recipient as socially inferior. In some cases, most notably in England, a person who received public assistance became "pauperized" and, therefore, ineligible to perform various civil functions. In addition, paupers often were sent to workhouses. Not only social but legal sanctions were imposed on those who had to turn to public welfare assistance.

Thus far we have tried to demonstrate that the range of state activity during the sixteenth through eighteenth centuries was quite extensive. Indeed, in some cases it was apparently as comprehensive as that of the twentieth-century modern nation-state. Nevertheless it is important to point out one fundamental difference between the role of the state during this period compared to our own. Traditional rulers often found it difficult, and in some instances impossible, to enforce their policies. While the reasons for this are complex, two factors stand out. The first was the absence of a fully developed modern bureaucracy to administer, oversee, and enforce the wishes of the ruler. The second and related factor was the absence of the necessary communications and transportation facilities to enforce the will of the state. The reader should not conclude, however, that the early state was completely impotent. Obviously European and Asian rulers collected sufficient revenues, raised large enough armies, and regulated enough behavior to support themselves and protect their nations. Nevertheless, there is this important difference in the enforcement capability of the traditional and fully modern state.

In sum, the image that emerges from this brief account of the early modern state is one in which government was actively involved in a full range of regulatory, extractive (e.g., taxation, conscription), and distributive policies. The early state is distinguished from the current social welfare state less in its assumption of the appropriate role of government than in its ability to enforce its will.

Laissez Faire: The Nineteenth-Century Attack on the Active State

In the nineteenth century the concepts of mercantilism and state activism that had characterized state behavior in the sixteenth through eighteenth centuries came under attack and, in many cases, were superseded by a new philosophy: the limited state. The set of ideas that supported this view was summarized by the phrase "laissez faire" or "laissez nous faire" ("let it be" or "let us alone") and was first advocated by English and French philosophers and economists during the late eighteenth and early nineteenth centuries.

The concept of laissez faire as articulated in the nineteenth century denoted a doctrine that opposed intervention by the state in the economic activities of a nation. It was predicated on the assumption that society and the economy were governed by "laws of nature" that imposed a "natural order and harmony" on life. Any tampering or interference by the state would upset this natural order. The state was to play a minimal role: to provide for the national defense, preserve internal order, and generally create an environment conducive to the operation of a free and competitive marketplace. Beyond this, the state was to withdraw and allow the laws of nature to operate.

The implications and prescription of laissez faire were clear: the mercantilist, interventionist policies of the sixteenth through eighteenth centuries interfered with the natural economic order. The writings of Adam Smith, and particularly his famous *Inquiry into the Nature and Causes of the Wealth of Nations* (1776), provided much of the basis for, and exerted enormous influence over, subsequent conservative doctrine—we will return to Adam Smith and his current disciples shortly.

The implications of laissez faire extended beyond the realm of economic policy and activity. Just as the advocates of laissez faire condemned state interference in the economy (except where it served their purpose), so too did they attack the social aspects associated with traditional state paternalism. Here again they argued that the laws of nature must operate unfettered by state interference. For example, advocates condemned the poor laws in England and elsewhere as an unnecessary and unwise interference with the social order. Thomas Malthus rejected the poor laws on the basis that poor people were "themselves the cause of their own poverty; that the means of redress are in their own hands, and in the hands of no other person whatever; that the society in which they live and government which presides over it, are without any direct power in this respect."[9] The notion that poverty is the result of personal defects rather than economic conditions or policies and, therefore, not a legitimate concern of the state was widely held in the nineteenth century.

The doctrine of laissez faire was consistent with the needs of the industrial revolution. The old mercantilist system that advocated controlling market forces—labor, trade, competition, capital, etc.—appeared to obstruct industrial growth and its requirements for a mobile labor force, free flow of capital, economic competition, and easy access to world markets and materials. Laissez faire emphasized natural laws and individual rights, rejected government paternalism and intervention, and, therefore, appeared better suited to the needs of the new economic order.

Although never fully adopted as the sole guide for formulating public policy, even in England, laissez faire did have a profound impact on the framework within which policy was made in England, on the Continent, and in the United States during the nineteenth century. The limited state, self-help, and individual liberty were exalted. It was in this atmosphere that industrial growth and the colonization of much of Asia and Africa took place. And it is to this period that modern conservative economists (e.g., Milton Friedman) and political practitioners (e.g., Margaret Thatcher and Ronald Reagan) turn to as a model of appropriate governmental behavior.

Historically, however, what occurred during the nineteenth century in the more advanced nations was that as industrialization proceeded it left in its wake a changing social, economic, and political environment. And, just as mercantilism and traditional paternalism appeared incompatible with or detrimental to industrialization, so too did laissez faire begin to appear inadequate in the face of political and social consequences of industrialization. Thus, by the latter part of the nineteenth century, a revised concept of state began to appear. This concept, embraced in theory and enshrined in constitutions, although not always in practice, was the idea of the general-welfare state. In a sense, the general-welfare state concept marked a revitalization of the active state concept. We now turn to an examination of its origins and manifestations.

The Emergence of the Positive State

The shift from a primarily agrarian to a primarily industrial economic base produced, and continues to produce, extraordinary social dislocations and profound social and economic changes.

Industrialization is a process that both requires and produces fundamental social change. Among its primary requirements is a relatively large and mobile labor force. Typically, the labor for industrial societies was recruited from rural populations within the nation itself (e.g., England, France, Germany, and Japan) or from abroad (e.g., the United States, Singapore, and Australia). The process of supplying the labor needs of industrialization in this manner caused an urban explosion. Between 1850 and 1900 cities such as Amsterdam, Berlin, Brussels, Chicago, London, Paris, Saint Petersburg, and Vienna, to name just a few, had population increases between 100 and 300 percent or more.

The nature and magnitude of the social changes that accompanied urbanization were even more dramatic. To begin with, housing conditions in the new industrial towns were deplorable. Overcrowded, rat-infested tenements could not accommodate the rapidly growing urban population. As a result, flimsy and unsafe structures were crowded even closer together, and all available "living" space, including hallways and cellars, was used.

Such overcrowded conditions produced serious public health and sanitation problems. There were inadequate supplies of safe water and food; infant and maternal mortality rates soared; cholera, typhus, and other epidemics were common in the nineteenth century throughout Europe and Asia. All these problems were exacerbated by the inadequacy or nonexistence of sewage and waste removal facilities. Human waste was frequently disposed of in the streets. Urban crime, in the absence of modern police forces, soared.

The movement from rural to urban areas caused another fundamental social change, one that further contributed to the hardships of urban life. Here we are referring to the decline of the extended family structure. In an extended family—parents, grandparents, married children, and their families—the welfare of the individual is the direct concern and responsibility of the family as a unit. During difficult periods, such as those involving physical injury, ill health, economic hardship, or marital disputes, it is the family in traditional agrarian society that provides social and economic security. The family also is expected to provide for the welfare of those in positions of "natural dependency": children, pregnant women, and old persons. The movement to cities often separated families and caused the breakdown of the extended family. Thus, urbanization helped undermine one of the very institutions that could have absorbed some of the shocks accompanying major social and economic dislocations.

Whereas many of the hardships of the nineteenth century derived from the urbanizing process, others could be directly attributed to the employment environment in industrial enterprises. Here the problems involved unsafe and unsanitary working conditions, and the use of young children as labor in mines and factories. From whatever source, the human costs of the industrial revolution were enormous.

During the course of the nineteenth century, it became clear to many that the social and economic dislocations and human misery spawned by industrialization required remedial action beyond that which was provided by private charities, existing poor laws, or "invisible hands." Increasingly there were calls for the state to provide protection, not only against external enemies and internal lawlessness, but also against the evils and insecurities of industrialization. Initially governments, when they responded at all, did so in gradual, piecemeal fashion. In the late nineteenth century, there was not as yet a coherent theory of a positive state that was committed to the general welfare. Only in the twentieth century would such a commitment emerge.

In the course of the nineteenth century, the governments of industrializing nations, hoping to maintain the national loyalty of the emerging and politically powerful urban working class (i.e., the proletariat), began introducing public health, labor, education, and social insurance legislation.

Government became actively involved in protecting individuals from the various problems and uncertainties associated with an urban, industrial environment. This protection was guaranteed the people not through Christian charity or paternalism, but because it was viewed as a right of citizenship. By the second decade of the twentieth century, the idea that the state exists to promote the interests and welfare of all its citizens had become established in theory, if not in fact, in most of the world.

In recent years, however, many of the assumptions and activities of the general-welfare state, much like those of its distant but recognizable relative, the early modern state, have come under attack. And, as was the case in the nineteenth century, it is the advocates of laissez faire or classical conservatism who have raised the issue of the appropriateness of state intervention to solve social problems. It is a debate, as we suggested above, which has been going on for generations. By the early part of the nineteenth century, in many countries, the debate was "won" in a practical sense by the proponents of the limited state: let the laws of nature operate unfettered and people and society will prosper. The debate was rekindled in the latter part of the nineteenth century following the enormous changes accompanying industrialization. In much of the industrialized world the proponents of the active, general-welfare state prevailed: the government must act to guarantee not only collective security but individual security and well-being. Today, the issue is once again being actively debated, not only by political theorists but by citizens and politicians. It is not clear, at the time of this writing, whether this debate too will (or can) herald in yet another era of limited government in our country or others. One thing, however, is certain; it will not be the last time such a debate will occur.

TWO VIEWS OF GOVERNMENT

It would be useful at this point to summarize the essence of this current debate. While there are certainly many important underlying philosophical issues involved—e.g., What is the nature of human beings?—in everyday political discourse and activity, the issue really comes down to the fundamental question of: What is the appropriate role of government? Should government be the ultimate guarantor of the well-being of its citizens, ensuring them adequate education, housing, income, jobs, health care, protection against economic uncertainty, and so on? Or are some or all of these the responsibility of the private sector? While we could not possibly answer all of the issues involved in this most fundamental of political debates, in the next few pages we would like to examine some general orientations toward this issue. In subsequent chapters we will look at specific areas of concern and see the responses, in a policy sense, of our government and those of other countries.

The two orientations or viewpoints which are presented below are those of the U.S. (and to a certain extent, Western European) political left and right. In the context of U.S. politics the terms "liberal" and "conservative" are used to describe and identify these orientations. There are, to be sure, important differences within each perspective—e.g., "old guard" conservatives like Barry Goldwater and Ronald Reagan, neoconservatives like Jeane Kirkpatrick and Irving Kristol, and "new right" conservatives like Reverend Jerry Falwell and Richard Viguerie—and these differences are often substantial. Nevertheless, while it clearly does some damage to reality to speak of either the U.S. political left or right as if they were monolithic, there is a good deal of common ground within each orientation. In this book we will use a sort of composite or idealized model of each perspective. Rather than litter the text with qualifiers such as "many," "most," or "some" (e.g., "Many conservatives oppose ERA"), we simply alert the reader here to the fact that not all liberals or all conservatives subscribe to all views associated with their particular orientation.

The View from the Right

Modern conservatism, whose genesis can be traced back to the writings of Adam Smith and Edmund Burke in the latter part of the eighteenth century, has been remarkably consistent in its overall view of the role of government. Adam Smith, in what has to be one of the most frequently quoted statements in the English language, wrote the following description of the appropriate role of government:

> According to the system of natural liberty the sovereign has only three duties to attend to; three duties of great importance, indeed, but plain and intelligible to common understanding: first, the duty of protecting the society from the violence and invasion of other independent societies; secondly, the duty of protecting, as far as possible, every member of the society from the injustice or oppression of other members of it, or the duty of establishing an exact administration of justice; and, thirdly, the duty of erecting and maintaining certain public works and certain public institutions. . . . [10]

Almost 200 years later, Barry Goldwater, a leading U.S.conservative, wrote that the legitimate functions of government are "maintaining internal order, keeping foreign foes at bay, administering justice, [and] removing obstacles to the free exchange of goods. . . ."[11] And, finally, Paul Johnson, a British journalist and prominent conservative, maintains that there are "three essential activities of government. First, the state has an absolute obligation to protect the nation's territorial and political integrity. Second, it must maintain internal order and administer justice impartially among its citizens. Third, it must issue and maintain a legal currency."[12]

For conservatives on both sides of the Atlantic, then, the message over the last 200 years has been clear, precise, and consistent. The activities of government should be limited to national defense, internal order, administering justice, and providing conditions for an effective and freely operating economy—hence Smith's concern with public works (e.g., roads, canals), Goldwater's with the free interchange of goods, and Johnson's with maintaining a legal currency.

To be sure, many practicing conservative politicians and theoreticians recognize that the changes which have occurred since Adam Smith's time may require government to go beyond these "essential" or "legitimate" functions—but not too far. Thus, according to Milton Friedman, "A fourth duty of government that Adam Smith did not explicitly mention is the duty to protect members of the community who cannot be regarded as 'responsible' individuals."[13] Aside from children, it is not clear to whom Friedman is referring (e.g., mentally ill, handicapped?). Margaret Thatcher is somewhat broader in her extension and modernization of the conservative view of government. According to Prime Minister Thatcher, "[T]he role of government in a free society should be to ensure that people can go about their business freely and without fear and to protect the weal of those in need." Prime Minister Thatcher goes on to say that "Both in Britain and in the United States the reach of government has far exceeded this limited role. Instead, governments in both countries have pursued policies of extensive and detailed intervention far beyond those one would have expected to find in a free society."[14]

Furthermore, conservatives contend that not only is government intervention beyond the essential functions of government inappropriate, it is counterproductive. "It is no coincidence," Ronald Reagan told us in his Inaugural Address, "that our present troubles parallel and are proportionate to the intervention and intrusion in our lives that result from unnecessary and excessive growth of government." Beyond this, however, conservatives argue that inappropriate and unwarranted government intervention erodes government's ability to adequately perform its essential functions. According to Paul Johnson, "When Caesar becomes a nursemaid, he ceases to be a soldier."[15] For conservatives, government clearly is the problem, not the solution.

The View from the Left

There are no Edmund Burkes or Adam Smiths around whom liberals can rally and find an historic standard. The view from the left, on both sides of the Atlantic, has not been as historically clear, precise, or durable as that from the right. Indeed, the term "liberal" means something quite different today than it did in the nineteenth century. And the Liberal party in Great

Britain historically has represented a more conservative position than contemporary U.S. liberals would allow. In addition, what goes under the name of liberalism in the United States is best understood in Western Europe as "social democracy." However, while there is admittedly considerable imprecision in treating the view from the left as a monolithic one, enough common ground does exist upon which U.S. liberals and European social democrats could feel comfortable. For purposes of convenience, the term liberal will be used throughout the following discussions. Finally, the reader is reminded that our purpose is not to deal with all of the threads of modern liberalism but rather only that one which deals with the appropriate role of government in society.

Modern liberalism in the United States is basically a twentieth-century product. It traces its origins back to the Progressive-Wilson era, although it was not until the New Deal of Franklin D. Roosevelt that it had its first substantial impact on U.S. public policy. From that time, the liberal position has been, in direct contrast to conservative wisdom, that government is and should be a positive, indeed indispensable, force for achieving the good society. This view, and its rejection of conservatism, is articulated by the late Robert Hutchins, a leading spokesman for the liberal cause in the U.S. "The notion that the sole concern of a free society is the limitation of government authority and that that government is best which governs least is certainly archaic. Our object today should not be to weaken government in competition with other centers of power, but rather to strengthen it as the agency charged with the responsibility for the common good."[16]

It is important to note here that liberals do not reject Adam Smith's three functions of government—they simply go beyond it. Particularly striking is the relationship between government and the economy. Conservatives, it will be remembered, view government as an instrument for ensuring and facilitating the free operation of the marketplace. Liberals, on the other hand, see the government as an active, indispensable agent in regulating the economy in order to protect the consumer as well as encourage economic growth and development. John Kenneth Galbraith, a liberal economist, argues that "big government" is in fact needed as a "counter-vailing power" in order to constrain big business and the increasing power it wields on behalf of its own selfish motives and to the detriment of the common good. Government thus becomes the protector and promoter of the weak against the strong. Government is seen by liberals as an active, positive force in the economy.[17]

This positive role extends, of course, to the area of social policy, where government is expected to come to the aid of citizens in their search for economic security and adequate food, clothing, housing, education, and health care. Here too, government intervention is viewed as a necessary counterweight to either private abuses or private neglect. Thus, according to Arthur M. Schlesinger, Jr., "The history of governmental intervention has been the history of the growing ineffectiveness of the private conscience as a means of social control. The only alternative is the growth of the public conscience, whose natural expression is the democratic government."[18] It is this perspective on government which came to dominate the policy-making processes of most industrialized nations of the world in the course of the twentieth century. Government, in this view, is not simply a "night-watchman"—a favorite conservative phrase—guarding against threats to society, but an active, positive promoter of the values to which society aspires. "Big government" is not only necessary, it may be desirable. Government is not to be feared because, reflecting as it does the will of the people, it will be benevolent.

In the previous few pages we have tried to examine the role of government from both an historical and philosophical perspective. In subsequent chapters we will see how both factors affect the choices and courses of public policy in the United States and, by comparison, other countries. Before turning to that task, however, we want to explain in greater detail the utility of a comparative approach to the study of government and policy.

THE COMPARATIVE STUDY OF PUBLIC POLICY

There are a number of reasons why U.S. public policy is best studied and understood within a comparative framework. The most important, from our perspective, was illustrated earlier in regard to the debate over gun control. United States policy makers, like their counterparts elsewhere, frequently look to other countries for policy inspiration, ideals, models, and support. The reasons for this comparative approach to policy making are not hard to find.

One of the most compelling reasons is simply expediency and convenience. Borrowing the ideas and/or policies and policy experiences of other nations, where appropriate, is considerably easier, more efficient, and less time-consuming than starting from scratch. Why, after all, reinvent the wheel? Thus, by way of illustration, in 1981 the Senate established a Special Committee on Aging, chaired by Senator John Heinz of Pennsylvania. The purpose of the committee was to examine the impact of an aging population on the U.S. social security system. One result of the committee's work was an information paper entitled "Social Security in Europe: The Impact of an Aging Population" (December 1981). As Senator Heinz explained in the preface to the paper, "[I]t is instructive for members of Congress and the American public to consider the experience of other countries as we debate the future course for our own social security program." The problems and programs of many European countries are not too dissimilar, if at all, from our own. It simply makes good legislative sense to use those experiences when considering policy solutions in this country. While such borrowing has long been practiced by U.S. state and local policy makers, and noted by students of comparative state and local public policy, it is also common among national policy makers.[19] The much criticized congressional junket, in which members of the U.S. Congress travel abroad—typically to warm climates during the congressional winter recess—is ostensibly to gather information and ideas from other countries to assist lawmakers in their jobs.

Second, policy makers frequently look toward the policy experiences of other nations to lend rhetorical support to their own policy positions. Clearly Congressman Ashbrook thought he had found evidence to support his anti-gun-control position in the case of Switzerland. Similarly, Mr. Rodino felt that the Swiss case provided support for his pro-gun-control position. Similar arguments are frequently offered. Advocates of social welfare legislation, in Congress and academia, often cite the case of Sweden to demonstrate how well such legislation works. And, both opponents and proponents of national health insurance often cite Canada, West Germany, or other nations to prove their point.

Third, U.S. policy makers use the policy experiences of other nations, and particularly policy failures, in order to avoid similar problems in this country. For example, in September 1981 Congressman Annunzio of Illinois reported to his House colleagues on a scandal involving the company authorized to issue Greek commemorative coins in honor of the 1982 Pan-European games. Apparently the company contracted to mint the Greek coins had engaged in certain questionable business practices and was under investigation by the Greek government. This same company was now under consideration for a similar contract to mint coins honoring the 1984 Summer Olympics in Los Angeles. The authorization to mint the Olympic coins was part of proposed House and Senate legislation dealing with the Los Angeles Olympics. Congressman Annunzio urged his colleagues, "Let us learn from others so that we can have a successful and profitable coin program not clouded by suggestions of scandal."[20] The desire to avoid the mistakes of others plays an important role in the cross-national orientation of U.S. policy makers.

Fourth, U.S. policy makers take a cross-national perspective when the policies of other governments affect the United States, and particularly when they affect us adversely. Consider, for example, an amendment by Senator William Cohen of Maine to the Agriculture and Food Act of 1981. The first section of the amendment read, "The Congress finds that Canadian domestic production subsidies and European Economic Community subsidies are causing substantial displacement in the export sales of fresh and processed potatoes produced in the United States."[21] Mr. Cohen, whose state is second only to Idaho in producing potatoes, urged that the secretary of agriculture use his authority to implement a special standby export subsidy program to neutralize the effects of the Canadian and EEC subsidies. In sum, in order to be effective and protect the interests of their constituents, U.S. policy makers must be aware of the policies of other nations.

The above example suggests a fifth and related explanation for the tendency of national lawmakers, including U.S. congressmen, to look outside their own country when considering policy. This explanation involves what one scholar calls the internationalization of national politics. "A celebrated aspect of the technical, economic, and cultural development during the present century, and perhaps in particular during the post-World War II period, is that a great number of human activities have expanded more drastically than earlier across the borders of the national states: research, education, technology, sports, fashion, art, ideology, knowledge, and culture in general. This internationalization process is, perhaps, particularly strong for the economic system."[22] As trite as it sounds, it is nevertheless true that we have become a small world—and a highly interdependent and interrelated one. The residual influences of colonialism, the revolution in electronic communications, the plethora of international agreements ranging from air safety to plant protection, the widespread international traffic of influential people (e.g., scholars, legislators, bureaucrats, technical commissions), and the increasing number of international organizations have combined to make the borrowing of policies and policy ideas much more likely and more frequent than at any time in history.

In sum, for a wide variety of reasons, policy making, in this country and elsewhere, increasingly has become a comparative (i.e., cross-national) enterprise. To fully understand policy and policy making, therefore, we often must approach it from a cross-national perspective.

There is, however, another reason why U.S. students are best served by approaching U.S. policy from a cross-national perspective. This one is, in a sense, more personal and less academic. A knowledge and understanding of the public policies of other countries will allow each student to make more valid assessments of the public policies in this country. On the face of it, it seems absurd to reject national health insurance, for example, in favor of private health delivery, unless one actually has examined how well or poorly this policy has worked in other countries. If for no other reason, students who have knowledge about the policies of other countries can, if they so desire, be more effective advocates of the policies of this country. The Roman jurist Cato once said that "He who knows only his side of the argument, knows little of that." Whatever policy position you wish to defend, you will be a more successful advocate of that position if you are familiar with its alternatives. A cross-national approach to the study of public policy assures such familiarity.

CAUTIONS AND CONCLUSIONS

While there are obvious advantages to studying public policy from a comparative perspective, there are also some limitations.[23] For our purposes perhaps the most serious limitation is that not all comparisons are either logical, valid, or applicable and, therefore, can lead to simplistic or misleading conclusions. Some students and practitioners of the comparative approach to policy making have been mindful of these pitfalls. Senator Heinz, in the study noted above, warned that we cannot "seriously expect that approaches taken by foreign countries would always be considered acceptable here in the United States." Others, however, have not been quite as sensitive to this point. Thus, for example, the uses of Sweden as a policy model by liberals and Singapore and Hong Kong by conservatives are cases in point. Sweden is frequently extolled by scholars on the left as a model welfare state in which all citizens are guaranteed social, economic, as well as political justice and equity. Unemployment is low, poverty is almost nonexistent, economic productivity is high, all citizens have access to modern, competent health care regardless of income, and so on. The state, acting on behalf of and in response to its citizens, is promoting and protecting the well-being of all Swedes. Why, the liberal laments, can we not be more like Sweden? Why, indeed? Rarely does the liberal mention that Sweden only has as many people as New York City, and, unlike the United States and many other nations, it is a culturally, racially, linguistically, and religiously homogeneous country. As a result, reaching a consensus on public policy is a good deal easier, and societal resources do not have to be diverted toward dealing with problems inherent in pluralistic societies. Nor is it mentioned that Sweden, located on the periphery of the globe, has not participated in a major war since 1814, and is not a major power with all of the burdens associated with that dubious honor.

Conservatives too have their favorite role models. Milton Friedman, the Nobel Prize–winning conservative economist is apparently not immune from making downright irrelevant comparisons. For Friedman the question is, Why can we not be more like Hong Kong? Surely Adam Smith must have had a country like Hong Kong in mind when he wrote about the proper role of the sovereign. As Friedman describes Hong Kong, with obvious envy, "It has no government direction of economic activity, no minimum wage laws, no fixing of prices. The residents are free to buy from whom they want, to sell to whom they want, to invest however they want, to hire whom they want, to work for whom they want."[24] It sounds like heaven!

Of course, it may be worthwhile to emphasize that the United States has almost fifty times as many people as Hong Kong. It is also noteworthy that Hong Kong is not an independent nation, but a British crown colony—

and, therefore, not required to maintain its own armed forces, conduct foreign relations, etc. Furthermore, some of the success of Hong Kong's capitalist economy is in part attributable to its relationship to the People's Republic of China. Thus, for example, a substantial part of Hong Kong's inexpensive labor force is comprised of refugees from China. It is easier to "hire whom they want," and keep labor costs down, when there is an almost unlimited source of cheap labor on your border. In short, Hong Kong is so unique, in so many ways, that it seems ridiculous to hold it up as a model for most nations, let alone the United States.

All of this is not to say that Sweden, Hong Kong, or Lapland cannot be used to illustrate certain policies and policy experiences. It is necessary, however, for both the author and the student to acknowledge and understand the limits of comparison. Perhaps we should view Sweden or Hong Kong as models of policy behavior and accomplishment to which we should aspire. We must, and we will, recognize that ours is a much different society, and that reaching the goals reflected in the cases of Sweden or Hong Kong will entail different arrangements and that we will meet with different problems.

With these caveats in mind, we now can proceed to examine public policy in seven areas: the economy, health care, poverty, crime, education, housing, and women's rights. These areas were chosen for two reasons. First, they represent the research interest of the authors. Second, they deal with some of the most fundamental concerns of citizens throughout the world. Aside from national defense, it is difficult to imagine issues more important than jobs and income, health and security, poverty, crime, education, housing, and equality. Clearly other policy issues are important and could have been included, such as environmental and consumer protection, national defense, and energy. We chose, however, to emphasize our strengths and interests over breadth of policy coverage.

One final point must be noted here about our approach. The discussion of each policy area in a separate chapter is a distortion of political reality. Policy makers do not take one policy problem at a time, devoting their full energies and the nation's resources to each, and then move on to the next issue. Problems relating to public safety, education, housing, equality, health care, and so on often compete with each other for the attention and resources of policy makers and the public. In fact, the simultaneous existence of several issues on the nation's policy agenda is one of the major constraints imposed upon the policy-making process. There is simply not enough time, energy, or money available to address, much less solve, all of the nation's problems at once. Books about public policy can deal with issues separately, policy makers cannot. In the course of the book we will introduce other constraints imposed upon policy makers and the policy-making process in the United States. Primary among these are federalism, or the sharing of power and policy responsibility by different levels of government, and the separation of powers among the three branches of the federal government. Each of these structural features helps set the parameters within which public policy is made.

On occasion we remind the readers of these constraints. But in most instances you will have to remind yourselves that content and limitations of particular policies, and their adoption or rejection, were shaped by a variety of competing and constraining political forces.

In each chapter then we will examine the purpose and content of U.S. public policy and compare it to the policies, experiences, accomplishments, and failures of other, mainly western, industrialized nations. Our purpose is not to proselytize on behalf of particular policy orientations. We intend to present as balanced an approach as possible and let each student make up his or her own mind about the virtues of different approaches to common problems.

NOTES

1 *Cong. Rec.,* July 16, 1981, pp. E3533–E3534.

2 *Cong. Rec.,* July 23, 1981, pp. E3688-E3689.

3 The following three sections are based upon Howard M. Leichter, *A Comparative Approach to Policy Analysis: Health Care Policy in Four Nations* (New York: Cambridge Univ. Press, 1979), pp. 17–32 and are used with the permission of Cambridge Univ. Press.

4 Reinhold A. Dorwart, *The Prussian Welfare State before 1740* (Cambridge, Mass.: Harvard Univ. Press, 1971), p. vii.

5 Daniel Bell, "The Public Household—On 'Fiscal Sociology' and Liberal Society," *Public Interest,* 37 (Fall 1974), 35.

6 Barrington Moore, Jr., *Social Origins of Dictatorship and Democracy* (Boston: Beacon Press, 1967), p. 205.

7 R. T. Holt and J. E. Turner, *The Political Basis of Economic Development* (Princeton: Van Nostrand, 1966), pp. 72, 120–121.

8 See, for example, Eli F. Heckscher, *Mercantilism,* rev. ed., 2 vols. (New York: Macmillan, 1955).

9 Thomas Malthus, quoted in Sidney Fine, *Laissez-Faire and the General Welfare State: A Study of Conflict in American Thought, 1865–1901* (Ann Arbor: Univ. of Michigan Press, 1956), p. 167.

10 Milton Friedman and Rose Friedman, *Free to Choose: A Personal Statement* (New York: Avon Books, 1981), p. 20.

11 Barry Goldwater, *The Conscience of a Conservative* (New York: Hillman Books, 1960), p. 17.

12 Paul Johnson, *The Things That Are Not Caesar's* (Washington, D.C.: American Enterprise Institute, 1980), p. 1.

13 Friedman and Friedman, p. 24.

14 Margaret Thatcher, "Speech at Georgetown University," Washington, D.C., Feb. 27, 1981.

15 Johnson, p. 15.

16 Quoted in James Burnham, *Suicide of the West: An Essay on the Meaning and Destiny of Liberalism* (New Rochelle, New York: Arlington House, 1975), p. 90.

17 John Kenneth Galbraith, *American Capitalism: The Concept of Countervailing Power* (Boston: Houghton Mifflin, 1956).

18 Arthur M. Schlesinger, Jr., *The Vital Center: The Politics of Freedom* (Boston: Houghton Mifflin, 1962), p. 176.

19 Ira Sharkansky, *The Routines of Politics* (New York: Van Nostrand Company, 1970).

20 *Cong. Rec.,* Sept. 23, 1981, p. H6577.

21 *Cong. Rec.,* Sept. 17, 1981, p. S9806.

22 Assar Lindbeck, "The Changing Role of the National State," *Kyklos,* 28 (1975), 28.

23 Leichter, pp. 8–10.

24 Friedman and Friedman, pp. 25–26.

CHAPTER 2

POVERTY AND SOCIAL WELFARE POLICY

Poverty policy evolved slowly over the course of U.S. history and has always been a subject of great controversy. During most of U.S. history the consensus was that care of the needy was not an obligation of the federal government. The prevailing belief was that local governments and private charities should bear the responsibility of assisting those among the poor who could be described as "deserving" (e.g., the aged, ill, handicapped, mothers, and small children). Only in the twentieth century (with the advent of the great depression) did a significant percentage of the public adopt the philosophy that the federal government should play a major role in succoring the unfortunate.

The main critics of an enlarged role for the federal government in combating poverty were conservatives, who, of course, espouse a belief in a limited role for government. Conservatives feared that welfare programs would destroy personal motivation, thus contributing to dependency and sloth, while burdening the economy. Liberals tended to argue that the government was not only morally obligated to aid the poor, but that the cost of neglect—in increased crime, lost productivity, etc.—would far exceed program costs. The gap between conservatives and liberals on this issue substantially reflects their different interpretations of the causes of poverty. Conservatives believe that it results from lack of personal effort, while liberals believe that most poverty is caused by defects in the social and economic structure. Despite these very important differences, by the 1960s both of the nation's major parties, including both conservatives and liberals, had come to believe that the federal government should play a significant role in promoting and ensuring the welfare of citizens. Over the years the policy differences between liberals and conservatives have narrowed in regard to this issue.

Ronald Reagan often articulates the new conservative view. During his first year in office he frequently stated his belief that the government has an obligation to maintain a safety net of protective programs for its most vulnerable citizens. Presidents Nixon and Ford shared similar views. In fact, both Presidents Nixon and Ford proposed that Congress guarantee an income base to most poor families. While President Reagan is thought to be less sympathetic to the poor, in his Inaugural Address he said:

> How can we love our country and not love our countrymen? And loving them, reach out a hand when they fail, heal them when they are sick and provide opportunity to make them self-sufficient so they will be equal in fact and not just in theory.

These views did not mean that Reagan had become a liberal on welfare issues. Reagan's actions as President frequently revealed that while he did not believe that welfare programs should be eliminated, he did believe that they assisted too many citizens and that many of the programs should be the responsibility of the states rather than the federal government. Liberals often argued that if Reagan's policies were adopted, the nation's welfare system would be destroyed.

Thus, the parameters of the welfare debate have narrowed, but the debate is far from over. In this chapter we trace the evolution of poverty policy in the United States, attempt to determine why particular policy options for dealing with poverty have been chosen, and evaluate the efficacy and impact of current welfare policies. Second, we examine welfare policies in Western European nations in order to highlight the different approaches adopted to deal with poverty and to consider the possibility that the policies, experiences, and successes of these nations might inform welfare reform in the United States. Last, we discuss both conservative and liberal proposals for reforming the welfare system.

STAGES OF POVERTY RELIEF

There were no official estimates of poverty before 1959, but there is ample evidence that poverty always has been extensive in the United States. Historical records and accounts document persistent poverty from the time of the U.S. colonies into the twentieth century.[1] The design and administration of poverty relief that began in the colonies was based on concepts implicit in the English poor laws. The Elizabethan Poor Law was passed in 1601 and long guided poverty laws and relief in England. As Rimlinger notes, the poor laws provided relief in a framework of repression.[2] The U.S. colonist agreed with the philosophy upon which the poor laws were based and designed U.S. relief to reflect the same values and goals.

The poor laws had three broad goals. The first was the paternalistic goal of promoting the public welfare by succoring those who because of misfortune legitimately could not adequately care for themselves. The second was to promote law and order by controlling vagrancy and by punishing those who were considered lazy, immoral, and parasitic. The last goal sought to place the burden for care of the poor on local communities. Local communities were required to take private or public action to deal with their most unfortunate members

Most of the English communities decided that the "legitimate or deserving" poor were the aged, handicapped, insane, and mothers and children. These poor citizens were given outdoor relief (food, clothing, small sums of money), or placed in almshouses or workhouses. Children of poor parents were sometimes placed with other families. Those poor considered "illegitimate"—able-bodied males—were beaten, thrown into workhouses or jails, or warned to get out of town.[3]

The colonies adopted basically the same approach. Modest outdoor relief generally was given to the "legitimate" poor, while the able-bodied unemployed were warned to get out, beaten, imprisoned, or even bound over to the highest bidder as indentured servants. In some instances children were placed in families that could take care of them, or placed in workhouses. Relief generally was given even to the "legitimate" poor in a manner that cast a stigma on the recipient. Paupers in the New York colony who received assistance had to wear the letters "N.Y." sewn on their clothing,[4] while those in Pennsylvania were required to wear a "P" on one sleeve.[5]

As an economy measure, and to increase the stigma and punishment associated with relief, communities increasingly cut back or ended outdoor relief and established almshouses or workhouses for the poor. The first almshouse was established in Boston in 1740.[6] During the next 180 years or so the almshouse became a primary method of dealing with the poor. By 1884 there were 600 almshouses in the New England area, and they were common in all the states. Conditions within the institutions were often deplorable. In hope of stimulating state regulations and other reforms, social critics, both in America and Europe, began to write accounts of the deplorable conditions that often prevailed. There is little doubt that the institutions were fertile grounds for exposé. As Trattner points out:

> [L]ittle or no regard was paid to the type of care provided within those institutions. Into most were herded the old and the young, the sick and the well, the sane and the insane, the epileptic and the feebleminded, the blind and the alcoholic,

the juvenile delinquent and the hardened criminal, male and female, all thrown together in haphazard fashion. Nakedness and filth, hunger and vice, and other abuses such as beatings by cruel keepers, were not uncommon in the wretched places, vile catch-alls for everyone in need, defined by one reformer as "living tombs" and by another as "social cemeteries."[7]

Reformers did force some improvements, and by the early 1900s many communities again were placing more emphasis on outdoor relief for the aged, the blind, and mothers and children. But the almshouse and workhouse were still important means of poverty relief. Poverty policy was little changed by the time of the great depression. As Piven and Cloward note:

> At the time of the Great Depression the main legal arrangement for the care of the destitute was incarceration in almshouses or workhouses. In some places the care of paupers was still contracted to the lowest bidder, and destitute orphans were indentured to those who would feed them in exchange for whatever labor they could perform. The constitutions of fourteen states denied the franchise to paupers. . . . By such practices the relief system created a cleverly demarcated and degraded class, a class of pariahs whose numbers were small but whose fate loomed large in the lives of those who lived close to indigence, warning them always of a life even worse than hard work and severe poverty.[8]

Conservatives did not see the workhouse or almshouse as necessarily evil institutions. They believed that such institutions both punished indolence and taught self-reliance. Many conservative groups believed that society had a Christian obligation to reform the poor, and they believed that punishment was necessary to achieve this conversion.

The great depression was the catalyst for historic changes in the government's role in the management of the economy, and in the promotion and protection of the welfare of citizens. The collapse of the economy was so massive that by 1933 one-fourth of all the nation's adult men were unemployed,[9] creating an increasingly volatile situation.[10] Millions of those who suffered from the economic crisis were registered voters, increasingly willing to support radical remedies. Still, the government's response was slow. Between 1933 and 1935 President Roosevelt centered his attention on emergency measures such as public works projects and the prevention of bank closures.

By 1935 the crisis had deepened. The Works Project Administration (WPA) had provided jobs for millions of U.S. citizens, but some 8 million males were still unemployed. It has been estimated that WPA provided jobs to only one of every four applicants.[11] Those millions who could not find work, along with the aged, handicapped, and orphans, turned to state and local governments for assistance. Many of the states, however, could not handle the burden. Some cut the size of grants so that more of the needy could receive assistance. Others abolished all assistance. The state of New

Jersey offered the indigent licenses to beg.[12] The continuing hardship spawned more and more radical critics of the Roosevelt administration. Under these pressures, Roosevelt launched what historians refer to as the "second New Deal." This New Deal had two primary thrusts. First, the government would use Keynesian economics to stimulate and regulate the economy, and increased assistance to business to promote an economic recovery. Second, the government would establish through the Social Security Act of 1935 assistance programs for those who were outside the labor force.

The Social Security Act consisted of five major titles. Title I provided grants to the states for assistance to the aged. Title II established the social security system. Title III provided grants to the states for the administration of unemployment compensation. Title IV established the Aid to Dependent Children (ADC) program. Title V provided grants to the states for aid to the blind. The Social Security Act represented a radical new role for the federal government. Congress previously had enacted programs to subsidize state and local assistance programs, but this was the first time that programs had been established which would be run by the federal government (social security) or in partnership with the states (ADC).

Thus, the Social Security Act was a historic step, a change in policy that was made possible because of the massive and sustained collapse of the economy. Conservatives denounced the act for two main reasons. First, they believed that a healthy economy would take care of most citizens, and that government spending on the poor would impose financial burdens on business and hinder economic recovery. Second, they believed that aid to the poor should be kept modest. The best way to achieve this was to leave relief to the states and private charity. Liberals, on the other hand, had much less faith in the market and felt an obligation to ameliorate the impact of the market's failures on society's most vulnerable citizens.

As radical a departure as the Social Security Act was, its benefits were originally quite modest. Benefits were extended only to those aged who worked in certain occupations and industries, and benefits were delayed until 1942. It was not until 1950 that half of all aged Americans received any benefits under the program.[13] In the same year the act was amended to provide assistance to the permanently and totally disabled.

Until 1950 only orphans and poor children received any assistance from the ADC program, and benefits were extended very slowly. In 1940 only 360,000 families received assistance under ADC for the care of one or more poor children or orphans. Nine states were extending assistance to less than 1,000 families. Texas had only 85 families on its ADC rolls.[14] In 1950 the program was changed to Aid to Families with Dependent Children (AFDC), allowing benefits to one parent (usually the mother) in a family with eligible children.

With the passage of the Social Security Act of 1935, the United States became the last of the major industrial nations to develop national welfare programs, which by European standards were quite modest. In addition to its modesty, the Social Security Act contained three features which had long-term and significant consequences for U.S. social welfare programs. First, benefits under the various social security titles were designed for only a select category of the needy. Even as social welfare programs expanded greatly, they continued to be categorical, rather than universal as they are in many other nations. The implications of this feature are detailed below.

Second, some of the social security titles allowed a great deal of local autonomy. ADC (or AFDC as it later became) allowed the states to determine who would receive assistance and how much they would receive. As AFDC expanded to become the nation's primary cash assistance program for the needy, this feature remained. Variations in state benefits under AFDC are huge, with some states being much more generous than others. Titles I and V also allowed a great deal of local autonomy in funding assistance to the aged and blind. Until these titles were superceded by the Supplemental Security Income (SSI) program in 1974, funding variations were substantial.

Last, the Social Security Act did not include health insurance. Most of the other western industrial nations already had health insurance programs by 1935. Roosevelt considered including health insurance in the Social Security Act, but opposition from the American Medical Association and southern congressmen was so intense he eliminated it.

It was the conservative southern members of Congress who insisted that, as much as possible, the programs under the Social Security Act be categorical and that each state have maximum control over the programs. As Piven and Cloward point out, the southern congressmen had two concerns: "that the grant levels, if set by the federal government, would undermine the low wage structure in the South; and that a federal supervisory agency, if vested with great authority, would curtail local prerogatives to say who should get relief, thus opening the rolls to blacks and undermining the caste economy of the South."[15] Thus, the south's determination to maintain racism and a low-wage structure had a major and long-term impact on the design of the U.S. welfare system. Conservatives in other parts of the nation also liked the categorical design of the programs and the states' role. They felt that these features would preserve state prerogatives and hold costs down.

Thus, the values of both liberals and conservatives were reflected in the nation's new welfare system. Liberals convinced the federal government to establish programs, but conservatives were able to influence the design of the programs. The programs would be for a select group of the nation's poorer citizens, benefits would be modest, and often state-supervised and controlled. At the time neither liberals nor conservatives put any significant emphasis on programs that might prevent people from becoming poor. Even the programs established were not designed to remove people from poverty. They were designed to provide the poor with modest, temporary financial aid that would help them meet some of their most pressing needs.

State control over the benefit levels under Titles I, II, IV, and V of the Social Security Act substantially limited growth in these programs through the 1950s. In 1960 there were only 803,000 families receiving benefits under AFDC, and only 144,000 blind or disabled citizens were receiving assistance under the Social Security Act.[16] Thus, by 1960, 25 years after the original act, U.S. welfare programs were still extremely modest and, as events would prove, poverty was still very severe.

The "Discovery" of American Poverty

Just as the great depression had served as the catalyst for the nation's first major social welfare programs, the civil rights movement and the ghetto riots of the 1960s served as the stimulus for the next substantial expansion of the welfare state. The civil rights movement, which developed in the late 1950s and early 1960s, centered attention on the economic conditions of millions of U.S. citizens. Civil rights workers often charged that many U.S. citizens of all races were ill-housed, ill-clothed, medically neglected, malnourished, and even suffering from hunger. Most of the nation's public leaders simply dismissed the suggestion that any significant number of U.S. citizens were suffering from hunger. Southern politicians, especially those in the Senate, were often extremely hostile in their denunciations of these charges.[17] But slowly the evidence of acute poverty, malnutrition, poverty-related disease, and even starvation began to be documented. One of the first prominent public officials to take these charges seriously was John F. Kennedy.

As President, Kennedy expanded the nation's modest Food Commodity program and convinced Congress to initiate a pilot Food Stamp program. In 1963 he ordered a number of federal agencies to develop the case for a full-scale attack on poverty. During the summer of 1963, Dr. Martin Luther King led a demonstration of 200,000 people to Washington, D.C., with the intent of focusing national attention on racism, unemployment, poverty, and hunger. By the time of President Kennedy's death in 1963, a great deal of attention was being focused on U.S. poverty.

In late 1963 President Johnson expanded on Kennedy's efforts by declaring a "war on poverty." The core of this "war" was the Economic Opportunity Act of 1964, consisting primarily of job and work-experience programs and small business loans. The Office of Economic Opportunity (OEO) was created to coordinate the attack on poverty. The "war," most observers agree, turned out to be more of a skirmish. President Johnson became absorbed by Vietnam, leaving very little money for the domestic war. Donovan calculated that "the [funding for OEO] from fiscal year 1965 to 1973 cost approximately $15.5 billion. Expenditures for the war in Vietnam during the same period totalled some $120 billion."[18]

Johnson's "war" and the tensions resulting from the civil rights movement had the effect of maintaining attention on the problem of U.S. poverty.[19] In 1967 the Senate Subcommittee on Employment, Manpower and Poverty held hearings on U.S. poverty. The testimony of many civil rights leaders contained graphic allegations of acute hunger in the south. This testimony stimulated two liberal members of the subcommittee—Robert Kennedy (D., N.Y.) and Joseph Clark (D., Penn.)—to conduct a personal tour of the Mississippi delta. They returned to Washington to testify to the presence of severe hunger and malnutrition in the area they visited.

The subcommittee's initial investigations also had encouraged the Field Foundation to send a team of doctors to Mississippi to investigate the health of children in Headstart programs. The team issued a report entitled "Children in Mississippi." The report documented extensive poverty, poverty-related diseases, and malnutrition among the children and their families.[20]

The most dramatic documentation of U.S. poverty was yet to come. In the mid-1960s the Field Foundation and the Citizens' Crusade against Poverty, two liberal groups, formed the Citizens' Board of Inquiry into Hunger and Malnutrition in the United States. The Citizens' Board conducted investigations, held hearings, and reported its findings in late 1967 and 1968. The findings confirmed the worst suspicions of welfare reform advocates. They discovered within the larger population of the United States a population that might best be described as an underdeveloped nation. They reported "concrete evidence of chronic hunger and malnutrition in every part of the United States where we have held hearings or conducted field trips."[21]

These findings contributed to the pressures on Congress for improvement in and expansion of welfare programs. There were still the issues, however, of how this might be done and who should deal with this problem. And there were still some who denied the problem, or at least its magnitude. The leaders of the civil rights movement continued to demand new programs for the poor, and between 1965 and 1968 literally hundreds of riots erupted in U.S. cities. Many conservatives saw the riots as evidence of a breakdown of morals in U.S. society and an attack on the nation's institutions.[22] In the final analysis, however, most conservative members of Congress agreed with liberal members that social programs had to be expanded. Both conservatives and liberals agreed that expanding social programs would at least help restore order. Thus, with the cities on fire, and media attention focused on the struggles of the black population and the poverty of millions of U.S. citizens, Congress passed a number of new civil rights laws and welfare programs during the 1960s.

Major civil rights acts were passed in 1964, 1965, and 1968. Also, in the 1960s and early 1970s Congress expanded existing welfare programs and created other major welfare programs. Below we will discuss these programs in depth, but here we will simply note the basic changes that took place. In 1960 Congress passed legislation providing some modest medical assistance to the aged. In 1961 an amendment to the AFDC title allowed states to provide benefits to two-parent families where both parents were unemployed. Less than half the states adopted this option. In 1963 a bill providing maternal and child care planning was passed. In 1964 Congress formally established the Food Stamp program, which twenty-two states initially opted to participate in. In 1965 both the Medicare and Medicaid programs were enacted by Congress, and federal funding for the AFDC program was increased substantially. In 1971 Congress adopted national standards for the Food Stamp program, but it was not extended to all the states until 1974. The Supplemental Security Income (SSI) program was passed in 1972 and went into effect in 1974. By 1975 a total of five new titles had been added to the original Social Security Act, and all the original titles had been expanded through amendments.

The 1960s and early 1970s, then, saw a great increase in social welfare programs. While there had been little attention or expansion of social welfare programs during the 1940s or 1950s, civil strife and liberal charges of terrible poverty had produced a spate of new programs. The changes that took place give credence to Christopher Leman's argument that the diffusion of power in the United States has made progress in social policy possible only under conditions of acute crisis. He calls this "innovation by the big bang."[23] The strife and national guilt of the 1960s had produced the second "big bang."

Social Welfare Programs

Social welfare program participation and costs grew rapidly during the 1970s. There were two major reasons for this. First, in the 1960s and 1970s the civil rights movement, and several related organizations, made millions of families aware of their eligibility for assistance. Second, in the 1970s the nation's economy turned sour, with significant increases in unemployment, subemployment, and inflation. These conditions prompted millions of new families to seek assistance. In 1965 there were about 1 million families on the AFDC rolls. By 1970 the AFDC rolls included 2.5 million families, and by 1982 the number had increased to 3.5 million.[24] The food stamp rolls grew in a similar dramatic fashion. In 1970 the food stamp budget was $577 million. By 1982 it was over $11 billion. Funding for the Medicare and Medicaid programs also increased very dramatically during the 1970s. (See Chapter 3.)

Table 2-1 provides an overview of the nation's major social welfare programs. The table shows the basis of eligibility, source(s) of funding, form of aid, and actual or proposed expenditures and beneficiaries in fiscal years 1981, 1982, and 1983. The figures for fiscal 1983 are estimates that reflect substantial cuts President Reagan pushed through Congress. The seven programs listed on Table 2-1 can be divided into three categories:

1 Social insurance programs such as social security, Medicare, and unemployment compensation. Social insurance programs are based on employee and/or employer contributions and benefits are sometimes wage related.

2 Cash assistance programs such as Aid to Families with Dependent Children (AFDC) and Supplemental Security Income (SSI). These programs are means-tested, with benefits going only to those who meet income and other qualifications.

3 In-kind programs such as Food Stamps and Medicaid, which provide a noncash service. These programs are also means-tested, and often have non-income-related qualifications that must be met by recipients.

Social insurance programs are by far the most expensive of the programs. Strictly speaking, they are not welfare programs because recipients made contributions during their working years and receive benefits which are roughly comparable to their contributions. The 1983 budget projects the expenditure for social security at $175.6 billion, making it by far the most expensive social welfare program. The next two most expensive programs are also social insurance programs—Medicare and unemployment compensation. The projected cost of these programs in 1983 is $55.4 billion and $22.6 billion, respectively. The total projected cost of these three programs in fiscal 1983 is $253.6 billion.

The two cash assistance programs are inexpensive by comparison. The AFDC program and the SSI program were projected to cost the federal government $6.8 billion and $8.9 billion, respectively, in fiscal 1983. The two major in-kind programs are somewhat more expensive, with projected combined costs of $31.3 billion in fiscal 1983. The total projected costs of the three types of programs in fiscal 1982 was $300.6 billion, with social insurance programs accounting for 84 percent of the total cost. Cash assistance programs account for 5 percent of the total; in-kind programs account for the other 11 percent of all expenditures.

In fiscal 1983 federal expenditures are projected to be $758 billion. The two cash assistance programs account for about 2 percent of the total. The two in-kind programs account for an additional 4 percent. If all the other federal payments for the poor were calculated, the total for all the programs

TABLE 2-1
FEDERAL EXPENDITURES FOR SELECTED SOCIAL WELFARE PROGRAMS

Program	Basis of eligibility	Source of income	Form of aid	Fiscal 1981		Fiscal 1982		Fiscal 1983
				Expenditures, billions	Beneficiaries' monthly average, millions	Expenditure, billions	Beneficiaries' monthly average, millions	Expenditures, billions
				Social insurance program				
Old-age survivors and disability insurance	Age, disability, or death of parent or spouse; individual earnings	Federal payroll taxes on employers and employees	Cash	$145.0	$36.0	$162.3	$36.5	$173.5
Unemployment compensation	Unemployment	State and federal payroll tax on employers	Cash	19.6	4.1 (per week)	25.2	3.4 (per week)	22.6
Medicare	Age or disability	Federal payroll tax on employers and employees	Subsidized health insurance	39.1	28.5	43.6	28	55.4

Cash assistance programs

Program	Beneficiaries	Funding source	Benefit type					
Aid to Families with Dependent Children (AFDC)*	Certain families with children; income	Federal, state, local revenues	Cash and services	7.9	11.1	7.6	10.4	6.8
Supplemental Security Income (SSI)*	Age or disability; income	Federal, state revenue	Cash	7.2	4.1	7.9	4.1	8.9

In-kind programs

Program	Beneficiaries	Funding source	Benefit type					
Medicaid*	Persons eligible for AFDC and SSI and medically indigent	Federal, state, local revenues	Subsidized health services	17.1	22.5	18.4	22.9	19.9
Food Stamps	Income	Federal revenues	Vouchers	11.4	22.4	11.3	22.2	11.4

* The figures represent the federal costs of these programs. The figures for 1983 are estimated.
Source: U.S. government budgets in brief, various years.

would be less than 10 percent of the federal budget. The more broadly oriented social insurance programs listed on Table 2-1, however, account for about 33 percent of the total projected budget.

Program Administration and Regional Variations   In addition to costs, Table 2-1 provides another important insight into the nation's approach to income maintenance. As both conservatives and liberals frequently point out, the nation actually does not have an integrated income security system. Instead it has a network of separate programs, administered by various agencies and levels of government, each with its own basis of eligibility and administrative rules. For example, the Social Security Administration administers social security and SSI, the Department of Agriculture administers food stamps, and Health and Human Services administers AFDC and Medicaid. The states play a major role in the administration of the Medicaid and AFDC programs, and they pay a substantial proportion of the total costs of these programs.

The nation's income security system then consists of a series of individual programs created in serial installments by various combinations of government in response to a particular problem or the perceived needs of a particular segment of the total poverty population. Benefits generally are keyed not just to need but to specific categories of the "legitimately" needy. In all but the Food Stamp program, beneficiaries must not only be needy, they must also fit into the "eligible" category of poor people allowed to qualify for a particular program. Some groups, such as mothers of small children and the aged, are much more likely to be able to qualify for assistance than male-headed households, couples without children, and single adults without children.

Welfare reformists claim that a number of consequences result from the categorical nature of welfare assistance. First, the programs lack horizontal equity—persons with the same degree of need do not receive the same degree of aid. Variations in levels of assistance from state to state also contribute to this outcome. Second, the programs lack vertical equity— those with the most severe needs do not necessarily receive aid before those with less severe needs. In fact, reformists argue, aid often goes to families whose needs are far less severe than those of individuals and families who never receive any aid. The reason for this, of course, is that some individuals and families fit into the classifications of people who may qualify for aid, while others (especially nonaged single adults and couples without children) often do not. Additionally, because state welfare guidelines are often not pegged to the federal government's definition of poverty, some persons who would not be considered poor by the federal standards receive aid, and other persons continue to receive aid after they have received enough assistance to cross the poverty threshold for their family size.

The only program for which a family or individual can qualify simply by being poor (provided they have little or no assets) is the Food Stamp program. A person who cannot qualify for any federal program, except perhaps food stamps, may qualify for state aid if the state he or she lives in has a general assistance program. Thirty-seven of the states, the District of Columbia, Guam, Puerto Rico, and the Virgin Islands have general assistance programs. Most of the individual programs assist a fairly small number of persons and provide modest benefits. For example, in June 1980 the programs assisted a total of 929,261 persons and provided average family benefits of $157.13 and average benefits to individuals of $26.58. The total costs of these programs in 1980 was $1.3 billion.[25]

One final explanation for inequities in welfare programs is severe variations in levels of spending.[26] The south, which has the largest number of poor residents, spends far less per recipient than does any other region of the country. In fiscal 1976 the south's total (state and federal) expenditure for each poor resident was $784. The midwestern states averaged $1,589, the western states averaged $1,512, and the northeastern states averaged expenditures of $2,425 per recipient—over three times the per-person expenditure in the south.[27]

One last characteristic of the welfare system should be emphasized. The nation's major welfare programs are not primarily oriented toward the prevention or alleviation of poverty. The primary emphasis of the programs is on subsistent benefits to meet the eligible poor's most pressing, immediate needs. When we examine the approach of the major European nations below, the contrast between the emphasis of the U.S. programs and those of the European nations will be quite obvious.

Program Impact   Having examined the costs and general characteristics of the nation's major social welfare programs, we can now turn to their impact upon the population and the problem of poverty. The evidence shows that the programs play a very large role in reducing the incidence of poverty in the United States. According to the government's measure of poverty, without social welfare expenditures the number of poor would almost double, leaving about one U.S. citizen in five in poverty.

Table 2-2 shows the impact of social welfare expenditures in fiscal 1976. Without any social welfare expenditures, 21.1 percent of the population (45.8 million persons) would have fallen below the official poverty line. After cash expenditures—social security, AFDC, SSI, etc.—12.8 percent of the population (24.7 million persons) remained below the poverty level. Thus, 46 percent of the pretransfer poor were moved over the poverty line. A pattern of studies shows that as expenditures increased through the 1960s and 1970s, a larger proportion of the pretransfer poor were rescued from poverty by cash benefits. For example, in 1965, 33 percent of the pretransfer

TABLE 2-2
HOUSEHOLDS BELOW THE POVERTY LEVEL UNDER ALTERNATIVE INCOME
DEFINITIONS, FISCAL YEAR 1976

Households in poverty	Pretax, Pretransfer income	Pretax, post-social insurance income	Pretax, post-money transfer income	Pretax, post-in-kind transfer income		Posttax, post-total transfer income
				I*	II	
Number, thousands	20,237	11,179	9,073	7,406	5,336	5,446
Percent of all families	25.5	14.1	11.4	9.3	6.7	6.9

* Excludes Medicare and Medicaid payments.
Source: U.S. Cong., Congressional Budget Office, *Poverty Status of Families under Alternative Definitions of Income* (Washington, D.C.: GPO, 1977), p. XV.

poor were moved over the poverty line by cash welfare.[28] Economists Plotnick and Skidmore found that in 1972, 17.6 million households, including 39.5 million persons, were poor before they received cash welfare assistance or social security. Cash benefits reduced the number of poor to about 23 million persons. Thus, 44 percent of the pretransfer poor were moved over the poverty line by cash benefits in 1972.[29]

As insightful as these data are, for at least two reasons they are misleading. First, the federal government does not attempt to calculate in-kind benefits (e.g., food stamps, Medicaid, housing assistance) in measuring a poor person's income. If in-kind benefits were included, many more of the pretransfer poor would be pushed over the government's poverty thresholds. For example, Table 2-2 shows that if all cash, in-kind, and tax programs were taken into consideration in fiscal 1976, only 6.5 percent of the population—14.7 million persons—remained below the poverty line. Similarly, another study showed that if income was adjusted for underreporting of cash assistance, taxes paid, and in-kind benefits, only 7 percent of all households, or 5.2 percent of all persons, would have been counted as poor in 1972.[30]

A second point is that social welfare expenditures are much more likely to remove some persons from poverty than others. For example, social security benefits are generally more generous than cash assistance benefits, and they go primarily to people (the aged) who can qualify for at least one aid program and generally more. Not surprisingly, social security removes more people from poverty than does any other program.

In both 1965 and 1972, the overwhelming majority of pre-transfer poor households that escaped poverty were dependent upon Social Security to do so. And the fraction of households kept from poverty by this program rose sharply from 21 percent in 1965 to 30 percent in 1972. . . . This impact has been mostly concentrated among the elderly—36 percent of the pre-transfer poor aged households were made nonpoor by Social Security in 1965, 51 percent of them in 1972.[31]

Welfare programs for the nonaged are not nearly as effective at reducing or preventing poverty. It has been calculated that only 3 percent of the pretransfer poor were made nonpoor by cash welfare in 1965. Even after substantial funding increases, the proportion increased only to 6 percent in 1972.[32]

Table 2-2 shows similar results for fiscal 1976. Before tax and transfer programs, 27 percent of those who would be counted among the poor are aged. But the impact of all available programs is to reduce aged poverty to 7.5 percent of the total. However, while 43 percent of the pretransfer poor are under 25, 55 percent of all the posttransfer poor are under 25. Similarly, 41 percent of all the pretransfer poor live in the south, but because of extremely low benefit levels in the region, 56 percent of all the posttransfer poor live in the south.[33]

THE OFFICIAL MEASURE OF POVERTY

Both conservatives and liberals, then, agree that the social welfare programs substantially reduce poverty. But, as we will see, they differ sharply over the number of persons left in poverty after assistance. To illuminate this controversy it is necessary to examine the government's measure of poverty.

There was no official measure of U.S. poverty until the mid-1960s. In 1964 the Council of Economic Advisors (CEA) formulated a crude measure of poverty based on the estimated cost of the minimum diet an individual or family would need to avoid nutritional deficiencies. In 1965, the Social Security Administration (SSA) attempted to improve upon the CEA standard, but decided to continue to base the standard on the estimated cost of an "adequate" diet for families of various sizes. Using a food budget formulated by the National Research Council, a poverty standard was computed for various family sizes, with an adjustment for urban or rural residence. It was assumed that food costs represented 33 percent of the total income needs of families of three or more, and 27 percent of the total income required by two-person households. This standard was quickly adopted as the federal government's official measure of poverty.

Table 2-3 shows the 1980 SSA poverty standard for various family sizes. Note that the standard varies by family size, the sex of the family head, and the family's place of residence. Farm families are presumed to need only 85 percent of the cash income required by nonfarm families. The rate for single persons and couples is adjusted to compensate for their higher

TABLE 2-3
POVERTY STANDARD: 1980

Family unit	Nonfarm				Farm		
	Total	Male head	Female head	Total	Male head	Female head
1 person							
(unrelated individual)	$ 4,184	$ 4,190	$ 4,379	$ 4,037	$ 3,539	$ 3,680	$ 3,392
15 to 64	4,286	4,290	4,441	4,109	3,693	3,773	3,492
65 and over	3,941	3,949	3,990	3,938	3,359	3,392	3,347
2 persons	5,338	5,363	5,373	5,316	4,502	4,513	4,302
Head, 15 to 64	5,518	5,537	5,568	5,415	4,714	4,721	4,497
Head, 65 and over	4,954	4,983	4,988	4,946	4,233	4,237	4,185
3 persons	6,539	6,565	6,608	6,386	5,573	5,587	5,271
4 persons	8,385	8,414	8,418	8,382	7,170	7,170	7,152
5 persons	9,923	9,966	9,976	9,878	8,472	8,474	8,373
6 persons	11,215	11,269	11,274	11,227	9,613	9,625	9,168
7 persons and more	13,883	13,955	13,886	13,767	11,915	11,889	12,133

Source: U.S. Bureau of the Census, "Money Income and Poverty Status of Families and Persons in United States: 1980 (Advance Report)," *Current Population Reports,* Series P-60, No. 127, 1980, p. 28.

costs. Female-headed families require slightly less, and two-person elderly families are presumed to need 8 percent less than nonelderly two-person families.

Table 2-4 shows the SSA poverty threshold for a nonfarm family of four backdated to 1959, and the number of people counted as poor by year using the specified standard. Taken at face value, the SSA standard suggests that substantial progress was made in reducing poverty during the 1960s with some reversals occurring in the 1970s. In 1959 there were almost 40 million U.S. poor, but the count dropped to 25.4 million by 1963. The count remained basically steady until 1973 and 1974, when poverty declined to about 23 million. However, in 1975 poverty increased by 2.5 million people and actually exceeded poverty for every year back to 1967. Between 1976 and 1978 the count dropped by some 1 million, but in 1979 it increased to 26.1 million. By 1981 the count had leaped to 31.8 million, the highest poverty count since 1965.

An analysis of the actual computation of the official poverty standard for one family size shows the assumptions on which the government measure is based. In 1980 the poverty threshold for a nonfarm family of four was $8,414. This standard allowed $2,103 per person per year, or $5.76 per day, one-third of which was the daily allocation for food ($1.92). The family could spend a total of $2.56 per meal for all four people, or $53.76 per week on food. A budget for a four-person family would look like this:

TABLE 2-4
POVERTY SCHEDULE—FAMILY OF 4 (NONFARM): 1959-1981

Year	Standard	Millions of poor	Percent of total population	Median family income	Standard as a % of median family income
1959	$2,973	39.5	22%	$ 5,620	53.0%
1960	3,022	39.9	22		
1961	3,054	39.9	22		
1962	3,089	38.6	21		
1963	3,128	36.4	19		
1964	3,169	36.1	19		
1965	3,223	33.2	17		
1966	3,317	30.4	16		
1966*	3,317	28.5	15		
1967	3,410	27.8	14		
1968	3,553	25.4	13		
1969	3,743	24.1	12		
1970	3,968	25.4	13	9,867	38.0
1971	4,137	25.6	12.5	10,285	40.2
1972	4,275	24.5	12	11,116	38.4
1973	4,540	23.0	11	12,051	37.6
1974	5,038	24.3	12	12,836	34.2
1974*	5,038	24.3	11.5	12,902	39.0
1975	5,500	25.9	12	13,719	40.0
1976	5,815	25.0	12	14,958	30.8
1977	6,200	24.7	12	16,009	38.7
1978	6,662	24.7	11.4	17,640	37.7
1979	7,412	26.1	11.7	19,680	37.6
1980	8,414	29.3	13	21,020	40.0
1981	9,287	31.8	14	22,388	41.5

Source: Derived from U.S. Bureau of the Census, "Characteristics of the Low-Income Population," *Current Population Reports,* Series P-60, various years.

$2,804.66 for food: $1.92 per day (64 cents per meal) per person; $13.44 per week per person.

$2,804.66 for shelter: $233.72 per month for rent or mortgage for four persons.

$2,804.66 for necessities: $58.43 per month per person for clothing, furniture, transportation, health care, utilities, taxes, entertainment, etc.

Liberals argue that the estimates on which the standard is based are quite low. They doubt that anyone consistently could prepare nutritious meals for four persons for $2.56, or that a family of four could be fed adequately on $53.76 per week. Allowances for rent or mortgages and other necessities, they note, are also modest.

Liberals believe that one intention of the SSA is to define poverty in a very restrictive manner—one that keeps the poverty count as low as possible. They note (See Table 2-4.) that the poverty standard has not kept pace with the growth in personal income. In 1959 the standard was 53 percent of median family income. By the 1970s it averaged only about 39 percent of median family income. Much of the decline in the poverty count between 1959 and 1980, liberals argue, is the result of the fact that the standard did not keep pace with the growth of personal income, rather than from families actually escaping poverty. The authors of a recent Organization for Economic Cooperation and Development (OECD) study provide support for this point:

> It is not surprising . . . that the percentage of the United States population that falls below the official poverty line has declined considerably over the last decade or more (from 22.4 percent of total population in 1959 to 11.9 percent in 1973). For, as long as poverty is defined in absolute terms, economic growth is likely to be enough to eliminate much of it without any special income maintenance programs.[34]

Liberals argue that verification of the inadequacy of the SSA standard is suggested by the research of another government agency.[35] The Bureau of Labor Statistics (BLS) annually estimates the income families need to live at a "lower-level," a "middle-level," and a "higher-level" standard of living. The BLS estimated that in 1978 an urban family of four needed to gross $18,622 to live at a middle-level or moderate standard. A lower-level standard of living, the BLS said, would have required $11,546—almost $5,000 more than the poverty standard. The BLS concluded that a lower-level standard in 1978 would have required $3,574 for food, $2,233 for housing, and $5,739 for such items as transportation ($856), clothing ($847), personal care ($302), medical care ($1,065), social security ($719), and taxes ($935).

Liberals note that for the same size and type of family, the SSA poverty standard for 1978 allowed only $2,221 for food, or $1.52 per person per day. The BLS standard allowed $2.44 per day for each person's food needs. As the above figures show, the BLS allowance for necessities other than food and shelter total more than twice the SSA's allowance for necessities. In fact, liberals argue, the assumptions of the BLS standard for lower-level families are quite spartan. For example, the BLS assumes that families at the lower-level live in rental housing without air conditioning, rely heavily on public transportation where it is available and own an 8-year-old car where it is not, perform most services for themselves, and utilize free recreational facilities.[36] Thus, by the estimates of the BLS the poverty standard represents a bare subsistence level, one that leaves the poor far below the living standards of even lower-income families, and far from a moderate standard of living.

Liberals point out that a number of studies have revealed that millions of people would be added to the poverty count if only modest changes were made in the SSA's standard. In 1976 the Department of Health and Human Services published a study showing the impact of modest increases in the food budget used by the SSA. The most minimal of changes increased the poverty count for 1974 from 24.3 million to 39.9 million.[37] If both the food budget and the multiplication factors are changed (to reflect more recent research on the percent of poor people's budget spent on food), the poverty count exceeds 50 million. The U.S. Bureau of the Census publishes figures which reveal how substantially an even minor alteration in the poverty measure would affect the poverty count. The U.S. Bureau of the Census concluded that if in 1980 the poverty threshold for various family sizes had been raised by only 25 percent, 40.6 million U.S. citizens, rather than 29.3 million, would have been poor even after cash social welfare benefits. This would have included 14.9 percent of all white U.S. citizens, and 40.2 percent of all black U.S. citizens.[38]

Similarly, liberals note, if the poverty count were based on the median income of average families, the count would increase very substantially. For example, in many nations it is common to define the poor as those who have less than 50 to 66 percent of the median income for their family size.[39] If this approach were adopted in the United States, it would substantially raise the poverty standard and the poverty count. For example, in 1980 the official poverty threshold for an urban family of four was $8,414. The median income for four-person families was $24,332. If half the median income was used as the poverty standard, the relative standard would have been $12,166—an increase in the poverty standard for four-person families of more than 40 percent. Roughly estimated, a relative standard of this type for all family sizes would yield a poverty count of 50 to 60 million poor U.S. citizens.

Has Poverty Actually Been Abolished?

In several recent, well-publicized books and articles a number of conservative scholars have argued that the government's failure to measure in-kind benefits covers up the fact that poverty has not just been lowered below the official poverty count, but has in fact been eliminated.[40] These scholars argue that the value of in-kind benefits is so much higher than the aggregate income gap of the poor that if in-kind transfers are considered, all the poor are pushed over the poverty line.

Liberals disagree vigorously, pointing out that these studies are based on five assumptions that are either wrong or highly questionable.[41] They are as follows:

1 That in-kind transfers go entirely to those who are counted as poor

2 That of the poor who receive in-kind transfers, none receive benefits from more than one in-kind program

3 That all the poor receive in-kind transfers

4 That in-kind transfers are worth their market value (the government's cost) to the recipient

5 That the poverty standard is reasonable and does not need to be adjusted by using an updated multiplication rate or a more adequate food budget

Liberals point out that the first three assumptions are factually wrong. First, they note that in recent years at least half of all in-kind transfers have gone to individuals or families that were not counted among the poor.[42] Thus, even if the other assumptions above were correct, only about half the cost of in-kind programs should have been considered. Second, of the official poor who do receive in-kind assistance, about 25 percent receive assistance from at least three programs.[43] AFDC families generally receive food stamps, Medicaid benefits, and often housing and school lunch assistance. SSI recipients are eligible for Medicaid assistance and food stamps in most states. Liberals argue that it is clearly wrong, then, to assume that the costs of in-kind programs can be equally apportioned to each poor person. Some of the poor receive a great deal more than an equal share. Third, a very significant proportion of all those persons counted as poor receive no in-kind transfers. For example, in 1979, 28 percent of the official poor did not receive any in-kind assistance.[44]

Liberals argue that the fourth assumption is highly questionable. It assumes that the value of in-kind transfers is equal to the government's costs. Medicaid services, liberals argue, provide a good example of why this is a dubious assumption. Medicaid services, which are often dispensed by Medicaid "mills," may be expensive yet worthless or even harmful to recipients. Additionally, a dying person who receives expensive Medicaid services would be pushed over the poverty threshold, perhaps even into some upper-income group. But the person could hardly be said to have escaped poverty because of an expensive lingering illness, or death.

Liberals note that about two-thirds of all in-kind expenditures are for medical services, and the government's estimate of the per capita expenditure for the aged (almost $3,000 each in 1979) itself is enough to push almost all the aged over the poverty threshold. Thus, if in-kind transfers are counted at their market value, almost no aged person in the United States could be considered poor. This is hardly realistic. It assumes that the aged obtain their yearly shelter, nourishment, and heat by visiting their doctor or by a stay in the hospital.

Some of the scholars who believe that in-kind benefits should be counted, but believe that medical transfers cannot realistically be counted at market value, have tried to estimate the actual value to poverty recipients of medical services. Smeeding estimates that it is about one-seventh of the government's cost.[45] When Smeeding recalculates the poverty count making this adjustment and includes all other in-kind transfers to the poor, he concludes that 13.7 million U.S citizens were left poor in 1980. If the medical transfers are not counted but all other in-kind transfers are, 18 million U.S. citizens were left in poverty in 1980.[46]

But, liberals note, even Smeeding's sophisticated reanalysis is based on the government's official poverty standard. While Smeeding's strictest assumptions reduce the official poverty count by half, government studies show that adjustments in food budgets and the multiplication factor would increase the poverty count by 15 to 31 million. Thus, liberals argue, a much improved measure which included in-kind benefits, taxes paid, and underreporting of income, while adjusting the multiplication factor and the food budget, would probably show from 5 to 20 million additional poor.

Thus, while many conservatives believe that the official poverty counts seriously overestimate the number of people left in poverty after welfare expenditures, liberals believe that the official figures actually underestimate poverty.

The Poor

Who are the U.S. citizens the government counts as poor? The most obvious thing the government's figures point out is that the poverty class in the United States is disproportionately drawn from minorities, the aged, the young, and women. While numerically a majority of the poor are white, only 10.2 percent of all white U.S. citizens were poor in 1980. However, 32.5 percent (nearly 1 in 3) of all black U.S. citizens were poor, and nearly 26 percent of all Spanish-origin citizens lived in poverty. In 1980, 13 percent of the poor were over 65, and 39 percent were less than 18 years old. If the aged and dependent poor are added together, they constituted 52 percent of all poor U.S. citizens in 1980.

One of the most dramatic changes in the composition of poverty in the United States in the last twenty-five years has been the "feminization" of poverty. Increasingly, women head families, and female-led families constitute a larger and larger share of all poverty families. Between 1960 and 1980 the percentage of all U.S. families headed by women increased by almost 80 percent. By 1980, 15 percent of all U.S. families were headed by a woman.

In 1980, over half of all the poor families in the United States were female-headed (female households without a husband, and married families headed by females). In 1959, 77 percent of poor families were headed by a male. By 1971, the percentage of poor, male-headed families had dropped to 60 percent, and by 1980 males headed only 49 percent of all poor families. Female-headed families suffer a much higher rate of poverty than do male-headed families. Only 6.2 percent of male-headed families were poor in 1980, but 32.7 percent of all female-headed families lived in poverty.

Race plays a major role in predicting whether a family will escape poverty. The rate of poverty among white families is rather low (8 percent). Of the poor white families, most are headed by a couple. Of the white, female-headed families the rate of poverty is high (26 percent), but not as high as for other racial groups. Among black families the trend is quite different. Twenty-nine percent of all black families live in poverty. Seventy-one percent of all poor black families are headed by a female, and almost half of all black, female-headed households live in poverty. A somewhat similar trend prevails among Spanish-origin families. One-fifth of all Spanish-origin families live in poverty, and women head about half of all poverty families. As with black families, half of all Spanish-origin families headed by a female live in poverty.

One last prominent feature about poverty is that there is considerable regional variation. In 1980, 42 percent of all the poor lived in the south, 20 percent lived in the northeast, and 22 percent lived in the north central states. Only 17 percent of the poor lived in the west. The south's high poverty is a function, in part, of a low wage structure, especially for minorities and women, and more modest welfare expenditures.

Summary

Conservatives and liberals may disagree about the number of people left in poverty after welfare expenditures, but both groups tend to agree on at least two points. The first is that the nation's welfare programs are expensive, and getting more expensive all the time. Second, both groups tend to believe that our welfare programs are not as effective as they should be. The criticisms of the welfare system put forth by conservatives and liberals sometimes merge. For example, both conservatives and liberals often make the following points:[47]

1 Welfare programs and rules often discourage poor people from working. Multiple benefits, high tax rates on some earnings, and exclusion of some working poor from in-kind programs such as Medicaid often discourage some of the poor from working.

2 There are far too many individual welfare programs. The numerous programs often fail to mesh, creating duplication and even dysfunctional impacts on the poor.

3 Assistance is narrow in coverage, unresponsive to the needs of many poor people, and often detrimental in its impact. The categorical nature of welfare programs allows the neglect of single persons, couples without children, and intact male-headed families. The result is not only inadequate response to the needs of many of the poor but also the frequent destruction of the family unit.

4 Much of the overlap, waste, and ineffectiveness of welfare programs is attributable to the fact that they are administered by too many levels of government (federal, state, local).

5 Because each state has considerable latitude over the number of state and federal dollars its poor will receive, there are extreme interstate variations in welfare aid. Conservatives believe that the states should play a major role, but they often agree that variations in benefits by state are too extreme.

6 Welfare programs lack horizontal equity—those with the same need do not receive the same degree of aid.

7 Welfare programs lack vertical equity—those with the greatest need do not receive aid before those with less severe needs.

In addition to these specific points, liberals often argue that the whole structure and approach of welfare programs are self-defeating. The argument is often made that the programs, individually and collectively, are not designed to end poverty by transferring out of poverty those poor families who could support themselves with the right help and under the right circumstances. Nor are they designed to make certain that the children of the poor do not suffer the handicaps that plague many of their parents. Instead, most welfare programs are oriented toward providing some minimal level of resources to certain groups of the poor, while the problems that handicap them—lack of job skills, inadequate education, low self-confidence, unemployment and subemployment—are left unaddressed. Many believe that maintaining the poor at a subsistence level through assistance may actually encourage or allow the poor to continue to ignore the basic problems that keep them in poverty.[48]

Both liberals and conservatives have promoted many welfare reforms in recent years, and, as we will describe below, they have often agreed on certain fundamental reforms. But before these proposals are reviewed, we will examine welfare programs in some western nations to determine if the experiences of these nations suggest policy alternatives that might inform welfare reform in the United States.

SOCIAL WELFARE PROGRAMS: THE EUROPEAN APPROACH

Studying social welfare programs in the western industrialized nations provides an important comparative perspective to the analysis of U.S. antipoverty efforts. This is not because these nations have succeeded in eradicating poverty. A few nations, such as Sweden, West Germany, Austria, Switzerland, and Norway, do have very little poverty, but other nations, such as France and Britain, have a rate of poverty quite similar to the rate in the United States.[49] What is important is that the variety of antipoverty strategies employed by these nations provides a basis for weighing alternatives to U.S. approaches. This is an important undertaking because almost the entirety of poverty research undertaken within the United States has been narrowly framed, most often evaluating programs only in their own terms with little, if any, in-depth consideration to the advantages and disadvantages of alternative strategies.

Below we discuss three major antipoverty strategies and programs found in Western Europe. These include the preventive and universal design of many European social welfare programs and Sweden's labor market strategy.

1. Prevention

European social welfare programs generally are designed to prevent social problems rather than respond to the consequences or manifestations of those problems. The European programs are based on the belief that to be preventive, social welfare programs must be comprehensive. Programs must be designed, in other words, so that citizens cannot fall through the cracks. There are at least three major policy areas which demonstrate the commitment of various European nations to the prevention of social ills. They are family, health care, and housing policies.

Family Policy   All the European nations have been more committed to supportive services for families than has the United States. In the European nations there is a firmer belief that a healthy environment is essential to a stable family life and good child development. Kahn and Kamerman make a typical liberal argument about these programs:

> What the Europeans apparently know but what many Americans do not yet perceive is that social services may support, strengthen, and enhance the normal family—and that failures in social provision may undermine our most precious institutions and relationships. The issue is not whether or not government will intervene. It will. The question is will it intervene for enhancement and prevention or to respond to breakdown, problems, and deviance alone.[50]

There is also a belief in Europe that family policy can promote specific societal goals such as childbearing, low infant mortality rates, and women's equality.

Family policy in Europe starts with paid maternity leaves for working women, prenatal and postnatal mother and child care, family allowances, and child care. In most of the nations there are also specific programs designed to assure families of adequate housing. In all the Scandinavian nations and Britain, West Germany, France, and Belgium, among others, working women receive maternity benefits under the national insurance scheme. Sweden's program is one of the most comprehensive. Mothers normally receive 36 weeks leave, but this can be extended under some circumstances. After the birth of the child, either the mother or father can take the leave. The parent on leave is assured 90 percent of his or her normal pay. In West Germany leaves are 14 weeks in duration and are extended only to women who belong to an approved sickness fund (which includes most workers). The mother receives 100 percent of her normal income. In England the leave is for 18 weeks, and in France it is 14 weeks. In France the mother only receives 50 percent of her normal income.[51]

As part of their medical systems, all the major Western European nations have special programs to administer to the health care needs of pregnant mothers and young children. The benefits under these programs include prenatal and postnatal mother and child care. In the Scandinavian nations there are maternity centers where expectant mothers receive free prenatal and delivery care. Once the child is born the centers provide regular checkups and care. For mothers who cannot travel to the centers there are health visitors (trained nurses) who make home visits. Almost all mothers in these nations use the maternity centers. The Scandinavian nations have the world's lowest rate of infant mortality, and many believe that the availability of care significantly accounts for this fact.

The French also have a system of maternity centers. Parents cannot receive their family allowances unless they take their children to the centers for periodic checkups.[52] In England, West Germany, and Belgium prenatal and postnatal services are provided as a regular part of the nation's health care system.

Another common feature of European family policy is family allowances. These are designed to encourage population growth and good family environments by paying part of the cost of child support. In the Scandinavian nations, Canada, and Belgium, among others, the allowances are universal and tax free. All families, in other words, receive the allowance, regardless of the family's income. In Britain and France only families with two or more children receive an allowance. West Germany's program provides the least coverage because only families with two or more children are covered, and the program is means-tested. Only families below a certain income are eligible.

One last feature of family policy is the existence in many nations of a network of state-administered and subsidized child care centers. The most universal network of child care centers is found in Sweden, Norway, and Denmark.[53] In these nations child care facilities are still inadequate but have been developing rapidly since the 1960s. The child care centers tend to be neighborhood-based and supervised by a board of parents and professional child care workers.

The centers are designed primarily to meet the needs of working parents, but they also serve other groups as well. In all the centers the children receive educational, nutritional, and medical care. The educational program varies according to the age of the children, and becomes rather sophisticated by the fourth and fifth year. Good nutrition is stressed and medical and dental checkups are scheduled throughout the year. The centers care for preschool children, and also provide after-hour care for schoolchildren. Some centers are open 24 hours a day to accommodate families that work night shifts. Parents also may leave children at a center for only a few hours while they run errands. The fees charged the parents vary by the number of children the family has in the center and the parents' income. The fees are kept modest so that the center's use will not be discouraged.

France also has a system of child care, but the centers are primarily designed for children 3 to 5 years old. The centers serve as preschools, or kindergartens.[54] In recent years France, England, and West Germany have been expanding child care facilities, but in the latter two countries parents still rely primarily on private care for their children.

The child care systems free parents for work or education and they provide a wide range of beneficial services to children. Good child care also makes it easier for parents (both mothers and fathers) to combine parenthood with a career. Where single parents are concerned, child care programs allow single parents to work, instead of staying at home on welfare.

Housing Policy   Most of the European nations have concluded that it is in society's best interest to see that all citizens have good-quality housing. These governments use a variety of methods to expand the base of decent housing. In addition, they often provide housing allowances to help low-income citizens obtain better housing. Chapter 8 examines these policies in some depth. While the housing policies of these nations are far from perfect, there is no doubt that the programs have greatly improved living environments. None of the countries with housing programs have the type of big city ghetto areas found in the United States, where housing problems are acute. England and France do have housing that is grim, but it is still superior to the worst U.S. neighborhoods. In Sweden, West Germany, Switzerland, Norway, Austria, and Denmark, among other nations, rural housing is on average far superior to that found in the United States, and there is little or no real slum property in the cities of these nations.

Health Care Policy   All the Western European nations have adopted health care programs that extend comprehensive medical services to all citizens, regardless of their income level (See Chapter 3.) These health programs include benefits such as maternity and sickness allowances, and prenatal and postnatal care. The programs are designed, in part, to prevent poverty by promoting good health. They also prevent poverty because a family cannot be bankrupted by medical expenses, and they help the poor who do fall ill get back on their feet through medical and other supportive services. Some of the nations, such as West Germany, have oriented their health care systems toward preventive health care, rather than the acute health care system found in the United States.[55] The preventive orientation seeks to reduce productivity losses and even poverty through a healthy and medically informed public.

2. Universality

Social welfare programs are generally less categorical in Europe than they are in the United States. Rather than being designed just for the poor, they are often designed for all citizens, regardless of wealth. This is true of European housing and health care programs, and, as noted above, generally true of policies designed to assist families.

Many scholars argue that there are at least three advantages of universal, as opposed to poverty-specific, programs. First, a universal program is much more likely to be acceptable to the public. A program designed just for the poor carries a stigma and generally receives less political and public support than does a program designed to assist all the public. The stigma associated with a poverty-client program also can discourage even the needy from utilizing it because of the shame associated with participation. Some argue that the stigma associated with poverty programs in the United States explains, in part, why only about one-half the families who could qualify for food stamps apply for them.

Second, because the programs are universal they tend to be designed better than the poverty-specific programs in the United States. This is because the programs have stronger public support and do not have the punitive orientation of poverty-client programs. Being more broadly oriented, the goals of a universal program can be more positive, and policies can be designed to achieve those goals. This helps explain why housing and medical programs in Europe have a more positive impact on poor citizens than do poverty programs in the United States such as Medicaid and public housing.

Third, universal programs do not require people to stay poor to receive needed benefits. George Gilder, a conservative scholar, argues that millions of U.S. citizens remain unemployed or subemployed and on the dole because they would lose their Medicaid benefits if they worked.[56] Liberals tend to agree with this point.

3. Labor Market Strategy

A labor market strategy is a series of techniques designed to promote public well-being and equality through the economy. A good market strategy creates a healthy economy that meets the needs of most citizens and thereby decreases the need for social welfare programs, allowing the nation to deal more effectively and generously with those citizens who cannot meet their needs through the market. The strategy also may be designed to contribute to public growth and dignity by allowing the public to shape the economy to meet their needs.

Sweden has one of the best articulated and most successful strategies of any major nation. Sweden's strategy is based on three major principles: full employment, a decent wage combined with job satisfaction, and economic efficiency.[57]

Full Employment   The Swedish practice maximalist full employment. This policy involves two major elements. First, they try to provide a job for every citizen who wants one. Second, the job should pay a decent wage and be satisfying. The Swedish feel that every citizen should have the right to quit a job and train for a new one if he or she is seriously dissatisfied with his or her job. The Swedish, in fact, are concerned that a constant effort be made to upgrade the work environment of all employees. A 1976 law requires all firms to earmark 20 percent of net profits for improvements in the workplace environment.[58]

The Swedish have been quite successful in ensuring full employment. The unemployment rate averaged 1.8 percent between 1960 and 1973, and 1.9 percent between 1974 and 1980.[59] Employment policy is in part a critical form of preventive social policy. By assuring citizens of a good job, the nation avoids much of the costs associated with unemployment compensation and the social problems spawned by economic deprivation.

Economic Efficiency   The Swedish believe that their economy must be economically efficient. This means that industry must innovate to promote productivity, and that weak, inefficient businesses must be weeded out. Union featherbedding is not allowed because it reduces productivity. Workers and unions do not have to struggle to protect obsolete jobs because if workers' jobs are abolished, they are assured of other equally good jobs. The Swedish goal is a modern, highly productive economic system that enables businesses to successfully compete in international markets.

The Swedish do not emphasize economic efficiency to encourage materialism. They encourage it to produce the surpluses needed to provide a wide range of supportive human services. Thus, efficiency is employed to enhance human welfare.

Summary

European social welfare policies differ from U.S. policies in some important ways. First, European social welfare programs are often designed to prevent rather than respond to poverty. Second, European social welfare programs tend to be universal. Unlike U.S. programs, they are designed for all individuals and families, not just the poor. This removes the stigma from social programs and broadens public support for them. These two design features are perhaps the most important program differences between European and U.S. welfare programs. Individual European programs do not work perfectly by any means, and the growth of welfare programs and their costs is as much a concern of continental governments as it is in the United States. But it is often argued that European nations get more for their welfare dollar because their programs are better designed.

Last, the concept of a market strategy, epitomized so well by the Swedish approach, helps eliminate poverty. A viable market strategy not only takes care of most of the public's needs, it also creates the surpluses needed to succor those citizens who cannot participate in the market.

Of course, as noted in Chapter 1, it would be naive to assume that economic problems in the United States and Sweden are of equal magnitude. Still, a review of Sweden's labor market strategy is insightful because it emphasizes the critical relationship between a nation's economic system and its ability to deal with public needs. Sweden's policy makers concluded that a welfare state required an extremely viable economy. The economy would have to be wisely designed to create the surpluses needed to finance the welfare state while remaining competitive on the world scene. Sweden has had a broad measure of success, and the basic option of a market strategy is one that any nation could adopt. But, of course, the problems that would have to be overcome, and the strategies that could effectively be employed, would vary considerably from one nation to the next.

OPTIONS FOR REFORMING THE U.S. WELFARE SYSTEM

Starting with the Nixon administration, there have been a number of major efforts to reform the U.S. welfare system. Presidents Nixon, Ford, and Carter all recommended major welfare reforms to Congress. Interestingly, all the reform proposals involved substituting a negative income tax and/or guaranteed income for most of the nation's current welfare programs. None of the proposals sought to emphasize family policy, and none placed major emphasis on policies to improve the economy. While the reform proposals were seriously debated during both the Nixon and Carter presidencies, they eventually failed in Congress. Perhaps the most interesting feature of the long reform effort is that for some 10 years both conservatives and liberals pursued basically the same types of reform.

Before we examine the specific reform proposals it would be helpful to clarify the basic design and intent of the two major proposals. First, a guaranteed income plan is a very simple concept. It is designed for individuals who cannot participate in the job market (e.g., the aged, the ill or disabled, mothers of small children). Under such a plan, the government would establish an income level that citizens of a certain age and circumstance would be guaranteed. If the individual or family had the specified level of income from such sources as a retirement plan, savings, or earnings, no assistance would be given. If their income fell below the specified level, they would receive enough assistance to bring them up to the guaranteed level.

A negative income tax (NIT) is a more complicated idea. The NIT is a concept generally accredited to conservative economist Milton Friedman.[60] Since its introduction by Friedman in 1962, it has been proposed in many forms.[61] While individual plans vary, the basic characteristics are constant. All NIT proposals include a cash floor for poor individuals and families. For example, a proposal could specify that a family of four needs an income of at least $7,500.00. A family whose earnings fell below the floor would receive a supplementary grant to bring them up to the floor and no more. Up to this point the NIT works like a guaranteed income proposal.

However, to encourage the poor to work, a NIT plan allows recipients to receive some type of matching aid for earnings above the floor up to some cutoff or break-even point. For example, a break-even point might be set at $12,500.00 for a family of four. A family that earned $8,500.00 ($1,000.00 more than the floor) would receive some proportion of the deficit between earnings and the break-even point ($12,500.00 − $8,500.00). The rate at which the deficit would be funded is generally called the tax rate. Most proposals call for a tax rate of 0.50. Thus, the family that earned $8,500.00 would receive 50 percent of the deficit between $12,500.00 and $8,500.00 ($4,000.00), which would be $2,000.00. This $2,000.00 would give the family a total income of $10,500.00.

NIT proposals, then, provide a basic floor of income for all families, a cutoff point for aid, and work incentives based on a funding scheme for those earning above the floor but below the break-even point.

The first attempt to establish a NIT plan as a substitute for the traditional welfare approach was the Family Assistance Plan (FAP) recommended to Congress by President Nixon in 1969.[62] Although the FAP stirred considerable controversy and was twice passed by the House of Representatives, it was finally rejected by Congress in 1972.

The demise of FAP led to a more sophisticated and comprehensive NIT proposal developed by the Joint Economic Committee of Congress.[63] In

1974 the committee proposed a NIT plan based on cash grants, tax reform, and tax credits. The plan was entitled Allowances for Basic Living Expenses (ABLE); it was estimated that it would cost about $15.4 billion if fully operational in 1976, with about half the cost in the form of tax relief to low-income working families.

Shortly after the Joint Economic Committee put forth the ABLE proposal, the Ford administration formulated a plan entitled the Income Supplement Program (ISP). Like ABLE, ISP proposed a NIT program, consolidation of some programs, and tax breaks. Like ABLE, the plan provided $3,600.00 in cash assistance to a penniless family of four. However, because of high inflation and unemployment during Ford's administration, all reform proposals were set aside.

In the fall of 1977, President Carter forwarded to Congress a major welfare reform proposal.[64] Carter's plan emphasized a dual strategy: the poor would have been divided into those who could work and those who could not. Those designated as capable of work were expected to accept a public- or private-sector job, which the government would have supplemented through the use of a NIT program if wages fell below levels established for varying family sizes. Many workers also would receive some tax relief (the cutoff point for a family of four would have been $15,600.00). Those unable to work would be eligible for a guaranteed income based on family size. The income programs and the job programs would cover all the poor, including two-parent families, single persons, and childless couples.

The Jobs Component

To provide employment for the poor, the plan proposed the creation of 1.4 million public-sector jobs, some 300,000 of which were part-time. The jobs would have paid the minimum wage. To qualify for one of the public-sector jobs, an individual had to be unemployed for 5 weeks. All holders of the newly created jobs were required once every 12 months to engage in a thorough search for private-sector employment.

Those required to work would have included parents with children above 14 and those healthy, nonelderly adults with no children. Single parents with children aged 7 to 14 were expected to work full-time if child care facilities were available, part-time if they were not. Single parents with preschool children were exempt from the work requirement. Some 42 percent of the public-sector jobs were reserved for heads of AFDC families. Additionally, many low-income workers (the major exceptions being those holding the public-sector jobs created under the plan and families without children) would receive some tax breaks. Families with children could claim a 10 percent tax credit on earnings up to $4,000.00. Above $4,000.00

in earnings an additional credit of 5 percent could be claimed up to a cutoff point at which the family would have ceased to be eligible for cash assistance. The various supplements were designed to make employment more attractive than welfare and to encourage workers to earn above the threshold point. The denial of the tax credit to those holding the public-sector jobs was designed to encourage them to obtain employment in the private sector.

The Guaranteed Income Component

Those who could not work would receive a cash grant under a guaranteed income plan. The grant would replace the AFDC, SSI, and Food Stamp programs. The cash grants would be small and vary by family size. A family of four would receive a total grant of $4,200.00, about $1,615.00 less than the poverty threshold for a nonfarm family of four in 1977. (In 1977 only twelve states, mostly in the south, paid less than $4,200.00 a year to a four-person family.) An aged, blind, or disabled individual would receive only $1,100.00; a couple without children would receive $2,200.00.

The cash grants were modest for two reasons. Most obviously they were meant to force as many adults as possible to work. Second, the low grants were designed to encourage state supplements. The federal government would pay 75 percent of the first $500.00 in supplements for a family of four, and 25 percent of all additional supplements.

Congressional Rejection

For a variety of reasons, Congress rejected Carter's reform plan. Critics pointed out that benefits to nonworkers under the plan were quite low, that the jobs it would have created were only minimum-wage jobs, that there was little emphasis on quality child care, and that it was not based on a market strategy.[65] Many members of Congress also feared that during periods of high unemployment, Carter's welfare plan would have greatly raised welfare costs. And, as we will detail below, many members of Congress have severe reservations about the efficacy and impact of NIT plans.

The Failure of Reform

Both conservatives and liberals often argue that welfare reform has been stymied because it must meet a number of seemingly conflicting goals. Martin Anderson, for example, argues that "to become a political reality the plan must provide a decent level of support for those on welfare, it must contain strong incentives to work, and it must have a reasonable cost. And it must do all three at the same time."[66] Anderson, Friedman, and

Gilder all argue that it would be impossible for any plan to achieve all the necessary conditions.[67] All the major welfare reform proposals discussed above scared off some supporters because it was feared that the new plan would be more expensive than the old system.[68] Many moderates, and even some liberals, also refused to support the various plans because benefits to many recipients would have been lower under the substitute plan.[69]

Liberals, however, raise two points. They often argue that the reform dilemma discussed above occurred for two reasons. First, the cost problems occurred because the reform proposals were not comprehensive enough. They argue that if a reform proposal included social security, social welfare costs could be reduced. The social security program, liberals argue, should be turned into a genuine insurance program based on a guaranteed income concept. Only those elderly persons with resources or incomes below a guaranteed level would receive any benefits. A guaranteed income for the elderly would be considerably less expensive than social security, and the savings here would reduce social welfare expenditures.[70]

Second, liberals argue that the reform proposals failed because too little attention was paid to the economy. They suggest that the reform plans might very well have expanded the welfare rolls because the unemployment rate was high and growing throughout the 1970s. Liberals believe that genuine reform can occur only if it is coordinated with a market strategy designed to greatly reduce the unemployment rate and improve the overall performance of the economy.[71]

The major welfare reform efforts failed for one reason not included in the reform dilemma discussed above. They failed in part because many members of Congress are skeptical of the negative income tax proposal. Their fear is that the NIT would encourage millions of poor U.S. citizens to quit their jobs and stay at home. Although the NIT is not an untested proposal, most would agree that it has not been adequately tested. The Institute for the Study of Poverty did conduct a number of experiments in urban and rural areas to determine how well the NIT concept would work.[72] Selected families were enrolled in a NIT program and their work habits and other social behavior were studied for the duration of the experiment.

The studies showed that male heads of households reduced their work efforts very little (about 5 percent). Female heads of households also reduced their work efforts very little (about 8 percent). Wives dropped out of the job market at a rather high rate—reducing their work effort by 22 percent. Children in the families reduced their work role by some 46 percent. Interpretation of these findings is to some extent a matter of value judgment. Reduction of work effort by wives and children might be considered positive if it promoted the family or improved the educational performance of the children. But the reductions in work effort by heads of households clearly worried many policy makers. This may seem puzzling since the work reductions were small. But the concern of many policy makers grows out of the fact that the NIT recipients were aware that they were part of a closely observed experiment. Each family was interviewed twenty-two times a year. Many policy makers feared that a less closely observed set of recipients would reduce their work effort much more substantially.[73] The experiments were clearly not extensive enough to address these fears. As a result, many members of Congress, including conservatives, moderates, and even some liberals, simply are not convinced that the NIT is a viable reform alternative.

Conservative and Liberal Reform Proposals

Fears of the NIT have convinced many conservatives that our present welfare system is reasonably effective and that it should be reformed in only minor ways. Martin Anderson, a policy advisor to both Presidents Nixon and Reagan, provides the following assessment:

> There may be great inefficiencies in our welfare programs, the level of fraud may be very high, the quality of management may be terrible, the programs may overlap, inequities may abound, and the financial incentives to work may be virtually nonexistent. But if we step back and judge a vast array of welfare programs by two basic criteria—the completeness of coverage for those who really need help, and the adequacy of the amount of help they do receive—the picture changes dramatically. Judged by these standards our welfare system has been a brilliant success.[74]

Anderson believes that the idea of substantially reforming our welfare system should be abandoned and that we should try instead to make the current system work better.

Another prominent conservative, George Gilder, basically agrees. Gilder argues that the NIT would be a disastrous substitute for the nation's current welfare programs. He argues that the poor can escape poverty only through work, family, and faith. Gilder argues that many poor U.S. citizens simply do not work hard enough. He believes that this is true because many poor families (especially those headed by a woman) often live better on welfare than on the incomes they can earn in the market. He believes that a NIT would only enhance this problem. Gilder does not believe that women will ever do very well in the job market because their family responsibilities will always keep them from devoting full attention to their jobs. Women, he believes, should stay home and let the men work.[75]

Gilder believes that the welfare system drives fathers away from their families because they often cannot support them as well as they can be supported by the welfare system or even by the wife. This is a particularly critical problem for black families. Young black males are discouraged from working because they have been denied the opportunity to support their families. Steps must be taken so that young males learn to accept their responsibilities and work harder. Gilder would have women stay home so that the husband could have the psychological satisfaction of fulfilling his need to be the breadwinner. Welfare support would be lowered, aimed primarily at emergencies, and limited to in-kind aid (like food stamps) rather than cash. To keep Medicaid from being a work disincentive, a fee system would be established to make the program less desirable, and working mothers would not have their benefits reduced or taken away.

Since Gilder believes that the families of poor citizens must be strengthened if poverty is to be overcome, he supports the adoption of a universal system of family allowances.[76] He feels that the evidence indicates that family allowances have greatly aided families in Europe and have spared the countries that employ them many of the social problems that plague this nation. The allowances would be universal so that people will not have to be poor or stay poor to receive them.

Last, Gilder argues that the poor must be given faith in their ability to improve their lot. Faith in one's ability to improve one's future through hard work, often lacking among the poor, is important to all people. It is wrong, he says, for the message to be spread that racism, for example, holds back black citizens. Gilder argues that there is almost no racism in the United States today and that to lead blacks to believe that there is only discourages them.[77]

Some conservatives, such as Milton Friedman, still believe that the best alternative would be to adopt the NIT proposal. Friedman believes that the NIT experiments vindicated the proposal, and that there is still a good chance that the NIT concept will be adopted. The benefits under the NIT must be lower than under current welfare programs, Friedman believes, to keep program costs down and to encourage work.[78]

Liberals tend to be critical of many of the conservative assumptions and proposals, but there are areas of agreement. First, they tend to believe that a guaranteed income for the aged and disabled is both necessary and humane. It is necessary to replace the social security system—which they view as an outdated and unnecessarily expensive program—in order to fund other social welfare programs. Liberals are divided over the NIT proposal. Some believe that it would be best to give AFDC a uniform benefit level and extend it to all poor families, regardless of whether they are headed by a male or female. Others would prefer to give the NIT proposal a national trial.[79]

A fundamental flaw that most liberals find in the conservative critiques and proposals is that they pay little attention to the economy. Most liberals feel that many poor citizens are poorly integrated into the job market because there are no decent jobs for them, because they cannot get needed job training, or because they cannot obtain or afford the child care services they require. It will be necessary, they argue, to establish job training programs to teach the poor the skills they need, and perhaps even for the government to become the employer of last resort.[80]

Many liberals also contend that a national family policy that included universal maternity leaves, prenatal and postnatal child care, and family planning and child care could play a large role in preventing poverty. They note that the largest group of welfare recipients in the United States is single women and their dependent children. Over 3.5 million women and about 7.5 million children constitute the major recipient group of the AFDC program. In recent years some 99 percent of all AFDC families also have received Medicaid services, and about 75 percent have received food stamps. Mothers and their children are, then, the largest and most expensive group of welfare recipients in America.

Many liberals note that if the European approach was followed, family policies could be designed to serve the needs of all families. The intent would be to promote women's equality, prevent families from falling into poverty, and provide the poor with the support they need to achieve independence. A universal system of child care, for example, would free parents to work, or to obtain the education and job training they need for work. A system of child care that addressed the educational, nutritional, and health needs of poor children would help to break the cycle of poverty by ensuring that the poor start life without many of the typical poverty-related handicaps. Most liberals would be quite sympathetic to Gilder's family allowance proposal.[81]

Liberals do not agree with Gilder's call for women to quit the job market and their professions in order to return to the home. The entry of women into the job market reflects healthy and inevitable alterations in lifestyles and family structures, a lowering of discriminatory barriers, and outright economic necessity. They feel the evidence indicates that most women, including those who are married, work out of compelling economic necessity.[82] Liberals do not accept the argument that some men always will be discouraged from working as long as women are in the job market. The type of man that Gilder refers to will accept family responsibilities when our society provides him with opportunities to earn a decent living in the job market.

Liberals do not accept Gilder's argument that racism is a thing of the past in the United States. They do, in fact, argue that current and past racism accounts for many of the problems that continue to plague minorities and women in the United States. True, racism is a much less severe problem now than it once was, and in some cases being a minority can open opportunities. But liberals believe that discrimination is still a significant problem. They are sympathetic to Gilder's argument that faith is an important motivation, and that many poor people have less faith in their abilities and future than they should have. But there are many features of the political and economic system that serve to discourage the poor. Until job opportunities, housing, and many other conditions in our society are improved, many people will have good reason to doubt their ability to join the great American dream.

Liberals, then, believe that ending poverty in the United States means designing better welfare programs and providing certain services such as good housing, equal educational opportunities, health care, and child care to all citizens. They also believe that these programs must be based upon, and backed up by, a healthy economy that meets the needs of all citizens.

CONCLUSION

The nation's response to its poor and financially pressed citizens has created a large, complex, and very expensive welfare system. Most scholars and policy makers, and much of the public, believe that the current welfare system is less efficient and effective than it should be. But as this chapter has shown, there is no consensus about the reforms or alternatives that should be pursued, and efforts to radically reform the welfare system under both Republican and Democratic administrations have failed. It is interesting to note, however, that all major political groups in the United States now believe that the nation is obligated to assist its less fortunate citizens. Some conservative welfare reform proposals, such as Milton Friedman's negative income tax proposal and George Gilder's family allowance proposal, have a distinctly radical ring to them.

Both conservatives and liberals tend to believe that most of the able-bodied poor must be moved into the job market, and that the welfare system should strengthen the family. Conservatives tend to put more stress on designing programs to encourage the poor to develop self-reliance, on keeping programs and their costs as modest as possible, and on allowing state and local governments as much participation as possible. Liberals place more stress on reforming the economy so that there will be better job opportunities, and on more universal social welfare programs to provide all citizens with child care, housing assistance, and other basic services.

Thus, while the policy differences between conservatives and liberals over the issue of poverty have narrowed over the last couple of decades, the differences between them are hardly trivial. The differences reflect divergent philosophies about the obligations of society to its citizens and the impact of government on individual freedom and growth. And these, of course, are the fundamental differences that have always divided conservatives and liberals.

NOTES

1 Walter I. Trattner, *From Poor Law to Welfare State: A History of Social Welfare in America* (New York: The Free Press, 1979); and Joe R. Feagin, *Subordinating the Poor: Welfare and American Beliefs* (Englewood Cliffs, New Jersey: Prentice-Hall, Inc., 1975), pp. 15–47.

2 Gaston Rimlinger, *Welfare Policy and Industrialization in Europe* (New York: John Wiley & Sons, 1971), p. 20; and Howard M. Leichter, *A Comparative Approach to Policy Analysis: Health Care Policy in Four Nations* (New York: Cambridge Univ. Press, 1979), p. 22.

3 Rimlinger, pp. 22–34; and Feagin, pp. 25–29.

4 Raymond A. Mohl, *Poverty in New York, 1783–1825* (New York: Oxford Univ. Press, 1971), p. 42.

5 Edgar May, *The Wasted Americans* (New York: Signet Books, 1964), p. 16.

6 Frances Fox Piven and Richard A. Cloward, *Regulating the Poor: The Functions of Public Welfare* (New York: Vantage Books, 1971), p. 47.

7 Trattner, pp. 53–54.

8 Francis Fox Piven and Richard A. Cloward, *Poor People's Movements: Why They Succeed, How They Fail* (New York: Pantheon Books, 1977), p. 42; and Feagin, pp. 25–34.

9 Piven and Cloward, *Regulating the Poor*, p. 49.

10 Paul Samuelson, *Economics* (New York: McGraw-Hill, 1967), p. 170.

11 Piven and Cloward, *Regulating the Poor*, p. 98.

12 Ibid., p. 109.

13 Robert T. Kudrle and Theodore R. Marmor, "The Development of Welfare States in North America," in *The Development of Welfare States in Europe and America*, ed. Peter Flora and Arnold J. Heidenheimer (New Brunswick, N.J.: Transaction Books, 1981), p. 94.

14 Piven and Cloward, *Regulating the Poor*, p. 117.

15 Ibid., p. 116.

16 *Social Security Bulletin*, 44, No. 8 (Aug. 1981), 40.

17 Nick Koltz, *Let Them Eat Promises: The Politics of Hunger in America* (New York: Doubleday, 1971), pp. 1–18; and Mark J. Green, James M. Fallows, and David R. Zwick, *Who Runs Congress?* (New York: Bantam Books, 1972), p. 79.

18 John C. Donovan, *The Politics of Poverty* (Indianapolis: Bobbs-Merrill, 1973), p. 178.

19 For a good summary of studies see Kirstein Gronbyerg, David Street, and Gerald D. Suttles, *Poverty and Social Change* (Chicago: The Univ. of Chicago Press, 1978), p. 60.

20 Koltz, pp. 8–9.

21 *Hunger, USA: A Report by the Citizens' Board of Inquiry into Hunger and Malnutrition in the United States* (Boston: Beacon Press, 1968), p. 16.

22 See Robert Kennedy's report in *Hunger, USA*, p. 7.

23 Christopher Leman, "Patterns of Policy Development: Social Security in the United States and Canada," *Public Policy*, 25 (Spring 1977), 261–291.

24 *Social Security Bulletin*, 44, No. 8 (Aug. 1981), 40.

25 *Social Security Bulletin,* 44, No. 3 (March 1981), 53.

26 Joel Havemann and Linda E. Demkovick, "Making Some Sense out of the Welfare 'Mess'," *National Journal,* Jan. 8, 1977, p. 44.

27 Ibid, p. 54.

28 Robert D. Plotnick and Felicity Skidmore, *Progress against Poverty: A Review of the 1964–74 Decade* (New York: Academic Press, 1975), p. 159.

29 Ibid., p. 51.

30 Ibid., pp. 85, 180–181.

31 Ibid., p. 145.

32 Ibid., p. 148.

33 Harold Watts and Felicity Skidmore, "An Update of the Poverty Picture Plus a New Look at Relative Tax Burdens," *Focus: Institute for Research on Poverty Newsletter 2,* No. 1 (Fall 1977), p. 5.

34 Organization for Economic Co-operation and Development, *Public Expenditure on Income Maintenance Programmes* (Paris: OECD, 1976), p. 63.

35 "New BLS Budgets Provide Yardstick for Measuring Family Living Costs," *Monthly Labor Review* (Apr. 1969), pp. 3–16; *Monthly Labor Review* (Jan. 1980), pp. 44–47.

36 *Monthly Labor Review* (Jan. 1980), pp. 44–47.

37 U.S. Dept. of Health, Education, and Welfare, *The Measure of Poverty* (Washington, D.C.: GPO, 1976), p. 77.

38 U.S. Bureau of the Census, "Money Income and Poverty Status of Families and Persons in the United States: 1980 (Advance Report)," *Current Population Reports,* Series P–60, No. 127, March 1981, p. 32.

39 OECD, *Public Expenditure on Income Maintenance Programmes,* pp. 64–67.

40 See E. K. Browning, "How Much Equality Can We Afford?" *The Public Interest,* July 1976, pp. 90–103; Martin Anderson, *Welfare* (Palo Alto, California: Hoover Institution Press, 1978); and G. W. Hoagland, "The Effectiveness of Current Transfer Programs in Reducing Poverty," paper presented at Middleburg College Conference on Economic Issues, Apr. 1980.

41 Harrell R. Rogers, Jr., *The Cost of Human Neglect: America's Welfare Failure* (White Plains, New York: M. E. Sharpe, 1982).

42 U.S. Cong., Congressional Budget Office, *Poverty Status of Families under Alternative Definitions of Income* (Washington, D.C.: GPO, 1977), p. 5.

43 U.S. Bureau of the Census, "Characteristics of Households and Persons Receiving Noncash Benefits," *Current Population Reports,* Series P–32, No. 110, March 1981, p. 20.

44 Ibid.

45 T. M. Smeeding and M. Moon, "Valuing Government Expenditures: The Case of Medical Care Transfers and Poverty," *Review of Income and Wealth,* Sept. 1980; and T. M. Smeeding, "The Anti-Poverty Effect of In-Kind Transfers: A Good Idea Gone Too Far, p. 17, memo.

46 Smeeding, "The Anti-Poverty Effect of In-Kind Transfers . . .," p. 17.

47 See, for example, Laurence E. Lynn, Jr., and David de F. Whitman, *The President as Policymaker: Jimmy Carter and Welfare Reform* (Philadelphia: Temple Univ. Press, 1981), pp. 35–37; and Milton Friedman and Rose Friedman, *Free to Choose: A Personal Statement* (New York: Avon Books, 1979), pp. 82–118.

48 Harrell R. Rodgers, Jr., *Poverty Amid Plenty* (Reading, Mass.: Addison-Wesley Publishing Co., 1979), pp. 173–204; and Rodgers, *The Cost of Human Neglect,* Chapter 8.

49 OECD, *Public Expenditure on Income Maintenance Programmes,* p. 67; and Peter Townsend, *Poverty in the United Kingdom: A Survey of Household Resources and Standards of Living* (Berkeley, California: Univ. of California Press, 1979).

50 A. J. Kahn and S. B. Kamerman, *Not for the Poor Alone* (New York: Harper Colophon Books, 1977), p. 172.

51 Social Security Administration, *Social Security Programs throughout the World 1977* (Washington, D.C.: GPO, 1977), p. 78.

52 Ruth Jordan, "Child Care: The Need for Commitment," *American Federationist,* sec. 2 (1977), p. 20.

53 M. Wagner and M. Wagner, *The Danish National Child-Care System* (Boulder, Colorado: Westwood Press, 1976).

54 Jordan, pp. 18–19.

55 Leichter, pp. 110–156.

56 George Gilder, *Wealth and Poverty* (New York: Bantam Books, 1981), pp. 151, 153.

57 This summary is drawn from Norman Furniss and Timothy Tilton's excellent study, *The Case for the Welfare State: From Social Security to Social Equality* (Bloomington, Indiana: Indiana Univ. Press, 1979), see especially Chapter 6.

58 Ibid., p. 127.

59 New York Stock Exchange, *U.S. Economic Performance in a Global Perspective* (New York: Office of Economic Research, 1981), p. 43.

60 Milton Friedman and Rose Friedman, *Capitalism and Freedom* (Chicago: Univ. of Chicago Press, 1962), Chapter 7.

61 See, for example, Theodore R. Marmor, ed., *Poverty Policy* (Chicago: Aldine-Atherton, 1971); Christopher Green, *Negative Taxes and the Poverty Problem* (Washington, D.C.: The Brookings Institute, 1976); Robert J. Lampman, *Ends and Means of Reducing Income Poverty* (New York: Academic Press, 1971); Michael C. Barth, George J. Carcagno, and John L. Palmer, *Toward an Effective Income Support System: Problems, Prospects and Choices* (Madison, Wisconsin: Institute for Research on Poverty, 1974); Kenneth E. Boulding and Martin Pfaff, *Redistribution to the Rich and the Poor: The Grants Economics of Income Distribution* (Belmont, Calif.: Wadsworth, 1972); and Joseph Pechman and P. Michael Timpane, eds., *Work Incentives and Income Guarantees* (Washington, D.C.: The Brookings Institute, 1975).

62 For an outline of the plan see U.S. Cong., House, *Welfare Reform: A Message from the President of the United States,* 91st Cong., 1st sess., H. Doc. 91–146, (Washington, D.C.: GPO, 1969).

63 U.S. Cong., Joint Economic Committee, Subcommittee on Fiscal Policy, *Income Security for Americans: Recommendations of the Public Welfare Study* (Washington, D.C.: GPO, 1974).

64 Lynn and Whitman, pp. 193–226.

65 Ibid, pp. 90–116.

66 Anderson, p. 135; and Henry J. Aaron, *Why Is Welfare So Hard to Reform?* (Washington, D.C.: The Brookings Institute, 1973).

67 Anderson, pp. 133–152; Friedman and Friedman, *Free to Choose*, pp. 116–117; and Gilder, p. 153.

68 Daniel Patrick Moynihan, *The Politics of a Guaranteed Income* (New York: Random House, 1973).

69 Lynn and Whitman, pp. 227–261.

70 Rodgers, *The Cost of Human Neglect*, Chapter 8.

71 Ibid.

72 For an overview, see Anderson, pp. 87–151.

73 Ibid., pp. 105–108.

74 Ibid., p. 39; see Friedman and Friedman's critical reaction in *Free to Choose*, pp. 98–100.

75 Gilder, pp. 88–171.

76 Ibid., p. 153.

77 Ibid., p. 86.

78 Friedman and Friedman, *Free to Choose*, pp. 110–117.

79 Rodgers, *The Cost of Human Neglect*, Chapter 8.

80 Lester T. Thurow, *The Zero-Sum Society* (New York: Basic Books, Inc., 1980), pp. 204–205.

81 See Kahn and Kamerman, *Not for the Poor Alone*; Kamerman and Kahn, eds., *Family Policies in Fourteen Countries* (New York: Columbia Univ. Press, 1978); and Carolyn Teich Adams and Kathryn Teich Winston, *Mothers at Work: Public Policies in the United States, Sweden and China* (New York: Longman, 1980).

82 U.S. Cong., House Committee on Education and Labor, Subcommittee on Equal Opportunities, pt. 5, March 1976 (Washington, D.C.: GPO, 1976), p. 167; and U.S. Bureau of the Census, "A Statistical Portrait of Women in the U.S.," U.S. Department of Commerce, *Current Population Reports*, Special Studies, Series P–23, No. 58.

CHAPTER 3

HEALTH, HEALTH CARE, AND PUBLIC POLICY

It is difficult to conceive of anything more important or basic to human happiness, dignity, and freedom than good health. Surely we all have been told, or at least heard, "If you have your health, you have everything." The importance that people in the United States, individually and collectively, attach to maintaining and regaining good health, and preventing ill health, is reflected in the billions of dollars we spend ($287 billion in 1981, or more than $1,125 for every person in the country) and in our expressed opinions on the subject. A 1981 Gallup poll found that among the social values prized by U.S. citizens, the two most frequently cited as being very important were a good family life (82 percent) and good physical health (81 percent).[1] There has never been, to our knowledge, any serious political debate over the desirability of being and staying healthy.

There has been considerable debate, however, over the question of how best to provide the means for maintaining and, when necessary, regaining one's health. Is health care a civil right and, therefore, something that government should guarantee each of us? Should the cost, quality, and accessibility of medical care be a responsibility of the public or private sector? How far should government go in preventing people from unnecessarily exposing themselves to health risks? For example, should the United States government require people to use seat belts as do several other countries? Should it ban cigarette smoking, the single most serious danger to the health of U.S. citizens? In short, what is the appropriate role of government in the area of health care policy?

In this chapter we examine the debate over health, health care, and the role of government. We begin the chapter by examining the issue of the relationship between health, health care, and individual responsibility. We then examine five general, historical, and cross-national models of health care systems. The discussion of these models will reveal the ideological or philosophical assumption underlying each, as well as the relationship between health care and government. The models will demonstrate some alternative directions in which U.S. health care policy and the health care system may travel. Following this discussion, we examine the major issues— many observers call it a crisis—in U.S. health care: quality, accessibility, and, most critically, the cost of health care. Conservative and liberal policy proposals for dealing with these problems are then discussed and evaluated in the light of the experiences of other nations.

HEALTH, HEALTH CARE, AND THE INDIVIDUAL

Any discussion of an appropriate health care policy for the United States must begin with an understanding of the relationship between health and health care. Most people tend to equate the two. In the equation, an increase in one (i.e., health care—more doctors, hospitals, and money spent on these) will produce a corresponding increase in the second (i.e., health—longer lives, less illness, and fewer premature deaths). In recent years, however, a rather lively debate has taken place, in the United States and other countries, over how best to improve the health status of people. We briefly examine this debate not only because of the implications for health care policy but because it illustrates the sharing of policy ideas among nations. In addition, the debate, to a certain extent, reflects liberal and conservative differences in this policy area.

In recent years a ''new perspective'' on health care and health care policy has developed in the United States and several other industrialized nations. The term ''new perspective'' derives from a highly influential 1974 Canadian government working paper, ''A New Perspective on the Health of Canadians,'' by the then Minister for National Health and Welfare, Marc Lalonde.[2] The Lalonde report outlined the primary causes of mortality and morbidity in Canada (among them motor vehicle accidents, ischemic heart disease, other accidents, respiratory diseases, lung cancer, and suicide— a profile virtually identical to the United States) and identified their major underlying causes as self-imposed, environmental, or the result of living habits (i.e., lifestyle). The report went on to note that ''personal decisions and habits that are bad, from a health point of view, create self-imposed risks. When those risks result in illness or death, the victim's lifestyle can be said to have contributed to, or caused, his own illness or death.''[3]

Thus the Lalonde report placed lifestyle and the environment on a par with the more traditional concerns of health care policy—human biology and health delivery systems. The report also shifted at least part of the responsibility for health care from the health delivery system to the individual.

The Lalonde report inspired official reaction in the form of reports or legislation in Great Britain, Sweden, and the United States. In 1976 the U.S. Congress passed the National Consumer Health Information and Health Promotion Act, which granted authority to the Secretary of Health and Human Services to "undertake and support necessary activities and programs to . . . increase the application and use of health knowledge, skills, and practices by the general population in its pattern of daily living."[4]

It is not at all surprising that financially strained nationalized health delivery systems (Canada and Great Britain) or private systems with a large subsidized component (the United States) would embrace the notion of health promotion, disease prevention, and individual responsibility. First, preventing disease and promoting health are allegedly less costly than curative medicine. Second, from the policy makers' viewpoint, the new perspective has the virtue of diffusing criticism of government health policies and delivery systems—a point to which we shall return. Finally, emphasizing individual responsibility in health care is justified medically— imprudent lifestyles *do* contribute, significantly, to premature mortality and increased morbidity.

The new perspective on health care makes certain assumptions about the relationship between lifestyle and disease, and carries with it certain explicit or implicit policy proposals and philosophical premises which need to be made clear. The most basic assumption is that contemporary lifestyles or daily habits are prominent among the causes of major diseases today: "[M]any of today's most important health problems are either self-induced due to hazardous lifestyles, or the result of congenital defects which could be prevented through better prenatal care, genetic counseling, family planning and abortions."[5]

A second assumption is that the costs of individual irresponsibility in health care are enormous. "The greatest portion of our national expenditure goes for caring for the major causes of premature, and therefore preventable, death and/or disability in the United States. . . ." If people followed more prudent lifestyles, "savings to the country would be mammoth in terms of billions of dollars, a vast reduction in human misery, and an attendant marked improvement in the quality of life."[6]

A third assumption follows directly from the first two. "Society cannot and should not assume the costs for medical and dental care, for illness or injury attributable to individual self-indulgence."[7] The assumption here is that those who foolishly and voluntarily expose themselves to certain health risks create an extraordinary health care debt. Suggestions for amortizing this debt have included substantially higher alcohol and tobacco duties, or some form of "your-fault" or "yes-fault" insurance. Presumably the revenues raised by these taxes or premiums would be spent on health care.

While the new perspective arguments are compelling, they have not been accepted uncritically. In fact, both liberals and conservatives at times have attacked different facets of the perspective. First, there are important political implications associated with the new perspective. One political scientist, with a political orientation toward the left, has labeled the new perspective "victim blaming" and charges that it is largely an ideological ploy that tries to cope with runaway medical costs, increased demands for more accessible and equitable medical care, and increased recognition of occupational and environmental sources of ill health. In this view, the emphasis on individual responsibility in health care is an attempt to convince people that greater prudence in lifestyle rather than more accessible health care or greater responsibility on the part of government and industry is the key to good health.[8] In particular, liberals are concerned that the new perspective will divert attention and resources from improving access to health care facilities for the poor. We will return to the issue of access later in this chapter.

Conservatives offer a second criticism of the new perspective. While not challenging the assumption of the "ideology of responsibility," they do question some of the implications for implementing policy along these lines. Specifically there is concern over how far and frequently the state should impose on personal freedom in order to affect lifestyles. While acknowledging that certain behavior patterns contribute to ill health, conservatives argue that—except in extraordinary circumstances such as those involving children or mentally incompetent persons—government should do no more than educate the public to the dangers inherent in imprudent personal behavior.[9] Thus, for example, conservatives in the United States and Great Britain have opposed mandatory seat belt–use laws and policies which discourage the use of tobacco or alcohol (e.g., cigarette warnings, higher taxes).

Finally, there are those who question the extent to which true voluntarism exists in many injurious behavior patterns.[10] In a society in which modern advertising and merchandising techniques, government crop subsidies, peer group pressure, and the addictive nature of the substance all conspire to encourage smoking, how voluntary is this high-risk habit?

Thus far little has been done in this country beyond more health education efforts such as the National Consumer Health Information and Health Promotion Act mentioned above. The new perspective clearly must be given credit for raising the level of consciousness of the general public and policy makers to the issue of self-inflicted health problems and to the limits of health care. However, it also has raised the serious issue of the extent to which this new perspective deliberately diverts attention and resources from needed improvements in the nation's health delivery system.

Health care systems and policies throughout the world continue to focus on the issues of health care delivery and curative medicine. It would be useful at this point to examine the basic approaches to providing health care in the world today—and in the past.

MODELS OF HEALTH CARE DELIVERY

While it may appear that there are a staggering number of approaches to providing for the health care needs of a people, the various permutations and combinations can be distilled into five basic models. By presenting these models or approaches we hope to show not only how other nations deal with such issues as access, quality, and cost containment, but also the policy alternatives available to the United States.[11]

Table 3-1 summarizes the most salient features of five types of health care systems and provides examples of each. Not all the features of these systems are displayed in the table, nor are they examined in the discussion.

Medicine as Free Enterprise

The first model depicted in Table 3-1 (the market model) represents the dominant approach to providing health care in most nations of the world up to the latter part of the nineteenth century. Health care in this case was viewed, with minor exceptions, as something to be sought, paid for, and practiced in the private sector—outside the jurisdiction of government. It was like any other good or service in the economic marketplace. Those who could afford to do so, and there were a great many who could not, went to a private physician (or hospital) and paid for the medical care they received. While the financing of medical care was primarily an individual effort, there were some early collective, but private, approaches as well. These typically took the form of workers' self-help or mutual aid societies in which workers set aside a small part of their earnings in a common fund. When a worker became ill he was given money from the fund to compensate for his loss of income. In addition, but less frequently, the fund paid for medical care.

It must be emphasized, however, that these were private, not public, arrangements and involved only a small proportion of the urban workers; children and spouses, as well as the large rural population, did not, as a rule, benefit from these programs. Those who could not afford to go to a private physician and did not belong to one of the few programs mentioned above relied for their medical care on charitable institutions—or went

TABLE 3-1
MODELS OF HEALTH CARE SYSTEMS

Characteristics of the system	Market, free enterprise (1)	Mixed (2)	Insurance, social security (3)	National health system (4)	Socialized (5)
Philosophical assumptions	Health care is a personal responsibility	Health care is a shared public and private responsibility but primarily private	Health care is a shared responsibility but primary concern of the government	Health care is an absolute right of citizenship	Health care is an absolute right of citizenship
Role of government	Minimal	Decentralized, indirect	Centralized, direct	Centralized, direct	Total
Position of physician	Private enterprise (PE)	PE	PE	PE	State employees
Ownership of health care facilities	Private	Private and public	Private and public	Mostly public	Entirely public
Financing	Direct patient to doctor	Some direct and indirect*	Mostly direct	Mostly direct	Entirely indirect
Examples	U.S., W. Europe, Tsarist Russia in 19th century	U.S. and South Africa	Sweden, France, Japan, Canada, Italy, Switzerland	Great Britain	Soviet Union, Eastern Europe

* Includes public and private insurance.

Source: Adapted from Mark Field, "The Health System and the Polity: A Contemporary American Dialectic," *Social Science and Medicine,* 14A (October 1980), p. 401, and used with the permission of the author and Pergamon Press.

without. Indeed, many of the most famous hospitals in Europe began as charity-supported institutions.

While medical care typically was received, paid for, and practiced in the private sector, there were some minor exceptions to this. In certain instances, governments either directly provided or paid for the medical care of various exceptional groups. Thus, in the United States the federal government established, as early as 1793, the Maritime Hospital Service which provided health care to merchant seamen. Aside from these minor exceptions the only sustained involvement of government in the area of health care dealt with matters of public health like sanitation ordinances, quarantines, and innoculations.

With regard to the practice of medicine, this too was essentially private. In most nations physicians owned their own equipment and charged the patients directly on a fee-for-service basis. There were, of course, exceptions both within and among nations. In many countries the government hired a small number of physicians to serve in the military or in public health agencies. In addition, some nations had a tradition of large scale government involvement in the health field. Tsarist Russia was one outstanding example where, since the mid-seventeenth century, the state financed all medical education. In return for this, new physicians had to enter government service for a specified period of time. Despite the fact that the service was not attractive, financially or otherwise, about three-fourths of all Russian doctors worked for the government even after fulfilling their obligations. The reason for this was that few Russians could afford private medical care, and there were few employment opportunities for doctors in private practice.[12] In general, however, medical care under the first model was private.

State Assistance in Medical Care—The Mixed Model

The second model represents the current medical care system in the United States (as well as South Africa). It is described as a mixed system because both the public and private sectors are responsible for the financing and delivery of medical care, the ownership of medical equipment and facilities, the training of medical personnel, and the conduct of medically related scientific research. In this mixed system, however, the private sector is predominant. The overwhelming majority of the 440,000 physicians in this country are in private practice: the federal government, for example, employs fewer than 20,000 physicians, mainly in military and veterans' hospitals. Most U.S. citizens are cared for by a private physician in private offices, hospitals, or nursing homes. About 60 percent of the people finance their medical care either by direct payments to the doctor or hospital or through private health insurance. Most physicians set their own fees and are free to practice, within the parameters set by a state medical board, as they wish. Similarly, most patients are free to choose whichever physician they wish.

In addition to the dominant private component, there is also an important and growing public dimension to medical care in the United States. This involvement has taken several forms. First, at the federal level there has been a demand for the government to recognize that certain exceptional categories of people merit assistance in obtaining medical care. The justifications for these departures from the free market system have been: (1) sacrifices on behalf of or service to the country (e.g., veterans, current civilian and military employees), (2) vulnerability due to significantly diminished income and increasing medical needs (the elderly), and (3) inability to purchase medical care privately (the poor). In the case of the poor and elderly, the government helps purchase medical care, typically from the private sector, through Medicaid or Medicare. Both programs were enacted in 1965 during the Johnson administration. Medicare, which operates through the social security system, provides hospital care insurance for elderly people. During our working years each of us contributes, along with our employers, to a social security fund. Upon reaching retirement age we become eligible for a monthly retirement allowance (i.e., social security) and money, when needed, to pay hospital bills. In addition, elderly persons may purchase supplementary medical insurance under Medicare to cover physicians' expenses. Medicaid, discussed in Chapter 2, provides state and federal funds to meet the health care needs of persons who fall below the official poverty level.

Finally, the federal government owns and operates hospitals which provide medical care to present and former military personnel and some nonmilitary personnel as well. In the case of the military, approximately 40 million U.S. citizens, or about 18 percent of the population, receive their medical care in VA or Department of Defense hospitals. The Veterans Administration, in fact, runs the single largest hospital system in the country, accounting for 5 percent of all hospital beds.

Federal government involvement in the mixed-model approach also takes the form of financial assistance for biomedical research, medical schools, and hospital construction. From 1946 to 1974 the federal government, under the Hill-Burton Act, financed local hospital construction in communities throughout the country. In addition, since 1938, when the National Cancer Institute was established, the federal government has spent billions of dollars on biomedical research. Today there are eleven National Institutions of Health conducting medical research on heart disease, aging, mental health, as well as cancer and other health problems.

State and local governments too are involved in providing medical care, primarily through the ownership and operation of state and local hospitals.

These hospitals account "for one out of every four hospitals in the country, 15 percent of all hospital beds, and over 20 percent of all hospital admissions."[13]

While public sector involvement in medical care is significant and growing—the proportion of public spending on health care has increased from just 2.7 percent in 1950 to 42 percent in 1980—it is still the case that ours is a primarily private medical care system. Most physicians, hospitals, nurses, pharmacists, etc., are in the private sector, although a significant portion of their income originates in the public sector. Private practitioners exercise control over professional matters (e.g., medical practices), set their own fees, determine how many patients they will treat and where they will practice with only minimal government involvement. The United States is one of the few countries in the world where this is the case. Some argue that this illustrates our good sense and virtue; others say that it reflects poor sense and insensitivity. In any event it is the system in the United States.

Medical Care through Social Insurance

The introduction of social insurance represents one of the most important changes ever accomplished in the relationship between citizens and the state. Introduced in Europe in the latter part of the nineteenth century, social insurance represented an expansion of both the obligations of the state toward its people and the degree of interaction between the state and the people. Although the proximate impulses for the introduction of social insurance policy varied, the underlying assumption was that the state had an interest in, and a need to respond to, the insecurities created by modern industrial life. While the problems of old age, illness, accidents, and unemployment had long existed, traditional social mechanisms, like the family or a paternalistic aristocracy, partly assuaged the anxiety attending them. With the erosion of these traditional social remedies, and with the seeming increase of social problems, new measures had to be found, and a social insurance policy became the answer for much of the modern world.

National health insurance was one form of social insurance. It was first introduced 100 years ago in Germany and adopted, over the years, by almost all modern nations. As in other areas of social insurance, the assumption here was that the state had an interest in helping people obtain necessary medical care. The particular nature of that interest varied in both place and time. In the case of Germany it was an effort by an authoritarian, conservative regime to undermine the increasing attraction of socialism and the Social Democratic Party. In the words of its primary architect, Chancellor Otto von Bismarck, national health insurance was intended, in large part, "to bribe the working classes, or, if you like, to win them over to regard the state as a social institution existing for their sake and interested in their welfare."[14] Thus, in Germany and other early adopting countries like Austria (1888) and Hungary (1891), state-sponsored health insurance was a policy weapon of conservative regimes aimed at preserving the existing political order. The hope of these policy makers was to convince the working class that the current regime was beneficent, interested in their well-being, and, therefore, worthy of their continued support.

A second and related impulse behind these early programs was that the nineteenth century monarchs of Europe (Germany, Russia, Austria, Hungary, Luxembourg) and Asia (Japan) continued to take seriously their religious and paternalistic obligations. Monarchs were stern but benevolent parents who were responsible for the well-being of their people. Social insurance in general, and health insurance in particular, was a modern manifestation of noblesse oblige.

Third, some nations which adopted national health insurance saw it as a way to improve national security and economic productivity. British officials, for example, were dismayed by the poor physical condition of working class military recruits during the Boer War (1899–1902), as were Japanese military authorities in the early 1930s as Japan embarked on an era of military adventurism. In both countries, the establishment and extension of national health insurance were seen as contributing to a strong national defense.

In addition, in both countries a healthy working class was viewed as necessary to improved national economic productivity. At the turn of the century, British experts attributed their country's declining economic productivity to the sorry physical condition of the working class. Similarly, in Japan the high rate of tuberculosis among workers in the critical textile industry was a major factor behind that nation's first national health insurance law.

We have detailed the motivation and circumstances behind the introduction of national health insurance to demonstrate that in its formative years it was very much a conservative, not liberal, policy idea. It was aimed at deflating worker discontent, fortifying established regimes, and contributing to national military and economic strength. Later on, other factors, including the notion of health care as a right of citizenship, replaced these more conservative impulses. But in its origins national health insurance was very much an "establishment" idea.

How then does this system, which is found in most modern, democratic nations, work? First, there is the issue of eligibility. Historically, most countries began with a program that only covered a small proportion, perhaps 10 percent, of the total population, representing the poorest, most unskilled segments of the urban working class. Self-employed persons, including farmers and rural laborers, and dependents were not insured. In the course of the twentieth century, early adopting countries such as Germany, Austria, Luxembourg, Norway, and Great Britain, as well as the more than fifty nations which adopted state-sponsored health insurance later on, extended coverage to all or most segments of the population. Today, a majority of the people in at least seventy-five nations are covered by a national health insurance program.

Second, there is the question of financing national health insurance. One approach is to require employers and employees to contribute to an insurance fund. This system, which is similar to our Medicare program, is used in Belgium, West Germany, France, Italy, Luxembourg, and the Netherlands. A second approach is to finance the system through general tax revenues. Tax revenues can be used either to finance virtually all costs, as in Canada, Sweden, and New Zealand, or to pay part of the costs, as in Japan and Australia. The third major source of financing is cost sharing by patients, typically used in conjunction with the other two financing mechanisms. In countries using this approach, part of the insurance money comes from either compulsory contributions or general tax revenue, and part comes from the patients. In the Netherlands, Germany, and most Canadian provinces patients only pay a small part of the costs, and this is typically for such things as drugs or medical appliances (e.g., crutches, eyeglasses). In Belgium, France, and Australia, on the other hand, patients pay a rather substantial portion of the doctor's bill.

Third, there is the issue of the range of benefits provided by national health insurance systems. All countries provide coverage for physician and hospital services. Beyond this, it is difficult to generalize about medical benefits under national health insurance. In some countries benefits include prescribed drugs, dental care, nursing care, and other medical services. In addition, many countries, including France, Austria, Canada, West Germany, the Netherlands, and Sweden, pay cash sickness and maternity benefits for specified periods of time.

National health insurance systems are administered in a variety of ways. For example, the program in some countries is under the general supervision of a central department (e.g., Ministry of Public Health and Social Security in France, or the National Social Insurance Board in Sweden) but is administered by local or regional bodies. The central government typically sets the rules governing eligibility and benefits, while the localities deal with the day-to-day operation of the programs. In addition, in many countries private insurance carriers, similar to our Blue Cross and Blue Shield, act as insurance agents for the program.

Finally, it should be noted that under most national health insurance systems physicians remain free to practice medicine as they wish, although the government may specify certain conditions of practice particularly as they relate to fees.

In essence national health insurance represents a belief that the good health of individuals, and the attendant hardships associated with illness, is the concern of society and not just that of the individual. Thus, under this system virtually all persons are guaranteed access to medical care and protected from the material hardships associated with illness. For many conservatives in the United States, the compulsory nature of some, but not all, such programs, the high costs, and the public bureaucracy which goes with a national health system are among its objectionable features. Perhaps the most eloquent testimony to the support national health insurance enjoys throughout the world is the fact that about seventy-five nations have adopted national health insurance systems, and no nation, once having done so, has abandoned it.[15]

National Health Service and Socialized Medicine

The differences between the last two models—national health service and socialized medicine—are minimal, although in some respects important. In both systems there is the explicit assumption that medical care is an absolute right of citizenship and, therefore, must be guaranteed by the state. In both systems the national government establishes health care policy and administers health care delivery, and in both the entire population is covered—eligibility is simply a function of permanently living in the country. Medical care is financed entirely in the socialized system and predominantly in the British National Health Service from general revenue funds rather than through cost sharing or designated insurance funds. Financing health care through general taxation represents a philosophical commitment to equal medical care for all citizens regardless of ability to pay; millionaires and the unemployed receive precisely the same public benefits under both systems despite the fact that one paid a great amount in taxes and the other nothing. Under many health insurance systems, differences in payment and benefits often exist.

Where the two systems differ is in the continued adherence of the national health service model, in use in Great Britain, to certain facets of the private market model. From the patients' perspective this means they may still choose to avoid the national health system and make private arrangements for their health care. In practice, in Great Britain only about 2 percent of the population chooses to obtain their medical care outside of the National Health Service, although an increasing number are supplementing their benefits through private insurance. Thus, one purchases extra insurance from a private company and uses that insurance to get a private room, as opposed to a ward, in a hospital. In a fully state-run or socialized system, as in the Soviet Union and other Eastern European countries, this option is not *legally* available, although there is evidence that in some of these countries a small number of people enter into private arrangements with state physicians to receive more prompt and attentive medical care.

From the perspective of the physician the differences between a national health service and a socialized system are greater and more consequential. First, the physician under national health service remains a private entrepreneur rather than a government employee. Physicians own or rent their own offices and equipment. They are free to practice where they want and how they want. They may, if they choose, practice in whole or in part outside the National Health Service (NHS) in Great Britain—although as a practical matter this is quite difficult since few people seek medical care outside of the NHS.

In addition, general practitioners under the British NHS receive payment for their services from the government primarily in the form of a "capitation fee," that is, a set monthly fee for every patient registered with them, regardless of the number of times they see that patient. Hospital physicians (i.e., specialists) are generally full- or part-time salaried employees of the nationalized hospitals. In the socialized system, all medical personnel are salaried government employees who work in government clinics or hospitals.

Finally, and of considerable importance, in contrast to the socialized systems of the Soviet Union and eastern Europe, physicians in Great Britain belong to a politically influential medical interest group, the British Medical Association, which very actively and successfully promotes and protects the interests of the medical profession. Thus, government policy concerning the NHS is arrived at through formal consultation between, and participation by, both government and the medical community. No such independent interest group activity exists under the socialized systems of eastern Europe.

In terms of the medical benefits, both systems offer virtually the entire range of medical care, including physician, hospital, dental and nursing services, drugs, physical therapy, etc., to the entire population regardless of income or social position. Many critics claim that under both systems the quality of medical care has suffered as a result of guaranteeing universality of care. Available evidence, either refuting or confirming the charge, typically says more about the ideology of the researcher than the reality of the system examined, and is therefore of questionable utility.

Summary of Health Care Models

These five models represent historical and contemporary approaches to the delivery of health care. Each model is premised on certain philosophical assumptions about individual and collective responsibility and interest; each involves a different set of relationships between the providers of medical care, the consumers, and the government. The purpose of each system is to allow citizens access to competent and affordable medical care when it is needed. Conservatives in the United States argue that this can best be achieved by adhering as closely as possible to the principles and practices of the market model (model 1), while most liberals favor the national health insurance model (model 3). It is now time to examine the issues involved in this current debate and the implications of the two alternative models for the U.S. health care system.

THE CRISIS IN U.S. HEALTH CARE

The recent debate over the appropriate direction of U.S. health care policy—either toward greater competition and less government involvement, or guaranteed access and financial protection through government regulation—has occurred in the context of a purported crisis in U.S. health care. This "crisis"—and the term must be qualified in deference to those who deny its existence—has several features.

Accessibility

There is, to begin, the problem of accessibility and distribution of health services. This aspect of the U.S. health care crisis has a number of facets. First, there is the issue of the geographical distribution of health services. Doctors in the United States, like their colleagues throughout the world, prefer the financial, professional, and social advantages and amenities associated with urban medical practice. As a result one finds a greater concentration of, and more sophisticated medical personnel and equipment in, cities than rural areas. In 1978, for example, there were 17.1 physicians per 10,000 people in metropolitan areas compared to 7.4 in nonmetropolitan areas in this country. What is more, there are still many rural counties in this country and many urban ghettos with no physician or only one physician in residence. According to Senator Edward Kennedy (D., Mass.), "[M]ore than 20 million Americans reside in medically underserved areas where the poverty level is so high that physicians cannot make a living or where physicians have been unwilling to locate because they could make a more comfortable living in wealthy, medically overserved suburbs."[16] In addition, the geographical maldistribution of medical service has had a regional dimension as well. In general, the northeast has had a greater supply of physicians and medical facilities than other parts of the country, especially the south and north central regions. While these differences have declined over the years, in 1978 the northeast still had 37 percent more physicians per 10,000 people than these other regions, although it had only slightly more than the west—17.9 compared to 16.8 physicians per 10,000 people.

The second facet of the accessibility issue involves the relationship between health and health care on the one hand and race and economic status on the other. Critics of the U.S. health care system charge that poor people and minorities suffer higher rates of mortality and morbidity than more affluent, white U.S. citizens because of poorer access to quality health care. Although, as we noted earlier, the relationship between health and health care is not always a direct one, there is substantial evidence in some areas to support this criticism. We should note, by the way, that being white and affluent is no guarantee of good health. In fact, in several significant health areas, including heart disease (excluding hypertension), several forms of cancer, and automobile accidents, nonpoor whites have significantly higher mortality and morbidity rates than the poor or nonwhites. These differences are obviously not a function of access to health care but are related to certain aspects of lifestyle—lack of exercise, type of diet, and greater automobile ownership.

There are, however, certain critical areas in which race and economic status are a determining factor in health. The most glaring, unconscionable and significant is the persistent difference between white and black infant mortality rates. The infant mortality rate of a collectivity, be it a nation or racial group, is among the most important measures of that group's overall health status. According to one authority, it is

> [p]erhaps the most sensitive single index of health conditions within a community. . . . This rate has traditionally been widely used to classify communities or populations in terms of their overall health. . . . Further, the infant mortality rate has generally been used as an indicator of the level of social and economic well-being within a country.[17]

The data on infant mortality rates in the United States are disturbing: black infants are almost twice as likely as whites (23.1 per 1,000 live births compared to 12.0 per 1,000 live births) to die within their first year. And even more disturbing is the fact that while the rate has declined for both groups (down from 73.8 per 1,000 for blacks and 43.2 per 1,000 for whites in 1940), the ratio of black-to-white infant deaths has remained constant (2:1) for the past four decades.

There appear to be two main reasons for this phenomenon. The first is the much higher incidence (about twice the rate) of low-birth-weight infants among blacks. Low birth weight, one of the major causes of infant deaths, is in large part the result of poor overall maternal physical condition, stress, and poor nutrition. The second factor is that nonwhite women are much less likely to have early prenatal examinations. In 1978, for example, 78.2

percent of all white women visited physicians within their first 3 months of pregnancy, while only 60.2 percent of all black women did so. If one defines health care broadly, including health education and adequate diet as well as access to trained medical personnel, the differences between black and white infant mortality can be attributed to unequal access.

Another major health area in which economic status clearly affects access to health care is that of dental disease. Here the evidence is unambiguous and direct. As noted in Table 3-2, poor people, both white and nonwhite, are much less likely to have visited a dentist within the past 2 years than nonpoor people. And if you are poor *and* nonwhite you are least likely—55.1 percent of the nonwhite poor had not been to a dentist between 1976 and 1978. While the data do show improvement for all categories of persons from 1964 to 1978, the intereconomic status and interracial differences remain strong.

The result of the difference in access is predictable: poor people have nearly twice as many decayed and missing teeth as nonpoor people, and nearly half the number of filled cavities. "The greater number of filled teeth among those in the higher income group is consistent with the higher rate of contact that the nonpoor have with dentists."[18]

We should note one final area of interracial difference in mortality rates. In 1978 the death rate from homicide for white males was 9.2 per 100,000 people, while for black males it was 58.7 per 100,000 people. In some age groups—e.g., 25- to 29-year olds—blacks were eight times as likely to be murdered, and this accounted for more than one-half the excess of black-to-white deaths. Homicide is a major cause of death among black males, especially younger ones. In this area decreases in the mortality rate are more likely to be a function of social change (e.g., better job opportunities, housing, and overall life chances) than improved access to health care.

We do not want to leave the reader with the impression that the health

TABLE 3-2

PERSONS WITH NO DENTAL VISITS WITHIN PAST TWO YEARS, BY COLOR AND ECONOMIC STATUS

Year	White		Nonwhite	
	Poor	Nonpoor	Poor	Nonpoor
1964	57.7	39.2	72.8	59.2
1973	51.0	34.4	59.4	51.2
1978	47.3	32.2	55.1	44.4

Source: Jennifer Madans and Jack Kleinman, "Use of Ambulatory Care by the Poor and Nonpoor," in U.S. Dept. of Health and Human Services, *Health, United States: 1980* (Washington, D.C.: GPO, 1980), p. 47.

of, and access to health care among, the poor and minorities have shown no improvement in recent years. Clearly they have. While the *ratio* of black-to-white infant mortality has remained constant, the *rate* of infant death for all groups has declined significantly over the years. So too has there been a decline in death rates from tuberculosis, influenza, diphtheria, and several other infectious or communicable diseases. Nonwhites have shared, although not equally, in the advance in medical science over the past several decades.

In addition, the introduction of Medicaid and Medicare in 1965, both of which were intended to remove barriers to obtaining needed health care, has improved the access of needy persons to health care. Table 3-3 indicates the increased use made by poor people, of all races, of ambulatory health care. Part of the reason poor people go to physicians more frequently is because they suffer more illnesses. What Medicaid and Medicare apparently have done is to improve the access that these people have to health care.

This is not to suggest that the level of access is commensurate with the need for medical care among the needy, or that the care they receive is equal in quality to that of the more affluent. Medical care for the poor is often provided in hospital outpatient departments—those earning under $7,000 a year in 1978 were 2½ times as likely to have visited a physician in an outpatient department as someone earning over $25,000 a year—in a hurried, uncaring manner, often by inexperienced and harried medical attendants. Or it is provided by private physicians in urban ghettos or rural areas where one is unlikely to find either the most skilled practitioners or modern facilities.

A recent government publication summarized the progress in and status of health care for the needy:

> In summary, although substantial progress has been made in reducing barriers to medical care among the poor, no definitive evidence exists as to whether or not the poor are receiving adequate care, in terms of both quantity and quality,

TABLE 3-3
PHYSICIAN VISITS PER PERSON, PER YEAR, ACCORDING TO COLOR AND ECONOMIC STATUS, 1964, 1973, 1978

	White		Nonwhite	
Year	Poor	Nonpoor	Poor	Nonpoor
1964	4.2	4.9	3.3	3.9
1973	5.4	5.1	5.3	4.6
1978	5.7	4.7	5.6	4.5

Source: Madans and Kleinman, p. 45.

relative to their need. Furthermore, the poor are much less likely to receive dental care. Poor children have significantly greater unmet need for treatment of dental caries as measured by direct examination than do non-poor children.[19]

Quality

A second dimension of the health care crisis involves the quality of medical care. While there is no doubt that the United States has one of the best medical establishments in the world, perhaps *the* best, there are still serious criticisms concerning the quality of health care. Frequently mentioned is the allegation that U.S. doctors expose patients to unnecessary and often dangerous medical procedures and medications. One highly publicized report by a congressional subcommittee claimed that in the year studied there were 2.4 million unnecessary surgical procedures resulting in 11,900 deaths.[20]

Another study, prepared by the National Center for Health Statistics, examined the use of cesarean section delivery of infants in six countries between 1970 and 1978—the United States, Canada, Sweden, England, Norway, and the Netherlands—and found that while the use of cesareans had gone up in all countries, physicians in the United States throughout this period had used them more frequently than their colleagues in any other country. Thus, for example, in 1978, 15.2 percent of all deliveries in the United States were by cesarean section compared to 7.5 percent for Norway. While 1978 data were not available for the Netherlands, in 1975 only 2.8 percent of the deliveries in that country were by cesarean section.[21] A more recent study found that physicians in New England performed two to four times the amount of common surgery as their colleagues in England and Norway.[22] The explanation for the alleged overuse of surgical procedures in the United States is that since almost one-third of all U.S. physicians are surgeons the supply of surgeons creates an artificial need for surgery.

The issue of the quality of medical care is also related to the mushrooming of malpractice suits against U.S. physicians. To give just one example, in 1960, the average malpractice insurance premium paid by surgeons was $229; in 1972 it was $2,307 per year, and by 1979 it was $7,190 per year. Several factors, other than increasing incompetence by the medical profession, explain these extraordinary increases—although incompetence and carelessness cannot be ruled out. Among the more prominent factors are (1) a general increase in consumer willingness to hold "sellers" accountable for actual or perceived poor services; (2) "the growth in skepticism toward social institutions in furthering the public interest";[23] (3) greater use of medical services, which allows for greater error; (4) a changing legal environment that has facilitated, and perhaps encouraged, recourse to litigation; (5) a bandwagon effect produced by the publicity about malpractice suits and particularly about highly celebrated big settlements. Whatever the reason for their growth, malpractice suits both reflect and contribute to the disillusionment and increasing hostility toward the medical community, and they constitute part of the U.S. health care crisis.

The Explosion of Health Care Costs

When citizens and policy makers refer to the crisis in U.S. health care the dimension to which they most frequently refer is the explosion in the cost of health care. In 1981, national health care costs alone increased almost $40 billion: from $247.2 billion to $287 billion. This 15.1 percent increase was the second largest in 15 years and represented an increase to 9.4 percent of the gross national product (GNP). It also should be noted that the 15.1 percent increase came on the heels of a 15.8 percent increase in the previous year and represented a 2-year increase from 8.9 to 9.8 percent of the GNP spent on health care. While the growth in health care costs "slowed" to just 11 percent in 1982, the overall rate of inflation in that year was 3.9 percent. Reflecting what has to be a consensus among most observers of all political persuasions, Richard Schweiker, former secretary of Health and Human Services, recently said, "We cannot allow health costs to keep climbing, because we simply cannot afford to pay the bill."[24] Because the explosion in health care costs is so important and so central to the national debate on the direction of U.S. health care policy, we will examine it in some detail.

There are several points worth underscoring with regard to the trends revealed in Table 3-4. The first is that while health care costs have risen at immodest rates throughout the period 1950–1980, it is only in the last 15 years (1966–1980) that they really have taken off. Thus, for example, the annual average rate of increase for the period 1966–1980 was 12.6 percent compared to the 8.3 percent increase for the period 1950–1965. The period 1975–1981 is particularly noteworthy because of the increase (from 8.6 to 9.8 percent) of the GNP spent on health care. In addition, it is important to note that public spending has risen more sharply than private spending for health care. This, as we shall see shortly, was due mainly to the introduction in 1965 of the Medicare and Medicaid programs. The relatively more rapid growth of public spending on health also is reflected in the proportion of total spending on health care from the public and private sectors. Public sector spending, as noted earlier, has increased from approximately 2.7 percent in 1950 to 42 percent in 1980.

There is one final issue concerning the nature of health cost increases which is not reflected in the data in Table 3-4, namely, the relationship between hospital care costs and physician and other medical care costs (e.g., dental services, drugs). Three points need to be made in this regard.

TABLE 3-4
THE GROWTH OF HEALTH CARE COSTS (1950–1981)

	1950	1960	1965	1975	1981
Total health expenditures:					
In $ billions	12.7	26.9	41.7	132.7	286.6
As % of GNP	4.4	5.3	6.0	8.6	9.8
Per capita	81.86	146.30	210.89	603.57	1225.00
Annual % increase	12.2	8.7	9.2	14.0	15.1
Public expenditures:					
In $ billions	3.4	6.6	10.8	56.2	122.5
Per capita	22.24	36.10	54.57	255.49	524.00
Annual % increase	15.5	7.8	10.2	19.2	16.2
Private expenditures:					
In $ billions	9.2	20.3	20.9	76.5	164.1
Per capita	59.62	110.20	156.32	348.08	701.00
Annual % increase	11.2	9.0	8.8	9.7	14.3

Source: *Health Care Financing Review*, 4 September, 1982

First, hospital costs constitute the largest proportion of health care expenditures. In 1980, 40.3 percent of all money spent on health care went to hospitals compared to 18.9 percent for physicians' services.

Second, that proportion has increased over the years: 30.4 percent in 1950 compared to 40.3 percent in 1980. The third point is a function of the first two. "Since hospital care has accounted for an increased share of the total health care dollar, it has been responsible for a disproportionate share of the relative growth of the health care sector during the past 15 years."[25] The significance of this will be discussed later in the chapter when we examine various proposals for containing health costs.

The profile of health care spending that emerges then is one of rapid and accelerated increases in absolute and relative spending on health care; the public sector portion increasing more rapidly and accounting for a larger portion of the bill, over time, than the private sector; and hospitals consuming an increasing portion of the resources allocated to the health care sector.

Why have medical care costs risen so precipitously and persistently? There are several reasons which explain the rise in health care costs in the United States and in other industrialized nations as well. For purposes of analysis, it is useful to organize the reasons into three broad categories: pricing and financing factors, utilization factors, and service factors.

Pricing and Financing Factors   It has been estimated that 70 percent of the astronomical increase in health expenditures in 1981 was due to inflation and especially increases in wages and salaries. The medical industry is a highly labor-intensive enterprise and over the last decade it has become even more so. Thus, in 1971 there were, on the average, 272 hospital personnel per 100 patients, whereas by 1978 the number had increased to 323 per 100 patients.[26] Increased labor intensity combined with increased labor costs are major factors in health cost inflation. It must be remembered, however, that medical cost increases have been running at a rate two to three times as high as overall inflation and, therefore, one has to look beyond general inflation to explain these increases.

A second price-related factor involves the mechanisms for financing medical care. Many policy makers and academic observers have identified these as the culprits in the health cost crisis. There are three issues here that need to be identified. These are third-party and fee-for-service reimbursement practices, and the unique market arrangement between the actors in the medical marketplace. We will examine each of these.

By 1976, 90 percent of the people in the United States had some form of health insurance. Today approximately 90 percent of all hospital costs and 60 percent of all physicians' fees are paid by either private (e.g., Blue Cross, Blue Shield) or public (e.g., Veterans Administration, Medicaid, Medicare) third-party insurance carriers. A majority of U.S. citizens never see or touch the money (or at least not very much of it) which goes to physicians and hospitals. Hence, it is argued, there is no incentive for either the patient, the physician, or the hospital to be cost-conscious because the insurance company or the government, not the individual, is paying the bill. Doctors order, hospitals perform, and patients have come to expect more tests, more amenities (e.g., private rooms, color TVs), and more attention because it will be paid for by an unseen third party. As former Congressman Al Ullman put it, "With the invisible 'third party' insurer paying more than 90 percent of the cost, the consumer and the doctor rarely spare the expense."[27]

Doctors and hospitals rarely "spare the expense" not only because of the intervention by third-party insurers but also because of the fee-for-service reimbursement procedures which dominate medical practice in the United States. Basically, doctors and hospitals are paid a fee for every service they perform or provide—every office visit, every test, every injection, etc. The more they do, the more they earn. This, combined with third-party payments, leads to little cost-consciousness. Alain Enthoven, a severe critic of the system, says it "is a totally inappropriate way to finance medical care."[28]

Another facet of this third-party payment mechanism is that the tax system tends to encourage more generous and, critics charge, more inflationary coverage. Under current federal tax laws employers can deduct from their taxable income all health insurance costs they pay on behalf of their employees. Offering employees more generous health insurance coverage—i.e., plans that cost more, cover more, and push the nation's health bill up ever higher—is good for employee morale and is a very attractive tax incentive. Ultimately, of course, someone has to pay the bill. General Motors estimates that health care costs for their employees (which in 1980 cost $1.5 billion) added $315.23 to the cost of every GM car and truck.[29] Finally, it also should be noted that these benefits currently are not calculated as part of the employee's taxable income, although in 1983 President Reagan proposed changing this.

The final feature of the financing mechanism which contributes to spiraling health costs is the nearly unique nature of the medical marketplace. In most economic relationships cost is typically a function of supply and demand. In general, the greater the demand by buyers, the higher the cost. In medical care, however, the supplier (i.e., the physician) also determines the demand. It is the physician, not the patient, who orders the tests, determines if and for how long the patient will stay in the hospital, and prescribes the medication. The functional equivalent would be if the local Ford dealer determined that every family needed three automobiles—and Fords at that. The typical restraints that supply and demand impose on costs in other areas are simply absent in the U.S. health care market.

Utilization Factors   Pricing and financing mechanisms are not, however, the only factors contributing to the extraordinary growth in medical care costs. Important changes in utilization patterns also have contributed to the problem. In particular, increases in the number and relative proportion and health care usage of three groups—women, nonwhites, and the elderly—each of whom tends to use medical services more than their opposites, have increased the nation's health bill. Of the three, however, the elderly have had the most profound impact on the system.

To begin, there are over 13 million more U.S. citizens 65 years old or over today than there were in 1950—25.5 million compared to 12.5 million. Furthermore this represents an increase from 8.1 percent of the population in 1950 to 11.3 percent in 1980. By the year 2030 it is estimated that there will be 50 million elderly people, comprising 17 percent of the population. Not unexpectedly, the elderly make greater demands on the health care system and account for a disproportionate share of the health care bill. Gibson and Fisher, examining age differences in health expenditures for the fiscal year 1977, found that "total per capita spending for the elderly was more than two and a half times that for persons aged 19–64 and nearly seven times that for those under age 19. Thus, expenditures for the aged, comprising 11 percent of the population, totaled 29 percent of personal health care spending."[30] The elderly become ill more frequently than other age groups. They see physicians more often and take up more time when they do. It has been estimated that it takes three times longer to x-ray an elderly person than a younger one.[31] They are more likely to require costly medical procedures than other age groups. And the demand for these more costly procedures is going up faster for the elderly than other groups. "Surgery rates for the country as a whole rose by 25.5 percent between 1965 and 1978; but for people 65 years of age and over, the rate increased by 64.7 percent."[32]

The reasons for the rapid growth in the consumption, and hence costs, of medical care for the elderly are not hard to find. First, and foremost, was the introduction of Medicare in 1965 which had as its purpose the removal of financial barriers to acquiring necessary medical care. The impact of Medicare was profound: In 1967 the federal government spent $4.5 billion on Medicare for the aged; in 1982 the cost was $50 billion. The increase in the demand (and coincidentally the costs) for health care by the aged is in no small measure the result of deliberate, and benevolent, government policy.

The increased demand is also a function of the success of the medical and scientific community in preserving life and conquering illness. In the decade 1965–1975 the death rate for people 65 years old and over declined 11 percent, from 6,008 per 100,000 to 5,432 per 100,000.

In sum, what has happened is that the success of the United States in terms of achieving better and more accessible health care for the elderly, improved nutrition, greater health awareness among its people, and scientific advances in dealing with such diseases as hypertension, arthritis, etc., has combined to increase demands made upon the health care system and increase the costs of running it.

Service Factors Another factor which has contributed to the cost explosion in health care is the revolution in medical technology. This technology has introduced into U.S. medical practice, in just the last few decades, extraordinarily sophisticated *and costly* life-saving and life-sustaining diagnostic equipment, drugs, and procedures. In fact, Victor Fuchs, one of the foremost students of the U.S. health care system, has argued that "the most important thing that drives up costs, over time, is new technology."[33] Such diagnostic procedures or equipment as the CAT scanner (computerized aerial tomography), the colonoscope, and stress tests; surgical procedures such as heart bypass and kidney transplants; the use of a treatment procedure like kidney dialysis; and the introduction of intensive care units and coronary care units in hospitals all have contributed to the ability of the medical profession to sustain life and treat illnesses in ways that were beyond the reach of medical science just a few years ago. But the cost of this technology has been enormous. Consider some of the following examples:

1 In 1982 it cost approximately $1.056 billion for kidney treatments, dialysis, and transplant operations for the 59,125 kidney patients enrolled in a special federal program. This group constituted just .025 percent of the U.S. population.

2 With the introduction of intensive care units to treat premature infants the mortality rate for those born earlier than 7 months declined from 80 percent to 20 percent, while the cost for such care increased from $10,000 per care to $120,000 per care.[34]

3 CAT scanners are modern medical miracles which allow physicians to observe any part of the body in three-dimensional detail and to locate medical problems which heretofore could only be found, if at all, through surgery. Currently CAT scanners cost about $1.2 million to buy and about $300,000 to $400,000 a year to operate.

As more and more hospitals, physicians, and patients utilize these technological innovations the cost of health care mounts higher and higher—and so does consumer demand. And herein lies the last, and in some sense most important, explanation for the continued explosion in health care costs.

Health—At Any Cost   In the final analysis it is the extraordinary value we attach to good health, and the often emotional atmosphere within which medicine is practiced, that makes any effort to effectively contain costs so very difficult. As David Mechanic, an able student of health care, has noted, "The psychology of illness, and the importance that consumers give to their own medical care, make policy formulation particularly difficult. Reasonable consumers can see the logic of more efficient distribution and organization of services, more parsimonious use of laboratories and technologies, and allocating resources in some relation to expected benefits, but when sick they want the best that medical sciences make possible."[35] In effect, when it comes to our own and our family's health, none of us are "reasonable" consumers. Cost, particularly since most of it is paid by third parties, is no object.

From a macroeconomic or societal perspective, of course, cost is a matter of concern. How much can we as a nation afford to spend on health care? In 1950 4.4 percent of the GNP was devoted to health care, while in 1981 it was 9.8 percent. How much is enough to do the job, or is politically acceptable? Alain Enthoven concedes: "There is no magic number. The right number is the number people want it to be."[36] Thus far the U.S. public seems not to have reached the point where they are willing to concede that "enough is enough."

Price factors, utilization patterns, technological advances, and the extraordinary value attached to health care combine to make for a seemingly unabated and uncontrollable explosion in health care costs. While consumers appear, at least for the time being, willing to pay the bill, policy makers, who must set priorities each year and suffer the consequences of their decisions, see the issue as an intolerable one.

THE WORLDWIDE EXPLOSION IN HEALTH CARE COSTS

For whatever comfort it may offer, data from other industrialized nations during the 1960s and 1970s indicate that the United States was by no means alone in suffering the burdens of increased health care costs. In fact, a recent study by Joseph Simanis and John Coleman of the Social Security Administration found that among nine industrialized nations during the period 1960–1976 the United States, which ranked fourth in the percentage of GNP devoted to health care in 1975 (see Table 3-5) in unadjusted expenditure figures, "had the lowest average annual rate of increase in actual expenditures during the entire study period."[37] When the authors adjusted the annual rate of growth for change in the consumer price index for the nine countries, the United States ranked next to last. The annual rate of increase for each country (in percent) for the period 1969–1976 was:

West Germany	11.30	Canada	6.65
The Netherlands	9.69	Sweden	6.29
Australia	9.55	United States	5.93
France	7.39	United Kingdom	5.13
Finland	7.31		

TABLE 3-5
HEALTH CARE EXPENDITURES AS A PERCENTAGE OF GNP FOR NINE
INDUSTRIAL NATIONS, SELECTED YEARS 1960–1976

Country	1960	1965	1970	1975	1976
Australia	5.0	5.2	5.6	7.0	7.7
Canada	5.6	6.1	7.1	7.1	7.1
France	5.0	5.9	6.6	8.1	8.2
West Germany	4.4	5.2	6.1	9.7	NA
Netherlands	NA	5.0	6.3	8.6	8.5
Sweden	3.5	5.8	7.5	8.7	NA
United Kingdom	3.8	3.9	4.9	5.6	5.8
United States	5.3	5.9	7.2	8.4	8.6
Finland	4.2	5.2	5.9	6.8	7.2

Source: Joseph G. Simanis and John R. Coleman, "Health Care Expenditures in Nine Industrialized Countries," *Social Security Bulletin* 43 (Jan. 1980), 5.

Finally it should be noted that Simanis and Coleman found that, as in the case of the United States, in each country the annual growth of health care costs exceeded both the overall rate of inflation and the growth rate of the GNP. Although the relative rank-order of these countries may have changed since 1976, the problem of rapid increases in health care costs has not. And, while there are undoubtedly some idiosyncratic factors which might account for some of the increase, for the most part they are attributable to the same sources as in the United States: overall inflation, aging population, increased use of new and expensive medical technology, the importance attached to health and health care, as well as fee-for-service and third-party reimbursement procedures.

TO REGULATE OR DEREGULATE? APPROACHES TO SOLVING THE HEALTH CARE CRISIS

Whether or not it is in a state of crisis, there are clearly problems with the U.S. health care system. Policy makers in the United States have responded to these problems in a variety of ways. In terms of basic policy orientation, liberals have recommended, and in some cases implemented, greater government intervention in, or regulation of, the health care system, while conservatives have favored deregulation and increased reliance on the free market. We will examine and evaluate both approaches now, as well as look at the experiences of other nations in dealing with these issues.

Liberal Approaches to the Health Care Crisis

In the area of health care policy, as in others, liberals have favored the intervention of government to protect the interest of the public. In the case of cost containment, two specific proposals have emerged. The most publicized and persistent is the recommendation that the United States adopt national health insurance, including a cost containment provision. While there have been several such proposals recently, the best known of these is that of Senator Edward Kennedy. Kennedy's proposal for a national health insurance program has known several cosponsors and formulations. In one of its most recent incarnations it was cosponsored by Congressman Henry Waxman (D., Calif.) and developed in conjunction with the labor coalition Committee for National Health Insurance. The proposed bill ("Health Care for All Americans"), whose non-cost-related details will be discussed below, contained several proposals for reducing health care costs. Specifically, the bill proposed the following cost control mechanisms. First, Congress would set the overall annual budget for the national health care system—so-called "global budgeting." Annual increases in the budget could not exceed the growth rate in the GNP—something which they have done for a decade or more.

Second, physicians' fees, which would be paid by the health insurance system, would be negotiated between the medical profession and a national advisory board. These fees, like all other facets of the health care system, would be a part of, and limited by, the annual budget for the entire system. Third, hospital budgets would be set a year in advance, and physicians and hospitals would be held responsible if those budgets are exceeded. Fourth, the federal government would reimburse capital expenditure outlays only for *approved* medical projects. This latter provision is aimed at controlling unnecessary increases in hospital construction and hospital bed expansion. Finally, restrictions would be placed on the use of high-risk and costly medical procedures.[38] The Kennedy approach, which would mandate health insurance for everyone, is the most comprehensive proposal for dealing with all facets of the cost crisis. It is also the most difficult to sell politically.

A more modest, but ultimately no more successful, proposal was introduced by President Carter in 1977 and again in 1979. The Carter proposal was aimed at the largest and fastest growing facet of the health care bill, namely, hospital costs. The original Carter-sponsored bill contained two major provisions. The first would have limited hospital cost increases in fiscal year 1978 to 9 percent and to smaller increases in subsequent years. Any hospital that exceeded the 9 percent limit would have to put the exceeded amount in escrow and reduce the following year's budget by the appropriate amount. The second provision would have set a limit of $2.5 billion a year for new hospital construction. The money would be allocated among the states based upon population and need.[39] The bill met with strong opposition from the hospital industry and had only lukewarm support from members of Carter's own party within Congress. Some, like Senator Kennedy and Congressman Paul Rogers (D., Fla.), felt the bill did not go far enough. In any event, the bill died in committee in both houses.

The bill was revived and revised in 1979 and made more attractive to the medical industry by including certain voluntary cost control efforts. Voluntary controls would be replaced by mandatory controls if the industry could not hold down costs. This bill proved no more popular than its predecessor and suffered a similar fate. In 1980 the Democrats lost control of the White House and the Senate. The regulatory path to health cost containment seemed a less likely, but not impossible, policy option.

Another regulatory effort, aimed at both cost and quality control, was the introduction in 1972 of professional standards review organizations (PSROs). These organizations were intended to encourage doctors within a geographical area to monitor the professional practices and procedures of their colleagues in dealing with Medicaid or Medicare patients. If the

PSRO determines that the physician is not conforming with the treatment standards set by the organization, it may warn the physician and, if there is no behavioral change, exclude him or her from participating in Medicaid and Medicare. The original law (PL 92-603) provided that if local physicians did not voluntarily set up their own PSRO, the government would designate a group. The medical profession vigorously opposed the system and was able to win postponement of its implementation. Even today, a decade after its passage, the PSRO law has not been fully implemented, and in the areas where it has, the results have been mixed in terms of improved quality of care and decreased costs.

Lastly, in dealing with maldistribution of health care personnel, the main government effort was to establish, in 1970, the National Health Service Corps. The NHSC, which is under the Bureau of Health Personnel Development and Service, was set up to improve the availability of health services in areas of urban and rural poverty. The agency provides scholarships for medical, dental, and nursing students. These students, in turn, promise to join the corps upon completion of their training, and serve in medically underserved areas for a period of one year for each year that they are on government scholarship. The NHSC pays the salaries of medical personnel while they serve the corps.

Assessments of the corps, thus far, have been rather mixed. A 1978 General Accounting Office report found that only 42 of the 800 physicians that had served in the corps up to that time had remained in the area in which they had worked.[40] This was disappointing to the program's supporters who had hoped, and argued, that these people would stay in the areas, thereby solving the problem of inadequate medical care on a more permanent basis. Nevertheless, it is true that at least for a finite period of time many locations across the nation, but especially rural areas, are being provided with medical services for the first time. In closing, we might note that under the Kennedy-Waxman bill, Congress would establish a health resources distribution fund which would support the creation of medical centers and other medical resources in, and hopefully attract medical personnel to, underserved areas of the country.

Conservative Approaches to the Health Care Crisis

The advent of the Reagan presidency and a strong conservative bloc within Congress opened the prospect that quite a different approach to health care policy might be taken. Indeed, in June 1981 then Secretary of Health and Human Services Richard Schweiker announced that "this Administration is committed to trying something new. We intend to loose the forces of the market to make the health care system more competitive."[41] What Secretary Schweiker had in mind, specifically, was the problem of runaway health care costs, although market forces were expected to remedy quality and distributional problems as well. How could increased competition and reliance on the marketplace help bring health care costs down? Reagan administration officials such as Schweiker, Director of Office of Management and Budget David Stockman, a number of congressional advocates, and academic economists like Alain Enthoven argued that the main problem was in the system's financing mechanism and particularly in third-party carriers. It will be recalled that the major criticism of this mechanism is that consumers and providers have no incentive to become economically prudent because the tab is picked up by the third party—Blue Cross, Blue Shield, Medicare, etc.

The Reagan administration developed a package of legislative plans, the essential parts of which were already embodied in the Health Incentives Reform Bill (1981) sponsored by Senators David Durenberger (R., Minn.), David Boren (D., Ok.), and John Heinz (R., Pa.). According to this proposal there would be a three-pronged attack on health care costs. First, the bill would limit the amount that employers could deduct from their taxable income for their employees' health benefits package. This would eliminate the tax incentives for employers to increase health care benefits. It would also, presumably, put a cap on the amount allocated to health insurance benefits because beyond a certain amount there would be no incentives at all. Second, it would encourage employers to offer not one, as is generally the case now, but multiple and competing health care plans. Here it is hoped that employees, who would be allowed to choose among plans each year, would shop around for the best buy in medical coverage. Theoretically health insurance providers would have to offer plans with good coverage at reasonable rates to attract and keep members. Third, employees would get a fixed and equal amount toward their health care plans. This would mean that if people choose plans more costly than the employer's coverage, they would have to pay the difference themselves. On the other hand, if they choose a plan that costs less than the employer's contribution, they could keep the difference. The assumption is that employers will offer, and employees will choose, less costly and, therefore, less comprehensive plans in which there would be more out-of-pocket payments—and more cost consciousness when seeking medical care.

In a related plan the Reagan administration proposed the introduction of a voucher system whereby Medicare recipients would be given a voucher equal to the amount of money for which they were eligible under Medicare. Recipients would then shop around for medical coverage. If they choose a plan that costs less than their allocation, and which undoubtedly would require greater out-of pocket expense, they could keep the difference. If they choose a more costly and comprehensive plan, they, not the government, would pay the difference. Here too the assumption is of greater frugality, more out-of-pocket payments, and greater cost consciousness.

The final part of the package was a proposed tax credit to employers who offered low-cost group health plan options. These plans, called Health Maintenance Organizations or HMOs, are prepaid medical programs in which members pay a set monthly fee regardless of the actual medical services received. HMOs provide an alternative to the fee-for-service approach. When individuals need medical attention they go to the HMO medical center, where they are seen by one of the staff physicians from a wide variety of medical specialties. The fees paid to the HMO become, in effect, its budget. It is in the interests of the HMO to keep costs within budget to avoid deficits and enjoy profits. Theoretically there are no unnecessary tests, office visits, or hospitalization because the physicians and staff have an interest in keeping costs down.

The Reagan proposals were not well received, either in Congress or among various interest groups. In a rare show of agreement, almost all the participants—major businesses and organized labor, medical groups and the insurance industry—attacked some or all of the proposals. No action was completed on any of the proposals during the Ninety-seventh Congress, although the administration resubmitted parts of its health program to the Ninety-eighth Congress.

The sense of frustration that the administration felt and their perception that the continuing problem required some action, even if that action was ideologically obnoxious, was reflected in a statement at the time by an assistant secretary for planning and evaluation in the Department of Health and Human Services. "The health-provider industry is betting that if we cannot get competition, we're going to do nothing. They are making an error. If we have to make a choice between regulating or deficit financing, we're going to get to regulation."[42] Similar sentiments were being expressed at the time by Senate Finance Committee chairman Robert Dole (R., Kans.) who said that Congress may have made a mistake in rejecting President Carter's hospital cost control act.[43]

In the latter part of 1982, the Reagan administration proposed yet another cost containment plan—and one which seemingly abandoned a free-market approach to controlling health care costs. The plan was in response to a congressional mandate that the secretary of Health and Human Services propose a cost containment program for Medicare by December 31, 1982. Congressional and administrative concern with Medicare was based upon the fact that it has become one of the most expensive and fastest growing of all federal programs. Begun in 1966, Medicare cost $4.7 billion in its first full year of operation. By 1981 the program cost $44.8 billion. The 1981 figure represented a 21.5 percent increase over the previous year.

"The primary reason for this increase is the rapid escalation of outlays for hospital care."[44]

The Reagan proposal to contain Medicare hospital costs is based upon two practices widely used outside the United States: prospective budgeting and diagnostic-related group (DRG) reimbursement. Under the proposal, the federal government would pay all hospitals treating Medicare patients the same amount, fixed in advance, for particular diagnoses. The administration proposed establishing 467 DRGs—e.g., heart attack, hip replacement, cataract removal—and each hospital would be paid a predetermined fee for each although some regional variation in charges would be allowed. Currently, hospitals and physicians treating Medicare patients are reimbursed for the "customary, prevailing and reasonable charges" with no limits on procedures and tests. This system has led to both rapidly rising and virtually uncontrollable cost increases and remarkable national variation. For example, Medicare has been charged as little as $2,100 for a hip replacement and as much as $8,200; it has paid $450 for cataract removal at one hospital and $2,800 at another—and with no apparent difference in the quality of the health care provided.

By standardizing reimbursement for specific diagnoses, the administration expected to eliminate such disparities, as well as control the growth of health care costs. Each hospital in the country would receive, for example, $3,200 for a heart attack patient covered by Medicare, regardless of how long the patient remained hospitalized—currently the range for treating heart attack patients is $1,500 to $9,000. If a hospital's costs for treating a heart attack patient were less than $3,200, the hospital would keep the difference; if higher, it would swallow the loss. Under no circumstances could a hospital bill a patient if its costs exceeded the Medicare fee. Hospitals, it is argued, would have a strong incentive to control costs under this system.

The Reagan proposal for prospective budgeting represented a retreat from the free-market approach to Medicare cost containment exemplified by the voucher system and to which Reagan had been so philosophically attached. That he swallowed his ideological pride and even considered what is essentially a regulatory approach to health cost control was a measure of the frustration felt by the administration to this seemingly intractable problem.

While conservative policy makers have not addressed the issues of the quality and distribution of medical services directly, Milton Friedman has. According to Friedman, while licensing of physicians and hospitals is often justified in the name of protecting the public, it was originally intended, and continues, to be the main means of protecting physicians from increased competition. Friedman, therefore, advocates doing away with licensing. According to Friedman:

I am myself persuaded that licensure has reduced both the quantity and quality of medical practice; that it has reduced the opportunities available to people who would like to be physicians, forcing them to pursue occupations they regard as less attractive; that it has forced the public to pay more for less satisfactory medical service, and that it has retarded technological development both in medicine itself and in the organization of medical practice. I conclude that licensure should be eliminated as a requirement for the practice of medicine.[45]

Eliminating licensure would increase the number of physicians and hospitals, forcing them to be more competitive in their rates and, thereby, reducing physicians' and hospital fees. In addition, less qualified physicians will be driven from the marketplace, in the same manner as less qualified automobile mechanics, by the more competent ones. We might add that Friedman is not at all clear, at least in *Capitalism and Freedom,* how this system would work. He does not explain, for example, if he would favor allowing anyone to "hang up a shingle" and practice medicine or just those who graduate from medical school.

In sum, conservatives argue that health care costs could be controlled, and the quality improved, if physicians, hospitals, and other health services were compelled to compete with one another for patients, and if the patients too were thrust into a more market-oriented system. It is time now to evaluate the liberal and conservative proposals for dealing with health care problems in the United States. In doing so we will be able to draw upon the experiences of other nations in dealing with similar problems.

Evaluating Liberal and Conservative Policy Proposals

Let us begin with the liberal faith in national health insurance as the cure for the nation's health care ills. If the experiences of other nations such as West Germany, Japan, Canada, and France are relevant, then national health insurance, even if it includes appropriate and attractive incentives, is not likely to lure physicians out of middle- and upper-class urban and suburban areas into urban ghettos or rural towns. Senator Kennedy is accurate in his concern that "it is now virtually impossible to find a physician in private practice in the south Bronx, in Roxbury, in east Los Angeles, in east St. Louis, in south Philadelphia."[46] But national health insurance, which Senator Kennedy supports, is unlikely to solve the problem. One of the authors, in a comparative study of health care systems, found similar problems of maldistribution in Great Britain, West Germany, Japan, and even the Soviet Union despite the latter country's substantial coercive capability. Physicians in the United States, like their British, German, Japanese, and Soviet counterparts, prefer the professional and personal amenities of urban practice.

Second, there seems to be no reason to expect national health insurance to improve the quality of health care. The experiences of countries such as West Germany, Japan, and Canada suggest that a fee-for-service national insurance system—which is probably the route the United States would follow if it were adopted—by no means discourages unnecessary surgery, office visits, and overprescribing of medicine. As we have seen, in a fee-for-service system physicians are paid for every service they perform. Hence, the more they do, the more they earn. In Japan, for example, each medical procedure is assigned a number of points—e.g., an examination is 45 points, an x-ray is 100 points—and physicians are reimbursed by the insurance companies a specified amount per point. The more points they accrue, the more money they get. And there have been many complaints that Japanese physicians "overdoctor" and "overprescribe."

Lastly, in terms of health care costs, the evidence seems most clear—and damning.[47] There is no doubt that health care costs can be limited by imposing annual ceilings, either on all expenditures as proposed in the Kennedy plan, or on hospitals only as proposed by President Carter, or on Medicare as proposed by President Reagan. This is not to say that costs would not rise. In most proposals it is stipulated that growth in health expenditures would be pegged to some economic indicator or standard such as the consumer price index or growth rate of the GNP. Then they would continue to rise but not, as they have over the past decade, at a rate exceeding that of other goods and services.

The real issue in the use of either mandatory global or sectoral cost controls is not their economic or technical feasibility but rather their political acceptability. First, there is now, as there has been for the last half century, strong and enormously successful opposition from the medical industry. The American Medical Association in particular, but also the American Hospital Association, the Federation of American Hospitals, and the private insurance industry, has demonstrated remarkable success in preventing either national health insurance or mandatory cost restraints. To achieve mandatory expenditure limits, particularly within the framework of national health insurance, would be a political achievement of rather significant proportions.

Second, it should be recognized that setting and maintaining fiscally prudent health expenditure ceilings will require legislative statesmanship of the highest order. Public pressure for more and better health services, not curtailment of those services, will be enormous, as will the temptation to politicians to satisfy public demands in this incredibly important and sensitive policy area. In this effort, the public will find a willing ally in the medical industry. The experiences of nations such as West Germany, Canada, and Japan demonstrate that the medical community can be a formidable adversary even under national health insurance.

Finally, it should be recognized that truly effective cost containment may result in a decline in the quality of medical care in the United States. The industrialized nation that has been most successful in containing the growth of health care costs is Great Britain. (See Table 3-5.) However, the British National Health Service has been criticized, on both sides of the Atlantic, for the long lists of patients waiting to see specialists or find an available hospital bed for noncritical surgery. It is not at all unusual for someone to wait months to see a specialist and years for a vacant bed in a hospital. It would be wrong to suggest that successful cost containment in the United States would result in the medical resource problems experienced by the British. There are too many differences between the United States and Great Britain, which we cannot go into, to make such a conclusion valid. Nevertheless, global or sectoral cost containment, as envisioned in the Kennedy bill or Medicare prospective budgeting, would require some adjustments in the medical resource consumption patterns of U.S. citizens: e.g., fewer diagnostic tests, shorter hospital stays. Some of these, one might add, may be beneficial, such as less surgery.

We might note here that since passage in 1977 of a Health Care Cost Containment Act, West Germany has used global budgeting to contain costs, apparently with some success. Nevertheless, the overall record of national health insurance systems in controlling health care costs is not an impressive one.

We would hasten to add here that liberal support for national health insurance goes beyond monetary issues. First, liberals argue that while improved access to medical care may not substantially improve the health of a majority of U.S. citizens—although it will do so for some of our poorest citizens—it can alleviate the physical pain and mental anguish that often accompany illness. There are still many in this country who postpone or avoid seeing a physician because of financial considerations. According to a 1982 national survey, one-third of all those interviewed reported avoiding going to a doctor to save money.[48] Many illnesses resolve themselves without long-term implications for the health of the individual. But in many instances, the individual needlessly has suffered pain and anxiety which could have been minimized by medical attention. In addition, there are certainly cases when delay in getting such attention has serious, and sometimes fatal, consequences.

A second liberal justification for adopting national health insurance relates to the individual financial consequences of illness. There are still millions of U.S. citizens without any medical or hospital insurance at all for whom a major illness would be financially catastrophic. Many people in the United States without hospital insurance are not poor enough for Medicaid, but they are too poor to pay over $200 a day for a hospital stay. In addition, the national health survey mentioned above found that one out of five persons reported losing private health insurance coverage during some period of time in the year because of being unemployed.[49] Beyond the dollar costs of medical care there are, of course, the incalculable costs associated with the fear of a mammoth and ruinous medical bill. One of the major achievements of the British National Health Service, acknowledged by both its critics and admirers, is that it has "removed a burden of anxiety about ability to meet doctors' bills or hospital charges, which in the past preyed heavily on many people of low or modest means."[50]

A third reason that liberals offer in defense of national health insurance is both the most fundamental and controversial. In 1981, Congressman Robert A. Roe, a liberal Democrat from New Jersey, introduced a national health insurance bill (the Health Security Act). In the preamble to the bill, Congressman Roe asserted that "adequate health care for all our people must now be recognized as a right." This assertion, subscribed to by Senator Kennedy and most other liberals as well in all other industrialized nations, is central to any defense of national health insurance. If one accepts their assertion, then health care, like the rights of speech, assembly, and religion, must be guaranteed by the state.

In the final analysis, however, while there are certainly persuasive arguments in favor of a state-sponsored national health insurance system, the experiences of other nations and, indeed, our own experiences with Medicaid and Medicare suggest that those arguments do not include the likelihood of ending the health care crisis.

It is somewhat more difficult to evaluate the conservative prescription for curing the nation's health care ills. There are few contemporary experiences outside the United States upon which to make a judgment about the efficacy of greater reliance on market forces. Indeed, much of the attraction of these proposals is that they are untested and, therefore, as yet to be found wanting. Thus, a *New York Times* editorial (March 6, 1982) on the issue of health cost containment, while advising caution, concluded: "The economy cannot long endure runaway medical costs. It's time to find out whether a competitive health care market will make the bill more affordable." A critique of the market-competition proposals must be somewhat more speculative than a critique of the liberal approach.

To begin, it is difficult to take seriously Milton Friedman's suggestion that we cease licensing physicians and hospitals in order to increase their numbers, competition, and quality while reducing costs. The assumption that poorly qualified physicians will be abandoned by the consuming public, in much the same way that poorly qualified shoe repairmen are rejected, seems either naive or cruel. For one thing, it is not always possible for the public to know when it is getting incompetent medical care. If the pain does not go away or the rash does not clear up, is it the physician's fault, the medication, an untreatable problem, or what? In addition, one shudders to think of the harm an incompetent physician might do before he or she is driven from the marketplace. It is one thing to get a pair of shoes that have been improperly repaired; it is quite another to have an appendectomy which is improperly done. Finally, Professor Friedman's proposal is politically unacceptable. The medical profession will not allow it, and the public does not want it.

Proposals for reducing health care costs by increasing competition must, however, be taken more seriously. The proposal submitted by Senators Durenberger, Boren, and Heinz, endorsed by President Reagan and given scholarly legitimacy by Alain Enthoven, is the most thoroughly articulated and serious of the policy proposals in the area. The basic issue, in the words of a *New York Times* editorial, is: "Can a Free Market Cut Health Costs?"[51] To begin with, as *The New York Times* editorial noted, a limitation on tax deductability for health care benefits will not be as dramatic as supporters predict because it will not affect that many employers. "Merely limiting tax deductability would not alter the behavior of nonprofit and public agencies, employing 40 percent of the workers; they have no tax liability to begin with."

Second, competition advocates assume that if given the choice, U.S. citizens will opt for less extensive health coverage at a lower price and with more out-of-pocket payments. The evidence on this, however, is at best mixed. *The New York Times* conducted a national health survey and found that 45 percent of the people were willing to enroll in less expensive programs even if it meant more out-of-pocket payments. However, 44 percent were unwilling to do so and the remainder had no opinion.[52] In theory then, there does appear to be some support expressed for purchasing less costly insurance. Actual experience with the Medicare program, however, casts some doubt on this hypothetical commitment. The House Committee on Aging found that in 1978, 15 million of the 23 million older U.S. citizens covered by the Medicare program spent nearly $4 billion to supplement their Medicare coverage.[53] Furthermore, the desire for more health care security, in the form of more comprehensive insurance, is not restricted to the elderly. A study of federal employees found "that many younger people, too, would rather pay high premiums for high-option health coverage than pay medical costs out of their own pocket."[54] The evidence does not appear to give strong support to the theory that if given a choice among competitive programs, people will opt for the less costly plans.

In addition, one may question the average citizen's ability to make a rational economic choice among competing health plans. Clearly, the bottom line dollar figure is not the only relevant factor in making a decision about health insurance. The House Committee on Aging found that "nearly $1 billion of the $4 billion Medicare beneficiaries spent on supplementary coverage in 1978 went for overlapping coverage, with the elderly purchasing

double or triple coverage for some things while omitting others completely."[55]

The limitations of the market-competition approach to cost containment
appear most obvious in the case of hospital costs. Competition proponents
seem to assume a direct relationship between the patient and the hospital,
where, in fact, none exists. Two critics of the market approach have noted
that:

> Hospital care is characterized by a complex four-actor relationship, in which
> Person A (the patient) is treated by Person B (the hospital staff) at the behest of
> Person C (the attending physician) and paid for by Person D (the insurer). No
> other market in the U.S. has these characteristics. To presume that patients can
> discipline hospital staffs and doctors through a market relationship with insurers
> is to ignore the indirect structure of the relationships, not to mention the highly
> specialized nature of medical expertise and the life-threatening consequences
> of inadequate care. In short, the competition model is flawed economically
> because patients cannot control physicians and hospital costs through their
> choice of insurers.[56]

In short, it does not appear that the conservatives' market-competition
answer is any more convincing or promising than the liberals' national
health insurance–regulatory approach.

CONCLUSION

Where then does one go from here? We do not presume to have an answer
but would suggest that at this point we may not yet have reached the point
where anything *has* to be done. The reason for this lies in the nature of
health and health care as a policy issue.

Take the issue of the cost explosion, which is generally recognized as
the most serious problem facing the U.S. health care system. The problem
with devising an appropriate and acceptable health care policy is that in
many respects it is a politically, economically, and psychologically unique
issue area. It is the extraordinary importance that people attach to health
care that makes arriving at a consensus, on even the most fundamental of
policy points, so difficult. While it is true, for example, that health costs
are rising more rapidly than other items, that is not the same as saying that
they are rising too rapidly or that we are spending too much for health
care. Is 9.8 percent of the GNP too much or is 12 percent? The right
number *is*, as Alain Enthoven has said, the number people want it to be.
Thus far there does not appear to be as much public concern as there is
elite concern over the size of the nation's health care bill. Until the time
that health care costs so crowd expenditures in other areas that other

desired goods and services must be sacrificed, it is not likely that policy makers will be able to overcome the resistance of organized interest groups like the AMA or AHA. As long as people in the United States give a "higher priority to the growth of medical investment than to expenditure for education, transportation, or urban problems,"[57] a fundamental assault on health care costs is unlikely.

Finally, with regard to the other two facets of the health care crisis—access and quality control—it appears that these problems may be partly remedied through professional and socioeconomic factors. For example, while physicians (and hospitals, nurses, etc.) continue to favor urban and suburban practices over rural practice, the supply of rural physicians has increased significantly over the years. This is in part a function of the increased attractiveness of rural areas as a place to live compared to the metropolitan areas. In addition, medical schools, responding to this problem as well as that of too much specialization in the profession, are encouraging new physicians to enter general or family practice. This type of practice is much more common in the rural areas of the country than is the specialty-based practice, which tends to require an urban setting. In terms of improving access, the reader should be alerted to the fact that public policy in the form of national health insurance and other publicly provided health services can only go so far in improving the health care of poor people. Students of the British National Health Service have found, much to everyone's dismay, that despite nearly 40 years of a universal, free, and generally equally accessible health care system, differences in mortality and morbidity between social classes have remained—and in some instances actually have increased.[58] This fact illustrates a point made by Odin Anderson. "In general, it would seem to be a reasonable assumption that health services as such have less influence on mortality rates than general social conditions in economically developed countries."[59] Significant gains in the health of poor people in the United States will occur when public policy addresses *both* the health delivery system and the poverty system.

Finally, in terms of quality, the medical profession, fearing government intervention, has begun to police itself, starting in medical schools, over the issue of overdoctoring and overprescribing of medication. Thus, for example, in 1981 there was a dramatic drop in the number of Valium tablets—the most commonly prescribed tranquilizer in the country—sold in the United States. Medical observers attributed this to the greater consciousness on the part of physicians to the issue of overdoctoring in general.

Clearly, however, health and health care in the United States—its cost, quality, and distribution—will continue to be a central policy issue for years to come.

NOTES

1 *Gallup Report* #198, March 1982.
2 This section relies heavily upon Howard M. Leichter, "Voluntary Health Risks and Public Policy: The British Experience," *Hastings Center Report,* 11 (Oct. 1981), 32–39.
3 Marc Lalonde, "A New Perspective on the Health of Canadians" (Ottawa: Department of National Health and Welfare, 1974), p. 32.
4 Public Law No. 94-317.
5 R. M. Battistella, "Disease Prevention and Health Education," in *Health Care Policy in a Changing Environment,* ed. R. M. Battistella and T. G. Rundell (Berkeley: McCutcheon Publishing Corp., 1978), p. 276.
6 John H. Knowles, "The Responsibility of the Individual," in *Doing Better and Feeling Worse: Health in the United States,* ed. John H. Knowles (New York: W. W. Norton and Company, 1977), p. 75.
7 H. W. Merchant, "Economic Pressures to Promote Self-Care," *New England Journal of Medicine,* 295:2 (July 1976), 119.
8 Robert Crawford, "You Are Dangerous to Your Health: The Ideology of Victim Blaming," *International Journal of Health Sciences,* 7:4 (1977), 663–680; and "Sickness as Sin," *Health/Pac Bulletin,* 80 (1978), 10–16.
9 Daniel Wikler, "Persuasion and Coercion for Health," *Health and Society,* 56:3 (1978); see also H. L. Laframboise, "Toward a Solution to Life-Style Health Problems in a Free Society," paper delivered at the Ninth International Conference on Health Education, Pan American Health Organization, Washington, D.C., 1978.
10 See, for example, Robert M. Veatch, "Voluntary Risks to Health," *Journal of the American Medical Association* (Jan. 1980); and Thomas McKeown, "Behavioral Environmental Determinants of Health and Their Implications for Public Policy," in *Future Directions in Health Care: A New Public Policy,* ed. R. Carlson and R. Cunningham (Cambridge, Mass.: Ballinger Publishing Co., 1978), pp. 31–33.
11 There is a voluminous literature on the health care systems of other nations. For those interested in pursuing the subject, see Howard M. Leichter, *A Comparative Approach to Policy Analysis: Health Care Policy in Four Nations* (New York: Cambridge Univ. Press, 1979); and Milton Roemer, *Comparative National Policies on Health Care* (New York: Marcel Dekker, 1977).
12 Nancy M. Frieden, "Physicians in Pre-Revolutionary Russia: Professionals or Servants of the State?" *Bulletin of the History of Medicine,* 49 (Spring 1975), 24–25.
13 Charles E. Phelps, "Public Sector Medicine: History and Analysis," in *New Directions in Public Health Care,* ed. Cotton M. Lindsay (San Francisco: Institute for Contemporary Studies, 1980), p. 131.
14 Quoted in Leichter, *A Comparative Approach,* p. 116.
15 In 1978 Australia changed from a compulsory to a voluntary national health insurance system. In addition, Great Britain, in 1948, changed from a national health insurance system to a national health service. This change, however, represented a greater, not lesser, degree of government involvement.

16 *Cong. Rec.,* Apr. 1, 1981, p. 5346.

17 Monroe Lerner, "Social Differences in Physical Health," in *Poverty and Health: A Sociological Analysis,* ed. John Kora, Aaron Antonovoskv, and Irving K. Zola (Cambridge, Mass.: Harvard Univ. Press, 1969), p. 91.

18 Jennifer Madans and Jack Kleinman, "Use of Ambulatory Care by the Poor and Nonpoor," in U.S Dept. of Health and Human Services, *Health, United States: 1980* (Washington, D.C.: GPO, 1980), p. 48.

19 Ibid., p. 49.

20 Mary W. Herman, "Health Care and the Patient's Needs," *Current History,* 73 (July–August 1977), 3.

21 U.S. Department of Health and Human Services, *Health, United States: 1980* (Washington, D.C.: GPO, 1980), p. 73.

22 Kline McPherson et al., "Small-Area Variations in the Use of Common Surgical Procedures: An International Comparison of New England, England, and Norway," *New England Journal of Medicine,* 307 (1982), 1310–1314.

23 Douglas Conrad, "Medical Malpractice Suits," *Current History,* 73 (July–August 1977), 22–26, 36–37.

24 *New York Times,* July 12, 1981.

25 *Health, United States: 1980,* p. 101.

26 Ibid., p. 216.

27 Quoted in Linda E. Demkovich "Cutting Health Care Costs—Why Not Let the Market Decide?" *National Journal,* Oct. 27, 1979, p. 1798.

28 Quoted in *Congressional Quarterly, Health Policy: The Legislative Agenda,* (Washington, D.C.: GPO, 1980), p. 36.

29 *New York Times,* March 28, 1982.

30 Robert M. Gibson and Charles R. Fisher, "Age Differences in Health Care Spending, Fiscal Year 1977," *Social Security Bulletin,* 42 (Jan. 1979), 12.

31 See Linda Demkovich, "Who Can Do a Better Job of Controlling Hospital Costs?" *National Journal,* Feb. 10, 1979, pp. 219–223.

32 *Health, United States: 1980,* pp. 106–107.

33 *New York Times,* March 28, 1982.

34 Demkovich, "Who Can Do a Better Job?" p. 223.

35 David Mechanic, "Some Dilemmas in Health Care Policy," *Health and Society,* 59 (1981), 3.

36 *Cong. Rec.,* Feb. 3, 1981, p. 845.

37 Joseph G. Simanis and John R. Coleman, "Health Care Expenditures in Nine Industrialized Countries," *Social Security Bulletin,* 43 (Jan. 1980), 3–8.

38 See *Health Policy: The Legislative Agenda,* pp. 14–15 for a complete description of the Health Care for All Americans bill.

39 Ibid., p. 23.

40 Ibid., p. 56.

41 *New York Times,* June 12, 1981.

42 *The Oregonian,* March 14, 1982.

43 Ibid.

44 Robert M. Gibson and Daniel R. Waldo, "National Health Expenditures, 1981" *Health Care Financing Review,* 4 (Sept. 1982), 11.

45 Milton Friedman and Rose Friedman, *Capitalism and Freedom* (Chicago: Univ. of Chicago Press, 1962), p. 158.

46 *Cong. Rec.*, Apr. 1, 1981, p. 3117.

47 See, for example, Uwe E. Reinhardt, "Health Insurance and Cost-Containment Policies: The Experience Abroad," *The American Economic Review,* 70 (May 1980), 149–156.

48 *New York Times,* March 29, 1982.

49 Ibid.

50 J. F. Sleeman, *The Welfare State: Its Aims, Benefits, and Costs* (London: Allen and Unwin, 1973), p. 279.

51 *New York Times,* March 29, 1982.

52 Ibid.

53 *Health Policy: The Legislative Agenda,* p. 37.

54 Ibid.

55 Ibid.

56 David Young and Richard Saltman, "Can Competition Really Lower Health Costs?" *Wall Street Journal,* Dec. 22, 1981.

57 Mechanic, p. 2.

58 Leichter, *A Comparative Approach,* p. 193.

59 Odin Anderson, *Health Care: Can There Be Equity?—The United States, Sweden and England* (New York: John Wiley & Sons, 1972).

CHAPTER 4

WOMEN'S EQUALITY: PUBLIC POLICY IN TRANSITION

The twentieth century has witnessed a protracted and often tense struggle on the part of women to change their role and status in U.S. society. There is no doubt that the movement has produced changes that have dramatically altered the social and economic structure of U.S. society. But it is also obvious that the conflict and controversy over women's rights is far from over. It is often said, in fact, that the women's movement is now in its second phase.[1] Most agree that the first phase occurred during the first half of the twentieth century when women successfully struggled to gain such fundamental rights as the franchise, the right to own property, and standing to sue in a court of law. Victories in these areas ended women's status as property.

The second, and current, phase involves women's struggles for legal and social equality. Groups differ, of course, over the parameters of this movement. Still, the vast majority of women (and men) have agreed in recent years that women should be granted such rights as equal employment opportunities, equal access to credit, and equal educational opportunities.[2] Other goals of the organized women's movement have been more controversial, although many now enjoy majority public support.[3] These more controversial issues include equal pay for work of equal value, reproductive freedom, and supportive social services for working families.

This chapter will analyze the political and policy conflicts that have grown out of the latest phase of the women's movement, with emphasis on the implications of the struggle for the role of government in our society.

We will be interested, in other words, in the role that conservative and liberal groups believe the government should play in achieving specific policy goals. We begin by examining recent changes in women's roles in U.S. society. Second, we review the problems facing the nation's female population that organized women's groups believe are major. Third, we examine the major laws that have been passed to deal with some of the problems facing women. Fourth, we contrast liberal and conservative perceptions of women's roles and needs, including the protracted struggle over the equal rights amendment. Last, we review the conditions and progress of women in the other western industrialized countries and evaluate programs that have been passed to support women's equality in these nations.

WOMEN'S CHANGING ROLES

The role of women in the United States has changed drastically in the last 20 years, and, of course, these changes have had a broad impact on the family, the economy, the political system, and society in general. Women's changing role in the economy alone has been substantial enough to alter many aspects of life in the United States. The trend has been for women to enter the work force, including professions that were long closed to them. In 1960 women comprised 33.4 percent of the labor force. By 1980 they comprised some 43 percent of the total work force. (See Table 4-1.) In 1960 about 38 percent of all women were employed. By 1980 almost 52 percent were employed, bringing the female work force up to 45 million. Between 1950 and 1980 the number of women in the work force increased by over 135 percent. By 1980 there were more families with a husband and wife working than there were families with only the husband working.

Not only are more women in the work force, but the type of women currently working also has changed. In 1940, 64 percent of all employed women were single, widowed, or divorced. By 1980 single, divorced, and widowed women were even more likely to be in the work force, but married women had increased their participation rate to the extent that they comprised 60 percent of all working women. (See Table 4-1.) Increased employment rates have been greatest for women with children. In 1950 only about 20 percent of all women with children were in the labor force. By 1980 over half of all women with children were employed.[4] The largest proportional increase has been among women with children under the age of 6. Between 1950 and 1980 the employment rate for these mothers tripled from 14 to 46 percent.[5]

Women have entered the work force for a variety of reasons, but a major one has been economic need. In 1980 some two-thirds of all working women were single, widowed, divorced, or separated, or had husbands

TABLE 4-1
WOMEN AND EMPLOYMENT

Year	Female work participation as percent of total female population	Female workers as percent of total work force	Female work force in millions	Marital status of female workers		
				Single	Married	Widowed, divorced
1960	37.7	33.4	23.3	24.0	59.9	16.1
1965	39.3	35.2	26.2	22.8	62.2	15.0
1970	43.3	38.1	31.5	22.3	63.4	14.3
1975	46.3	39.9	37.1	23.1	62.5	14.4
1980	51.6	42.6	44.7	24.8	59.9	15.3

Source: U.S. Bureau of the Census, Statistical Abstract of the United States: 1981 (Washington, D.C.: GPO, 1982), pp. 379, 381, 388.

whose earnings were less than $12,000.[6] About 40 percent of all employed women were heads of households. The two-paycheck family is also not only increasingly common, it is increasingly necessary. In 1940 only 14.7 percent of women living with their husbands were in the work force. By 1980 the employment rate for such women was 50.2 percent. In 1982, 41 percent of all families had two earners. Two-parent families in which only the husband works are three times as likely as two-earner families to live in poverty.[7]

The increasing entry of women into the labor market reflects in part some substantial changes in the U.S. family. Divorce and separation have become more common. Between 1950 and 1980 the rate of divorce more than doubled, leaving more women as heads of households. In 1950 women constituted 9.4 percent of all family heads. By 1981, 15 percent of all families were headed by a woman. Women currently head about 12 percent of all white families and slightly over 40 percent of all black families.

WOMEN'S POLICY ISSUES: THE CONSENSUS ISSUES

While women have made many important gains in recent years, they frequently point to inequities in the employment sector, in the political system, and in public policies that they believe continue to discriminate against, or disadvantage, them. As we will detail below, there are disagreements among women over many issues, but there is a core of conditions and issues that at least a majority of all women believe reflect inequities that require remediation. Below we will discuss the most obvious of these problems.

Job Isolation

One of the most striking features of the U.S. labor market is the occupational segregation of the sexes. The federal government classifies jobs into 420 categories. Only 20 of these categories account for the professions of about 80 percent of all employed women.[8] Women tend to be employed in low-wage clerical and service jobs, while being poorly represented in skilled blue-collar occupations and the most prestigious professions. Women have made major employment gains during the last 15 years, but, as the figures below reveal, they are still poorly represented in the better paying and more prestigious professions. At the current rate of progress, women will continue to be segregated within the job market for a very long time. The figures below provide examples of the traditional employment segregation of women:[9]

Percentage of Jobs Held by Women (1980)

Typists	96.9
Bank tellers	92.7
Registered nurses	96.5
Librarians	81.4
Kindergarten teachers	98.4
Billing clerks	90.2
File clerks	86.4
Engineers	4
Lawyers and judges	12.8
Carpenters	1.5
Physicians and dentists	12.9
Life and physical scientists	20.3
Auto mechanics	0.7

Earning Gap

Female workers earn considerably less than their male counterparts. There are a number of reasons for this earning disparity. Major reasons include the following:

1 Many more women work only part-time or part of the year.

2 Women tend to change jobs and move in and out of the work force more frequently.

3 The mean age of working women is considerably younger than that of male employees (which means that women tend to have less seniority).

4 Women employees tend to be concentrated in jobs traditionally considered "women's work" and these jobs usually pay a rather low wage regardless of the skill and training required.

5 There is pay discrimination.

Most experts tend to agree that job segregation, inadequate compensation for jobs traditionally performed by women, and the broken pattern of women's work histories are the major reasons for the gap between male and female incomes.[10] Most studies show that these factors are considerably more important than discrimination. Darling, for example, writes:

> Discrimination in the labour market, as has been shown by a number of careful studies, is one important cause of sex segregation in occupations and the male-female differential in earnings. But a more fundamental factor lies in society's assignment of sex roles. For although employment discrimination undoubtedly stems in part from employers operating in terms of their personal conception of the role of women in society, they are only one of the actors in the system and labour market discrimination is but one manifestation of social relations and attitudes as they apply to women in society. Whatever the study, a substantial

part of the differential in the earnings of the sexes is generally recognized as resulting from differences in "objective criteria"—differences between men and women in education, experience, labour force attachment which cannot be related to the influence of discriminatory employer practices.[11]

Even in the last 10 years, most women entering the job market have continued to take traditional "women's jobs"—teachers, clerical workers, and nurses. These jobs, even when they require a college education, often pay wages that are considerably below those paid in traditionally "male" positions such as assembly line workers, plumbers, electricians, and sales.

Thus, in recent years women with a college education have on average earned less than male high school dropouts.[12] Women who have completed high school tend to earn less than men who failed to complete elementary school. Men's incomes tend to increase considerably with the addition of a college degree, while the impact on women's incomes is modest. Women, in fact, need considerably more education to reach the middle- to upper-income categories than do men.

In recent years women who worked year-round full-time on average have earned about 59 to 60 percent of the income earned by similarly employed males. In 1980, for example, males who worked year-round full-time had a median income of $19,173, compared to $11,591 for similarly employed women.[13] Men with 4 or more years of college earned a median income of $25,849, compared to $16,362 for women. Male white-collar workers on average earned $21,880, compared to $11,974 for women in white-collar jobs.[14] Similar disparities appear for all job and education classifications. Some of the difference in income reflects seniority, but a substantial proportion reflects women's segregation even within employment categories. In 1981, for example, women in sales earned on average about 52 percent as much as male sales workers.[15] The disparity reflects the fact that women tend to be in sales positions that pay a much lower commission. Women tend to sell clothes and household goods while men hold most of the positions involving expensive items such as heavy equipment.

The Feminization of Poverty

In recent years a number of factors have combined to greatly increase the poverty rate for women. The most immediate contributing factor has been the increase in the divorce and separation rate, which has produced a much larger number of female-headed families. As recently as 1955, some 77 percent of all poor families in the United States were headed by a male. By 1980 over half of all the families living in poverty had a female head (female households without a husband and married families headed by females). Because women with children often receive little help from the fathers of their children, often cannot obtain the support services they need to participate in the job market, and generally receive low wages when they do work, the poverty rate for female-headed families is very high. Only 6.2 percent of male-headed families were poor in 1980, but 32.7 percent of all female-headed families were below the poverty level. The poverty rate is particularly high for minority families headed by a woman. For example, in 1980, 26 percent of all white female-headed families were poor, while over half of all black female-headed families lived in poverty.[16] Women, in fact, currently constitute two out of every three adults living in poverty in the United States. As Ehrenreich and Stallard note:

> All other things being equal, if the proportion of the poor in female-householder families were to continue to increase at the same rate as it did from 1967 to 1978, the poverty population would be composed solely of women and their children before the year 2000.[17]

Lack of Supportive Institutions

Surveys of women who are employed, or who would like to be employed, indicate that most of them believe the political system has failed to provide women and families with the supportive services they need.[18] Women note that their role in society has been changing quite drastically but that public policies have not been designed to facilitate the combination of family and work responsibility. The most frequently mentioned problems are the need for child care assistance, maternity leaves, and pension and social security plans designed for working women and mothers.

The lack of adequate child care assistance is the most frequently cited problem of women in the work force. Women often point out that their inability to obtain adequate child care keeps them from taking jobs, or forces them to accept part-time jobs that pay low wages and offer little chance of advancement. A study by the U.S. Commission on Civil Rights concluded that lack of child care often keeps women from accepting job promotions, training for advancement, and opportunities for participation in federal employment, training, and education programs. The study also concluded that child care problems often conflict with a woman's ability to do her job.[19] Of course, women's disproportionate responsibility for home and children accounts in substantial part for their more fluid attachment to the job market.

A number of studies indicate that between 18 and 20 percent of all unemployed women are out of work because they cannot obtain adequate child care.[20] A congressional study also indicated that 2 million children between the ages of 7 and 13 are simply left alone without any supervision while their parents are at work.[21]

Limited Representation in Positions of Power

Despite progress in recent years, women are still poorly represented in positions of power in the United States. For example, despite the fact that women constitute a majority of all U.S. citizens, they hold a relatively small percentage of all elective and appointive political positions. In 1982, 19 women served in the U.S. House of Representatives (out of 435 members), while there were only 2 female members of the Senate (out of 100 members). Women are also poorly represented in the other branches of the federal government. Dye and Strickland report that in 1980 only 20 of the top 258 positions (7.7 percent) within the federal government were held by women. Women hold only 12 percent of the elective positions at the state and local level. Only 10 percent of the members of state legislatures are women, as are 6 percent of county commissioners, 1 percent of all mayors, and 3 percent of city council members.[22] These figures represent substantial improvements over the last decade, but still reveal that women are represented in the political system far below their proportion of the total population. Surveys do reveal increasing levels of public support for female political activity.[23]

Women are even less well represented in positions of power within the nation's major economic, educational, legal, and military institutions. A recent study by Dye and Strickland found that women constituted only about 4 percent of the leaders of the nation's largest and most prestigious institutions. By 1980 the 100 largest corporations in the United States had promoted only 36 women to top positions (out of 1,499 positions). Dye and Strickland noted:

> The educational level of our top women leaders was very high; nearly half possessed earned Master's degrees or doctorates and an additional quarter possessed law degrees. . . . A total of 71.0 percent of women leaders earned advanced degrees; the comparable figure for male leaders was 49.5 percent. This strongly suggests that women need more education than men to compete effectively for top posts.[24]

Interestingly, Dye and Strickland found that 75 percent of the women leaders were married and over 60 percent had children. "Most of the women at the top combined marriage and family with careers. . . ."[25]

In summary, then, most women believe that there are at least five major women's issues that need to be addressed. They are job isolation, disparities between male and female earnings, the economic hazards facing female-headed families, the lack of supportive institutions and services for families, and the limited representation of women in positions of power.

RECENT ANTIDISCRIMINATION LAWS

As women's roles in society and the economy have changed, there have been increasing pressures on government and the private sector by organized women's groups and their supporters for policies that protect women against discrimination. While minor actions were taken earlier, meaningful laws designed to protect women against discrimination were not passed until the 1960s.[26] Since the early 1960s, however, there have been numerous important laws, administrative rulings, and court decisions on women's rights. These laws, rulings, and decisions resulted from the pressures that women's groups have brought to bear on federal, state, and local officials. The major women's groups interested in convincing the government to protect and accommodate women's changing roles primarily have been interested in convincing the federal government to pass desired laws, enforce existing laws, and create supportive programs. The federal level has been the focus of most attention because the national government has the most resources, and its decisions are sweeping, extending protections and benefits to all women, regardless of the state in which they live. While the women's groups have not achieved all their goals, since the 1960s they have won many important victories.

The first important law was the Equal Pay Act of 1963. This law required that men and women doing basically the same job had to be paid the same wage. In deciding whether jobs were equal, the law required that the skill, effort, and responsibilities of the job be considered. Originally this law was enforced by the Department of Labor, but during the Carter administration responsibility was transferred to the Equal Employment Opportunity Commission (EEOC).

Title VII of the 1964 Civil Rights Act provided much more sweeping legislation to protect the rights of women. The 1964 act grew out of the struggle of minorities to gain basic civil rights. One section of the act prohibited discrimination in employment on the basis of race, color, religion, national origin, or sex. This same provision made it illegal to discriminate in hiring or firing, compensation, or fringe benefits. Employers also were prohibited from discriminating in classifying, referring, assigning, or promoting employees. The Equal Employment Opportunity Commission was established to enforce the provisions of the act, but originally was given only very modest enforcement powers. An amendment in 1972 substantially increased the EEOC's enforcement powers and expanded the jurisdiction of Title VII to state and local governments, educational institutions, and any business or union with fifteen or more employees.

In 1965 President Johnson issued Executive Order 11246 which prohibited all federal contractors (any company doing work under a federal contract) from using race, color, religion, or national origin as a basis of discrimination. This order required contractors to undertake affirmative action (positive steps) to eliminate all vestiges of discrimination. The Office of Federal Contract Compliance Programs (OFCCP) was created to supervise the enforcement of the standards by the twenty-six federal agencies responsible for contracts. The order was amended in 1967 to include discrimination based on sex. The potential sweep of Johnson's executive order is suggested by the fact that about one-third of the total work force is employed directly or indirectly by the federal government.[27]

By 1971 regulations designed to enforce Executive Order 11246 required the larger contractors to carry out specific affirmative action plans. These contractors were required to conduct internal investigations to determine why minorities and women were not equally represented in all job classifications and to eliminate practices that discriminated against them. They were also ordered to establish goals and timetables for expanding job opportunities for groups previously discriminated against and specific plans for remedial recruiting, hiring, and training.

In 1972 Congress passed Title IX of the education amendments, prohibiting sex discrimination in federally assisted education programs. Title IX specified that "no person in the United States shall, on the basis of sex, be excluded from participation in, be denied the benefits of, or be subjected to discrimination under any education program or activity receiving Federal financial assistance." Under Title IX any educational institution receiving federal funds is required to offer physical education classes on a coeducational basis, and girls' and women's athletic programs must be given equal support and encouragement. The law did not require sexual integration of contact sports teams or identical sports programs for each sex.

During the 1960s and early 1970s there were many important administrative guidelines and court cases designed to enforce and interpret these laws. In interpreting the Equal Pay Act the courts held that jobs needed only to be substantially equal (not identical) to merit equal pay. The courts also ruled that wages included overtime, fringe benefits, and such items as uniforms and travel. Under Title VII the courts ruled that virtually all jobs had to be open to both sexes, and that women could not be denied a job because it involved travel, night work, the supervision of men, or heavy lifting or other strenuous physical activity. The court ruled that an employer could require a potential employee to pass a physical test to determine if he or she could do a job, but the test could not be sexually biased. The courts also ruled that women could not be denied a job because of the preferences of coworkers or customers.

By the mid-1970s a few thousand cases had been filed against contractors, other businesses, and educational institutions to prompt the administration of affirmative action plans or to end specific discriminatory acts or programs. The settlements reached in some of these cases were large enough to command wide attention. In 1973 American Telephone and Telegraph Company agreed to distribute $12 million in back pay to thousands of its minority and female employees. AT&T also agreed to pay for promotion adjustments that would cost another $40 million. Similarly, nine major steel companies agreed to back pay for their minority and female employees totaling over $30 million. General Electric, Chase Manhattan Bank, and dozens of other major businesses also agreed to large settlements. Under the Equal Pay Act hundreds of smaller businesses have been required each year to make back payments to employees who have been discriminated against. In a typical year during the 1970s, employees were awarded $16 to $18 billion in back pay.[28]

In 1978 the EEOC was reorganized and its authority broadened. This reorganization transferred to the EEOC the Office of Personnel Management's jurisdiction over job discrimination within the federal government, the Department of Labor's responsibilities for enforcing the Equal Pay Act and the Age Discrimination in Employment Act, and the Equal Employment Opportunity Coordinating Council's responsibility for coordinating all federal employment activities (this latter agency was abolished). The newly bolstered EEOC also reorganized its national office and established new procedures designed to process complaints more quickly and reduce its backlog. The Early Litigation Identification program also was established. This program was designed to identify small companies with a pattern of discriminatory behavior. Once identified, EEOC brought a class action suit if necessary. This strategy was designed to enhance EEOC's impact by broadening its approach and by reducing the time it spends on the more passive complaint processing approach.

In a number of cases in the late 1970s the courts upheld the right of the government to require affirmative action plans by contractors, state and local governments, and employers operating compensatory programs to rectify past bias. A 1979 case, *United Steelworkers v. Weber* (99 U.S. 2721), also raised the question of whether a company could voluntarily establish an affirmative action program even though it had never been officially charged with racial or sexual discrimination. In an effort to bring more of its black employees into skilled jobs, the Kaiser Aluminum Company had established an affirmative action program at its Gramercy, Louisiana, plant. The program, with union backing, set aside 50 percent of the slots in a training program for black employees. Weber, a white employee, charged that he had been discriminated against because he had more seniority than some of the blacks admitted to the program. The case was of interest to both minorities and women because men had charged that many of the programs designed to assist women involved reverse discrimination and were thus illegal under Title VII of the 1964 Civil Rights Act.

Both the district and the fifth court of appeals ruled in favor of Weber, but the Supreme Court reversed these decisions and upheld the plan. The Court ruled that a literal reading of Title VII's prohibition of discrimination might sustain Weber's complaint, but that the purpose of the act, not its literal language, was the issue. The Court thus interpreted Title VII as encouraging voluntary and local remedies for employment discrimination. In 1979 the EEOC published a set of affirmative action guidelines that employers and policy makers could follow and still stay within the boundaries established by the Court's interpretation of Titles VI and VII.[29]

The courts also have rendered a number of other decisions in recent years that should have an important impact on the rights of both minorities and women. In 1981 the Supreme Court rendered a decision with implications for the equal pay for equal quality work issue. In *Washington County v. Gunther* the Supreme Court ruled that women could file suit under the 1964 Civil Rights Act without having to prove they were denied "equal pay for equal work" as forbidden by the 1963 Equal Pay Act.[30] "All that is necessary," the Court said, "is for a woman to show that her sex was used against her in the determination of her pay scale." Gunther and three other jail matrons sued because they were being paid less than male jail guards. While the job performed by the matrons was not identical to that of the guards, it was so similar that the women charged that the pay discrepancy was unjustified. The Supreme Court agreed.

A 1979 California case, *De la Cruz v. Tormey* (99 U.S. 2416, 1979), raised the issue of whether women's childbearing or child-rearing role constitutes a barrier to equal employment or educational opportunity. This is an issue that often has been raised by women but has received limited support from the courts or from policy makers. The EEOC did rule that an employer could not refuse to hire a woman because she was pregnant, nor could a woman be discharged simply because she was pregnant. Both the Supreme Court and Congress also ruled that women who are able and willing to work may not be denied unemployment compensation. However, in 1976 the Supreme Court ruled that companies were not engaged in sex discrimination when they excluded pregnancy as a medical disability.[31]

In 1978 Congress responded by amending Title VII to prohibit discrimination based on pregnancy. Under this amendment companies are not required to establish specific health care and leave plans for women, but they are required to treat pregnancy and pregnancy-related health problems like any other medical problem. Child care leave must be granted for a medically necessary period after childbirth. Many of the nation's major companies, however, have voluntarily developed leave policies for women that go beyond the requirements of the law. In 1982, 359 major companies offered maternity leaves and 34 offered paternity leaves.[32]

The *De la Cruz v. Tormey* case broadened the childbearing issue by raising the question of whether a community college district was engaging in sexual discrimination by refusing to use any of its funds to establish a child care center. A number of low-income mothers charged that the failure of the district to provide child care denied them equal educational opportunities. The mothers argued that the district, which received federal funds, was in violation of Title IX. The United States Court of Appeals for the Ninth Circuit ruled that the plaintiffs raised a valid issue and remanded the case to the United States District Court for trial. In doing so the court said:

> There can be little doubt that a discriminatory effect, as that term is properly understood and has been used by the Supreme Court, has been adequately alleged. The concrete human consequences flowing from the lack of sufficient child care facilities, very practical impediments to beneficial participation in the District's educational programs, are asserted to fall overwhelmingly on women students and would-be students.

The Supreme Court allowed the district court's decision to stand, thus allowing the case to go to trial. The case was settled out of court when the college district agreed to establish child care centers. Even though the case was settled out of court, the actions of both the district court and the Supreme Court suggest that colleges and universities receiving federal funds are providing equal educational opportunities for women only when they provide child care facilities. The potential for the extension of this principle to many other areas seems rather obvious.

Women and minorities did suffer one setback in a 1982 Supreme Court case. In *American Tobacco Co. v. Patterson* (454 U.S. 1136) the Supreme Court ruled that minorities and women challenging a seniority system under the 1964 Civil Rights Act were required to prove not only that the system had an adverse effect on them, but also that it was designed with the intent to discriminate. The Court pointed out that the 1964 Civil Rights Act allows bona fide seniority or merit systems as long as they are not designed with the intent to discriminate because of race, color, religion, sex, or national origin.

Federal agencies have given attention to one last issue that women often raise—sexual harassment on the job. In 1978 and 1979 the Office of Federal Contract Compliance Programs issued guidelines to federal contractors requiring them to maintain an environment free of sexual harassment, intimidation, and coercion. In 1980 the EEOC followed suit by publishing guidelines informing employers that sexual harassment is illegal. The EEOC guidelines encouraged employers to establish policies to prevent sexual harassment. The EEOC suggested that employers define sexual harassment for its employees, make it clear that it will not be tolerated, and establish sanctions for violations.

It should be noted that some of the Supreme Court's decisions have favored men.[33] For example, in a 1972 case the Supreme Court ruled that a state law which presumed that an unwed father was an unfit parent was unconstitutional. A provision of the Social Security Act which allowed payment to widows with small children but not widowers with small children was also unconstitutional. Under the law, the Court said, men received fewer benefits from their social security contributions than did women. Justice Brennan said in part, "It is no less important for a child to be cared for by its sole surviving parent, when the parent is male rather than female." In 1982 the Court ruled that the Mississippi University for Women could not deny a male entry into its nursing program. The state claimed that its single-sex policy was designed to compensate for past discrimination against women. But the Court ruled that the real effect of the rule was to "perpetuate the stereotyped view of nursing as exclusively a women's job."

The laws, rulings, and court decisions reviewed here reveal that a great deal of attention has been given to sexual discrimination since the early 1960s, and most observers would agree that a great deal of progress has been made in promoting women's equality. The women's movement, however, continues to point out many deficiencies in the laws, and argues that the Reagan administration has deemphasized the federal attack on both racial and sexual discrimination. There is little doubt that the Reagan administration is pursuing a somewhat less vigorous attack than some other recent administrations. Reagan, for example, refused to support the equal rights amendment, which failed to gain ratification in 1982. Supporters of the ERA believed that its adoption was important because they believe that it would have given women a better legal base from which to attack discrimination. They believe also that a constitutional amendment would provide permanent protections, while laws and court interpretations can more easily be changed.

Reagan's administrative appointments also have created unease within the women's movement. Reagan's initial nominee to head the EEOC was so unqualified that even most Republican Senators would not approve him. The Senate's refusal to accept this nominee left the EEOC without a head for 18 months. When Reagan finally sent the Senate another nominee, it was a conservative black attorney whom many civil rights and women's leaders did not trust. Nevertheless, the Senate approved this nominee. Reagan's appointee, Clarence Thomas, announced that he would deemphasize systemic or pattern-and-practice cases for a return to processing of individual complaints. Thomas did announce that goals and timetables for industries would continue to be used, but that they would be used less rigidly than in the past.[34] The Assistant Attorney General for Civil Rights, William Bradford Reynolds, announced an even more restrictive policy for the Justice Department. Reynolds announced that the department would no longer advocate goals and timetables to remedy discrimination under

Title VII.[35] President Reagan also has made clear his reservations about affirmative action, and, as we will note below, a number of the Republican members of Congress are sponsoring a constitutional amendment to prohibit affirmative action plans. Thus, civil rights and women's groups fear that some of the progress that has been made may be reversed, and that little in the way of additional progress will be made while Reagan is in office.

CONFLICT BETWEEN THE LEFT AND RIGHT

Philosophies about the roles, rights, and needs of women are as diverse as they are on any other major issue in U.S. society. Liberal women's groups believe either that women should alter their roles or that women's roles are inevitably changing because of alterations in modern society. In either case, liberal groups believe that laws should be designed to overcome all vestiges of discrimination against women, while providing the support that will allow them to choose the type of role they wish to pursue (e.g., housewife, career woman, or both). Liberal groups argue that they are not antifamily, but they tend to believe that in a modern society women's traditional role as housewife and mother is often not a full-time or completely fulfilling role. When viewed as a lifetime position, rather than a more temporary role shared with the male, they often view this role as a dependent, subservient, vulnerable, and unfulfilling trap that imprisons and stifles women's abilities to reach their full potential as human beings. Liberals sometimes argue that efforts are made to keep women in this position to provide cheap labor in the home and in the economy, while denying women their fair share of political and economic power. Liberal groups also believe that since it is the woman who must bear the burden of childbearing, who must interrupt her career or education to do so, and who often must support children, she should have full control over her childbearing decisions. Thus, these groups generally support sex education, access to contraceptives, and abortion on demand. Because liberal groups do not believe that government should regulate the private sex lives of adults, they also oppose discrimination against adults simply because they have chosen a homosexual lifestyle.

The most articulate and active conservative women's groups believe that women should resist the pressures of modern society which are altering their role in society. They argue that being a housewife and mother is the highest role to which women should aspire. The mother, they believe, is the foundation upon which the U.S. family is based, and alterations in women's traditional roles will undermine the integrity of the family. Preservation of the traditional family is a core value of the conservative movement. Conservatives believe that without the woman in the home, the family cannot work well, and without the traditional family, society will not work well. Thus, if women leave the home, the family will be destroyed because mothers will not be able to give children the love and supervision they need, and, most likely, the man's role as provider will be destroyed.

Conservative groups often express a fear that the women's liberation movement is designed in part to deny women the male care and support that they believe women need and deserve. Conservative groups often base their concerns on religious principles. They often argue that the "liberation" of women will not only destroy the family but in doing so will create unconventional and un-Christian lifestyles. Thus, conservative groups express alarm about the increasingly large number of single adult, single parent, and openly homosexual lifestyles. They believe that to support gay rights would only encourage depraved and un-Christian couplings. Similarly, conservative groups oppose abortion, and often sex education, on religious grounds and because they believe it allows women to neglect their most important role—the keeper of hearth and children.

The differences between conservative and liberal women's groups, then, are major. Liberal groups see women as victims of historical suppression in U.S. society and believe that it is high time that women gained a full measure of legal, economic, and political rights. Conservative groups seek to defend traditional women's roles, often believing that the changes sought by liberal groups will destroy the foundation upon which U.S. society is based. Below we will review in detail the major policy positions of conservative and liberal women's groups.

Policies Supported by the Left

Liberal groups want women to have an equal share of economic and political power. To obtain this goal they believe that women will have to overcome laws, stereotypes, traditions, and customs that discriminate against them, and that women must obtain the educational, occupational, and political skills necessary for advancement. These groups believe that women can overcome legal barriers through an issue-by-issue, case-by-case approach, but that the adoption of the ERA would provide a foundation upon which a broader, more expeditious and successful attack could be launched. Including a guarantee of women's equality in the Constitution would provide women with more security than laws or court decisions that can easily be changed.

Liberals support a variety of policies designed to promote the advancement of women in the workplace. They support both equal pay for equal work and the more complex policy of equal pay for work of equal value. Job evaluations should classify occupations by training, skill, and responsibility rather than by traditional conceptions which tend to undervalue jobs commonly held by women. Also needed are job training programs that will qualify women for good jobs, including jobs traditionally held by men. Training programs should be made available to women at any time that they might be needed in their life cycle. For example, liberals support programs for women just out of school who wish to develop careers, women who have left the employment market for a period of time and wish to reenter, and women who because of divorce, abandonment, or death of a spouse find they must support themselves. This latter group is increasingly common, and these women often are referred to as displaced housewives.

Liberal groups also support counseling programs to enlarge the career options that young women consider. The evidence indicates that young women are still much less likely than males to consider careers in such fields as business, the sciences, or engineering. Women college students still tend to major in the social sciences and orient themselves toward traditional women's jobs. Women are also less likely to finish college, and they are much less likely than males to pursue advanced degrees.[36] When women do receive advanced degrees, they are less likely than males to use those degrees to pursue a career in the chosen field. These facts suggest that women need to be counseled earlier about opportunities in less traditional fields. Finally, women should be protected from sexual harassment on the job; the law should protect women and businesses should take active steps to prevent this problem from occurring.

The left also supports a range of policies designed to allow women to combine work and family responsibilities. High on the list are child care services, maternity leaves, and tax breaks for families that have to hire household help. As noted in Chapter 2, the U.S. government provides much less support for child care services than many of the other western industrialized nations. In fact, in 1982 there were only 467,000 government subsidized day care slots across the nation.[37] The left believes that child care should be provided to all families, both to improve the development and education of children and to give both mothers and fathers greater freedom to seek education, job training, and employment. It is also noted that "where child care is perceived as part of the educational stream, the ideological argument over whether care is 'good' or 'bad' for children has been replaced by concern for the quality of the care given."[38]

Maternity leaves are critical if women are to be able to combine both careers and motherhood. The left generally supports the type of automatic, paid maternity leave that is so common in Western European and Scandinavian nations. Tax breaks for working families who must hire extra help would also facilitate the combination of parenthood with a career.

In addition there is also a need for flexible work schedules to help parents deal with dual family and career responsibilities. Often called flextime, this policy would promote nontraditional work schedules, such as the 4-day week or shorter-hour workweek, for women pursuing additional education or training, or those trying to maintain both a career and family role.

The left also has been concerned about pension rights for women. Social security and most private pension plans leave women, especially those who spent many years as housewives, disadvantaged. The social security system, for example, provides benefits based on earnings and years of employment. Typically women have jobs that pay a lower wage, and they are generally in the labor market for a shorter period of time, with the result that they receive modest benefits. The left believes that under private plans women should continue to earn retirement credit during periods of maternity leave. Social security, they believe, should be designed to base benefits on need. One frequently proposed reform would be to convert social security to a guaranteed income program for the aged, with no attention paid to work history.

Last, as noted above, the left supports reproductive freedom for women, plus complete civil protection for homosexuals.

Counterresponses by the Right and Left

The organized right supports a package of policies designed to restore, maintain, and promote the patriarchal family and traditional moral values. At the core of the right's philosophy is the belief that the strains of modern society and the policies of the left are destroying both the nation's families and the moral structure of society. While the left hardly agrees, the right has labeled its policies as "pro-family" while charging that the left is antifamily. To promote its philosophy the right supports policies to return and keep women in the home, a prohibition on abortions, the defeat of the ERA, a constitutional amendment to allow prayers in the public schools, and laws and policies designed to discourage homosexual lifestyles.

The right believes that the efforts of women to develop careers outside the home have both a negative impact on the family and a debilitating effect on men. Gilder has popularized the argument that female employment injures men. "The main impact of feminism," says Gilder, "is to take jobs and promotions away from men and give them to educated women."[39] Gilder, in fact, completely rejects the left's charge that women are discriminated against in the market. "Everyone seems to want indoor work with no heavy lifting, but only women nearly always get it, thus driving down their pay."[40] Gilder argues that female employment has a particularly destructive impact on poor families, especially poor black families. In such families, Gilder says, the male ego is emasculated by the fact that the woman can earn almost as much as the man, or may even be able to receive more assistance from welfare than the husband can provide.

According to Gilder:

> The man has the gradual sinking feeling that his role as provider, the definitive male activity from the primal days of the hunt through the industrial age and on into modern life, has been largely seized from him; he has been cuckolded by the compassionate state.
>
> His response to this reality is that very combination of resignation and rage, escapism and violence, short horizons and promiscuous sexuality that characterizes everywhere the life of the poor. But in this instance, the pattern is often not so much a necessary reflection of economic conditions as an arbitrary imposition of policy—a policy that by depriving poor families of strong fathers both dooms them to poverty and damages the economic prospects of the children.[41]

Thus Gilder believes that female employment takes jobs from men, destroys families, and promotes irresponsible, even criminal behavior on the part of men who have lost the ego gratification derived from the provider role. If men cannot be providers, says Gilder, "they have to resort to muscle and phallus."[42] Gilder also argues that expecting women to be completely devoted to their careers is futile.

> Once a family is headed by a woman, it is almost impossible for it to greatly raise its income even if the woman is highly educated and trained and she hires day-care or domestic help. Her family responsibilities and distractions tend to prevent her from the kind of all-out commitment that is necessary for the full use of earning power. Few women with children make earning money the top priority in their lives.[43]

At the core of Gilder's philosophy is a belief that men and women are genetically coded to play certain roles in society and that policies which conflict with this biological pattern are wrong. Gilder does not, for example, accept the argument of the left that custom and tradition, not biology, account for male and female roles, and that these role patterns subordinate women because they grew out of a male-dominated society. Nor does Gilder, or other members of the right, accept the argument that men can and should play a larger role in child rearing, while women assume greater responsibility for the financial support of the family.

The left basically accepts Gilder's argument that when men cannot obtain a job which pays enough to support a family, they often abandon wives and children. The left's response, however, is that it is not female employment that deprives these men of good jobs. Instead, the left simply believes that the economy provides a large percentage of the population with inadequate employment opportunities. Thus, the left supports economic policies that would greatly reduce unemployment and subemployment. The left also believes that society socializes men to feel like failures when they cannot play the role of provider, even when the economy does not offer them adequate job opportunities. It is this unfairness that causes men to abandon their families and sometimes engage in irresponsible, even criminal behavior. Gilder's response to the left is that when women leave the job market there will be ample jobs for men, and that men *should* feel like failures when they cannot provide for their families. It is this sense of obligation, says Gilder, that lies at the core of the male motivation to be the provider, and thus it is both healthy and natural.

Another argument of the right is that when women work, the relationship between the husband and wife in traditionally patriarchal families is disrupted by changes that women undergo. One consistent theme is that working women begin to expect to play a larger role in family decision making, thus creating tensions. For example, Kathleen Teague, founder of the Virginia Stop-ERA, echoes a familiar theme: "Once a woman is earning some money, she tends to want to have some say in how it's spent. Finances become a cause of problems."[44] Since the right does not support careers for women or other alterations in women's roles, they believe that policies which encourage or accommodate such changes should be appealed. Thus, the right supports the repeal of antidiscrimination and affirmative action laws which promote female careers. They also favor a substantial reduction in welfare support for single women and their children, since such programs only encourage women to engage in single parenting and divorce. The only viable way to deal with the feminization of poverty, conservatives say, is for women to get and stay married. The right also believes that publicly supported programs that give low-income women legal assistance should be abolished, since they are often used to obtain divorces.

The left's response is that marriage is often not a practical option for women who have been abandoned with children. Men are often frightened away by the financial obligations they would have to assume. In addition, neither men nor women necessarily have to be married to raise a family or lead a happy and productive life. The philosophy of the left is that people should have more freedom to select a lifestyle which suits them. The right, of course, believes that only the patriarchal family is suitable for child rearing and that single lifestyles are deficient and often immoral. The right also believes that women have the power to make marriage a more viable option. The mistake many women make is that they allow men to fulfill their sexual needs although they are not married. Women, in other words, need to be more virtuous. As Onalee McGraw puts it, "We need to make it tougher for men to get divorced," and we need to make it tougher for them to remain single or stray by "withholding sexual favors until they're married."[45]

The right has strong allies within the Reagan administration and in Congress, especially in the Senate. President Reagan opposes the ERA, supports a constitutional amendment to allow voluntary prayer in the public schools, and supports legislation to prohibit abortion on demand. In the spring of 1982, President Reagan announced that his assistants were drawing up an amendment to submit to Congress that would, if approved, allow public schools the option of voluntary prayers. Two conservative members of the Senate also have introduced legislation to abolish or severely limit abortions. Orrin Hatch (R., Utah) has introduced a constitutional amendment which would give the states and Congress joint authority to restrict or prohibit abortion, with the more restrictive statute to prevail. The amendment also specifies that the Constitution does not secure the right to an abortion to anyone.

The Hatch amendment is designed to undercut the Supreme Court's controversial decision in *Roe v. Wade* (410 U.S. 113, 1973). In *Roe v. Wade* the Supreme Court held that during the first 3 months of a pregnancy, the state could not interfere with a woman's decision to obtain an abortion. During the second trimester, a state could regulate abortion only to the extent necessary to protect a woman's health.

Another bill before the Senate also seeks to void the *Roe v. Wade* decision but intends to do so through a regular congressional bill, rather than through the more difficult constitutional amendment process. This bill declares that human life begins at conception and entitles a fetus to the guarantee of right to life under the Fourteenth Amendment. The bill would allow the states to pass antiabortion laws and would prevent federal courts from striking down any new antiabortion laws. This bill has less support in the Senate than the Hatch amendment because many doubt its constitutionality. Many supporters of antiabortion legislation in Congress believe that the *Roe v. Wade* decision could be overturned only by an amendment to the Constitution.

Senator Hatch has also introduced into Congress a proposed constitutional amendment that would bar the use of quotas, timetables, goals, or preferential treatment to overcome discrimination against minorities and women. In doing so Senator Hatch said:

> I believe affirmative action is an assault upon America, conceived in lies and fostered with an irresponsibility so extreme as to verge on the malign. If the government officials and politicians who presided over its genesis had injected heroin into the bloodstream of the nation, they could not have done more potential damage to our children and our children's children.[46]

Senator Roger Jepsen (R., Iowa) has also introduced the Family Protection Act. This bill is designed to meet several objectives of the right. First, it would prohibit the federally funded Legal Services Corporation from accepting any case which involves "the issue of homosexual rights, and ban monies to any individual or organization which presents homosexuality as an acceptable lifestyle." Second, the bill would prohibit the same corporation from giving poor women legal advice about abortions or divorce proceedings. Last, the Community Participation in Religious Instruction and Education clause calls for the withdrawal of federal funds from the development of any educational programs that do not reflect traditional relationships between men and women and do not contribute to the American way of life as it historically has been understood. The left has labeled the Jepsen bill an effort to engage in censorship and promote stereotypes with the intent to brainwash children.

The Battle over the ERA

The protracted struggle over the ERA also provides important insights into the philosophical differences between the left and right. The ERA was passed by Congress in March of 1972—some 50 years after its introduction in Congress—and sent to the states for ratification. The primary clause of the amendment was only one sentence long. It read: "Equality of rights under the law shall not be denied or abridged by the United States or any state on account of sex." The amendment passed both houses of Congress by overwhelming margins. The ERA long had enjoyed the support of both major parties, and this support was reiterated each presidential year until 1980. The Republican party decided in 1980 to reverse its long-standing support for the amendment, and Ronald Reagan became the first U.S. President to openly oppose the amendment. Despite the Republican party's reversal on the issue, polls consistently showed that a clear majority of the public supported the amendment throughout the 1970s. By the early 1980s some 70 to 75 percent of the public believed that the amendment should be adopted.[47]

Despite widespread public support, the amendment officially was rejected in mid-1982 when it fell three states short of being ratified by the requisite thirty-eight states. It failed because of an intense and well-financed campaign by the political right, including many women and women's groups. The right's interpretation of the ERA was that it would cause drastic alterations in male and female roles, with a devastating impact on U.S. society.

The sparsity and vagueness of the proposed amendment made it possible for critics to interpret its impact as they might. The amendment, however, was purposefully written in a short, general form to make it consistent with the rest of the Constitution. The federal Constitution, unlike most state constitutions, is a short, general document designed to grow with, and meet the needs of, a changing society. The practice throughout U.S. history has been for the courts to adapt the Constitution to the needs of the day, but not without restraints. The general rule is that the courts interpret the Constitution by considering the original intent of Congress.

The ERA developed over such a long period of time, and was based on such detailed documentation within the Senate Judiciary Committee, that there really should have been little doubt about the congressional intent behind the ERA. The Senate judiciary report, in fact, was written by a team of Yale Law School professors and was widely circulated and cited by members of Congress.[48] The report spelled out the anticipated effect the amendment would have on a variety of important policies. Since interpretation of the amendment became such an important issue, it is illuminating to summarize some of the relevant sections of the report.[49]

Domestic Relations   The impact of the amendment on domestic relations was one of the most controversial topics. The amendment definitely was designed to bring about some important changes in this area. The amendment would have required that domestic relations laws be based on sexually neutral principles. State laws, in other words, could not have assumed that the man was the breadwinner while the wife was a dependent housekeeper. Each partner in a marriage would have been assumed to have a support obligation based on such factors as earning power, wealth, or the agreement reached by the marriage partners. If one partner agreed to accept the obligation of maintaining the home, the other would have the obligation to support that partner. Alimony and child-support laws also would have been sexually neutral. The spouse who looked after the home and children would have the right to receive support from the other spouse. In case of divorce the parent best suited to raise the child would have been given custody.

The amendment would not have required that each parent make an equal financial contribution to the family, nor would it have required that spouses work. A couple would have been free to make any role arrangements it desired. But support for the family would have been based on the couple's agreement and the ability of each partner to make a financial contribution. Men would most likely have had a better chance of being awarded the children in a divorce, and, when the woman was the superior earner, the husband would have been more likely to win temporary financial support.

Military Service   Both sexes would have been allowed to volunteer for the draft and, in cases of emergency, both could have been drafted. Military assignment would have been based on ability, including selection for service in combat. Congress would have retained the right to make reasonable exemptions from the draft. During the congressional floor debate the ERA backers noted that Congress could exempt all parents with children under a certain age, or that it could exempt the parent designed to care for the children. Women who served in the military would have been eligible for the same benefits as male soldiers, including the G.I. bill and preference in federal hiring.

Homosexual Marriages   The states would not have been required to legalize homosexual marriages. However, states would have been required to be sexually neutral on the subject. If a state recognized marriages between women, it would have had to legitimatize male marriages as well.

Privacy   The states could have required reasonable separation of the sexes in the interest of protecting the privacy of men and women. The state, in other words, would have retained the authority to require separate facilities for single men and women in coeducational institutions, or in prisons or military barracks. The state also could require separate restroom facilities for men and women.

Criminal Law   The criminal code would have had to be sexually neutral on most topics. That is, both men and women would have received similar punishment for specific crimes. Laws, such as those punishing forcible rape, would not, however, have been invalid simply because they primarily protect women.

Education   Educational institutions would have been required to have sexually neutral admission, scholarship, and aid programs. Women's athletic programs would have had to receive the same financial support as men's sports.

Labor Legislation   The amendment would have prohibited sexual discrimination in employment. A job qualification might eliminate most members of one sex, as long as the qualification was motivated by nonsexist criteria. An employer could, in other words, require a strength test for a job, as long as the test could be shown to be relevant to the job, and as long as men and women who passed the test were given equal consideration. Enforcement of Title VII had already dealt with many of these problems. The amendment would, however, have extended the law to employers with fewer than fifteen employees.

Conservative Interpretations of the ERA   Liberal groups accepted the above interpretations as the proposed intent of the ERA. Conservative groups were often quite upset by the changes that everyone agreed would have been brought about by the ERA, and they often argued that the ERA would have consequences quite at variance with the standard interpretations. Conservatives correctly perceived that the amendment would have required laws to treat men and women equally, thus making it easier for couples to avoid the traditional male-dominant, female-dependent relationship. The law, in fact, would have accommodated any woman who wanted to develop a career, rather than a traditional housewife role. Women would have also lost some preferential treatment, such as in child-custody cases, and women would have often been expected to play a larger role as provider. In time of war, women most likely would have been called upon to play a much broader military role than they have in the past. Sports for women (a form of activity that many on the right consider to be unladylike, even unnatural) would have been encouraged. Thus, the ERA would have played an important role in bringing about changes that conservative groups often abhor.

Conservatives also often argued that despite official interpretations, the ERA would make it more difficult for men to get good jobs, that it would make it easier for men to divorce their wives, and that it would be harder for women to get child support. Thus, the right charged, the ERA was distinctly antifamily.

Conservatives often leveled another series of rather emotional charges against the ERA. Organizations such as Stop-ERA, the John Birch Society, the Daughters of the American Revolution, the American party, the National States Rights party, the Ku Klux Klan, American Women Already Richly Endowed (AWARE), Happiness of Womanhood (How), the League for the Protection of Women and Children, the League of Housewives, Humanitarians Opposed to Degrading Our Girls (HotDog), and Protect Our Women (POW) spent a great deal of money to publicize their belief that the ERA would bring about harmful and even immoral changes in American life. These groups often charged, for example, that the amendment would require Congress to draft mothers of small children, that public restrooms would be integrated, that universities would be required to house males and females together, that women would be required to leave the home and take a job, that states would be forced to recognize homosexual marriages, and that women would be able to obtain an abortion on demand right up to the day of delivery. Phyllis Schlafly, leader of Stop-ERA, even charged that the ERA would prevent states from enforcing antipornography laws.[50] These very emotional charges often inflamed the debate over the ERA to the extent that rational, dispassionate analysis was often impossible.

Why the ERA Failed   Given the broad public support for the ERA, why did it fail? Analysts differ on this question, but four points are widely accepted. First, it is generally agreed that the intense, well-organized, and well-financed campaign that the right carried out against the amendment was effective in inflaming opinion, polarizing the population, and diluting support for the amendment. Second, ERA supporters were disadvantaged because women have so little power in state legislatures. Women make up only 10 percent of the members of state legislatures. It has been calculated that a shift of only a dozen votes in three state legislatures would have given victory to the ERA. Third, many women were clearly frightened by the impact that they believed the ERA would have on them. Ironically, perhaps, polls rather persistently showed that more men than women supported the ERA. The reason for this difference was that some women tended to believe that the ERA would have a negative impact on them or their families. Spitze and Huber, for example, conducted research which showed that women who opposed the ERA were older, less educated, and more often worried about the impact of the amendment on their economic well-being. These women tended to believe that the ERA would endanger their husband's job, that it would make it easier for men to get a divorce, and that women would have more difficulty getting child support.[51]

Spitze and Huber believe that their research supports the claim that a lack of "concern for housewives has hurt the ERA."[52] Some supporters of the ERA argued all along that the left had paid too little attention to the concerns and fears of housewives. It was frequently suggested that the left undertake a campaign to convince housewives that the ERA would not be detrimental to them, and that the women's movement was not hostile to women who choose a traditional housewife role.

The fourth reason is more controversial. In a best-selling book, *The Cinderella Complex,* Colette Dowling argues that

> . . . personal, psychological dependency—the deep wish to be taken care of by others—is the chief force holding women down today. . . . The Cinderella Complex . . . a network of largely repressed attitudes and fears that keeps women in a kind of half-light, retreating from the full use of their minds and creativity. Like Cinderella, women today are still waiting for something external to transform their lives.[53]

Dowling's argument is not exclusively directed at women on the right. She believes that there is abundant evidence that women of all political persuasions and levels of education perform at a lower level than they should and have deep-seated fears about success. She believes that as children girls are socialized to play a dependent, submissive role with the result that many women come to believe that to be supported and taken care of by someone else is their right. This dependency role limits women's ability to achieve. "Dependency," says Dowling, "by its very nature, creates self-doubt, and self-doubt can lead all too quickly to self-hatred."[54] Dowling cites evidence to show that while I.Q. has a fairly close relationship to accomplishment among men, it does not correlate with accomplishment among women.[55] She also points out:

> Academically talented girls are less likely to enter college and complete the undergraduate degree than equally bright young men; they are less likely to take advanced degrees; they are less likely to use the Ph.D.'s they do take; they are less productive than men even if they do take the Ph.D., remain unmarried, and continue to work full time.[56]

Dowling cites considerable evidence to support her argument that many of the problems that women suffer can be traced back to child-rearing practices.

> Since the little girl has (a) less encouragement for independence, (b) more parental protectiveness, (c) less cognitive and social pressure for establishing an

identity separate from mother, and (d) less mother-child conflict, which highlights this separation, she engages in less independent exploration of her environment. As a result, she does not develop skills in coping with her environment nor confidence in her ability to do so.[57]

Dowling argues that for women to gain a full measure of success and power in life they must recognize the fear that controls their lives. She also believes that there needs to be a serious alteration in the preparation of young girls for adulthood. It should be noted that most conservative women reject Dowling's thesis, arguing that female children are properly socialized to play their ideal role in society. Even some liberal women reacted negatively to the book. They agreed that female children are socialized to accept a role that they considered to be submissive and inferior, but they believed that the book overemphasized the deficiencies of women in accounting for their lack of progress. They argued that Dowling's thesis amounted in part to nothing more than putting the blame on the victim.

The Federal Role: A Role Reversal

This review of the policy goals of both conservative and liberal groups illuminates an interesting point. As with the other policy areas analyzed in this book, the differences between conservatives and liberals sometimes do not result from their traditional attitudes toward the proper role of government. As one would predict, liberal groups do want the government to play a major, aggressive role in passing and enforcing laws designed to both overcome discrimination against women and promote their equality. Conservative groups oppose most of these efforts but want the government to use its authority to preserve their preferred image of society. Thus, conservatives support a government role in regulating women's reproductive decisions, in promoting religion in the public schools, in socializing children to accept traditional lifestyles and morals, and in the prohibition of homosexual lifestyles. Liberals argue that government has no right to get involved in any of these areas. Thus, in reality, the differences between conservatives and liberals, on this issue, reflects their policy goals, not their philosophical position on the role of government.

WOMEN'S EQUALITY IN THE MAJOR WESTERN INDUSTRIALIZED NATIONS

Western European women and families have been going through the same transitions that have occurred in the United States. Women in most of the European nations have been leaving the home to seek education and jobs in greatly increased numbers. To promote their new roles European women have lobbied for educational assistance, job and pay equality, and better support programs for families. Women have been more active and successful in some of the nations than others, but the problems that European women point to are remarkably similar from one nation to the next. They are also quite similar to those problems that liberal women in the United States have been concerned with.

European women who enter the job market tend to take jobs traditionally reserved for women, and they generally earn considerably less than male workers. On average, European women also obtain less education than men, suffer higher rates of unemployment, and are more inclined to work part-time. As in the United States, the female work force in Europe is younger than the male work force.

While similar trends are apparent across Europe, there are some significant national differences. Women in the Scandinavian nations have the highest work participation rates, and they are also most likely to continue working after having children. For example, in a recent year the work participation rate for women was 70 percent in Sweden, 67 percent in Denmark, and 65 percent in Finland. The participation rates for women in the larger Western European nations were similar to the United States: 50 percent in France, 48 percent in West Germany, and 57 percent in the United Kingdom. In some of the smaller European nations the rate was lower: 31 percent in Luxembourg, 32 percent in the Netherlands.[58] As we will note in more detail below, the participation rate for women reflects the cultural attitude of the nation toward women's labor, the progress made in extending protections to women, and the extent of support services to working parents.

Working women tend to earn less than working men in all the nations, but there are significant national variations, and the gap between the wages of men and women employed full-time, year-round is often significantly less than the discrepancy between similarly employed male and female workers in the United States. In some of the nations women earn almost as much as men. For example, the ratio is .87 in Sweden, .86 in France, and .85 in Denmark. In the other nations the ratio is generally .70 or above. It is .73 in West Germany, .72 in the United Kingdom, and .74 in Austria.[59]

The more equal earning power of women in the European and Scandinavian nations is not for the most part the result of job integration. In most of these nations women are as segregated by occupation as they are in the United States.[60]

Equal Opportunity Policies

As the women's movement has developed in Europe and Scandinavia many policies have been debated and instituted to promote women's rights. Some of the policies are quite similar to those currently in force in the United States. Other policies have evolved that reflect the cultural differences of the various nations, and some reflect the power of various national groups, especially the labor unions. The major policies being employed and debated are worth review because some suggest policies that might be employed in the United States.

Below we will review seven major types of policies that have been developed to promote equal opportunities for women.

Collective Bargaining   It is no accident that the gap between male and female income is considerably less in the Scandinavian nations than in many other nations. In the Scandinavian nations most of the work force is unionized, and the unions negotiate yearly salary agreements and working conditions with industry and the government. Equal pay for employees doing the same job has been an accepted principle in these nations since the 1920s, but in the 1960s these nations also adopted the goal of equal pay for work of equal value. The labor unions have accepted the obligation of promoting this goal in yearly negotiations, with the result that the wage gap between men and women has been closing at the rate of about 1 percent a year. The unions have also promoted job counseling and training programs to help women improve their employment status. The solidaristic wage policies pursued by the Swedish unions (see Chapter 5) have also had the effect of reducing the gap between male and female incomes.[61] The unions have supported women because they are committed to equality of all citizens, and , in part, because traditionally there has been a worker shortage in Sweden.

Training and Education   Many of the nations have instituted programs designed to provide a variety of types of education and training to promote equal employment opportunities. In their most comprehensive form the programs have been designed to enable women already in the labor force to move into different areas of work, to encourage and train older women not currently in the labor force to enter employment in nontraditional sectors, and to encourage younger women to train for and enter nontraditional jobs. The Scandinavian nations, Austria, and West Germany have adopted the most comprehensive programs, but all of the nations have programs of one type or another.

The Scandinavian nations also have adopted programs which give preferential treatment to anyone interested in a profession that normally has been dominated by members of the opposite sex. The laws in these nations clearly state that during a transitional period "preferential treatment" is not discriminatory. Sweden has developed an empirical guideline against which progress in job integration can be measured. Equal employment opportunity between the sexes requires that at least 40 percent of all those doing a particular job are male, and at least 40 percent are female. The labor unions use this measure to promote continued or expanded funding for education and training programs designed to overcome job segregation. West Germany passed the Work Promotion Act which provides financial aid to housewives seeking to obtain training in order to reenter the paid work force. West Germany also has implemented a number of pilot projects to train women for traditionally male occupations.[62] Austria has adopted a number of programs to provide job training for women, including training for nontraditional jobs.

Antidiscrimination Laws   All the nations have passed numerous laws designed to overcome discrimination against women, including statutes requiring equal pay for equal work. As noted above, the Scandinavian nations have long required equal pay for men and women. However, in the European nations it was generally legal to pay women less until the mid- and late 1960s. This was especially true in the private sector. The new antidiscrimination laws have been enforced in some nations by labor agreements, in France by litigation, and in both France and the United Kingdom by administrative enforcement.

Two major nations have begun to tackle the more complex problem of requiring equal pay for work of equal value. The Canadian Federal Human Rights Act passed in 1978 requires an equal rate of pay and benefits for "the same work," or "similar or substantially similar work," or "substantially the same work performance which requires equal education, skill, experience, effort, responsibility, and working conditions." The law requires that job analysis and job evaluation be carried out to determine when tasks carried out in dissimilar jobs are of equal value.[63] Since the law is rather new, there is limited empirical evidence on its impact. The evidence that is available indicates that enforcement has gotten off to a slow start, and that many technical problems remain to be resolved. One recent study of Canada concluded:

> A general weakness of equal pay laws is that employers have a financial incentive to delay compliance with the law, and as the penalties concern only the payment of arrears of earnings, there is no real loss. It is necessary therefore to make the law as comprehensive as possible in defining how "equal work" is to be determined, and not limiting the comparison of male and female workers to one establishment. Otherwise, it is too simple to circumvent the law by making minor alterations in job content or keeping males and females separate in different locations.[64]

West Germany also has recently passed legislation requiring equal pay for work of equal value. This legislation was based on the West German constitution which nullifies any collective wage agreement that violates the principle of equal rights. It was simply decreed that unequal pay for work of equal value violated this provision. The unions have accepted the responsibility of representing women's rights on this issue during collective bargaining agreements. Enforcement of the law has run into a number of snags. The most prominent has been that German pay scales generally provide a lower wage rate for "light work." While this classification does not affect all jobs performed by women, they are disproportionately affected by the law. One result has been the appointment of a number of study commissions to decide how jobs can be classified without discriminating against women.[65]

Equal Legal Rights   Only one of the European nations has passed a specific equal rights law which provides a broad foundation for a general strategy for assaults against laws and practices which discriminate against women. The Austrian constitution declares that both sexes are entitled to complete equality. In 1975 a new law, based on the constitutional principle, was passed requiring equality in marriage. Much like the disputed ERA amendment in the United States, the law provides that husbands and wives bear joint responsibility for the care and support of their family and each other. The law requires the couple to mutually decide on how roles will be shared, with the stipulation that any decision made must be in the best interest of their children. If both parents work, they are obligated to share all household duties. The article of the Austrian constitution guaranteeing both sexes equality and the new law have been used to support a broad strategy to ensure women equal employment opportunities. The West German basic law also requires sexual equality, but the specific clause seems to refer primarily to pay and benefit equality for workers. The Scandinavian nations guarantee equality to both males and females in their constitutions, and the acceptance of this principle has made pro-women policies much less controversial in these nations.

Family Policy   As noted in Chapter 2, both the European and Scandinavian nations place a great deal more emphasis on family policy than does the United States. These nations generally provide family allowances; they all have comprehensive medical care programs; paid maternity leaves are common; and child care programs are often more extensive than in the United States. These types of supporting policies obviously enhance the women's ability to handle both a career and a family, and they also make it easier for couples to share these responsibilities.

The service that mothers report that they need most is child care. While none of the nations has been successful in meeting the complete public need for child care services, as noted in Chapter 2 some of the nations have made major advances in this area. The Scandinavian nations, along with Canada, have developed rather comprehensive child care programs that provide both allowances and widely available facilities in a deliberate effort to encourage mothers to work. In recent years France has made considerable improvements in its child care programs and has plans for even more comprehensive policies. Child care has become an issue in all the other European nations, and the indications are that this policy issue will receive a greater priority as more women pursue jobs and professional careers.

One innovative program being tested in France is the introduction of wages for low-income mothers who elect to stay home with their children until they are 3 years old. The French program is a pilot project but has attracted attention in a variety of other nations. A number of other nations have welfare programs for mothers of small children, but women's groups have been lobbying for more general programs that would allow mothers of small children to choose between receiving a salary while they stay home for 1 to 3 years, or placing the child in publicly supported child care and returning to work or education.

Retirement Policy A few countries have responded to women's concerns about inequities built into their social security system. In most nations a woman continues to earn her social security rights through her husband's career, or, if she works, her benefits reflect her lower pay and intermittent work history. Four major nations have instituted reforms which sever the relationship between work and retirement benefits. In Australia, Canada, Denmark, and Sweden pension plans simply extend basic benefits to all citizens upon retirement, regardless of marital status or work history. This is the basic type of reform supported by women's groups in many nations.

SUMMARY AND CONCLUSIONS

The women's movement in the industrialized nations has many parallels. The role of women is changing in all the western industrialized nations, yet there are important national differences and women have clearly made more progress in some of the nations than others. A major difference results from the cultural attitude toward women's roles. In some nations women are expected to play the primary role in raising children, and thus less effort has been made to develop policies to accommodate mothers who wish to enter the work force. The Netherlands provides a good example of a nation in which mothers are simply expected to stay home with their children. In several other nations, including the United States, there is clearly an ambivalent national attitude on this question. While it is recognized that for financial reasons many mothers cannot stay home, there is reluctance on the part of policy makers to provide the type of supportive services that would assist those parents who have to remain in the labor force. At the other extreme are the Scandinavian nations. These nations have developed policies deliberately designed to encourage mothers to work.

A second major factor which seems to have a significant impact on women's policies is the size and power of the nation's labor movement. In those nations with powerful labor unions, such as the Scandinavian countries, West Germany, and Austria, the collective bargaining process has been used to promote pay and job equality for women. In these nations the labor unions also have worked to obtain passage of supportive legislation for parents who need, or wish, to be in the labor force. In the Scandinavian nations, and in Austria, France, and a number of other nations, socialist parties have also played a significant role in promoting both the labor movement and women's equality policies.

In terms of specific policies, the industrialized nations are administering and experimenting with policies with potential applications in the United States. At the most fundamental level are the rather extensive counseling, education, and training programs in operation in nations such as Austria and Sweden. Similar programs exist in the United States, but on a more limited scale. Additionally, the unemployment rate in the United States tends to be higher than in most other western nations, and thus graduates of training programs often have been unable to find a job. In one respect, however, the United States is considerably ahead of the other western nations. The United States provides opportunities for a college education, and especially advanced degrees, to a larger percentage of its population than does any other western nation.

A rather simple policy with important policy applications is the Swedish decision to define equal employment as requiring at least 40 percent males and 40 percent females in a job category. Equal employment in the United States has not been defined this precisely. American policy has simply reflected a concern for providing opportunities for women to move into nontraditional jobs through training programs or as a result of antidiscrimination laws. The Swedish standard, however, establishes a specific goal and thus is more likely to serve as the base and spur for equal employment policies.

Perhaps the most important and innovative policies in effect in the western nations are the laws in West Germany and Canada which require equal pay for work of equal value. This is an issue of primary concern to the U.S. women's movement. The organized women's movement in the United States believes that the equal value issue is critically important because they believe that many valuable jobs performed by women are undercompensated, and that even with recent laws women are likely to remain segregated for a very long time. The experiences of West Germany and Canada indicate that implementation of such a policy is highly complex.

The social security reforms that have been instituted in Australia, Canada, Denmark, and Sweden reflect a policy option that is currently being debated in many nations. In the United States a guaranteed set of basic benefits for all aged citizens is a policy option that has been suggested not only to overcome discrimination against women, but also as a long-term, comprehensive reform of the social security program. (See Chapter 2.)

The French program which pays a wage to low-income mothers who elect to stay home with their infant children is a policy that the organized women's movement in the United States has long supported. Many nations, including the United States, have welfare programs for mothers with infant children, but these programs generally have a welfare stigma attached to them, and they are generally designed to support mothers for a relatively short period. The French program is designed to give low-income mothers a nonstigmatized option of either staying at home during the child's first 3 years or opting for child care and reentering the labor market.

Many of the western nations have developed family policies that greatly enhance the options of women and provide support for all families. The differences between these nations and the United States are discussed in detail in Chapter 2. It is clear that in those nations with the most extensive family policies, a much larger percentage of the female population is engaged in education and the work force.

One last point that is obvious from this review is that those nations that rely on multiple strategies to advance women's equality have made the most progress. As one major assessment of the progress of women's groups concludes:

> There is no ideal method or universally applicable programme for achieving complete equality in the field of pay and employment. Each approach has its limitations, which vary in degree according to national circumstance. However, the strength of one policy option can complement the weakness of another, and it is for this reason that countries are now adopting more comprehensive approaches. Though tailored to their own needs, the programmes of each country therefore are increasing in similarity.[66]

There is little doubt that women's roles will continue to change in all the western industrialized nations, and that these changes will be the source of controversy, public debate, and genuine concern. The changes in progress undoubtedly will alter the structure and role of families, greatly increasing the public responsibility for child development, and perhaps altering traditional male and female roles in very substantial ways. Liberal groups will continue to try to convince the government to use its power to accommodate and capitalize upon what they see as inevitable, overdue, enlightened changes. They will also continue to argue that for government to try to ignore the changes that have already taken place, plus those in motion, will only weaken the U.S. family, while continuing to deny women opportunities to achieve their full potential.

The right—deeply wedded to the traditional family—will continue to express concern that the changes taking place will in the long run be quite harmful. The right will continue to argue that the government should use its power not to accommodate what they see as an ill-advised fate, but instead to reinforce and strengthen the traditional U.S. family.

NOTES

1 Gloria Steinhem, "The Stage Is Set," *Ms.*, Aug. 1982, p. 78; William H. Chafe, *The American Woman: Her Changing Social, Economic and Political Role, 1920–1970* (New York: Oxford University Press, 1972); Jo Freeman, *The Politics of Women's Liberation* (New York: Longman, 1975); Susan C. Ross, *The Rights of Women* (New York: Avon Books, 1973); Irene L. Murphy, *Public Policy on the Status of Women* (Lexington, Mass.: Heath, 1973); and Ralph E. Smith, ed., *The Subtle Revolution: Women at Work* (Washington, D.C.: The Urban Institute, 1979).

2 Steinhem, p. 226; Janet K. Boles, *The Politics of the Equal Rights Amendment* (New York: Longman, 1979), p 102; Glenna Spitze and Joan Huber, "Effects of Anticipated Consequences on ERA Opinion," *Social Science Quarterly*, 63, No. 2 (June 1982), 327–332.

3 Steinhem, p. 226; Susan Welch, "Support among Women for the Issues of the Women's Movement," *Sociological Quarterly*, 16 (Spring 1975), 216–227; and Glenna Spitze and Joan Huber, "Changing Attitudes Toward Women's Nonfamily Roles: 1958–1980," *Sociology of Work and Education*, 7 (Aug. 1980), 317–336.

4 U.S. Bureau of the Census, *Statistical Abstract of the United States: 1981* (Washington, D.C.: GPO, 1982), pp. 387–388.

5 Ibid., p. 388.

6 Ibid., pp. 384, 388; U.S. Commission on Civil Rights, *Child Care and Equal Opportunity for Women* (Washington, D.C.: Clearinghouse Publication No. 67, 1981), p. 9.

7 *Statistical Abstract of the United States: 1981*, p. 388; Barbara Ehrenreich and Karen Stallard, "The Nouveau Poor," *Ms.*, Aug. 1982, p. 220; and U.S. Bureau of the Census, "Money Income and Poverty Status of Families and Persons in the United States: 1980," *Current Population Reports*, Series P-60, No. 127, March 1981, p. 27.

8 Ehrenreich and Stallard, p. 220; and U.S. Bureau of Labor Statistics, *Perspectives on Working Women: A Databook* (Washington, D.C.: Department of Labor, 1980).

9 *Statistical Abstract of the United States: 1981*, pp. 402–404; Women's Bureau, *Women Workers Today* (Washington, D.C.: GPO, 1976). See also Barbara B. Reagan, "De Facto Job Segregation," in *Women in the Labor Force*, ed. Ann Foote Cahn (New York: Praeger Publishers, 1979).

10 U. S. Commission on Civil Rights, *Child Care and Equal Opportunity for Women*, pp. 3–4; Collette Dowling, *The Cinderella Complex: Women's Hidden Fear of Independence* (New York: Pocket Books, 1981), pp. 36–40; and Women's Bureau, *The Earnings Gap Between Women and Men* (Washington, D.C.: GPO, 1976).

11 Martha Darling, *The Role of Women In the Economy* (Paris: OECD, 1975), p. 111.

12 Women's Bureau, *The Earnings Gap Between Women and Men* (Washington, D.C.: GPO, 1979), p. 3.

13 "Money Income and Poverty Status of Families and Persons in the United States: 1980," p. 11.

14 *Statistical Abstract of the United States: 1981,* p. 388.

15 Ibid., p. 386.

16 "Money Income and Poverty Status of Families and Persons in the United States: 1980," pp. 26–27.

17 Ehrenreich and Stallard, p. 217.

18 U.S. Commission on Civil Rights, *Child Care and Equal Opportunity for Women,* pp. 10–15.

19 Ibid., p. 12.

20 See, for example, Dorothy Burlarge, "Divorced and Separated Mothers: Combining the Responsibilities of Breadwinning and Childrearing," Unpublished Diss. Harvard Univ. 1978, pp. 295–296; and Suzanne Woolsey, "Pied Piper Politics and the Child-Care Debate," *Daedalus,* 106, No. 2 (1977), p. 138.

21 *Cong. Rec.,* Jan. 15, 1979, p. S-77, remarks of Senator Cranston (D., Cal.).

22 *Statistical Abstract of the United States: 1981,* p. 496.

23 Susan Welch and Lee Sigelman, "Changes in Public Attitudes Toward Women in Politics," *Social Science Quarterly,* 63, No. 2 (June 1982), 312–322; Robert Bernstein and Jayne D. Polley, "Race, Class and Support for Female Candidates," *Western Political Quarterly,* 28 (Dec. 1975), 733–736; Laurie E. Ekstrand and William A. Eckert, "The Impact of Candidate's Sex on Voter Choice," *Western Political Quarterly,* 34 (March 1981), 78–87; and Susan MacManus, "A City's First Female Officeholder: Coattails for Future Female Officeholders," *Western Political Quarterly,* 34 (March 1981), 88–99.

24 Thomas R. Dye and Julie Strickland, "Women At the Top: A Note on Institutional Leadership," *Social Science Quarterly,* 63, No. 2 (June 1982), 337.

25 Ibid., p. 340.

26 Leo Kanowitz, *Women and the Law: The Unfinished Revolution* (Albuquerque, New Mexico: Univ. of New Mexico Press, 1969).

27 U.S. Commission on Civil Rights, *Federal Civil Rights Enforcement Effort* (Washington,D.C.: GPO, 1970), p. 12.

28 Darling, p. 99.

29 U.S. Commission on Civil Rights, *The State of Civil Rights* (Washington, D.C.: GPO, 1980), p. 24.

30 *Washington County v. Gunther,* 450 U.S. 970 (1981).

31 *General Electric Co. v. Gilbert,* 429 U.S. 125 (1976).

32 Steinhem, p. 78.

33 The 1972 case was *Stanley v. Illinois,* 405 U.S. 645; the social security case was *Weinberger v. Wiesenfeld,* 420 U.S. 636 (1975); the nursing school case

was *Mississippi University for Women v. Hogan,* 73 L.Ed. 2nd 1090 (1982). See also Harrell R. Rodgers, Jr., "Fair Employment Laws for Minorities: An Evaluation of Federal Implementation," in *Implementing Civil Rights* eds. Charles S. Bullock, III, and Charles Lamb (Monterey, California: Brooks/Cole, Spring 1983).

34 "The Conservative at the EEOC," *Business Week,* Aug., 1982, pp. 54–55.

35 *Report for the World Conference on the United Nation's Decade for Women 1976–1985,* "Employment Goals of the World Plan of Action: Developments and Issues in the United States" (Washington, D.C.: GPO, 1980), p. 17.

36 Dowling, p. 36.

37 Ehrenreich and Stallard, p. 219.

38 Darling, p. 113.

39 George Gilder, *Wealth and Poverty* (New York: Bantam Books, 1981), p. 166.

40 Ibid., p. 57.

41 Ibid., p. 140.

42 Ibid., p. 142.

43 Ibid., p. 89.

44 Ehrenreich and Stallard, p. 222.

45 Ibid., p. 223.

46 "Affirmative Action Assailed in Congress: Administration," *Congressional Quarterly,* 39, No. 37 (Sept. 1981), 1749–1753.

47 Steinhem, p. 79.

48 Thomas I. Emerson et al., "The Equal Rights Amendment: A Constitutional Basis for Equal Rights For Women," *Yale Law Journal,* 80 (Apr. 1971), 871–985; U.S. Citizens' Advisory Council on the Status of Women, *Interpretation of the Equal Rights Amendment in Accordance with Legislative History* (Washington, D.C.: GPO, 1974). For the minority interpretation see Paul Freund, "The Equal Rights Amendment Is Not the Way," *Harvard Civil Rights–Civil Liberties Law Review,* 6 (March 1971), 234–242; and U.S. Citizens' Advisory Council on the Status of Women, *The Equal Rights Amendment—Senator Ervin's Minority Report and the Yale Law Journal* (Washington, D.C.: GPO, 1972).

49 This review is based on the Emerson et al. *Yale Law Journal* article and Janet K. Boles, pp. 31–37. See also Barbara Brown et al., *Women's Rights and the Law: The Impact of the ERA on State Laws* (New York: Praeger, 1977); and Claire Safran, "What You Should Know About the Equal Rights Amendment," *Redbook,* 141, June 1973, pp. 62–65.

50 See John G. Schmitz, "Look Out: They're Planning to Draft Your Daughter," *American Opinion,* 15 (Nov. 1972), 1–16; "What's Wrong with Equal Rights for Women?" *Phyllis Schlafly Report 5,* Feb. 1972:3; "The Precious Rights ERA Will Take Away from Wives," *Phyllis Schlafly Report 7,* Aug. 1973:1. See also Jaquie Davidson, *I Am a Housewife* (New York: Guild, 1972); David W. Brady and Kent L. Tedin, "Ladies In Pink: Religion and Political Ideology in the Anti-ERA Movement," *Social Science Quarterly,* 56 (March 1976), 564–575; Catherine Arnott, "Feminists and Anti-Feminists as 'True Believers,' " *Sociology and Social Research,* 57 (Apr. 1973), 300–306; Lisa Cronin Wohl, "White Gloves and Combat Boots: The Fight for ERA," *Civil Liberties Review,* 1 (Fall 1974), 77–86; and Lisa Cronin Wohl, "Phyllis Schlafly: The Sweetheart of the Silent

Majority," *Ms.*, 2, March 1974, pp. 54–57.

51 Spitze and Huber, "Effects of Anticipated Consequences on ERA Opinion," pp. 327–332.

52 Ibid., p. 331.

53 Dowling, p. 21.

54 Ibid., p. 162.

55 Ibid., p. 32.

56 Ibid., p. 36.

57 Ibid., pp. 108–109.

58 Organization for Economic Co-operation and Development, *Labor Force Statistics: Demographic Trends 1950–1990* (Paris: OECD, 1979), p. 22.

59 Organization for Economic Co-operation and Development, *Women and Employment: Policies for Equal Opportunities* (Paris: OECD, 1980), p. 32; and Alice H. Cook, *The Working Mother: A Survey of Problems and Programs in Nine Countries* (Ithaca, New York: New York State School of Industrial and Labor Relations, 1975).

60 OECD, *Women and Employment*, p. 45.

61 Ibid., p. 57; and Organization for Economic Co-operation and Development, *Equal Opportunities For Women* (Paris: OECD, 1979), p. 111.

62 OECD, *Women and Employment*, p. 65.

63 Ibid., p. 64.

64 OECD, *Equal Opportunities For Women*, p. 98.

65 Ibid., p. 90.

66 Ibid., p. 111.

CHAPTER 5

THE ECONOMY AND THE POLICY PROCESS

The 1970s were a period of economic malaise and frustration for the United States. Not since the 1930s has the economy performed so badly. Both inflation and unemployment increased significantly and remained stubbornly high. The growth of the economy (increases in the production of goods and services) was modest across the decade and negative in some years. Productivity growth (the efficiency with which goods and services are produced) was so modest that the competitive advantage of the United States in international markets was seriously reduced.

The record of the 1980s thus far has not been encouraging. The only positive news has been a significant decline in the inflation rate. In 1980 the inflation rate was 12.4 percent, down slightly from 13.3 percent in 1979. In 1981 the inflation rate declined to 8.9 percent, still a very high rate by U.S. standards. However, by 1982 the inflation rate declined to 3.8 percent. The reduction in the inflation rate was achieved through record high interest rates which brought on a severe recession and other severe economic problems. Productivity growth remained negative. Unemployment reached record post-World War II highs. By the fall of 1982 and into the spring of 1983 the unemployment rate stood at 10.4 percent, representing over 11 million unemployed. Government deficits were at record levels, exceeding $110 billion in 1982. And in 1981 and 1982 the nation had the highest rate of small business failure in 40 years.[1] Most economists were predicting that unemployment would remain very high in 1983, that

TABLE 5-1
REAL ECONOMIC GROWTH, 1960–1973 AND 1973–1980, AVERAGE ANNUAL
PERCENT CHANGE

Country	1960–1973	Country	1973–1980
1. Japan	10.6	1. Japan	4.4
2. France	5.7	2. France	2.9
3. Canada	5.4	3. Italy	2.8
4. Italy	5.2	4. Canada	2.7
5. West Germany	4.8	5. United States	2.4
6. United States	4.0	6. West Germany	2.3
7. Sweden	3.6	7. Sweden	1.9
8. United Kingdom	3.3	8. United Kingdom	0.5

Source: Data from New York Stock Exchange, *U.S. Economic Performance in a Global Perspective* (New York: Office of Economic Research, 1981), p. 10.

economic growth would be modest, and that the federal deficit might reach $175 to $200 billion. Almost no one believed that broad economic recovery was just around the corner.

COMPARISONS TO OTHER WESTERN NATIONS

Surprisingly, perhaps, U.S. economic performance during the 1960s and 1970s was considerably worse than the performance of most of the other western industrialized nations. In fact, several other industrialized nations substantially outperformed the United States. Table 5-1 compares the economic growth rates of the eight major industrial nations between 1960 to 1973 and 1973 to 1980. Notice that the United States ranked sixth in rate of economic growth during the first period, and fifth during the second period. The Japanese growth rate was more than double the U.S. rate during the first period, and almost double the U.S. rate during the second period.

Table 5-2 compares the eight nations in terms of rates of inflation. This is the variable upon which the U.S. record is the best. From 1960 to 1973 the United States and Canada tied for the lowest rate of inflation. During the period 1973–1980 the inflation rate increased substantially for all the nations except West Germany. The U.S. rate of 9.1 percent was the second best of all the nations, although the rates for Canada, Japan, Sweden, and France were fairly similar. The inflation rate in Italy and the United Kingdom was absolutely staggering.

Table 5-3 compares the eight nations in terms of rates of unemployment. Here the United States has the next to the worst record. During the period 1960–1973 unemployment in the United States was far higher than in West Germany, Japan, Sweden, or France, and considerably higher than in the

TABLE 5-2

INFLATION RATES, 1960–1973 AND 1973–1980, AVERAGE ANNUAL PERCENT CHANGE

Country	1960–1973	Country	1973–1980
1. Japan	6.0	1. Italy	16.8
2. United Kingdom	4.7	2. United Kingdom	16.0
3. France	4.6	3. France	10.9
4. Sweden	4.6	4. Sweden	10.3
5. Italy	4.5	5. Japan	9.6
6. West Germany	3.2	6. Canada	9.3
7. Canada	3.1	7. United States	9.1
8. United States	3.1	8. West Germany	4.7

Source: Data from New York Stock Exchange. *U.S. Economic Performance in a Global Perspective* (New York: Office of Economic Research, 1981), p. 10.

United Kingdom or Italy. During the second period the U.S. rate is also the second worst, even though unemployment increased in all the nations. Still, the rate of unemployment in the United States was triple that of Japan or Sweden, double that of West Germany, and considerably higher than Italy, France, or the United Kingdom.

Comparatively, then, in terms of economic growth and unemployment, the U.S. economy has performed poorly. The rate of inflation in the United States has been high by U.S. standards, but fairly low compared to major competing nations. In a 1981 study the New York Stock Exchange's Office of Economic Research used the above data to create an economic performance index (EPI) for the industrial nations. The EPI represented a

TABLE 5-3

UNEMPLOYMENT RATES, 1960–1973 AND 1973–1980, AVERAGE RATE FOR PERIOD

Country	1960–1973	Country	1973–1980
1. Canada	5.3	1. Canada	7.3
2. United States	4.9	2. United States	6.8
3. Italy	3.2	3. United Kingdom	5.4
4. United Kingdom	2.9	4. France	5.0
5. France	2.1	5. Italy	3.8
6. Sweden	1.8	6. West Germany	3.3
7. Japan	1.3	7. Japan	2.0
8. West Germany	0.8	8. Sweden	1.9

Source: Data from New York Stock Exchange, *U.S. Economic Performance in a Global Perspective* (New York: Office of Economic Research, 1981), p. 10.

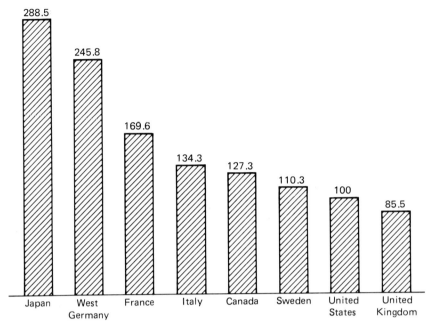

FIGURE 5-1
Comparative economic performance index: 1960–1973. *(Source: New York Stock Exchange,*
U.S. Economic Performance in a Global Perspective. New York: Office of Economic
Research, 1981, p. 12).

ratio between a nation's growth rate and the combined rates of inflation
and unemployment.

Figures 5-1 and 5-2 show the computed index for each nation during
each of the two study periods. In these figures the EPI for the United States
has been set at l00, and then the EPI for each of the other nations has been
set relative to that base. This computation allows the U.S. economic
performance to be compared to the other nations. What the EPI indexes
show is quite clear. During the period 1960–1973 only the United Kingdom's
economy performed worse than the U.S. economy. The Japanese and West
German economies greatly outperformed the U.S. economy, while the
French, Italian, and Canadian economies performed substantially better.
During the period 1974–1980 only two nations demonstrated a worse
economic performance than the United States. Again, Japan and West
Germany greatly outperformed the United States, while the French and
Canadian economies performed somewhat better.

While many of the industrial nations continued on average to outperform
the United States in 1980, 1981, and 1982, economic conditions deteri-

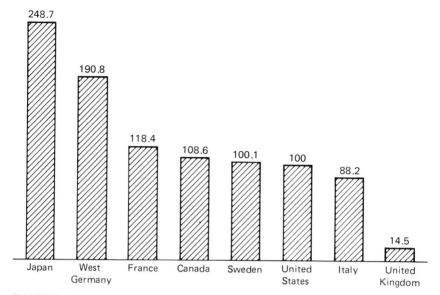

FIGURE 5-2
Comparative economic performance index: 1974–1980. *(Source: New York Stock Exchange,* U.S. Economic Performance in a Global Perspective. *New York: Office of Economic Research, 1981, p. 12).*

orated in most of them. All the nations struggled to hold down inflation while keeping their economies growing. Unemployment increased significantly in West Germany and France and more modestly in Japan. The leaders of these nations blamed the United States for many of their problems. They argued that high interest rates in the United States forced them to raise interest rates to keep their investment money from flowing to the United States. These high interest rates, they argued, caused their economies to stagnate. They also noted that in the United States high interest rates boosted the exchange value of the U.S. dollar in foreign markets. Since the U.S. dollar is the currency of foreign exchange in Europe, the strong dollar decreased the value of other currencies and made imports (e.g., oil and gas) much more expensive for European nations.

Policies adopted by the United States clearly have had an impact on European nations (just as their policies affect our economy), but these nations also may be suffering some of the same problems that have caused economic woes in the United States. There may be, in other words, problems indigenous to advanced capitalist nations which periodically cause even carefully managed economies to malfunction. This is a question we will try to address as we proceed. In the analysis that follows we emphasize the reasons why the federal government has become involved in the U.S. economy, and conservative and liberal reactions to the nature of the relationship between the economic and political order. In analyzing conservative and liberal perspectives, we also will analyze the major economic policies of the European nations in order to determine if they might be used to deal better with U.S. economic problems.

THE FEDERAL ECONOMIC ROLE

The economic problems that the United States has suffered during the last 20 or so years have been unsettling to both public and political leaders. Yet, in reality, economic problems are nothing new to the United States. In fact, the economy has performed much better since the end of World War II than at any other period in our history. Depressions, panics, recessions, and other economic problems have occurred throughout U.S. history.[2] The period since World War II has been marked by reoccurring economic problems, but they have not been as severe as the periods of depression and panic that occurred with great regularity throughout the nineteenth and first half of the twentieth century.

The most calamitous period of economic strife in the twentieth century was the great depression, which began in the late 1920s. The inability of President Hoover's policies to deal with the nation's economic problems led to the election of Franklin Roosevelt in 1932 and the beginning of the New Deal. The New Deal was an improvised and incremental approach to the severe problems the nation faced in recovering from the general collapse of the economy. By 1935 Roosevelt had decided that the economy would not recover unless the government played an even larger role. This conclusion lead Roosevelt to embrace Keynesian economics.

Keynes, a British economist, argued that capitalism would perform more smoothly with government management. The strategy Keynes suggested was basically quite simple. He recommended that the government increase spending to stimulate the economy and that it manipulate interest rates, taxes, and spending to keep the economy in tune. If the economy needed stimulation, Keynes suggested that spending be increased and taxes and interest rates lowered. The effect would be to put more money into the economy, thus stimulating spending and production. If the economy needed to be cooled off because prices were going up too quickly, the strategy could be reversed. Tax rates could be increased, interest rates raised, and government spending reduced.

Keynes' recommendations are broadly referred to as a stabilization policy—a set of activities that governments can utilize to minimize economic fluctuations and deal with more serious economic disturbances. Keynes' theory basically involves three types of strategies. The first is fiscal policies

applications of Keynesian economic techniques were based had changed, rendering some accepted wisdoms obsolete.

The nation's continued economic problems created considerable concern and set off a national debate about the causes of the nation's economic woes. Below we detail the major conservative and liberal theories of the nation's economic distress. After each major theory is explained, the opposition's critique of this theory is presented. We begin by examining some problems that both conservatives and liberals agree have contributed to the nation's economic woes.

PROBLEMS THAT BOTH SIDES IDENTIFY

While both conservatives and liberals agree that certain problems have contributed to the nation's poor economic performance, they disagree about the causes and cures for these maladies. We will first identify those problems and then discuss some of the differences between liberals and conservatives over their origins and solutions. There are at least four major areas in which problems are often identified: growth and productivity, energy and agriculture, coordination of government policies, and low rates of savings.

Growth and Productivity Problems

The terms "economic growth," "productivity," and "productivity growth" are often confused. Economic growth refers to increases in the nation's real output of goods and services. The "real" (GNP corrected for inflation) output of the economy increased at an annual rate of only 2.9 percent in the 1970s. This was substantially below the 4 percent rate that characterized the 1950s and 1960s. Both conservatives and liberals agree that the economy needs to grow at a faster rate to provide the jobs, goods, and services to improve the nation's standard of living. Below we will discuss the rather complex reasons that liberals and conservatives give for the nation's slower rate of economic growth.

The problem of productivity growth is a bit more complex. Productivity is simply a measure of the cost of producing goods and services. Rates of productivity in the United States are very high by world standards. Indeed, U.S. productivity in many industries is the highest in the world. The concern is that the nation's rate of growth in productivity has been below that of some of the other industrialized nations. During the period 1973–1979 Japan, France, and West Germany all had much higher rates of productivity growth than the United States.[4]

Higher productivity allows an industry to produce goods and services with less labor, capital, and resources. As Thurow says:

> If we produce more per hour, each of us can have more purchasing power to buy the things we want. If productivity does not rise, our money incomes can rise, but it is not possible to have more real purchasing power.[5]

Increases in productivity may result from something dramatic like a scientific or technological breakthrough, or from improved labor or management skills.

Conservatives tend to blame the nation's productivity growth problems on excessive wages for industrial workers (especially those represented by labor unions), government regulations that add to business costs (e.g., safety and pollution standards), and low capital investments. In relation to the last point, conservatives argue that in recent years high taxes and interest rates have discouraged investment.

Liberals blame the problem on the poor management of many U.S. industries, management's concern with short-term as opposed to long-term profits, and high interest rates. Liberals claim that U.S. companies are often managed so poorly that they fail to develop creative and productive relationships with their own employees, and that they have excessive layers of management that add to costs without improving products or services. They believe that the orientation of industry often causes management to chase short-term speculative profits rather than to invest in the long-term expansion or improvement of their own product and plant. Liberals agree that high interest rates have harmed industry, but, as we will see, they differ from conservatives in their explanations of why they are so high.

Some liberals also contend that the nation's high rate of unemployment has reduced productivity growth. They claim that productivity falls when the work force and industrial capacity are underutilized. Thurow, for example, argues that unemployment reduces productivity:

> This occurs because we have a large proportion of overhead labor and plants designed to operate most efficiently at capacity. Managers, research departments, salesmen, maintenance workers, and the like either cannot be or are not cut back proportionally when output falls. The result is a drop in productivity since more man-hours are now necessary to produce a unit of output. Conversely when output rises toward capacity, we do not have to expand the overhead labor force. Output goes up, but overhead man-hours do not go up, and the result is a rapid gain in productivity.[6]

Empirical studies have identified two of the causes of productivity decline. One has been the end of the shift from an agricultural to an industrial society. When rural workers were moving to the cities, productivity increased because industrial jobs were more mechanized and thus increased worker output.[7] This points up one of the truths about productivity; a worker's level of productivity is affected by the nature of his or her job. A plantation worker has one level of productivity, but the same individual working on an assembly line would have a much higher level of productivity. Second, these same studies show that about 14 percent of the decline in productivity has been due to increased manufacturing costs resulting from environmental and safety regulations.[8] Conservatives argue that these figures vindicate their belief that government regulations reduce productivity. Liberals counter that the figures show government regulations are an important, but not a major, cause of productivity decline. Government regulations, according to this view, have produced cleaner air and water, better work environments, and fewer days of work lost because of job injuries. These types of gains are not measured by productivity indexes.

Energy and Agricultural Shocks

The second major area of economic problems is not really very controversial. Both liberals and conservatives agree that the formation of the Organization of Petroleum Exporting Countries (OPEC) led to the tripling of the price of imported oil during the 1970s. This rapid increase in the costs of energy contributed significantly to inflation. Of all consumption in the United States 10 percent goes directly or indirectly toward the purchase of energy, and thus increases in energy costs have a very substantial impact on the whole economy. For example, a 100 percent increase in energy costs generates a 10 percent rate of inflation by itself.[9] During the late 1970s, the United States was importing almost one-half of all the oil consumed domestically. This represented $80 to $100 billion a year flowing out of the country.

Rapid increases in gasoline prices convinced the public to buy cars which were more fuel efficient, to cut back on their driving, and to exercise other conservation measures. The result was that by mid-1981 the nation's oil consumption was down, and by 1982 the OPEC nations were cutting the price of oil. This was good news for the U.S. economy and accounted in significant part for the nation's lower rate of inflation in 1981 and 1982. In addition, the recession contributed to the drop in demand and consumption.

Agricultural prices also increased rapidly during some periods in the 1970s. Ironically, better foreign markets for U.S. farm products created higher prices in U.S. markets and often drove consumer prices up. By 1981 farm prices had stabilized, and this also contributed to the lower rate of inflation in 1981 and 1982.

Coordination of Government Policies

Both conservatives and liberals tend to agree that the government's extensive involvement in regulatory and economic policies both promotes and harms the economy. There are two basic problems in this respect. First, conservatives argue that government regulations in such areas as safety and environmental quality are excessive, heavy-handed, unnecessarily complex, and burdensome. Liberals, while defending the need for regulation and dismissing some of these complaints as unfounded, often agree that federal policies and procedures could be better designed.

Second, both conservatives and liberals agree that the government's policies in such areas as the environment, energy, and urban affairs are poorly coordinated. Individually, the policies may be quite rational, but combined they constitute an untenable whole. Additionally, there is concern that neither the government nor the private sector carries out long-term studies on the impact of government on the economy. Below we will review some of the proposed solutions for these problems.

Low Rates of Savings

Both conservatives and liberals agree that people in the United States tend to spend too much and save too little. Excessive spending for consumer goods overstimulates the economy (contributing to inflation), while low rates of saving reduce the amount of capital available to finance industrial expansion. Among the major western industrial nations, the United States has one of the lowest rates of saving.[10]

In recent years all of the western industrialized nations have shown a concern for stimulating personal savings. Personal saving not only provides a pool of funds that can be used to finance capital investment, it also provides a more secure future for citizens who are able to save. Conservatives blame the nation's low rate of net saving on high taxes, especially those on higher income groups and investments. Of course, President Reagan's 1982 tax bill greatly reduced taxes on both investments and upper-income groups. Part of President Reagan's defense of tax breaks for wealthy citizens was that upper-income groups are the citizens who do save, and the nation must allow some citizens to become wealthy so that they can use their wealth to finance expansion and renovation of U.S. industry.

Liberals believe that the nation's low rate of savings can be traced to policies that discourage saving by average income earners and to tax laws that encourage excessive consumer purchases. Citizens who can save only modest amounts usually invest in savings accounts paying low rates of interest and then pay taxes on the small sums they earn. Normally, one has to invest as much as several thousand dollars to qualify for the more flexible and higher paying accounts. These policies, liberals argue, encourage average citizens to spend rather than save.

Liberals also argue that tax laws which allow citizens to treat common interest charges as a tax deduction simply encourage spending. As we will note below, liberals have proposed a ceiling on this deduction so that only a certain level of spending is encouraged. Last, liberals argue that while it is necessary to encourage saving to finance economic expansion, it is not necessary to promote and enhance the wealthy to do so. They argue that much of the necessary funds could be accumulated through encouraging savings by average citizens and through government policies that would create public funds that could be drawn upon. These policies are covered in more detail below.

Having covered a few points of agreement, we can now turn to the major areas of disagreement between conservatives and liberals.

CONSERVATIVE EXPLANATIONS

There are basically three major schools of conservative economic thought: supply-side, fiscal restraint, and monetarism.[11] Not all conservatives, however, subscribe to all three theories. For example, monetarists and supply siders rarely agree with each other's diagnosis of, or prescriptions for, the nation's economic woes.

The easiest of the schools to understand is fiscal restraint. It is also a philosophy that other conservatives may accept, especially monetarists. Fiscal restraint simply means that the government should limit its role and keep public spending under control. Normally this school believes that government spending should grow only in relation to growth in the nation's GNP.

Because it was embraced by the Reagan administration, supply-side economics has become one of the most prominent schools of conservative economic thought. Supply-side economics blames the nation's economic malfunctions on three major problems. First, in keeping with the fiscal restraint school, it holds that government is spending too much. Supply siders argue that large government budgets overstimulate the economy and thus fuel inflation. Second, burdensome tax rates, which finance excessive government spending, deny businesses and the public the funds that normally would be retained in profits and savings and consequently would be available for investment and capital improvements. Third, government overregulation of business imposes excessive costs that again deny businesses funds for plant improvements, research, and expansion. These arguments all center around a belief that businesses are being denied the capital needed for innovation and expansion.

Supply siders also believe that Keynesian economics is oriented too much toward regulating demand for private and public goods and too little toward helping industry supply those goods. Basically, supply siders believe that supply creates its own demand. That is, if there is an adequate supply of goods, there will be an adequate demand. The Keynesian school emphasizes the exact opposite approach. Keynesianism maintains that if government uses fiscal and tax policies to stimulate demand for goods, production will increase to meet demand. The Keynesians argue that if supply created its own demand, there would never have been depressions and recessions in the United States because goods were always plentiful during those periods.

The popularity of supply-side economics in the early 1980s probably can be traced to two factors. First, the failure of both traditional conservative and liberal economic policies in the 1970s fostered the development of new economic policies. During the 1970s conservative and liberal economic policies proved incapable of controlling inflation without creating a recession. Democratic administrations found that they could not use traditional Keynesian techniques to increase employment without causing inflation. Since both traditional schools proved a failure in the 1970s, conditions were ripe for a new approach. Second, supply-side economic theory is particularly attractive to conservatives because it justifies providing tax breaks and other assistance to businesses and upper-income groups— the Republican party's premier constituency. As George Gilder, a major advocate of supply-side economics, put it: "[T]o help the poor and the middle classes, one must cut the tax rates of the rich."[12]

During the 1980 election Reagan and his supporters popularized supply-side economics. They argued that the private sector would be invigorated if government expenditures were substantially reduced (especially those for social programs), if taxes were reduced (especially on wealthier citizens who can be expected to save and invest), and if expensive safety and environmental regulations on businesses were rolled back or eliminated.

The supply-side school developed primarily out of the writings of economist Arthur Laffer. Laffer makes two basic arguments: (1) that high tax rates discourage work and investment and (2) that high tax rates actually decrease tax revenues. On the first point, Laffer argues that when taxes become too high workers reach a point where work is unprofitable because increased income disproportionately goes to taxes. On the second point, Laffer argues that once taxes become too high they are counterproductive and actually depress business so badly that they reduce revenues (this is the Laffer curve). Thus, Laffer argues that if taxes were reduced 30 percent across the board over a 3-year period, government revenues would actually increase.[13]

The last major school of conservative economic thought is monetarism, and its chief spokesperson is economist Milton Friedman. Basically this school argues that inflation can be controlled only by careful management of the growth of the nation's monetary supply. The growth of the money supply should be proportionate to the growth of the economy. Friedman, for example, argues:

> In the modern world, inflation is a printing press phenomenon. . . . If the quantity of goods and services available for purchase—output, for short—were to increase as rapidly as the quantity of money, prices would tend to be stable. Prices might even fall gradually as higher incomes led people to want to hold a larger fraction of their wealth in the form of money. Inflation occurs when the quantity of money rises appreciably more rapidly than output, and the more rapid the rise in the quantity of money per unit of output, the greater the rate of inflation.[14]

Friedman and the other monetarists do not believe that there is a perfect correlation between inflation and increases in the money supply, but they do believe that growth of the money supply is the major cause of inflation. Friedman, for example, dismisses the idea that the salaries of labor union workers or the prices charged by businesses cause inflation:

> Unions may provide useful services for their members. They may also do a great deal of harm by limiting employment opportunities for others, but they do not produce inflation. Wage increases in excess of increases in productivity are a result of inflation, rather than a cause. Similarly, businessmen do not cause inflation. The rise in prices they charge is the result or reflection of other forces.[15]

Friedman does not even believe that government spending causes inflation as long as it is financed either through taxes or through borrowing from the public. But, of course, Friedman and other monetarists are generally fiscal conservatives because they do not believe that governments will take the politically unpopular route of financing expenditures through taxes and borrowing.

The monetarists, then, believe that if governments control the growth of their money supply, inflation will be controlled and government policies will not interfere with the natural dynamics of the economic market. But one common point of confusion should be cleared up. Friedman and other monetarists argue that public officials should not believe that they can control the growth of money by manipulating interest rates. The federal government normally increases the money supply by having the U.S. Treasury sell government bonds to the Federal Reserve System (another branch of the federal government). The Federal Reserve pays for the bonds either with newly printed money or by entering a deposit on its books to the U.S. Treasury. The U.S. Treasury can then pay its bills either with the cash or with checks drawn on its account at the Federal Reserve. It is this cycle that monetarists believe must be controlled, not interest rates.

It should be noted that supply siders and monetarists often do not agree with one another, despite the fact that both are conservatives. The supply siders believe that big government is here to stay and that if the Federal Reserve refuses to allow the money supply to grow to pay public debts, governments will finance debt by imposing higher taxes on businesses. The supply siders believe that the ultimate consequence of such actions is to bankrupt businesses, prompting government to either subsidize, regulate, or take over sectors of the economy.

Monetarists tend to reject the basic tenets of supply-side economics. They believe that government spending and taxes should be kept in check, but they do not believe that drastic tax cuts will greatly stimulate the productive sectors of the economy. Large tax cuts, they believe, will lead to large deficits. Milton Friedman, for example, supported President Reagan's tax cut bill only because he believed that it would cause huge deficits, thereby forcing Congress to cut government spending. In other words, Friedman thought Reagan's plan would fail, with one side effect being a deficit so large that congressional spending would be disciplined.[16]

The Liberal Critique of Conservative Explanations

Liberals tend to believe that government is the best friend that most people have. While they do not believe that government works as well as it should, they do believe that government action is often the best way to deal with societal problems, including deficiencies of the economy. Liberals, in fact, believe that the government's assumption of an enlarged role in the economy beginning in the 1930s has led to a much improved economy. Economist Lester Thurow emphasizes this point:

> Our own history shows that our economic performance since the New Deal and the onset of government "interference" has been better than it was prior to the New Deal. Our best economic decades were the 1940's (real per capita GNP grew 36 percent), when the economy was run as a command (socialist) wartime economy, and the 1960's (real per capita GNP grew 30 percent), when we had all that growth in social welfare programs. Real per capita growth since the advent of government intervention has been more than twice as high as it was in the days when governments did not intervene or have social welfare programs.[17]

Liberals reject supply-side economics as a flawed theory based on many inaccuracies. First, liberals reject the argument that the United States has been suffering from a shortage of goods and services. Liberals believe that the evidence shows that U.S. industry has been producing more cars, houses, appliances, and services than it can sell. Industries, in fact, have been burdened with surpluses rather than shortages. Second, liberals reject the idea that tax rates in the 1970s and 1980s were so high that they were discouraging work and investment. In fact, all of the western industrial nations impose higher taxes on the general population and the wealthy than does the United States. Taxes from all levels of government represent about 30 percent of Gross Domestic Products (GDP) in the United States, while they constitute around 40 percent of GDP in the larger western industrial nations and up to 50 percent in the smaller nations of Western Europe.[18] Additionally, most of the Western European nations spend a larger proportion of their nation's GDP on government operations and services than does the U.S. government. Yet most of these nations have been outperforming the United States.

Liberals do not believe that the nation's relatively high taxes on higher incomes have reached the point of lowering productivity. Economist Lester Thurow, for example, sees no evidence that current rates of taxation reduce work efforts.

> Repeated studies have shown that highly progressive tax systems (much more progressive than the tax system now in place) do not seem to reduce work effort. Income effects (the need to work more to regain one's living standard) dominate substitution effects (the desire for more leisure because of lower take-home wage rates), and individuals work for a variety of other rewards—power, prestige, promotions, satisfactions.[19]

Liberals note that the argument that high tax rates reduce productivity is related to another popular conservative theme: equality in incomes reduces efficiency. But a comparative analysis of the major industrial nations reveals there is no relationship between a nation's degree of income equality and its economic performance.[20] Japan, for example, has the most equal distribution of income and the best economic performance record, while the United States has the most unequal distribution of income and one of the worst records of economic performance.

Liberals also dispute another major supply-side argument: high taxes and excessive regulation have created a shortage of investment capital, restricting investment and productivity growth. Economist George Eckstein, for example, notes:

> [T]here is at present an overall surplus and not a lack of production capacity. Throughout 1980, industrial capacity has moved along a recession level, from 70 percent to 78 percent, well below the 90 percent level that is considered full capacity. Nor has there been a shortage of available investment capital, either from retained earnings or from outside sources; . . . Real fixed investment averaged about 9 percent of GNP during the 1950s, the time of our fastest economic growth, during the 1960s and early 1970s it rose to 10 percent, and to 10.5 percent in 1978.[21]

The other two major supply-side arguments are that government regulations and excessive government spending have been responsible for the nation's bout with stagflation. As noted above, liberals generally support government regulation of business to protect consumers and to promote other social goals such as job safety and environmental quality. They do not pretend that government regulations are as well designed or coordinated as they should be, but the evidence indicates that the costs imposed on businesses have not been nearly as high as conservatives claim. Last, as will be noted below, liberals reject the notion that the nation's inflation problems during the 1970s and 1980s were caused by government spending.

Liberals were particularly critical of President Reagan's economic programs in 1981 and 1982. They pointed out that in these 2 years Reagan did not actually decrease the cost of government; social welfare spending cuts were more than offset by increases in defense expenditures. Thus, in real dollars (adjusted for the rate of inflation) the cost of government increased. Yet Reagan's success in convincing Congress to cut taxes by 25 percent over a 3-year period significantly reduced the government's operating revenues. Falling back on the Laffer theory, Reagan argued that his tax cuts would so stimulate the economy that tax revenues actually would be higher than before the cuts. But by late 1982 the cuts had yet to stimulate the economic recovery that Reagan had been predicting, and federal deficits were the highest in the nation's history. Deficit projections for 1982 and 1983 were so large that Reagan supported a tax bill designed to raise about $100 billion a year. With Democratic support the bill passed Congress. Liberals labeled the Reagan tax hike an admission that his original tax cut had been too large.

Liberals generally argue that tax cuts cannot adequately stimulate productive investment.[22] Given the nation's tax code, there is no reason to believe that the rich will invest their tax savings in the productive sectors of the economy. The rich may use tax savings to invest in real estate and shopping centers rather than steel mills, auto production, energy, or technology. Worse yet, they might invest in short-term speculative ventures such as gems, gold, art, and rare wines. Or, if interest rates are high, they might simply put the money in super-safe government Treasury bills and reap high returns. Liberals would like to see the tax code changed to encourage investments in the productive sectors of the economy (by providing lower rates of taxation for "beneficial" investments and higher rates for speculative ones). But since this has not been done, there is no reason to believe that tax savings will be invested in ways that aid the economy. Secondly, the nation's high interest rates clearly conflict with Reaganomics. Reagan's tax cut was designed to stimulate investment, but the nation's high interest rates discourage investment.

During much of 1981 and 1982 Reagan seemed ambivalent about whether he should endorse high interest rates or blame them for the nation's continued economic problems. Liberals believed that the nation's high interest rates clearly had made Reaganomics contradictory. The contradiction arose from the conflicts between the supply siders and monetarists within the Reagan administration. Reagan represented the supply-side school, while many of his closest aides and the members of the Federal Reserve Board were monetarists. In fact, within the Reagan administration there were more monetarists than supply siders. Since the monetarists believe that the high deficits in 1981 and 1982 were inflationary, they supported high interest rates. They felt that President Reagan should have supported cuts in defense expenditures and even higher taxes to generate more revenues to reduce deficits.

Liberals also have fundamental problems with the monetarist approach. A basic difference is that liberals believe in using strategies to manipulate the money supply, but not exclusively to limit the size of government. And, of course, liberals believe that regulating the money supply should be part of a larger strategy, not an independent economic strategy. Liberals also express four specific disagreements with monetarism. First, because money takes so many forms it is difficult and perhaps impossible to efficiently control the money supply. Money can be currency, bank deposits, and lines of credit to name a few. Second, monetarism discriminates in favor of strong corporations that earn a high rate of profit and therefore can generate their own capital. Industries that must rely on low-cost money, such as the housing and auto industries, are thrown into a slump by tight money policies. Third, tight money cuts down on investment spending, adversely affecting productivity. Fourth, high interest rates actually fuel inflation. Liberals argue that higher interest rates may dampen consumer spending, but once people get used to the higher rates or are desperate for certain products such as cars, they often accept some of the higher costs. The result is that high interest rates include an inflationary cost, which both contributes to inflation and often stimulates further increases in interest rates. Charles Andrain makes this point:

> In all countries except Sweden, interest rates have successfully increased during each five-year period from 1960 through 1974; yet inflation has become more acute. Why? Rising interest rates probably constituted both a response to inflationary pressures generated from other sources and a cause of the continuing inflation. As inflation grew worse, interest rates tended to rise. Instead of restricting total spending and causing a drop in prices, interest rates raised costs incurred by consumers, business firms, and local governments. As the price of borrowing money escalated, the increased business costs of securing a loan became expressed in higher prices for the consumer. Higher interest rates thus pushed up costs more than they restrained demand.[23]

LIBERAL EXPLANATIONS

A fundamental difference between conservative and liberal explanations for the nation's economic problems can be clarified by contrasting the differences between demand-pull and cost-profit–push explanations of inflation. Conservatives tend to believe that inflation is caused by too much money chasing too few consumer goods. This is a demand-pull explanation of inflation. Monetarists believe that consumers end up with too much money because the government prints too much money. Fiscal conservatives believe that government spending overstimulates the economy and that labor unions inflate worker salaries, giving them too much money to spend. Supply siders believe that high taxes reduce productivity, thus creating shortages of goods that consumers are anxious to buy.

In all three cases, conservatives contend that consumers buy so many goods and services that they create shortages, driving up prices. The demand-pull explanations assume that the nation's economy is fully competitive and that supply and demand largely determine the price of goods. In its classic form, the explanation is based on four assumptions:

> (1) Each firm controls only a small part of the market; (2) A business enterprise has complete freedom to move to areas of the market where demand for a product is high and supplies of that good are low; (3) Each product, like a car or television set, produced by different firms has a similar design and style; consumers purchase solely because of price considerations; (4) Prices respond to changes in demand and quantities of the good supplied. When demand for the product declines, the firm lowers both wages and prices.[24]

By contrast, the liberal position is that inflation is best explained by a cost-profit–push explanation. This explanation assumes that all western industrial nations have markets in which price increases are essentially the result of imperfect competition. These market imperfections result from (1) the dominance of many product markets by a few large firms, (2) the ability of large, powerful firms to restrict new company entry into their field, (3) the role that style and design features play in determining consumer purchases, and (4) the ability of certain institutions (such as governments and labor unions) to increase business costs. As business costs increase, prices increase to reflect changes in costs rather than simply changes in demand.

Since business costs are pushed up continuously, a reduction in consumer demand may result in a production cutback rather than a reduction in prices. In market areas dominated by a few firms, a reduction in demand may result in a price increase. The increase reflects the company's determination to maintain profits by making a larger profit on each unit sold. Andrain summarizes these arguments:

> Unlike the demand-pull approach to inflation, the cost-push explanation assumes that prices do not necessarily fall when demand remains constant or declines. Rather, powerful institutions, such as concentrated industries, labor unions, and government agencies, create market imperfections and thereby push up prices. Large corporations administer prices that do not respond to changes in aggregate

demand. Rather than stemming primarily from excess total demand, increased prices reflect the higher costs of supplies, including labor, raw materials, capital, interest rates and taxes. The desire to maximize long-range profits encourages corporations to fix their prices at a certain level above these costs. When fully competitive markets do not operate, inflation partly represents a profit-push phenomenon.[25]

Liberals believe there is abundant evidence to support the argument that institutions persistently push up business costs and that businesses pass these costs along to consumers. For example, they believe that government policies play a large role in increasing business costs because throughout our history businesses and other groups successfully have lobbied the government to protect them from the rigors of the market. One result has been laws providing protective business regulations, tariffs, subsidies, welfare benefits, unemployment compensation, and hundreds, even thousands, of other protections and services to shield specific groups from the rigors and insecurities of the market.

Because of all these policies, liberals believe that the economy has been significantly changed. If the free market ever existed in the United States (and they doubt that it ever did), it certainly no longer does. All these protective measures (whether aimed at businessmen, employees, retirees, or the unemployed and ill) have changed the economy in a way that contributes to price increases. Thus, analysts on the left say that the nation's efforts to create a more humane and stable economy increasingly have built inflation into the system. It is naive to believe that the nation will ever repeal all the support systems. Therefore, dealing with our economic problems involves recognizing that the free market has been shackled in many important ways.

Liberals offer various kinds of evidence to back up their beliefs. For example, they note that since 1967 the economy has suffered from sluggish growth and slack demand, yet during this period prices increased over 100 percent. Unemployment was very high during the 1970s, especially during the second half of the decade, and excess productive capacity was in the 20 percent range. Yet prices continued to increase. The combination of excess supply, decreasing product demand, and rising prices is impossible in a competitive market because excess supply indicates falling prices.

Liberals also point out that the extent to which the economy is dominated by a few giant corporations is widely documented. For example, studies in early 1970 showed that the nation's 100 largest corporations controlled 52 percent of all industrial assets in the nation.[26] During the 1970s there were over 200,000 manufacturing corporations in the United States but 100 of them received almost 60 percent of all after-tax profits. In the mid-1970s the 500 largest corporations employed 75 percent of the industrial work force, received 72 percent of all profits, and made 66 percent of the sales of all U.S. industrial firms.[27]

The result of this economic concentration in U.S. markets is a condition economists call oligopoly—a shared monopoly. Economists define a market as being oligopolistic when four or fewer firms control 50 percent or more of all the sales in a given product line. Because of great increases in economic concentration, oligopoly characterizes much of the U.S. market. In a 1972 study a federal agency attempted to determine the proportion of the market characterized by oligopoly. After dividing all products into 422 categories, it was discovered that 110 were oligopolistic by margins of 50 to 97 percent. Divided by sales, 64 percent of the market was oligopolist.[28] The product lines found to be oligopolistic included numerous areas of the food, motor vehicles, computers, industrial chemicals, telephone equipment, and glass and gypsum products industries.

In separate studies economists John Blair and Gardiner Means found that oligopolistic industries are much less responsive to market forces than are competitive industries. Studying 32 product lines, Blair found that competitive industries reduced prices when demand decreased, while oligopolistic industries reacted by raising prices.[29] Means found that even some competitive industries increased prices as demand decreased, but oligopolistic industries increased their prices much more.[30] The ability of oligopolistic industries to target prices also gives them higher profits. Economist Howard Sherman found that the profit rates of competitive corporations during the 1960s was about 13 percent, compared to 20 percent for oligopolistic industries.[31]

In summary, liberals believe that a primary cause of inflation is imperfect market competition. Competition is distorted by government programs which impose costs on businesses—e.g., consumer protection policies and social welfare programs—and pro-business protective regulations. Liberals believe that the consumer protection and social welfare laws are necessary and humane, but they feel that these laws impose costs on businesses which are passed on to buyers. Pro-business regulations, such as licenses for truckers and peanut growers or subsidies for dairy farmers, distort the market by eliminating competition and by subsidizing inefficient and even unnecessary producers. Labor unions also force businesses to pay higher labor costs, and these costs are passed on to buyers. Oligopoly imposes direct market distortions by limiting competition.

Unemployment

Liberals also believe that unemployment is a significant cause of the nation's economic problems because it contributes to both stagnation and inflation. They see unemployment contributing to inflation because, while the unemployed do not pay taxes or contribute to the GNP, they do often receive services such as unemployment compensation, food stamps, or other welfare benefits. Numerous studies indicate that every 1 percent of unemployment above the 4 percent level costs the nation between $16 and $26 billion a year.[32] Therefore, a 10 percent rate of unemployment would cost between $96 and $150 billion a year. This is a staggering cost for the nation, and liberals believe it contributes greatly to inflation. Liberals note that if the unemployment rate had averaged 2 percent throughout the 1970s, the nation would never have had a deficit during the entire period. This evidence suggests to liberals that in the 1970s federal deficits were caused primarily by unemployment, not by excessive government spending.

Liberals believe that unemployment contributes to stagflation not only because of the costs it imposes, but also because it lowers the purchasing power of the public. The economy has been in trouble not because the public has been purchasing too much, but, in fact, because they have had too few funds to purchase cars, houses, and other consumer goods. High interest rates, declines in real purchasing power, and high rates of unemployment and subemployment have left the public with a greatly decreased capacity to buy the goods and services produced by industry. As evidence liberals note that the nation's industries have been performing far below capacity.

The Conservative Critique of Liberal Explanations

As might be expected, the various conservative schools react somewhat differently to the arguments made by liberals. There is, however, a core of agreement. Most conservatives agree that the government has passed many policies that impose costs on business, but they reject the assertion that these costs are passed on to consumers rather than absorbed. Conservatives also believe that most laws designed to assist businesses are necessary and beneficial to the economy. However, this is not always true. Some point out that business lobbies (such as dairy farmers, defense contractors, and energy producers) often have promoted legislation that unfairly and unwisely protects them from competition or provides them with unjustified subsidies and profits. In addition, conservatives agree that certain industries should be deregulated to increase competition and reduce prices. Thus, while conservatives generally defend those programs passed by Congress to assist business, they acknowledge that certain laws should be repealed or substantially amended.

Conservatives feel quite differently about the nation's social welfare programs. They believe that the nation's network of social welfare programs is excessive, wasteful, a financial burden for industry, and a disincentive to employment and thrift. While few conservatives would agree to completely dismantle the social welfare programs, most would favor substantially reducing their coverage and costs.

As noted above, most conservatives argue that inflation is caused by consumers buying too many goods and services, not by cost-profit–push. Many agree that government and labor unions increase business costs but believe that businesses must absorb all or most of these increases rather than pass them on to consumers. When businesses absorb the costs, their productivity is reduced, thereby creating shortages of goods and services. These shortages, conservatives argue, contribute to inflation.

Conservatives differ significantly in how they react to the argument that oligopoly contributes to the nation's economic problems. Some simply deny that any small group of businesses can so thoroughly dominate a market that they can ignore the laws of supply and demand. Others, including Milton Friedman, agree that a few firms do dominate critical markets and that the impact is unhealthy. Friedman's position is that increasing international competition will correct this problem over the next decade. The government, Friedman says, should take steps to increase international and national competition (such as abolishing all protective tariffs), but it should not use the antitrust laws to break up concentrated industries.[33]

Most conservatives concede that unemployment imposes significant costs upon the nation. During 1981 and 1982 President Reagan often argued that every 1 percent of unemployment cost the nation $25 billion a year. The difference between liberals and conservatives on this point involves the actions each group would support to lower the unemployment rate, the level of unemployment each believes is tolerable, and the relative seriousness each attributes to unemployment as a social and economic problem. Typically, conservatives believe inflation is a more serious problem than unemployment and that efforts to reduce unemployment must not increase inflation. Most conservatives see the traditional liberal policies designed to stimulate employment as inflationary. For example, they reject the typical Keynesian approach of increasing government spending to stimulate the economy when unemployment is high. Such actions impose costs on business, increase the federal budget, and are inflationary. Public employment programs are rejected for two reasons. First, social problems should be solved by an expanding economy, not government intervention. Second, government programs impose a drag on the economy.

Conservatives also believe that full employment is inflationary. When unemployment is low, workers have enough money to put serious pressure on the supply of consumer goods, thereby driving up prices. Unemployment in this view is simply one of the prices the nation must pay to keep prices down and to discipline labor. Labor unions are much less likely to fight for wage increases when unemployment is high, and, as in 1982, labor unions are inclined to make concessions to management when unemployment is high. Thus, conservatives generally argue that full employment should be defined as 6 to 7 percent unemployment, while liberals believe that full employment should be defined as 2 to 3 percent unemployment. As far as actions to increase employment, most conservatives believe that economic policies that create a more positive and supportive atmosphere for business will lead to improvements in the economy and reductions in unemployment.

In summary, liberals blame the nation's recent economic problems on high rates of unemployment, public policies and institutions (e.g., governments and labor unions) that increase business costs, and oligopolistic markets that stifle competition and thereby increase product costs. Liberals support labor unions, although they may disagree with specific labor demands and practices, and they support many of the social programs that they believe raise business costs. Liberals argue that economic reforms must compensate for the impact of labor unions and social welfare programs without destroying them. Liberals believe that some of the government regulations designed to protect business from competition are excessive and counterproductive and should be repealed.

Conservatives believe that the nation's recent economic problems have been caused by too much competition for too few consumer goods. Monetarists believe that the public has too much money because the government has overexpanded the money supply. Fiscal conservatives believe that Keynesian spending policies have overstimulated the economy, putting too much money into consumers' pockets. Supply siders believe that high taxes reduce productivity, creating shortages of goods and services, thereby fueling inflation.

ECONOMIC SOLUTIONS THAT BOTH CONSERVATIVES AND LIBERALS SUPPORT IN PRINCIPLE

Having examined and critiqued liberal and conservative explanations of the nation's economic problems, we can turn now to some solutions. We begin with a number of reforms that both conservatives and liberals support, although they differ over specifics. There are at least four general reforms that can be discussed here.

Increase Public Savings

Both conservatives and liberals believe that the government should encourage the public to save more. The conservative view is that the most efficient method of encouraging saving is to reduce the tax burden on upper-income groups. Liberals are more concerned with measures that would encourage middle- and lower-income groups to save. Liberals maintain that a certain amount of the interest earned on savings accounts should be tax exempt. This exemption could be designed to allow savings to grow at least as fast as the nation's rate of inflation. Another frequently discussed liberal reform would place a ceiling on the amount of interest costs that a taxpayer could use as a tax deduction. Some argue that allowing consumers to deduct all interest costs on homes and consumer goods only encourages them to buy. A ceiling in the range of $1,500, liberals argue, would allow consumers to make necessary purchases without encouraging unnecessary consumption.

Support R&D

Both conservatives and liberals favor government support for industrial research and development costs. The federal government already conducts a great deal of research which it turns over to industry, and it funds much of the nation's industrial research activity. It is often pointed out that in many competing nations, especially Japan and France, the government plays a much larger role in this area than it does in the United States. Many have speculated that the U.S. government's more modest role often puts U.S. industry at a competitive disadvantage, especially in international markets. Conservatives believe that the government should fund a larger percentage of R&D expenses, while liberals favor a larger government role in economic planning.

Increase the Efficiency and Productivity of Government

Analysts on both the left and the right acknowledge that the government should increase the efficiency and productivity of government. Conservatives tend to believe that government can be made more efficient by reducing its size. Liberals are more inclined to believe that planning should be used to coordinate government policies. Planning will be discussed in more detail below.

Resurrect the RFC

As the economy faltered in the 1970s and 1980s many economic analysts on both the left and the right began to suggest that the government assume a larger role in revitalizing the economy. A frequent suggestion from both sides was that the government resurrect a version of the New Deal Reconstruction Finance Corporation (RFC). The RFC provided equity capital and management assistance to industries during the great depression to help them get back on their feet. Analysts argue that a new RFC could provide select industries with equity capital, special tax breaks, management, and technological aid while helping industries obtain land, permits, and other resources. Liberal economist Lester Thurow has advocated that the nation create a national investment bank (such as the one in Japan) to work in coordination with the RFC.[34]

While both conservatives and liberals have been discussing this remedy in recent years, there are substantial differences between the two schools. Conservatives see the RFC as simply providing distressed industries with needed assistance, while not interfering with the company's autonomy. Liberals envision the government aiding industry and requiring a company to make management and administrative changes to help ensure that the company will be run well enough to repay the government loan. Many liberals also believe that government assistance to a corporation should result in equity shares in the firm that the government could sell on the private market once the corporation or new enterprise was on its feet. If the venture turned out to be profitable and a good revenue-generating device, the government should have the option of retaining the shares. Liberals, in other words, do not want the RFC to create a form of riskless capitalism, and they want the government to be able to profit from its efforts.

Many liberals also see the RFC proposal as a vehicle for achieving major economic reforms. For example, they believe the government should use its position within the company to stimulate reforms and market efficiencies. Thus, the RFC could play a role in developing new technology and could contribute to labor-management innovations by financing experiments in worker ownership and worker democracy. Or the RFC could be used to increase public control over (or democratize) the economy, to promote balanced regional growth, to help rejuvenate cities in the midwest and east, and even to encourage industrial competition.[35]

CONSERVATIVE SOLUTIONS

At this point it should be clear that neither conservatives nor liberals are in complete agreement about economic policies or governmental roles. Conservatives generally want the federal government to give business the assistance it needs without interfering too substantially in business activities. They want the government to keep social welfare expenditures low and to limit business regulation to the bare minimum. Because conservatives want the government to play a supportive but modest role in society, they do not have a long list of reforms they would like to see implemented.

The supply siders and the monetarists do, however, have specific policies they believe the government should adopt. Under the Reagan administration the supply-side economists have implemented many of the policies that they believe will improve the economy. They convinced Congress to substantially cut taxes, to reduce social welfare expenditures, and to cut back on many government regulations. They would like to see social welfare expenditures and government regulations reduced even more. As noted above, they have been ambivalent about the Federal Reserve's high interest rates. The high rates clearly have been the primary cause of the recession the nation has suffered since 1981. The recession in turn brought the inflation rate down. Through 1982 Reagan and his supply-side supporters were expressing pleasure that the high interest rates had brought down inflation, but they were beginning to show concern that the high interest rates were also holding back recovery. Many economists were predicting that the Reagan administration would be forced to convince the Federal Reserve to bring the interest rates down, or the economy would not recover. By the spring of 1983 the Federal Reserve had reduced interest rates, producing some modest signs of recovery.

By the spring of 1982 many conservatives who did not agree with the supply-side approach, and conservatives who believed that the Reagan policies had been excessive, were pressuring President Reagan to cut back on defense spending and increase taxes in order to reduce deficits. These conservatives argued that large deficits are inflationary because they force the government to either increase the money supply or borrow money in the private sector. The first option increases the amount of dollars that can be used to purchase goods (a condition that causes price increases), while the second increases the demand for private sector funds. When the government finances its debt by borrowing in the private sector it creates such a high demand for funds that interest rates are forced up. High interest rates in turn push up the nation's rate of inflation. Reagan's tax bill in 1982 was a partial concession to these critics.

The monetarists within the Reagan administration, including Chairman Volker of the Federal Reserve, had been insistent that interest rates could be lowered only when government spending was reduced and new tax revenues were generated. These conservatives pressured President Reagan to support a windfall tax on deregulated natural gas, or new taxes on such commodity items as alcoholic beverages and tobacco products, in order to raise government revenues. Reagan opted for the latter option, and, in response, the Federal Reserve lowered interest rates. Nevertheless, spring 1983 real interest rates were still, by historical standards, quite high.

LIBERAL SOLUTIONS

Like conservatives, liberals vary considerably in the economic policies they support. But unlike conservatives, they generally do not have much faith in unregulated markets. The economy functions better, they say, and is more attuned to the public's needs when it is guided by the government.

This difference leads liberals to support quite a range of specific economic policies. Below we will discuss five major proposals that liberal groups tend to support. Many of these proposals are drawn from the experiences of the other major western industrial nations.

Planning

Most of the Western European nations and Japan use economic planning as a method of improving both the general performance of their economies and the chances of meeting specific goals in such fields as housing and urban and rural development.[36] Planning is not a simple concept because there are numerous versions of planning, and each of the Western European nations has used it in different ways and with varying degrees of success. In a few nations, such as France, Sweden, and Japan, liberals would argue that planning has often been successful, at least in terms of specific objectives. However, most would admit that in such nations as Britain, planning has not been very successful.

At least four types of planning have been used by the Western European nations. The primary form of planning has been called educative or intellectual planning. Cohen explains this type:

> Educative planning consists of two simultaneous and interrelated processes. The first is analogous to an adult-education program designed to introduce top-level businessmen and ranking civil servants to modern managerial methods and attitudes: planning becomes a series of forums for the study of production techniques, industrial organization, government policies, foreign competition and similar concerns of progressive management. The second type of educative process, "indicative planning," transforms planning into a giant, cooperative market-research project: representatives of the major economic groups participate in the preparation of an input-output table for the principal sections of the economy. Both forms of educative planning depend upon one precondition: enlightened self-interest.[37]

Educative planning does not involve or depend upon any type of government coercion. Business and economic officials in and out of government rely on the information provided by planning to guide investment decisions only if they believe it is accurate and superior to their own research. Some governments, however, have used incentives to encourage businesses to rely on the plan. For example, the government may offer certain businesses tax incentives to modernize, expand, or move into a new product field. Incentives can be lucrative and often have served as a genuine enticement for industry cooperation. Tariff laws, state loans, and government contracts have also often been used as incentives.

Like many nations, France has used educative planning. Because the French government owns such a large proportion of the nation's industrial and financial institutions, a second form of planning has also been possible in France. In some instances the French Commissariat du Plan has used its influence over the public sector to guide the private sector toward goals established by the government. This is a form of planning that is possible, of course, only in a nation that has nationalized a significant proportion of the economy.

A third type of planning is cooperative management. Here the government brings the nation's major interest groups together and encourages them to develop cooperative agreements which will facilitate the accomplishment of economic goals established by the government. For example, in Sweden the government prompts meetings between industrialists, financiers, trade unions, and government departments to conclude a series of bargains about their future behavior.

The last type of planning involves the public sector in setting long-term plans for specific policy areas. For example, Sweden has used long-term planning to project the nation's housing goals. The plan includes coordinating government policies and developing strategies and incentives to encourage private sector cooperation in meeting those goals. In Sweden, for example, the government has used its taxing, licensing, and financing powers to guide the nation toward its housing goals.

Most of the Western European nations have attempted to use the first and last types of planning. France also has used the second type. The third type of planning has been attempted by several nations, most prominently by Sweden.

Liberals admit that planning has never been a panacea in any nation. The extent of its success is seriously debated. They recognize that when it has been successful, that success has been limited to certain time periods, types of plans, and specific nations. As the nations of Western Europe struggled to rebuild after World War II, educative planning helped public and private officials to make better decisions and eliminate production bottlenecks and other economic imbalances. Planning was used also to guide government subsidies and assistance to promote reindustrialization. Economists, such as Shonfield, writing about planning from the end of World War II to 1960, drew a fairly positive picture of the impact of planning and its potential.[38] But even Shonfield found that planning worked better in some nations than in others, even during a time in which events tended to stimulate a more united attack on economic problems. Great Britain, with an antistate tradition, used planning much less effectively than France, with its strong state tradition.

Since the 1960s planning has been used primarily to aid business and to improve general economic performance. Watson concludes that successful planning has been used "to complement business behaviour in tackling imbalances and obstacles threatening industrial expansion and profitability, implying a degree of collaboration, if not always complete agreement, with the private sector."[39] Liberals, like Watson, feel that in a mixed economy—one in which the government plays a significant role but investment decisions are still the preserve of private interests—planning is realistically limited to being a tool by which the private economic sector is given government assistance, subsidy, and guidance, or by which government policies are coordinated. Like most liberals, Watson believes that planning has been a success in helping these nations achieve limited but important goals.

Liberals see a limited but positive role for planning in the United States. They note that educative planning, which involves no government coercion, would probably be acceptable and beneficial if business became convinced of the quality of the information the government generated. At the very least planning might improve the economic performance of the nation. The government might also use planning to develop modest long-range plans for specific policy areas such as housing, health care, and urban policies. Along these lines Levinson has advocated that planning be used to coordinate federal programs, especially those concerned with regulation, taxes, credits, and subsidies. Levinson recommends

> a shift in emphasis from reliance on fiscal and monetary policies as the central tool of . . . policy to a broader approach based on coordinating all major forms of government intervention. Such an overall approach would establish a basic framework of social goals for the nation and the specific regulatory, tax and credit policies (as well as the detailed manpower and structural measures for particular industries and areas) needed to achieve them.[40]

Economist Lester Thurow goes a step further.

> We do not need central economic planning in the sense of an agency that tries to make all economic decisions, but we do need the national equivalent of a corporate investment committee to redirect investment flows from our "sunset" industries to our "sunrise" industries.[41]

Thurow also argues for a national investment bank that would work through private banks, much like the Bank of Japan. Thurow's intent is for this bank to provide business with financial, management, and planning advice in a noncompetitive and nonadversary fashion.[42]

Public Enterprise

In Western Europe public ownership of business is often used as a technique to improve the economy, to provide public services, and to increase public control over investments.[43] For the most part, public ownership did not result from ideological design, but rather as a result of war, economic depression, and general business failure. The government moved into the economy when it faltered or failed and stayed involved once the crisis was over. While some nationalization is common to all European nations, the most nationalized economies are those of France and Italy.

The French and Italians also have used public enterprise for the broadest range of purposes. Both have used it to aid in regional development. Italy has helped develop its south, and France has been concerned with the revitalization of its rural areas. Both have used public enterprise to stimulate exports, develop domestic markets where imports are considered to be too large, save companies threatened by multinational takeovers, promote advanced technology, restructure industry, increase investment, and stimulate growth. All the European nations have used public ownership to save critical industries that have failed in the private market. Great Britain especially has used public ownership to save steel, auto, aviation, gas, coal, rail, and electricity industries. Last, all the European nations have used public ownership to produce energy. In Europe it is quite common for oil, gas, coal, and electricity corporations to be publicly owned.

Liberals do not advocate that the U.S. government nationalize large sectors of the economy. Most believe that nationalization of industry would be both controversial and unnecessary. Rather than nationalization, they support more public control over major industrial investment decisions. For example, Congress might direct the oil industry to devote a certain percentage of its investment toward the development of solar energy. The energy field has been a primary concern of liberals because they have expressed doubt that the private energy sector's orientation is in the best interests of the nation. They believe that the private energy sector is concerned primarily with maximizing short-term profits, which lie in the field of petroleum. A sound energy policy requires a reorientation toward alternative energy sources. They do not believe that the energy industry will refocus without government intervention.

Some liberals believe that an alternative to public control of investment decisions would be for the government to establish a competing public corporation. For example, the government might redirect the energy market by establishing a Public Energy Corporation to compete with the private oil sector. As envisioned by liberals, this corporation would develop coal for both domestic and export sale, labor-intensive solar energy for both domestic use and in third world countries, and synthetic fuels. This corporation also could engage in energy exploration (especially on public lands), gas and oil production, and retail markets.

A Social Contract

Liberals contend that the economic performance of many nations, including the United States, suffers because of poor labor-management relations. In its most severe forms poor labor-management relations are marked by chronic strikes, worker slowdowns and other forms of employee recalcitrance, and, on the part of business, attacks on existing or potential worker organizations and unions. The United States, Great Britain, and France have long suffered labor strife, while in Sweden, Norway, the Netherlands, West Germany, and Japan labor-management relations in recent periods have been quite productive.

Some of the nations with positive labor-management relations have achieved this goal through social contracts between workers and industry. The two best examples are Sweden and West Germany. In both nations the work force is highly unionized, and workers use their power to negotiate contracts with industry. For example, in Sweden almost all the work force is unionized, and the Social Democrats (or Labor party) have been the ruling party in the government almost consistently since the 1930s. To avoid labor strife and the economic disruptions it causes, the Social Democrats negotiated a contract between labor and management. This contract established the principle that all workers have a right to a decent income, a fair share of company profits, and a dignified and safe working environment. In return labor agreed that it owed management loyalty and good service. Both agreed that, in discussions about wages and productivity, the good of employees, management, and the overall health and prosperity of the nation should be kept in mind. In a unique system the Swedish Employers Association (SAF) and the Swedish Labor Union Confederation (LO) meet once a year to hammer out wage increases. While there have been disagreements, all agree that this unique arrangement has worked quite well.[44]

The West Germans rely upon a similar arrangement. The nation's well-organized and militant unions have used their power to negotiate wage and profit agreements with industry that set wages at a rate agreeable to both workers and management. In 1951 the trade unions won passage of a law which requires that one-third of the members of the board of directors of large firms be employee representatives. Since 1951 this rule has been extended to many other corporations, often as a result of trade union bargaining.

The liberals contend that labor-management relations in the United States are less positive than they should be. Business resistance to unionization is still very intense, often creating a combative and noncooperative relationship between workers and management. Resistance has also resulted in a very low unionization rate. Only about 20 percent of the U.S. work force belongs to a union—the lowest rate among the major western industrialized nations. The tense relationship between business and workers often results in a rigid, unimaginative, top-down management and a work force that ranges from being mildly antagonistic to outright recalcitrant. Workers often show little loyalty or affection for companies they believe give them as little compensation, personal credit, and autonomy as possible. Management often responds by trying harder to regiment and supervise employees in hope of increasing or maintaining productivity by tight control. The negative nature of the relationship, liberals believe, only produces less cooperation and certainly stifles worker imagination.

Both business and labor would benefit, say the left, from a more creative, positive, and just relationship. A social contract could establish the right of workers to a fair wage, negotiate a wage rate for employees that fairly represented their skills, efforts, and contributions, while protecting business from unfair labor demands or wage rates that fuel inflation. Part of such an agreement should include labor representation on corporate boards and a more democratic work environment designed to stimulate worker growth, creativity, loyalty, and productivity.

Full Employment

In addition, liberals believe, the government should take the steps necessary to achieve and maintain full employment. The European nations tend to have less unemployment than the United States because they take specific actions to maintain high rates of employment. Andrain examines these policies:

> First, European governments took more active steps to establish flexible labor markets. Compared with North Americans, Europeans participated in more extensive job retraining programs, enjoyed greater opportunities for geographic mobility, and gained more information about available jobs. Second, until the 1974–75 recession occurred, European government leaders concentrated on expanding aggregate demand. Government expenditures as proportions of the GNP were higher in Europe than in the United States and Canada. European public officials stressed spending for both capital investment and for labor-intensive programs that created new jobs and maintained jobs held by employed workers. In contrast, U.S. officials emphasized tax reductions as the most appropriate technique for expanding total demand. Yet, cross-nationally, low taxes had less effect on reducing the jobless rate than did high government expenditures.[45]

Economist Lester Thurow has argued that the government should go beyond fiscal and job training programs to achieve full employment. Thurow proposes that the federal government establish a government corporation to employ the five to eight million persons who cannot find viable employment in the private market.[46] This corporation would build urban transportation systems, help rebuild the nation's decaying inner cities, build parks, and carry out other genuinely needed programs. Thurow proposes that the government provide a wide range of job and pay scales, from entry-level, unskilled workers at or near the minimum wage, to higher-paid skilled and professional employees. Thurow also recommends that the program be a permanent feature of the economy since unemployment is not, and perhaps never will be, a temporary problem in the United States.

Liberals reject the conservative argument that full employment is inherently inflationary. Levinson, for example, presents the liberal position on this point:

> [T]he notion that full employment will inevitably result in inflation is without foundation. There is a clear trade-off between unemployment and inflation when fiscal and monetary adjustments are the only policies employed, but not with regard to more focused policies. Manpower and regional policies, for example, are, in principle, anti-inflationary since they improve the "fit" between available workers and jobs. Focused policies to direct investment into areas where shortages exist also reduce price pressures, as do policies to stabilize private investment over the business cycle. (The latter policies serve to reduce "overheating" of the economy during expansion just as much as to reduce layoffs during downturns.) Finally, a broader role for trade unions improves the chances of achieving agreements that could limit the wage-price spiral. In short, there is in principle no reason why a mix of policies cannot be designed to reduce inflation as well as employment.[47]

Increasing Collective Savings

As noted above, it is a central belief of conservatives that as the size of government grows the tax rate becomes so high that too little money is left in the private economy to finance business expansion. This belief is central to supply-side economics, which argues that to make certain that there will be money to finance economic growth the tax rate on corporations and higher income citizens must be kept low. To liberals the evidence indicates that the size of the U.S. public sector is not yet having a negative impact on capital formation, and this was true before Reagan's tax and budget cuts.[48] But, as the public sector grows in the United States, it will be necessary for the government to assure the availability of adequate capital and encourage productive investment habits by private citizens. The experiences of the Western European nations suggest actions that can be taken to promote these goals. Some of the methods by which liberals believe that savings could be encouraged were discussed above. Additionally, they favor governmental action to encourage collective savings, such as worker funds or public funds raised through taxation.[49]

Collective savings are preferred over tax policies that allow a small percentage of the total population to become very rich. Liberals note that there are a number of collective ways in which capital can be accumulated for investment. One obvious way would be for the government to set aside tax revenues for investment. In Sweden, for example, the government uses the tax structure to raise funds that are then used to help finance certain areas of the economy. This technique forces saving on the public while allowing the government to pursue planned economic goals.

Liberals note that some nations are debating innovative policies to develop capital collectively. For example, in Sweden and the Netherlands there are proposals to transfer some proportion of corporate profits (about 20 percent) to regional or national funds owned by workers.[50] The funds would be managed by a board composed of representatives of industry, the government, and workers. Over a period of time the funds would become large enough to make the workers the dominant shareholders of Swedish industry, even though the industries would still be private. The funds accumulated would provide the capital for economic expansion and would be invested in those industries that would provide jobs while keeping the nation competitive in international markets.

The plan, which has stirred controversy in Sweden, would certainly be controversial in the United States. In Sweden it is quite likely that some version of the proposal will be adopted in the near future. Liberals do not expect a similar proposal to be acceptable in the United States for some time, but they do note that the proposal provides a viable alternative to enhancement of the rich as a method of developing capital. If a collective means of saving is used, the government would have a much better chance of using planning to influence the allocation of capital.

CONCLUSIONS

This chapter has analyzed differences between conservative and liberal economic approaches and policies. While both conservatives and liberals agree that the U.S. economy has not performed well over the last 10 or so years, they differ significantly over the causes and cures for the economy's maladies. The biggest difference between the two should be quite obvious. Conservatives believe in the efficacy of the economic market. They believe that government should play a modest role in the economy, and that if it does so, the market will function well enough to take care of most of the nation's social and economic problems.

Liberals are skeptical about the efficacy of the market. They believe that without government intervention the economy suffers drastic cycles of prosperity and bust, and that even during the best of times capitalism overcompensates a small percentage of the population (owners and managers) while inadequately compensating others. If business is not carefully monitored, it will pollute the environment, neglect the health and safety of its workers, and sell dangerous and deficient products. Liberals may worry about how to keep the government lean, efficient, and responsive to the public, but they believe in a collective approach to solving social problems.

It should be obvious from the above analysis that the differences between conservatives and liberals are a matter of degree. While each group has its extremes, both conservatives and liberals accept the need for a government that plays a large and important role in society. Most conservatives are reconciled to an important role for the government in the management and subsidy of the economy. As noted in Chapter 2, conservatives also support social welfare programs, but they generally believe that these programs should be more modest than liberals would like to see.

But, while the essential differences between liberals and conservatives are ones of degree, the differences are substantial. Liberals are concerned with the promotion of a more egalitarian society in which the public would control the economy. Conservatives promote a society that allows for inequality based on merit, with government providing a safety net that would be too modest to stifle initiative. The conservative society clearly would reflect more inequality, but conservatives believe that this inequality is both just and necessary to encourage endeavor.

While the long-term trend of all the nations in the western world is toward greater public involvement in the economy, the recent experiences in Great Britain under Margaret Thatcher, and in the United States under Ronald Reagan, suggest that the struggle between two major philosophies is far from resolved.

NOTES

1 *Business Week*, March 29, 1982, p. 66.
2 Douglas F. Dowd, *Modern Economic Problems in Historical Perspective* (Boston: D.C. Heath, 1965), p. 143.
3 Charles F. Andrain, *Politics and Economic Policy in Western Democracies* (North Scituate, Mass.: Duxbury Press, 1980), p. 30.
4 New York Stock Exchange, *U.S. Economic Performance in a Global Perspective* (New York: Office of Economic Research, 1981), p. 10.
5 Lester C. Thurow, *The Zero-Sum Society* (New York: Basic Books, Inc., 1980), p. 76.
6 Ibid., p. 86.
7 *The American Economy: Employment, Productivity, and Inflation in the Eighties* (Washington, D.C.: GPO, 1980), p. 32.
8 Ibid., p. 86.
9 Thurow, p. 41.
10 New York Stock Exchange, *U.S. Economic Performance in a Global Perspective*, p. 27.
11 See George Gilder, *Wealth and Poverty* (New York: Bantam Books, 1981); Milton Friedman and Rose Friedman, *Free to Choose: A Personal Statement*

(New York: Avon Books, 1979); John Chamberlain, *The Roots of Capitalism* (Indianapolis: Liberty Press, 1976); P. T. Bauer, *Equality, The Third World, and Economic Delusion* (Cambridge: Harvard Univ. Press, 1981).

12 Gilder, p. 224.

13 Arthur Laffer, "An Equilibrium Rational Economic Framework," in *Economic Issues of the Eighties,* eds. Nake M. Kamarany and Richard H. Day (New York: Longman, 1980).

14 Friedman and Friedman, p. 243.

15 Ibid., p. 251.

16 Ibid., p. 226.

17 Thurow, p. 8.

18 U.S. Bureau of the Census, *Statistical Abstract of the United States: 1980* (Washington, D.C.: GPO, 1980), p. 906.

19 Thurow, p. 168.

20 Ibid., p. 6.

21 George Eckstein, "Supply-Side Economics: Panacea or Handout for the Rich?" *Dissent* (Spring 1981), pp. 139–140.

22 Frank Ackerman, *Reaganomics: Rhetoric vs. Reality* (Boston: South End Press, 1982).

23 Andrain, p. 99.

24 Ibid., p. 88.

25 Ibid., p. 103.

26 Ralph Nader, Mark Green, and Joel Seligman, *Taming the Giant Corporation* (New York: W. W. Norton, 1976), p. 16.

27 Douglas F. Dowd, *The Twisted Dream* (Cambridge, Mass.: Winthrop Publishers, Inc., 1977), p. 70.

28 Ovid Demaris, *Dirty Business: The Corporate-Political Money-Power Game* (New York: Harper and Row, 1974), pp. 30–36.

29 John M. Blair, *Economic Concentration* (New York: Harcourt Brace Jovanovich, 1972), pp. 322–323.

30 "The New Monopolies: How they Affect Consumer Prices," *Consumer Reports,* June 1975, p. 378.

31 Howard Sherman, *Radical Political Economy* (New York: Basic Books, Inc., 1972), p. 108.

32 *U.S. Cong., House Committee on Education and Labor, Subcommittee on Equal Opportunities,* pt. 5, March 1976 (Washington, D.C.: GPO, 1976), p. 310.

33 Friedman and Friedman, pp. 231–232.

34 Thurow, pp. 96, 192.

35 Alfred J. Watkins, "Felix Rohatyn's Biggest Deal," *Working Papers* (Sept.–Oct. 1981), pp. 44–52.

36 Stephen S. Cohen, *Modern Capitalist Planning: The French Model* (Berkeley: Univ. of California Press, 1977); and Andrew Levinson, *The Full Employment Alternative* (New York: Coward, McCann, and Geoghegan, Inc., 1980), pp. 133–136.

37 Cohen, p. 3.

38 Andrew Shonfield, *Modern Capitalism: The Changing Balance of Public and Private Power* (New York: Oxford Univ. Press, 1965).

39 Michael Watson, "A Comparative Evaluation of Planning Practice in the Liberal Democratic State," in *Planning, Politics and Public Policy,* eds. Jack Hayward and Michael Watson (London: Cambridge Univ. Press, 1975), p. 447.

40 Levinson, p. 204.

41 Thurow, p. 95.

42 Ibid., p. 192.

43 William G. Shepard, *Public Enterprise: Economic Analysis in Theory and Practice* (Lexington, Mass.: Lexington Books, 1976); Richard Pryke, *Public Enterprise in Practice* (New York: St. Martin's Press, 1971); Stuart Holland, *The State as Entrepreneur* (London: Weidenfeld and Nicolson, 1972); and Martin Carnoy and Derek Shearer, *Economic Democracy* (White Plains, New York: M. E. Sharpe, 1980), pp. 60–62.

44 Norman Furniss and Timothy Tilton, *The Case for the Welfare State: From Social Security to Social Equality* (Bloomington, Indiana: Indiana Univ. Press, 1979), pp. 134–136.

45 Andrain, p. 80.

46 Thurow, pp. 204–205.

47 Levinson, p. 206.

48 David R. Cameron, "On the Limits of the Public Economy," unpublished paper presented at the Annual Meeting of the American Political Science Association, Sept. 1981, p. 5.

49 Bob Kuttner, "Growth With Equity," *Working Papers* (Sept.–Oct., 1981), p. 36.

50 Rudolf Meidner, *Employee Investment Funds: An Approach to Collective Capital Formation* (London: George Allen and Unwin, 1978); and J. C. Carrington and G. T. Edwards, *Financing Industrial Investment* (London: The Macmillan Company, 1979).

CHAPTER 6

CRIME, CRIMINAL JUSTICE, AND PUBLIC POLICY

When people in the United States discuss crime they tend to sound angry, shrill, and scared. Consider some of the following comments from political leaders and the general public:

> They [criminals] do really believe that they're better than the rest of us, that the world owes them a living, and that those of us who lead normal lives and earn an honest living are a little slow on the uptake. (Ronald Reagan in a speech to the International Association of Chiefs of Police)[1]

> We have allowed ourselves to degenerate to the point where we're living like animals. We live behind burglar bars and throw a collection of door locks at night and set an alarm and lay down with a loaded shotgun beside the bed and then try to get some rest. It's ridiculous. (B. K. Johnson, a former Houston Police Chief)[2]

> It is time for America to get mad. We need courts that work and laws that have teeth. We ought to be mad as hell and we ought not to take it any longer. . . . Let us make the punishment so severe that no one will dare to commit a crime with the use of a gun. [Congressman Gregory W. Carman (R., N.Y.)][3]

> Dear Congressman Rosenthal: I'm sick of it! Sick of the muggings, the robberies (we are one of the statistics), of the inability to wear hard-earned jewelry or carry a handbag, or go out at night alone. Sick, sick, sick of the liberal judges. . . . It's [sic] got to stop. We put a horrible, confining gate on our fire escape windows. We drilled holes in our windows near our terrace. (That's where our burglar made his 1:30 A.M. entrance while we were sleeping.) We put ourselves behind bars. Enough. [Constituent's letter to Congressman Benjamin Rosenthal (D., N.Y.)][4]

For the 574,000 people who were robbed, the more than 643,000 people who were assaulted, and the 81,500 women who were raped in 1981, enough is enough! For the 22,500 who were murdered it was obviously too much. There are few policy issues which are more fundamental to the interest of civilized society than crime and criminal justice. Unlike some of the other policy areas discussed in this book, there is no debate over whether government should or should not play an active role in this area. The protection of life, liberty, and property goes to the very definition of government itself and has been accepted by both liberals and conservatives as a requisite function of government. A government that cannot protect its members is failing to meet its most fundamental responsibility. Nevertheless, there are significant differences among people in the United States on how they feel the government can *best* achieve its primary responsibility of protecting the life, liberty, and property of its citizens. Liberals, as we shall see, define the problem of crime and, therefore, the role of government in this area more broadly than conservatives. Thus liberals believe that any effective criminal justice policy must include an assault on the underlying causes of crime—as they see them—such as unemployment, substandard housing, and racial or social class discrimination. Conservatives minimize or reject this causal explanation or approach. Conservative policy proposals tend to deal more narrowly with the manifestations of crime and how to deal with these—e.g., harsher sentences and more prisons. This, of course, suggests a more limited level of governmental activity. In this chapter then we examine the liberal-conservative dialogue over how best to deal with the "epidemic" of violence afflicting the United States.

The chapter begins with a discussion of the dimensions of crime, past and present. Are things as bad as people think? Are they, as most people apparently believe, worse now than they were in the past? And what about crime in other countries? Is the crime epidemic a worldwide phenomenon? Second, we examine the causes of crime. This discussion underscores differences in perspective between liberals and conservatives. It will also introduce the issue of what can be done to deal with crime in the United States. We will see that because liberals and conservatives disagree over what causes crime, they are led to different solutions to the problem. In turning to the critical issue of what can be done about crime, we will again look to the experiences of other countries.

DIMENSIONS OF THE PROBLEM

The year 1981 marked a rebirth of crime as a major public issue. On March 23, 1981, both *Time* ("The Curse of Violent Crime") and *Newsweek* ("The Epidemic of Violent Crime") ran cover stories on crime. In October, *U.S. News and World Report* ("Our Losing Battle Against Crime") joined the media chorus in proclaiming that crime was poisoning the very quality of life in the United States.

In the U.S. Senate conservative Senator Strom Thurmond (R., S.C.) and liberal Senator Edward Kennedy (D., Mass.) joined several of their colleagues in sponsoring a Senate resolution (No. 141) declaring that "it is the sense of the Senate that all appropriate action necessary to combat violent crime should be a national priority as well as a priority of the Senate and should receive immediate attention."[5] The preamble to the resolution expressed the mood of the time. The senators noted that "next to inflation, crime is the most important domestic problem facing the American people today."

Finally, public opinion polls indicated that whatever the reality of the situation, U.S. citizens felt that crime was bad and getting worse. A Gallup poll commissioned for the *Newsweek* story on crime found that 53 percent of the people polled nationally were afraid to walk alone in their neighborhoods at night; 58 percent believed there was more crime in their area in 1981 than in 1980; and 75 percent thought that criminals were more violent in 1981 than they were 5 years earlier.

Published reports indicated that the public's concern was justified. In September 1981 the FBI released the *Uniform Crime Report (UCR)* for 1980. The report confirmed what to most people in the United States seemed obvious—crime was up, and significantly so. The FBI's "Crime Index" of major crimes (i.e., murder, rape, robbery, aggravated assault, burglary, larceny-theft, motor vehicle theft, arson) was up 9.4 percent over 1979. Leading the increase were robbery (up 17.5 percent) and burglary (up 13.9 percent), while murder (up 7.4 percent) showed only a somewhat more modest increase. The murder rate of 10.2 per 100,000 was the highest since 1933, when the FBI began publishing the *UCR*.

How bad is crime in the United States today? Are U.S. citizens really more vulnerable today than in the past or than our contemporaries in other countries? Before we directly address these questions we must first take a slight detour into the rather uncertain world of crime statistics.

Crime Statistics

Scholarly assaults on crime statistics are almost as common as criminal assaults on innocent people.[6] While some of the concern about the validity and reliability of crime statistics is fairly esoteric and need not detain us, the issue is by no means irrelevant to an understanding of criminal justice policy. The heated demand that something must be done to stem the rising tide of crime is based upon the belief that there *is* a rising tide of crime. The basis of this belief lies in official crime statistics and especially the *UCR*.

These reports, which are the most widely used and publicized of crime data, are also the most roundly denounced. There is no need for us to deal with all the charges against and problems with the *UCR*. Certain criticisms and shortcomings of the data must be discussed, however, because they offer insights into understanding policy and policy making in this area.

The first point about official crime statistics in the *UCR* is that they reflect only a fraction—perhaps as little as one-quarter, certainly no more than one-half—of the actual crime committed in the country. Most crime in the United States is either unreported or uncounted. The reasons for this phenomenon are varied. First, the *UCR* only collects and publishes data on major or so-called "index crimes"—murder, forcible rape, burglary, robbery, aggravated assault, larceny-theft, motor vehicle theft, and, only since 1978, arson. Data on the remaining crimes (e.g., fraud, prostitution, drug offenses, embezzlement), which constitute the overwhelming majority of the crimes committed, are not included in the public reports.

Second, the majority of the crimes committed, including index crimes, are not reported to the police by the victims, although the more serious the crime the more likely it is to be reported. Why do people not report crimes? One explanation, reflecting a liberal perspective and certainly accounting for *some* of the unreported crime, is offered by former Attorney General Ramsey Clark. "Wherever crime is unreported we know the police are not effective, trusted or respected."[7] The belief that the police will not be responsive or might even be abusive leads some people not to report crime. The evidence, however, seems to suggest that this reluctance will prevail only when a second factor is present, namely, the crime is relatively unimportant—e.g., loss of property valued at under $50. Thus, Wesley Skogan found that in a survey of victims, people indicating that they had not reported a crime did so because "it wasn't worth the effort," "it was inconvenient," or "it was unimportant."[8]

A third explanation is that people are often victimized by persons they know (spouses, parents, and friends) and are thus reluctant to report crimes. A fourth explanation, which is often related to the third, is fear of reprisals, either in the form of physical reprisals or societal rejection. Studies indicate that rape victims often fear physical and social retribution.

It should be noted here that criminologists, and others who use crime data, are well aware of the problem of unreported and undocumented crime. In direct response to this problem the U.S. Bureau of the Census, under contract from the Law Enforcement Assistance Administration (LEAA), began, in 1973, to conduct an annual National Crime Survey of a scientifically selected sample of people across the country, asking them about their experiences as victims of serious crime. The surveys have consistently "revealed what many had long suspected—namely, that most crimes are never reported to the police and that the actual level of FBI index crimes was about four times the number reported by the FBI."[9] Since the victimization surveys are not without their problems—e.g., people forget details—they are generally viewed as a supplement to the *UCR* rather than a replacement of them.

There are, in summary, a variety of factors which weaken the utility of published crime statistics. The introduction of victimization surveys has improved the value of national crime data but serious problems remain. Nevertheless, despite the problems involved these data continue to be used, as they are here, with the appropriate caveats and disclaimers. Now that the reader is appropriately forewarned we can proceed to examine the central concern of this section: namely, U.S. crime trends in historical and comparative perspective.

Crime Trends

There is the widespread belief in the United States, fueled by media and government reports, that violent crime is increasing inexorably. One of the most frequently cited sources documenting both the magnitude and increasing frequency of serious crime is the bone-chilling "crime clock" produced by the FBI in the *UCR*. A comparison of the "crime clocks" for 1960, 1970, and 1980 (see Table 6-1) provides the rather ominous image of time running out for each of us as the clock of crime ticks on ever faster. Thus, while in 1960 a rape occurred once every 34 minutes, by 1980 it was occurring once every 6 minutes; a motor vehicle was stolen every 2 minutes in 1960 and every 28 seconds in 1980; and so on.

The popular perception of crime as an ever-increasing threat is not shared by all observers. There are some who claim that this kind of crime information is at best misleading and at worst fraudulent. Some critics argue, for example, that the "crime clock" figures are used by journalists

TABLE 6-1
THE FBI "CRIME CLOCK"

Type of offense	Frequency: One every . . .		
	1960	1970	1980
Murder	58 minutes	33 minutes	23 minutes
Forcible rape	34 minutes	14 minutes	6 minutes
Robbery	6 minutes	91 seconds	58 seconds
Aggravated assault	4 minutes	96 seconds	48 seconds
Burglary	39 seconds	15 seconds	8 seconds
Larceny-theft	60 seconds	18 seconds	4 seconds
Motor vehicle theft	2 minutes	34 seconds	28 seconds

Source: Uniform Crime Reports, 1960, 1970, 1980.

and politicians in a way that suggests that each person in the United States is equally vulnerable to each of these crimes—but they are not.

> The odds, however, vary immensely with the location and condition. Crime is not spread evenly over the nation. . . . The murder rate in big cities is four and a half times higher than in the suburbs and two and a half times above the rural rate. The big-city rates for aggravated assault, rape, burglary, larceny, and theft exceed both suburban and rural rates by two to four times. The rate of auto theft is fourteen times greater in urban than in rural areas.[10]

What then is the "truth" about crime trends? Are we more "endangered" today than in the past? The overall trend in the rate of index crimes (i.e., number per 100,000 people) over the last nearly one-half century provides an apparent picture of policy failure and social peril. Between 1933 and 1980, the incidence of every one of the seven index crimes increased, and some, like larceny-theft (5,000 percent) and rape (833 percent), increased by truly astronomical proportions. (See Table 6-2.) Before we can conclude, however, that the "crime clock" is indeed ticking ever faster, there are several points about the data presented in Table 6-2, and historical crime trends in general, which must be understood.

The first and most important of these points concerns the collection and reporting of crime data. In 1969, the U.S. National Commission on the Causes and Prevention of Violence reported, "Decreasing public tolerance of crime is seemingly causing more crimes to be reported. Changes in police practices, such as better recording procedures and more intensive patrolling, are causing police statistics to dip deeper into the large well of unreported crime. Hence, some part of the increase in reporting rates of violent crime is no doubt due to a fuller disclosure of the violent crimes actually committed."[11]

A decade after the commission report, a prominent criminologist echoed

TABLE 6-2
CRIME TRENDS: 1933–1980, SELECTED YEARS, RATES PER 100,000 POPULATION

Type of offense	1933	1940	1950	1960	1970	1980	Percent increase 1980 over 1933
Murder	7.7	6.6	5.3	5.0	7.8	10.2	33
Forcible rape	3.9	5.5	7.3	9.5	18.5	36.4	833
Robbery	108.8	53.6	48.5	59.9	171.4	243.5	124
Aggravated assault	56.4	49.0	71.6	85.1	163.0	290.6	415
Burglary	360.8	285.7	312.1	502.1	1071.2	1668.2	362
Larceny-theft	61.6	54.1	135.8	282.9	861.2	3156.3	5024
Motor vehicle theft	250.8	131.7	111.0	181.7	453.7	494.6	97

Source: Office of Management and Budget, *Social Indicators, 1973; Uniform Crime Reports,* 1980.

this sentiment by saying that what we were experiencing was not a "crime wave" but a "crime *reporting* wave."[12] People are more willing to report crimes, the police are better equipped to record crimes, and as a result there has been an increase in the amount of crime which finds its way into published and publicized crime statistics.

This is not to suggest that all of the reported increase in crime is simply the result of heretofore hidden or unreported crimes now being reported and recorded. It is impossible to deny the fact that the incidence of crime today is greater than it was, say, 10, 20, or 50 years ago. Murder, the most accurately reported and recorded of all crimes—it is, after all, difficult to hide the fact of a murder even if one can successfully hide the body itself—has increased over the years. And we can safely assume that other serious crimes also have increased. The point is that while some crimes have undoubtedly increased, it may not be as bad as it appears.

The second point follows from the first. That crime may not be getting worse as fast as we think may be irrelevant. Public attitudes and impressions about crime are often inaccurately related to the reality of crime or the likelihood of a person being a victim of crime. One study, for example, "found that people feel safer in their own neighborhoods than in others *even though* their own neighborhoods actually had a higher crime rate than surrounding areas."[13] Similarly, Richard Sparks, a professor of criminal justice at Rutgers University, claims, "[A]n enormous amount of fear has been generated for reasons I don't understand. If you take the long view, you wonder why in the 1980's we claim violent crime is a problem. Our best evidence shows it is no more a problem than it ever was. It's certainly not getting worse."[14] But there is certainly the feeling that it *is* getting worse. In 1965, 35 percent of the people in a national survey indicated that they were afraid to walk alone at night in their own neighborhoods. By 1976 the proportion had grown to 44 percent, and by 1981 it was 53 percent.[15] There is then both the reality of crime and the perception of crime. And, in a political and policy sense, perception may be more important than reality.

A third point about crime trends relates to the observation of Professor Sparks that by taking the "long view" things do not look as bad as we seem to think they are. Actually, a reexamination of Table 6-2 will indicate that crime in 1933 was worse than it was in subsequent years. In fact, it was not until 1970 that the 1933 murder rate was exceeded, not until 1968 that the robbery rate was exceeded, and not until 1965 that the motor vehicle theft rate was exceeded. Indeed, if one takes the long view, the image that emerges is not one of ever-increasing crime trends but rather cyclical ones. Professor Ted Gurr, who has studied long-term crime trends not only in the United States but in Great Britain, Sweden, and Australia as well, has found that in all four countries the rate of violent crime was substantially higher in the distant past and has shown an overall decline over the centuries. Specifically with regard to the United States, Professor Gurr has identified three great surges in violent crime in recent history. The first began shortly before the Civil War (ca. 1860) and lasted into the 1870s. The second began after the turn of the century and lasted into the early 1930s. The most recent surge began in the mid-1960s and *may* have peaked in the mid-1970s.

On the issue of whether or not crime is worse today than in the past, Gurr has this to say about the homicide rate: "Current national homicide rates are higher than any recorded previously, though only slightly greater than those of the 1920s. They are also greater than any indicated by the fragmentary nineteenth-century evidence."[16]

While there is fragmentary evidence that in certain specific locales and for certain groups (i.e., blacks) violent crime rates may have been higher during earlier periods of the century than now, there seems to be general agreement that for the entire range of serious crime, ours is a comparatively more crime-ridden time.

Although there may be some question that there is more crime today than in the past, there is absolutely no doubt that there is significantly more crime in the United States than in other comparable nations. For Professor Marvin Wolfgang of the University of Pennsylvania this is one of the most disturbing features of crime in the United States.

> Whatever our statistics may be, they are high relative to other civilized populations. We're two to 10 times more violent than any other country in Western Europe. And the comparison with Japan is even more dramatic. So whether our trend is up or down slightly over the past 10 years is not the important thing. It's the high baseline from which we are starting. It's dreadful. It's appalling.[17]

Complete, comparable, current cross-national crime statistics on a wide range of offenses are difficult to obtain. We will have to be content, therefore, with somewhat dated and fragmentary evidence. The first such fragment is offered in Figure 6-1. Here we see a comparison of homicide rates between the United States and six other industrialized nations. Two rather clear and dismaying trends are apparent. The first and most obvious is that the U.S. homicide rate is dramatically higher than that of other countries. Thus, the homicide rate in the United States for the period 1970–1975 averaged 9.3 per 100,000 people, while it averaged less than 1.5 per 100,000 people in France, the Netherlands, Norway, Austria, and Japan (as well as Belgium, Denmark, West Germany, Ireland, Italy, Sweden, and the United Kingdom which are not included in the figure). The nation closest to the United States was Canada and even there the average annual rate was only 2.3 per 100,000 people.

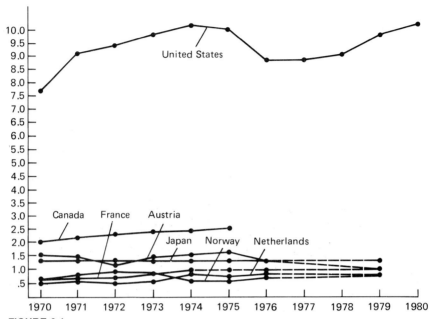

FIGURE 6-1
Homicide rates for selected countries, 1970–1980 (per 100,000 population).

The second trend that emerges from the data in Figure 6-1 is that not only do other countries have less violent crime but, in addition, they do not share our rapidly increasing homicide rate. With the exception of Canada, there was virtually no change in the rate of homicide in these countries for the period 1970–1979, while in the United States there was nearly a one-third increase.

Fragmentary evidence for other crimes reveals a similar pattern. For example, while the robbery rate in the United States in 1976 was 196 per 100,000 people, it was only 11.2 in Japan and 24.8 in England and Wales. In the same year the rate for forcible rape in the United States was 26.4 per 100,000 people while it was 2.7 in Japan and 2.2 in England and Wales. In fact, we could not find a single example over the last several decades involving major democratic, industrial nations in which the United States was not the undisputed leader in the rate of serious crime.

The obvious and critical question is why? Why is our society so much more violent than other advanced, democratic societies? To the extent that one can explain this phenomenon, the answer can be found both in the nature of our people and society and in our criminal justice policies. The remainder of this chapter, therefore, examines the causes of crime and the public policies and policy proposals to deal with crime.

CAUSES OF CRIME

Identifying the causes of crime is among the oldest and most earnestly pursued enterprises in the social sciences. The fact that the search continues is testimony to the inadequacy of the efforts thus far. To anticipate the following discussion, there is as yet no single theory of crime, but rather a large number of competing explanations, some of which owe their origins more to ideological commitment than scientific inquiry.

While one could go back to the ancient Greeks in search of explanations as to why people commit crimes, or why some societies have more crime than others, or why certain times are more violent than others, our quest will be more modest. The explanations discussed below are among the more prominent recent efforts to explain crime in the United States.

"America the Violent"

H. Rap Brown, a black militant, once said that violence is "as American as cherry pie." This sentiment was echoed, albeit in less prosaic terms, in the 1969 report of the U.S. National Commission on the Causes and Prevention of Violence: "Violence has been far more intrinsic to our past than we should like to think."[18]

If our nation was "conceived in liberty" so too was it conceived in violence, and as it was conceived so did it develop. "By the time of its first centennial, in 1876, the United States had already earned the persisting reputation as the most violent society in the Western world."[19] The violence was not only the collective violence of revolution, Indian wars, the Civil War, the Mexican-American War, and slavery, but also individual criminal violence. The fragmentary evidence available indicates that the homicide rate in the United States in the period 1860–1880 is comparable to the homicide rate in our own time—between 9 and 10 per 100,000 population.[20] The violence took different forms at different times and places: lynching of blacks after the Civil War in the south; range wars in the west; labor violence in the east and midwest; and robbery, murder, and rape throughout the country.

Not only were we a violent nation, but we tended to celebrate and even honor those who committed the violence. Vigilantes who took the law into their own hands and even outlaws, such as the James brothers and Billy the Kid, were as revered as, if not more revered than, law officers.[21] Later on the nation adopted, and Hollywood canonized, new heroes: Bonnie and Clyde, John Dillinger, and Charles "Pretty Boy" Floyd—murderers and thieves all. The celebration of villains and violence continues today and everyday on television. According to one expert, "Our children have been conditioned to an acceptance of violence as no civilized nation has ever been before. . . ."[22] Of course, the United States is not unique in its celebration of violence. Japanese "samurai" stories shown in movies and on television are replete with blood and gore—and are enormously popular in Japan. And yet Japan has one of the lowest crime rates in the world. We will return to the case of Japan and examine some of the social and political mechanisms which apparently counteract this tradition. Clearly, with regard to the United States, the celebration of violence cannot, by itself, explain our high crime rates or individual acts of criminal behavior. It is at best a partial explanation. It identifies a facet of our national culture which tolerates, sometimes encourages, perhaps even venerates criminal behavior, especially violence. This historical and cultural explanation also contributes to our understanding of why our society is so much more violent than some others. There is no evidence to suggest that the acceptance and celebration of violence in the United States is greater than every other nation in the world. But there is certainly reason to believe that we are close to the top.

"Invasion of Barbarians"

While criminologists continue to disagree about the causes of crime, there is one contributing factor upon which there is universal agreement: "All records of crime in Western societies, past and present, show that young males are disproportionately represented among offenders."[23] Young people (15 to 24 years old), and young males in particular, are "crime-prone." In 1980, persons 14 to 24 years of age constituted 20.5 percent of the population but accounted for 69.7 percent of all arrests for serious crimes in the United States. Any appreciable increase in the relative and absolute number of young people inevitably leads to an increase in crime. And this is precisely what happened in this country in the period 1960–1975—the period of our most recent crime surge. In 1950 there were about 24.5 million 15- to 24-year-olds in the country, constituting about 16.1 percent of the population. In 1960 the numbers were up (27.3 million) but the percentage was actually down (15.1 percent). By 1970, however, the "baby boom" postwar generation had come to "crime age": 40.3 million people, constituting 20.4 percent of the population, were now between the ages of 14 and 24 years old. The magnitude of this increase was nearly unprecedented; the increase in the proportion of young people was greater than at any time in the preceeding 70 years.[24] And, in 1970, this 20.4 percent of the population accounted for 75.9 percent of all the arrests for index crimes in this country.

Why are young people so crime-prone? "Daring, lack of foresight, uncritical enthusiasm, sheer physical strength and endurance, all play their part. You could say that these are perennial characteristics of youth in any age or time, enough in themselves to account for a big share in mischief, small and great."[25] When the "perennial characteristics of youth" were mixed with an extraordinary growth in the relative and absolute number of young people, the result was, in effect, a "system overload." The nature of this overload has been rather colorfully described by Professor Norman Ryder, a Princeton University demographer: "There is a perennial invasion of barbarians (e.g., young people, immigrants) who must somehow be civilized and turned into contributors to fulfillment of the various functions requisite to societal survival." In effect, society socializes these "barbarians," teaching them the rules of the game. Occasionally, as in the decade of the 1960s in the United States, however, the system is simply overwhelmed by the number of new "barbarians." "The increase in the magnitude of the socialization tasks in the United States during the past decade was completely outside the bound of previous experience."[26]

Obviously not all young people commit crimes and not all crime is committed by young people. But persons, especially males, in the 15- to 24-year age group are more likely to commit crimes than those in any other age group. It should also be noted that similar patterns—i.e., increases in the number and proportion of young people in conjunction with an increase in crime—have been reported in other nations and at other times in history.

Violence Begets Violence

The most recent surge in crime was not only coincidental with an increase in the size of the most crime-prone age group, it also was coincidental with a bloody and domestically divisive war in Southeast Asia. This association of events suggests a third, and again we emphasize partial, explanation for the elevated crime rates in the United States relative to our own past and to the current rates in other countries. Studies of the United States and other countries have identified increased patterns of criminality either prior to, during, or immediately subsequent to periods of war. Gurr, for example, found the relationship between war and increased criminality quite dramatic: "War is the single most obvious correlate of the great historical waves of violent crime in England and the United States."[27] This relationship has been identified not only in England and the United States but in most of Western Europe as well. And even in Japan, viewed by many as the paragon of the peaceful society, there was an extraordinary increase in homicides, robberies, and rapes following the end of World War II: The number of homicides increased more than 300 percent between 1945 and 1954 (from 919 to 3,081) before they began their gradual descent.[28]

There are several reasons why war may lead to an increase in violent crime.[29] One reason is that criminal activity typically declines during the war either because of "social solidarity" or because many of those who would commit crime (e.g., young males) are away doing mischief somewhere else. The end of the war is followed by an upsurge in crime because of the decline in the sense of solidarity and the return of the crime-prone age group. A related explanation is that many veterans who have returned from war have developed an appetite or habit for violence or have become insensitive to its use. One early study of Vietnam veterans, which seems to have been supported by subsequent events, noted that "some (veterans) are likely to seek continuing outlets to a pattern of violence to which they have become habituated, whether by indulging in antisocial or criminal behavior or by offering their services to the highest bidder."[30]

Another study, which reviewed and tested these and other theories, concluded that the most valid and convincing explanation for this relationship is that war tends to legitimize violence. According to Professors Archer and Gartner of the University of California, Santa Cruz, there is a "residual effect on the level of homicide in peacetime society."[31] In other words, young men are, in effect, given a license to kill during war—indeed, the most successful killers are often the most celebrated soldiers. Having been convinced by the state that taking life is acceptable, even desirable, there is apparently some difficulty in returning to civilian peacetime prohibitions against such behavior.

Of course, one need not look for erudite, social scientific theories to explain why there is a relationship between war and postwar levels of crime. In the case of the Vietnam war, many U.S. soldiers developed drug problems during the war which continued into civilian life. Criminal activity necessary to feed these drug habits has been widespread among returning veterans. So too have unemployment, mental problems, and general social and personal dislocation. In the United States, as well as in other countries at other times, war has often been the prelude to increased criminal behavior.

Crime *Does* Pay

In the 1964 presidential campaign Barry Goldwater introduced the issue of "law and order" into U.S. national politics. Until recently conservatives have enjoyed near preeminence in pursuing law and order as a policy issue. What then is the conservative explanation for crime? They begin with the nature of people. President Reagan, reflecting a traditional conservative position, spoke of a fundamental "truth" of human nature: "[M]en are basically good but prone to evil." He also spoke of "the darker impulses of human nature."[32]

Secondly, conservatives believe that people are free agents exercising free will. Human nature is not, as liberals would have it, somehow defined by social conditions. Rather, people are rational beings; they calculate costs and benefits and are free to make choices on the basis of their calculations. Criminal behavior, like all behavior, is essentially a rational, free choice, not a response to societally induced deprivations. According to Ronald Reagan, "The truth is that today's criminals, for the most part, are not desperate people seeking bread for their families; crime is the way they've chosen to live."[33]

The reason criminals have chosen to live this way, conservatives say, is that in rational, calculated economic terms the benefits of crime outweigh the costs. Crime, in other words, pays. There have been, in fact, several studies which have calculated the costs (e.g., time, purchase of equipment, costs associated with apprehension and conviction) and benefits of crime (e.g., monetary rewards and psychic satisfaction). After reviewing these, Luksetich and White concluded, "In most jurisdictions studied, property crime was found to be profitable."[34] Even where property is not involved, such as in rape or assault, there is some evidence to suggest that rational, cost-benefit analysis still applies. This assumes, of course, that not all benefits are financial or tangible but include such psychic benefits as revenge, "beating the system," and so on.

Another important feature that is often found in conjunction with the profitability argument is that crime is also more attractive than legitimate employment. James Q. Wilson paints a rather seductive picture of crime:

> One works at crime at one's convenience, enjoys the esteem of colleagues who think a "straight" job is stupid and skill at stealing is commendable, looks forward to the occasional "big score" that may make further work unnecessary for weeks, and relishes the risk and adventure associated with theft. The money value of all these benefits . . . is hard to estimate, but is almost certainly far larger than what either public or private employers could offer to unskilled or semi-skilled young workers.[35]

Presented in these terms, one wonders why more people do not turn to crime!

There are then two central assumptions to the conservative explanation of crime. The first is that people rationally calculate the costs and benefits of criminal behavior (or at least those crimes associated with tangible benefits). The second is that because people are rational, we can assume that those people who commit crimes have concluded that the benefits outweigh the costs. And several studies have indicated that, objectively, this appears to be true. All things considered, crime does pay.

There are, of course, important policy implications of this position. Although we will look at these in detail in the following section, we should point out that the most obvious one is that the best way to deter crime is to increase its costs. We will see shortly that conservatives, therefore, typically propose increasing the severity and certainty of punishment as the best way of increasing the cost of crime.

The Social Origins of Crime

While conservatives lay the cause of crime at the doorstep of the individual, liberals see the failings of society as the basis for criminal behavior, although they do recognize that individual pathology (e.g., insanity) may be responsible as well. The liberal emphasis on social rather than individual responsibility for crime is nicely summarized in the following statement by Ramsey Clark:

> Most crime in America is born in environments saturated in poverty and its consequences: illness, ignorance, idleness, ugly surroundings, hopelessness. Crime incubates in places where thousands have no jobs, and those who do, have the poorest jobs; where houses are old, dirty and dangerous; where people have no rights.[36]

Crime, in this view, is not the fault of the criminal but of a negligent society which allows those conditions which encourage crime to flourish. It is important to emphasize here that Clark's observation is absolutely critical to the liberal position on crime. No progress can be made in making society safer in the United States until one understands the root causes of crime. And of these, poverty and racism are the most urgent.

The policy implications of the liberal view are obvious and ambitious. To control crime one must eliminate, or at least substantially reduce, ignorance, poverty, poor nutrition, unemployment, slums, and discrimination. To accomplish these extraordinary tasks will require an extraordinary government commitment. Such a commitment is justified not only because of its crime-fighting implications but also because the elimination of poverty and racism is a moral imperative. Most liberals are not so naive as to believe that even if all of the above social maladies were eliminated crime would cease. There are, of course, too many examples of educated, employed, healthy, white suburbanites committing crimes, as well as examples of continuing crime (albeit at much lower rates) in countries which have all but eliminated these problems (e.g., Japan, Sweden, Switzerland). Nevertheless, there is the conviction that the reduction of poverty, in its various manifestations, will substantially reduce crime. We will examine this point more carefully shortly.

Before concluding this section, we would like to mention briefly a few additional explanations of crime which, while not necessarily of liberal origin, nevertheless tend to emphasize social context as the breeding ground for crime. The first of these, with the rather imposing title of "differential association," is probably the most widely recognized of all the theories of crime.[37] Shorn of its various subtleties, the notion of differential association suggests that crime is behavior which is learned through social interaction. In every society one interacts with a variety of people who communicate different information and provide competing models of behavior. Criminals are those who have received far more value cues and information conducive to criminal behavior than lawful behavior. And such interaction is more likely to occur in urban ghettos than in other locales.

A somewhat similar theory, which also enjoys considerable prestige, is Robert Merton's theory of anomie. According to this view, there are no competing cultures in the United States but a single culture or value system characterized by a high value placed on hard work, success, and material rewards and possessions. Unfortunately, not everyone in society is capable of realizing this "American dream," despite the enormous social pressures to do so. Blocked because of race, family background, or social class from realizing this dream in a legitimate way, some persons seek to achieve it through crime.[38] This position is, of course, quite consistent with the liberal view of the causes of crime.

Finally, there are a number of explanations or theories which relate crime, including differential rates across time and between nations, to various macroeconomic cycles such as recessions, depressions, and inflation. Gurr reports on one major study of the United States, Great Britain, and Canada between 1900 and 1970 which found a strong relationship between economic adversity and the rates of both property and personal crimes in all three countries.[39] These findings support the liberal contention that societal conditions are a breeding ground for crime.

The Cure Is As Bad As the Illness

There is one point on which liberals and conservatives agree. The criminal justice system itself—the police, the courts, the prisons, and the laws themselves—rather than deterring, actually contributes to crime. The agreement on this point is reflected in the comments of first, Ronald Reagan, and second, Ramsey Clark: "If you want to know why crime proliferates in this nation, don't look at the statistics on income and wealth; look at statistics on arrests, prosecution, conviction, and prison population. These data show that failure of the criminal justice system . . . [is] behind the crime rate." "In its most direct contacts with crime—prevention, detection, apprehension, conviction and correction—the system of criminal justice fails miserably."[40] The specific terms of the indictment of the criminal justice system differ depending on perspective. Since the next section of this chapter deals with actual and proposed policy solutions to the nation's crime problem and, therefore, extensively covers the failures of the criminal justice system, we will not deal with the particulars now. We will do nothing more here than simply list in the most general terms the charges of each perspective as they relate to the claim that the system is itself a cause of crime. We will develop each point in the next section.

Liberal critics say the system encourages or contributes to criminal behavior in the following ways: (1) By discriminating against the poor and minorities at every stage of the process, those involved in the criminal justice system (police officers, judges, prison officials) convince these people that working with or within the system is either impossible or futile. (2) Contrary to one of its alleged purposes, the prison system does not rehabilitate offenders so they may lead useful and legitimate lives once they have paid their debt to society; if anything the system reinforces criminal behavior. (3) Trial delays, capricious bail, sentencing, and parole practices reduce the deterrent effect of the process.

Conservatives complain that the criminal justice system contributes to crime in the following ways: (1) Supreme Court decisions over the last two decades have been more concerned with protecting the rights of criminals— and, therefore, making it more difficult to prosecute and convict them— than those of law-abiding citizens. (2) Various criminal justice procedures, including lenient bail, plea bargaining, or parole practices, unnecessarily and prematurely expose society to criminal elements. (3) The lack of certainty and severity of sentencing are undermining the deterrent effect of justice as well as unleashing criminals on society.

Summary: Causes of Crime

There is no single cause of crime. In this section we have looked at some of the explanations of crime in the United States, and particularly its recent upsurge. The history and celebration of violence in our country, the almost unprecedented increase in the crime-prone 15- to 24-year-old age group, the war in Vietnam, the attractiveness of crime for certain elements in society, poverty and its attending manifestations of poor housing, limited job opportunities, disease, and limited education all play some role in the origins of crime. Which factor or factors one believes to be the most important is, at this point at least, more a function of ideological commitment than scientific discovery.

Because the causes of crime remain murky and are subject to continuing debate, finding cures for the problem is particularly difficult. Nevertheless, society cannot and will not wait for a definitive academic ruling. People in the United States want something done now—and quite properly so. We will conclude this chapter then with a discussion of the policy responses to the problem of crime in the United States and abroad.

WHAT TO DO ABOUT CRIME

The Federal Context

Primary responsibility for criminal justice policy, constitutionally and historically, has rested with state and local agencies and actors—police officers, public prosecutors, judges, jail and prison personnel, and parole officers. Today, more than 40,000 state and local police agencies, employing over 580,000 persons, administer the nation's criminal justice system. The role of the federal government is quantitatively and qualitatively secondary to that of the localities; there are fewer than 50,000 federal law enforcement personnel. The overwhelming majority of the criminal laws and crimes, law enforcement officers, judges and court proceedings, prisons and prisoners are located within the jurisdiction of local and state boundaries.

Nevertheless, the federal government does have an important role in the area of criminal justice policy. To begin with, there are federal crimes—about 3,000 of them—for which federal law enforcement officers (e.g., FBI, Immigration and Naturalization agents, U.S. Marshals Service, Drug Enforcement Administration, and Bureau of Alcohol, Tobacco and Firearms), federal judges and courts, and federal prisons are responsible. These laws cover such areas as banking and postal service crimes, drug offenses, kidnapping, airplane hijackings, and attempts on the lives of federal officials like the President and members of Congress.

Second, the federal government influences criminal justice policy at the state and local level by providing a model of behavior and practices. It does this not only through making and administering federal criminal law, but also through its capacity as the criminal justice policy-making body for the District of Columbia. Thus in such areas as bail reform and preventive detention the federal government has provided a model, not always emulated, for criminal justice policy throughout the country. In addition, the federal government, typically in the person of the President or individual members of Congress, can set the tone for the criminal justice policy debate. The emphasis by Presidents Nixon and Reagan, for example, on "law and order" helped stimulate policy discussions and changes at the subnational level.

Third, the federal government provides assistance to state and local law enforcement agencies. While a certain amount of assistance has been provided for a number of years—e.g., FBI national fingerprint identification—it was not until 1968, with the Omnibus Crime Control and Safe Streets Act and the creation under that act of the Law Enforcement Assistance Administration (LEAA), that the federal government became more intimately involved in crime control throughout the nation. "The theory behind the bill was that, while the Federal Government should not and probably could not engage directly in local law enforcement, the Government should and could provide substantial financial and technical assistance to local police departments."[41]

The centerpiece of the act was the establishment of the LEAA to help states improve their crime fighting capacity. Originally, President Johnson proposed that these grants be made directly to local law enforcement agencies. Republicans, however, successfully opposed this allocation scheme and won approval instead of "block grants" to go to the states. A state planning agency, appointed by the governor, allocates monies to local communities. The act specified three types of grants: planning, law enforcement, and training and research. Under the planning grants states were given funds to establish a planning agency and develop a statewide law enforcement plan. Law enforcement grants were used for such purposes as training and recruiting of police officers, construction of law enforcement buildings, and developing methods and equipment to aid law enforcement officials. Finally, training and research grants were used to conduct training programs, run by the FBI's National Academy, for state and local law-enforcement officials. In addition, a National Institute of Law Enforcement and Criminal Justice was established to conduct research in the area of law enforcement.

In 1981 President Reagan ended what some observers admitted was a 12-year, $8 billion failure; LEAA was abandoned. Actually, the demise of LEAA began under President Carter, who, in his last budget as President, drastically reduced LEAA's budget. In a recent book on the rise and fall of the Safe Streets Act and LEAA, Professors Thomas Cronin, Tania Cronin, and Michael Milakovich examined the question of what went wrong. In effect, they concluded, just about everything. The act was an ambiguous legislative mandate; there was mismanagement within the agency, ineffective national leadership, and indirection and irresponsibility on the part of state and local officials.[42] In the preface to their book the authors summarized the implications of this failure:

> This is the story, for the most part, of a beleaguered, frustrated, and failed national effort—the kind of effort costly not only in terms of taxpayers' money and legislators' time but also to our sense of confidence in the ability of the national government to work, to solve problems, to govern.[43]

The fourth way in which the federal government is involved in the administration of criminal justice is through Supreme Court and lower federal court decisions.[44] Federal courts exercise influence over local law enforcement and criminal justice policy in several ways. First, the Supreme Court may hear appeals of state criminal cases in which a state law or procedure (e.g., capital punishment) is alleged to be in violation of the U.S. Constitution, or federal laws or treaties. Second, federal courts can review, through habeus corpus proceedings, state criminal justice standards and practices. Third, claiming that a fair trial in a particular state court is impossible, a defendant may petition to have the trial moved to a federal court.

Of these three, it is through the first procedure, Supreme Court reviews of state criminal laws and practices, that the Court has had the most profound impact on criminal justice policy across the country. This impact was most telling and controversial in the 1960s during the tenure of Chief Justice Earl Warren. In a series of cases beginning in 1961 the Court overturned various state laws and criminal justice practices, while at the same time expanding the rights of accused persons. The more prominent of these decisions were:

1961   *Mapp v. Ohio* (367 U.S. 643)
        Prohibited prosecution of a person based upon evidence acquired in an illegal search.

1962   *Robinson v. California* (370 U.S. 660)
        Prohibited cruel and unusual punishment.

1963   *Gideon v. Wainwright* (372 U.S. 335)
        Required that a person be represented by counsel, if necessary at state expense, during a trial for a serious offense.

1964   *Malloy v. Hogan* (378 U.S. 1)
        Protected persons in state criminal court proceedings from self-incrimination.

1964   *Escobedo v. Illinois* (378 U.S. 478)
        Required a person be provided an attorney during a police interrogation.

1965   *Pointer v. Texas* (380 U.S. 400)
        Guaranteed accused persons access to witnesses against them.

1966   *Miranda v. Arizona* (384 U.S. 436)
        Required that accused persons be apprised of their rights (e.g., the right to remain silent and to have an attorney) prior to questioning by the police.

1967   *Klopfer v. North Carolina* (386 U.S. 14)
        Guaranteed a speedy trial in criminal cases.

1969   *Benton v. Maryland* (395 U.S. 784)
        Prohibited a person from being tried twice for the same crime ("double jeopardy").

These decisions came during a time of urban disorder and increased crime and, as a result, produced a strong backlash in the country. Critics, including then presidential candidate Richard Nixon (1968), claimed the Supreme Court was more concerned with protecting criminals from society than society from criminals. Nixon, whose campaign stressed the issue of "law and order," promised that, if elected, he would appoint persons to the Court who would reorder the Court's priorities in order to safeguard the rights of law-abiding citizens. Liberals, on the other hand, defended the Court's actions, arguing that these legal safeguards were necessary to protect all citizens and particularly those most vulnerable, such as blacks and poor people, when confronted by the criminal justice system. In any event, Presidents Nixon, Ford, and Reagan appointed new members to the Court who had a more conservative philosophy. As a result, some recent decisions have tended to modify and relax some of the substantive and procedural rights of accused persons.

The area in which this "retreat" (or "remediation" depending upon one's perspective) has been most obvious deals with the Fourth Amendment prohibition against unreasonable searches and seizures. In 1980 the Court ruled (6 to 3 with Justice Blackmun and liberal Justices Brennan and Marshall dissenting) that illegally obtained evidence could be excluded only if the defendant in the case was the victim of an illegal search and seizure (*United States v. Payner*, 447 U.S. 727, 1980). In other words, evidence illegally obtained from Miss Jones may not be used against her but can be used against Miss Smith. In another case (*United States v. Ross*, 31 Ca.L. 3051, 1982), with Justices Brennan and Marshall dissenting again, joined by Justice White, the Court held that the police after arresting a person may conduct a warrantless search of an automobile which they have stopped and which they believe may have contraband. Any evidence found in the course of this search is admissible in court.

The specific rights extended by the Supreme Court to accused persons, as well as the appropriate role of the Court in the criminal justice policy-making process, continue to be a matter of debate. As we will see shortly, proposed reforms of the system include some which are directed at the courts themselves.

By way of summary then, the U.S. criminal justice system is a highly decentralized one in which the states and localities play the predominant role. There are, however, various opportunities for the federal government to influence the system even within the local and state context. Changes in the criminal justice system to help it deal more effectively with the problem of reducing crime, while still ensuring fairness in the administration of justice, must address both state and local, as well as national, institutions, laws, and practices. We can now turn to specific proposals for improving the criminal justice system.

Law and Order versus Social Reform

The criminal justice system consists of four major components: police, prosecutors, courts, and correctional institutions (jails and prisons). We will examine each of these in turn, identifying the major policy recommendations of both the left and the right.

The Police   The police "solve" very few crimes. The clearance rate for all index crimes for 1980, a typical year, was 19 percent. Stated differently, the police find sufficient evidence to identify, charge, and apprehend persons in only one out of every five serious crimes. Actually the clearance rate varies according to the crime: from a low of 14 percent for burglaries and motor vehicle thefts to a high of 72 percent for murder. The major concern, therefore, with the role of the police in the criminal justice system is how to improve police performance in preventing and detecting crime and apprehending criminals. In this regard, policy debate has focused on three areas: resources, laws governing police conduct and practices, and police-community relations.

Before looking at each of these, the reader should be reminded that crime prevention, detection, and criminal apprehension constitute only a small part of police work. Police officers, especially the "cop on the beat," spend most of their time performing non-crime-related services such as refereeing marital disputes, retrieving cats from trees, teaching bicycle safety to schoolchildren, directing traffic, and arresting drunks. From the very beginning of the organization of modern police departments, these noncrime service functions have been central to the role of police work, and they are a drain on the time and resources of police departments.

Having introduced the issue of limited resources as a cause of poor police performance, we can now pursue it more closely. During the 1960s there was a profound, and primarily liberal, conviction that in the area of criminal justice more money and equipment for police would equal less crime. There are few people today, including liberals, who believe that insufficient resources are at, or even near, the heart of the problem of poor police performance. There are cities, including Houston, Los Angeles, Boston, and Trenton, to name a few, in which there are far fewer police than the populations, geographic size, and crime rates demand. While bringing these police forces up to prescribed levels *might* have an effect on crime, it would not be significant. Empirical evidence on this issue suggests that increases in the number and visible presence of police does *not* reduce crime or make citizens feel safer. One major year-long study, the Kansas City Preventive Patrol Experiment, found that routine preventive patrol "had no effect on crime, citizen fear of crime [or] community attitude toward the police?"[45] This was the case, by the way, even when the number of patrol cars was doubled and tripled! More did not equal less. We should add here, however, that there is some evidence to suggest that while an increase in the number of police on patrol does not affect crime, patrolling strategies may. Apparently, more "aggressive" patrolling, in which officers do not wait for crime to happen but aggressively stop suspicious looking persons or pay extraordinary attention to persons with previous criminal records, does have a deterrent effect.[46] However, some of these practices, which have been shown to reduce crime rates, raise important constitutional issues.

If more police does not equal less crime, neither does more equipment. The largesse showered upon law enforcement agencies by the LEAA clearly helped to modernize many police agencies around the country. But there is little evidence that these efforts had a significant positive impact. Some, in fact, may have done more harm than good. For example, some LEAA money went toward more patrol cars, which took police officers off the streets and may have further estranged police-community relations. All this is not to say that money is unimportant or irrelevant. The point is that money is clearly not as critical to the police effort as was once thought.

If money has been the liberal hobbyhorse, then "handcuffing the police" has to be the conservative equivalent. A particular source of irritation to conservatives is the exclusionary rule. Under this rule, evidence which is illegally obtained may not be used in court. This rule was first applied in 1914 (*Weeks v. United States*, 232 U.S. 383) to the federal government and was extended to the states in 1961 (*Mapp v. Ohio*, 367 U.S. 643) where it was decided that evidence acquired during an illegal search and seizure was inadmissible in court. In the course of the 1960s the Warren Court extended this rule. Thus, for example, in the Miranda case the Court ruled that confessions were admissible in court only if made in the presence of an attorney or if, after being apprised of their rights, accused persons waived the right to have an attorney present. In the case of Ernesto Miranda, despite the fact that he confessed to raping an 18-year-old woman and was identified in a police lineup by the victim, his conviction was overturned by the Supreme Court because he was not informed by the police of his right to remain silent and to have an attorney present. Miranda, by the way, was retried and convicted. Conservative critics argue that strict adherence to this rule has allowed many guilty people to go free due to an unintentional error by the police. According to President Reagan's Task Force on Violent Crime, "Application of the rule has been carried to the point where it is applied to situations where police officers make reasonable, good faith efforts to comply with the law, but unwittingly fail to do so." The task force recommended a change in the exclusionary rule that would allow "tainted" evidence to be introduced if it could be demonstrated that it was acquired in good faith.

Support for such a change appears to be growing in Congress as well.

In 1981 conservative Senators Orrin Hatch (R., Utah) and Strom Thurmond (R., S.C.) introduced an amendment to the Federal Criminal Code which would eliminate the exclusionary rule. However, they proposed that persons whose Fourth Amendment rights (e.g., protection against unreasonable search and seizure) have been violated by the police be allowed to seek monetary damages. Furthermore, police officers who illegally obtain evidence could be disciplined for their actions. Thus under this proposed change police would be deterred from abusing a citizen's civil liberties, yet the courts and society would not be denied use of evidence to prosecute lawbreakers. While this change would apply only to the federal court and criminal justice system, there is some evidence of support on the Burger Court to allow similar changes by state legislatures as well. Chief Justice Burger has indicated that as long as some remedy against unlawful conduct by police officials is provided for, eliminating the exclusionary rule would find support on the Court. However, in 1982 the Court, with its four most conservative justices dissenting, once again upheld the exclusionary rule (*Taylor v. Alabama*, 31 Ca.L. 3118, 1982).

Liberals reject the idea that the exclusionary rule has impeded the criminal justice process.

> Repealing the so-called "exclusionary rule" would not make the police any more effective in their "war" against crime. Despite loud and frequent complaints, the police have not been handcuffed by the rulings of the Warren Court. Except for minor drug offenses, there is no evidence to suggest that policemen make fewer arrests, or that prosecutors secure fewer convictions, because of Supreme Court decisions safeguarding the rights of the accused; on the contrary, the evidence runs the other way.[47]

It should be noted that the liberal assertion that the exclusionary rule has not hampered law enforcement efforts has never been documented sufficiently. In any event, the exclusionary rule will be the focus of policy debate and scholarly review for some time to come.

The third area which has attracted policy attention is that of police-community relations. Here there is agreement among liberals and conservatives. Both acknowledge that relations are poor and that they have a deleterious effect on law enforcement. The importance of good police-community relations is emphasized by virtually all professional criminologists. One major reason is that it is very rare that a police officer actually sees a crime in progress or finds a condemning fingerprint at the scene of the crime. Rather, the police depend upon the public to report suspicious activity and thereby prevent crime, to report crimes in progress, and, after the event, to identify suspects and appear in court to testify. As Charles Silberman, in a self-acknowledged bit of exaggeration, has noted, "The police can solve a crime if someone tells them who committed it."[48]

Silberman's observation is supported by a Rand Corporation study of 153 law enforcement agencies: "The single most important determinant of whether or not a case will be solved is the information the victim supplies to the immediately responding patrol officers."[49] Unfortunately, relations between the police and the public have not been characterized on either side by the cooperation, support, and understanding which is necessary for successful police work. We have seen that a large proportion of crime goes unreported either because of fear of the police or a sense that they are either incapable or unwilling to help. Similarly, the police view citizens, or at least some of them, with contempt. Newsweek (March 23, 1981) reports: "Many cops feel friendless in a land they see filled with dumb judges and dangerous civilians." The article went on to quote a Bronx, New York, police supervisor: "My men don't want to do nothing. They don't want to get sued. They don't want to get shot. They have no incentive. They get no rewards." Why is this the case?

This is where liberal and conservative opinions part company. Liberals lay most, but not all, of the blame on the police. Either as a result of malevolence or inadvertence, police attitudes toward young, poor, and nonwhite citizens inhibit or prevent cooperative and supportive community relations. "With our history of racism and the deep tensions among minorities living in the high-crime areas of the slums, the use of poorly trained, undereducated, economically insecure white officers to police central city [sic] makes effective performance virtually impossible and frequently inflammatory."[50] Police bias toward minorities, in the form of street harassment and a greater readiness to arrest them than whites, causes conflict and unwillingness to cooperate with the police. National arrest data are often used to support this contention. Thus, for example, in 1980, 32.8 percent of all those arrested for index crimes were black, while blacks constitute only 11 percent of the total population.

Conservatives deny or underplay police bias. James Q. Wilson, for example, argues that to the extent a problem does exist it is concentrated among young black males and ghetto police, and not the entire black community. But more importantly, Wilson argues that it is neither racial conflict nor personal bias that causes conflict between police and citizens, but rather it is "inherent in the situation" of police work. "The police see conflict and unrecoverable losses where the citizen expects vindication and restitution. . . ."[51] This inherent conflict may be exacerbated by, but is not caused by, racial tension.

Recognizing that a problem exists, although differing over why the problem exists, policy makers have sought a variety of approaches to improve police-community relations. The LEAA supported programs to better educate police officers in community relations, ethnic history, and interpersonal relations, among other areas. Many police departments have experimented with community-relations units, ride-along programs, and "storefront" police substations. Other departments have begun to screen their police recruits with greater care in an effort to identify those most likely to handle both the physical as well as the sociological dimensions of police work. Reports of success in improving police-community relations are, however, infrequent.

What about the role of the police in other countries? We have already seen that crime is lower in virtually every other industrialized nation than in the United States. Can this be attributed to either more or better police, fewer restrictions on police conduct, or better police-community relations? To begin, it does not appear that any western industrialized nation has as high a per capita number of police as the United States. Japan, which has a much lower rate of crime than ours, in a recent year had 1 police officer for every 563 persons compared to 1 per 410 persons in the United States.[52] Lower police-to-population ratios exist in most Western European and industrialized Commonwealth countries. Nor does it appear that other countries equip their police departments as well as we do. The former Chief Inspector of the British Constabulary noted that "many American police forces are much better off than their English counterparts. The best of your departments, has much more and better equipment than we have."[53]

Foreign criminal justice policy is more supportive of the police in the area of the exclusionary rule. Stated most simply, no other nation in the world has an exclusionary rule. However, several authors have found that the need for the rule in other countries, to protect citizens from abusive police tactics, is not as great as it might be in the United States. For example, one study indicated that in Canada lower levels of violent crime and, therefore, fewer pressures on police, a greater tradition of discipline among police officers, sensitivity to civil liberties, and the relative lack of racial tension minimize the need for an exclusionary rule.[54] In addition, police officers in Canada are subject to and have been prosecuted for misconduct. Furthermore, in countries such as Sweden, West Germany, and France legislatures have played an active role in overseeing police behavior and using legislative remedies to deal with abuses. In the opinion of some, therefore, the absence of an exclusionary rule should not be viewed as a major advantage which other police forces have over their U.S. counterparts. What we accomplish through formal constraint (i.e., the exclusionary rule), they accomplish in other ways (i.e., self-imposed restraint).

James Q. Wilson, however, sees the absence of an exclusionary rule as the factor with the "greatest importance" to the effective operation of the British police. While it is true the police are liable to criminal, civil, or administrative punishment for misconduct in gathering evidence, "in theory, no one goes free because the constable has blundered."[55] By now the reader should have recognized that the Canadian and British systems are precisely what Senators Hatch and Thurmond are proposing for the United States.

The third area of interest, police-community relations, provides perhaps the most outstanding difference between the United States and other nations. The best documented and most envied illustration of this difference is that of Japan. Earlier in the chapter we noted that Japan not only has a crime rate considerably lower than our own, but that the rate is actually declining. Several scholars have studied the Japanese system in order to understand its success. One of the best such studies is Professor David Bayley's *Forces of Order*. Bayley found that on just about every dimension, Japanese police performance and community relations are far superior to our own, with the result that the police do make a significant contribution to maintaining domestic tranquility. Among the factors that Bayley found contributing to effective police performance and good community relations were the following. First, Japanese police officers are trained for a longer period of time—1 year compared to about 3 months in the United States—and that training not only involves professional skills but matters of personal behavior as well. Japanese police recruits receive training in managing their personal finances, in proper personal appearance, and in cultural traditions such as flower arranging and tea ceremonies. Second, there is greater police interaction with and penetration of the community. The Japanese police force is neighborhood-centered; police officers visit every home twice a year to survey its occupants and their possessions so they are completely familiar with the neighborhood and citizens for whom they are responsible. In addition, each neighborhood has a Crime Prevention Association which works closely with the police and with other citizens. There is, in fact, and in contrast to the United States, considerably less formal distinction between government and society (including the police) in Japan than in the United States. Japanese believe that both the police and citizens have a moral obligation to preserve public safety. Thus the Japanese police do not see themselves, and are not viewed by the public, as being "friendless" or "embattled" but rather as part of a cooperative community effort to preserve public safety.

The picture painted by Bayley is a nearly utopian one; indeed, one chapter of his book is entitled "Heaven for a Cop." Are there then any policy lessons to be learned from the Japanese experience? Bayley is not terribly sanguine about importing Japanese police practices into the United States. The Japanese success appears to be so firmly rooted in the Japanese social context—and so seemingly opposite the U.S. social context—as to make Japanese exports in this area nearly impossible. In what must be one of the most pessimistic passages on comparative criminal justice in recent years, Bayley notes:

[T]he levels of criminal behavior that Americans find so disturbing may be the inevitable consequences of aspects of national life that Americans prize—individualism, mobility, privacy, autonomy, suspicion of authority, and separation between public and private roles, between government and community. *The United States may have relatively high levels of criminality because it is inhabited by Americans.*[56]

While there are few countries which achieve the degree of community success of the Japanese, there are many others in which good police-community relations apparently contribute to police success. The unarmed British "bobby" is perhaps the best-known example, but others from Western Europe and Scandinavia are also prevalent. But in the final analysis it is hard to ignore Bayley's conclusion that the failure of cooperative and supportive police-community relations is anchored in U.S. culture—a factor not easily remedied by changes in public policy. It may be that Bayley is right when he says, "[G]iven American traditions, it is questionable whether law enforcement agencies can be much more effective in curbing criminality than they are now."[57]

There is one final policy change relating to police behavior which we have thus far ignored; namely, gun control. In Chapter 1 we noted that gun control is one of those policy issues over which honest and honorable disagreements exist among people in the United States. We will not examine the all too familiar debate in detail: the right to bear arms versus the harm that unregulated gun ownership brings. Few adults who have given the issue any thought are likely to be dissuaded from their pro- or anti-gun-control position. We will simply note some cross-national information on the subject. First, most nations control their citizens' access to guns and especially handguns. Even in the case of Switzerland, as we have seen, while guns are easily available, restrictions in the form of permits and sales records are required. In most industrialized countries, however, private ownership is either prohibited (e.g., Japan) or restricted through licensing or registration (e.g., Great Britain, Italy, West Germany, France, and Canada).

Second, in the area of the use of handguns in crimes the United States is the unchallenged leader. The figures in Table 6-3 indicate the number of handgun deaths per 100,000 people in various industrialized nations during 1980, and these figures clearly show our unparalleled position.

Third, it appears that handgun use is a function not only of the accessibility of guns, but cultural values as well. Japan is virtually completely disarmed, and Switzerland is just the reverse—at least for the adult male population. Yet in neither country are handguns used, in any significant number, in the commission of crimes. One study of the Swiss system concluded: "It appears that the Swiss do not have this tendency to use violence, in terms of a full 'subculture of violence,' which often involves using weapons to

TABLE 6-3
HANDGUN DEATHS, SELECTED COUNTRIES, 1980

Country	Number of deaths, per 100,000 population
Canada	0.20
Great Britain	0.01
Israel	1.50
Japan	0.04
Sweden	0.26
Switzerland	0.57
West Germany	0.07
United States	5.10

Source: Congressional Record, Nov. 10, 1981, p. E5225.

settle serious disputes. A quite different situation exists in the United States in relation to firearms, however, due to the far greater possibilities of using extreme violence in disputes."[58]

Whichever position one takes—and a June 1982 Gallup poll found that 66 percent of the people in the United States favored handgun registration— the handgun-control debate will continue to dominate policy discussions in the United States for the foreseeable future. Indeed, several localities, including San Francisco, have already passed laws prohibiting the possession of handguns. However, the efficacy and constitutionality of these measures are questionable.

Prosecutors and the Courts   In the vituperative finger pointing that has characterized the debate over the apparent failure of the U.S. criminal justice system, more often than not the finger is aimed, by both police and the public, at the court system—prosecutors and judges. The failure of the court system is often illustrated by a bone-chilling, anger-producing anecdote. Consider the case, reported in *Reader's Digest* (November 1981) and inserted separately, and presumably unknowingly, by two U.S. Senators into the *Congressional Record*. The Indianapolis police arrested a man, Stephen Judy, age 22, and charged him with raping and murdering Mrs. Terry Chasteen and drowning her three young children. At the time of this arrest Judy was out on bond following his arrest on an armed robbery charge. The armed robbery charge came at a time when Judy was out on parole for a prison term resulting from a previous abduction conviction. Stephen Judy had amassed quite a record of convictions for violent crimes by the time he murdered Mrs. Chasteen and her children. In the words of one participant in the case, "This is sad testimony of how our criminal-justice system has failed." Sixteen months after the Judy case the state of

Indiana changed its bond law. And, in March 1981, they executed Stephen Judy.

What can be done about the court system to make it more responsive to the public safety interests of the general public? The action by the state of Indiana touched upon one of several policy reforms that have been either proposed or initiated at the state and federal level. Of the many areas of policy change which have been debated, we would like to focus on three: plea bargaining, bail reform, and sentencing.

Plea Bargaining   Plea bargaining, the process by which prosecutors offer accused persons a reduced charge (e.g., unarmed rather than armed robbery) or a lighter sentence in return for a guilty plea, is a common feature of the U.S. criminal justice system. Currently, approximately 90 percent of all criminal convictions occur as a result of a guilty plea through bargaining. Defenders of the practice argue that it is necessary to help move cases expeditiously through overcrowded court systems, that it is a more certain way of getting convictions than taking a chance with a jury, and that it is cheaper. In addition, Charles Silberman points out that plea bargaining dates at least as far back as the nineteenth century and, therefore, can hardly be held responsible for the recent surge in crime.[59]

Critics, however, say the practice debases the system. Tricks like "swallowing the gun,"—i.e., reducing armed robbery to unarmed robbery— are expedients, not justice. The remedy for plea bargaining, critics suggest, is to abolish it. And this is precisely what the voters of California did in June 1982. Among the provisions of an omnibus anticrime public initiative (Proposition 8) was one that would, with few exceptions, prohibit plea bargaining for major felonies and drunken driving cases. At this writing it was not clear whether the prohibition was constitutionally or practically workable. As Silberman points out with regard to other, more limited, attempts to prohibit plea bargaining, there are other ways and other stages of the process in which deals may be made in order to expedite cases— e.g., prosecutors promise to drop other cases, or charges pending, in return for a guilty plea.[60] Nevertheless, the California action is one policy response to a perceived failure of the system.

Bail Reform   There are few things that anger the public more than cases like that of Stephen Judy, in which a person out on bail commits another, often violent crime. The purpose of bail is to allow accused persons who the courts feel are not likely to flee if released to be set free pending the disposition of their cases. The rationale behind bail is, first, that all persons are presumed innocent until proved guilty and, second, that this freedom is necessary for people to participate in their own defense. In addition, accused persons are able to continue to work, take care of their families, and so on. Thus a judge will set a sum of money as bond or security, guaranteeing the defendant's appearance in court. If the accused does not have the money, it can be borrowed from bail bonding agents at interest rates of from 5 to 20 percent.

One of the problems with the system is that poor people often find it impossible to personally, or through a bonding agent, raise the bond. Thus the poor more frequently remain in jail during the pretrial period than others. In 1966 Congress responded to this inequity by passing the Bail Reform Act which, except in murder cases or when there was a strong likelihood of the accused fleeing, severely restricted federal judges from imposing money bonds. Other forms of security, including release on one's own recognizance, were to be substituted. Money bonds still could be imposed, but under no circumstance except the two mentioned above would a person be denied pretrial freedom because of inability to raise bond. This reform pertained only to federal courts, although some states adopted similar practices.

The Bail Reform Act was, in a sense, a monument to liberal optimism and philosophy. But as crime rose and as cases like that of Stephen Judy came to light, the call for "reform" grew louder. In 1981 several members of Congress and the President's Task Force on Violent Crime recommended a change in federal bail procedures. Under the Bail Reform Act the only issue considered in pretrial release is the likelihood that the defendant will appear at the trial. Under both the proposed legislation and the task force recommendation, persons who, in the eyes of the court, are likely to pose a significant danger to the community if set free would be denied bail. This practice, sometimes referred to as "preventive detention," appears to have increased support among the general public: one of the provisions of California's Proposition 8 allows judges to refuse bail to accused persons whom they view as a danger to the community.

While Congress had not yet taken action on preventive detention as of this writing, the issue will undoubtedly continue to be debated at both the federal and state levels and be adopted in some jurisdictions.

Sentencing   The Task Force on Violent Crime found "widespread agreement that the present federal approach to sentencing is outmoded and unfair to both the public and persons convicted of crime." This is probably one of the few areas of criminal justice reform where the term "widespread" is justified. Both liberals and conservatives agree on the problem and what should be done about it—although they agree for different reasons. The object of greatest attention, at the state as well as the federal level, is indeterminant sentencing. Under this practice judges, typically within guidelines set by a criminal code, set minimum and maximum terms for incarceration—e.g., not less than 5 years nor more than 15 years. A parole board or commission then determines when a prisoner should be released. Underlying the system is the idea of prison as an institution for rehabilitation. But as the task force found: "Yet almost everyone involved in the criminal justice system now doubts that rehabilitation can be induced reliably in a prison setting and now is quite certain that no one can really detect when a prisoner does become rehabilitated.''

Conservatives generally oppose indeterminant sentencing, arguing that sentences of varying degrees, even for the same crime, do not provide an effective deterrent to crime, do not help protect the public, undermine respect for the law, and debase the seriousness of the crimes. Liberals, on the other hand, argue that indeterminant sentencing is just one more opportunity for racial and class bias to enter the system, leading to capricious, unpredictable, and unfair sentencing. In addition, it is unnecessarily cruel since prisoners can never be certain when they will be allowed to leave prison. Thus, for very different reasons, both liberals, like Senator Kennedy, who emphasize justice, and conservatives, like Senator Thurmond, who emphasize punishment, have supported *determinant* sentencing. Under this system judges, acting within statutory guidelines, would sentence defendants for a set or determinant period of time. Both the public and the offender will know precisely how long the sentence is. There will be, it is argued, greater uniformity, certainty, deterrence, and fairness. In addition, James Q. Wilson believes that keeping convicted persons in prison for definite periods will effectively incapacitate habitual offenders who account for such a high proportion of property-related crimes.

The ideological ecumenicalism which has characterized support for determinant sentencing at the federal level is likely to lead to its adoption. At the state level, eleven states already have adopted some variation of determinant sentencing and more are certain to follow. Whether the system will be improved or whether it can support what will undoubtedly be the resulting larger prison population remains uncertain.

Lessons from Abroad   While the United States appears to be moving toward adopting some criminal justice policies found in other industrial nations, in the main we are moving in quite the reverse direction.

Plea bargaining is one of the few areas of policy convergence. For all practical purposes plea bargaining is not practiced in countries such as Sweden, France, and West Germany. In fact, in West Germany a rule of ''compulsory prosecution'' for all cases of serious crime requires prosecutors to take a case to trial ''in the strongest and most inclusive form.''[61] On the other hand, in England, while plea bargaining as such is not practiced, it is possible for a defendant, in all but the most serious cases, to ask for a summary trial before a magistrate's court rather than a jury trial in a higher court. The advantage to the defendant is that magistrate's courts are limited in the severity of the sentences they may impose.[62] However, it should be noted that this ''deal'' must be approved by the court, which often rejects it.

Bail practices in Europe and Japan vary considerably. In countries such as Japan, the Netherlands, Sweden, Denmark, and parts of Switzerland, bail does not exist. Persons are either freed on their own recognizance, which occurs in the vast majority of the cases, or they are detained, because of the seriousness of the offense, pending trial. In England, where bail is still used, the courts take into account not only the likelihood of the accused appearing at the trial but also whether the person would pose a danger to the community. In the latter event, bail is denied. This is, of course, the direction toward which reformers in the United States would like to see the U.S. system move.

If we had to identify the one area of criminal justice in which European and Japanese practices differ most significantly from the United States, it is that of criminal punishment. While the move in the United States is toward surer and longer incarceration, in most other countries there is increased reliance on nonincarcerative penalties and punishment. The most popular alternative forms of punishment are monetary penalties and suspended sentences or probation. In West Germany, for example, almost 85 percent of all persons convicted of crimes pay fines rather than serve time in penal institutions. Fines are imposed not only for traffic violations but for burglary and theft as well. More serious crimes, such as manslaughter, sexual assault, and murder, do carry prison terms. In Japan, only 4 percent of all convicted persons are punished by imprisonment, while the remaining 96 percent pay fines. As in West Germany, only the most serious crimes are punished by incarceration. In comparison, in a recent year in the U.S. federal system, 44.7 percent of persons convicted for federal offenses were sent to prison, 41 percent were placed on probation, and only 6 percent paid fines. As Bayley has observed, "Jails are a last resort in Japan; in the United States they are more commonly a first response."[63]

It should be noted, however, that at least one state (Minnesota) and some localities (e.g., Quincy, Massachusetts, and Wilmington, Delaware) have introduced fines or, in a case where the criminal cannot afford it, community-work penalties for nonserious offenses. In the case of Quincy, the money collected, or credited through work, goes toward restitution to the victims of thefts or personal or property damage. These efforts are, however, the exception rather than the rule in the United States.

The second most commonly used alternative to imprisonment is to suspend sentence or place persons on probation. Thus, of the relatively small proportion (4 percent of the total) of convicted persons in Japan given jail sentences, almost two-thirds of those sentenced are given a suspended sentence or placed on probation.[64] In addition to West Germany, Switzerland, and Japan, Sweden, Norway, Denmark, and the Netherlands also rely heavily upon nonincarcerative penalties.

The rationale behind the depenalization approach is threefold. First, overcrowded and underfinanced penal institutions can be reserved for those who have committed the most serious crimes and who are likely to do so again. Second, since prisons are often the place where first-time offenders are turned into lifetime criminals, society is better served by keeping the less dangerous out of prison than by incarcerating them. Third, nonincarcerative penalties are far cheaper.

Thus far depenalization has not attracted much support in the United States. In fact, as we will see below, there has been greater reliance upon imprisonment, and for longer periods, in the United States in recent years.

Prisons We have already touched upon some policy issues affecting the prison system, but will look at them in more detail now.

Theoretically, prisons should serve one or more of the following functions: (1) deter crime, (2) rehabilitate criminals, (3) incapacitate criminals (i.e., "keep them off the streets"), and (4) punish criminal behavior (i.e., retribution). From the latter part of the nineteenth century onward, the dominant theoretical and practical emphasis in the U.S. correctional system was on rehabilitation. Today it is virtually impossible to find anyone involved in or knowledgeable about the criminal justice system who believes that prisons rehabilitate criminals. Similarly, while there are many who *believe* that the threat of imprisonment is an effective deterrent of crime, actual *proof* of this is either inconclusive or negative.[65]

The prevailing sentiment in the country today seems to favor the third model of punishment, incapacitation. If prison does nothing else, it takes persons who have already committed crimes, and who very frequently continue to commit crimes, out of the community. The leading and most influential academic proponent of this model is James Q. Wilson. Wilson begins with the assumption, generally supported by fact, that a few habitual criminals are responsible for a majority of the crime in the country. "Yet a large proportion of repeat offenders suffer little or no loss of freedom. Whether or not one believes that such penalties, if inflicted, would act as a deterrent, it is obvious that they could serve to incapacitate these offenders and thus, for the period of the incapacitation, prevent them from committing additional crimes."[66] While Wilson's views have been challenged in the academic world, they have won widespread support in the political world.[67] Wilson counts as his supporters such diverse politicians as Gerald Ford, Ronald Reagan, and Edward Kennedy. And, in practice, there has been greater recourse in recent years to imprisonment, and for longer periods, than in the past. In 1982 there were 405,371 prison inmates in federal (29,403) and state (375,968) facilities; in 1970 there were 196,000. In addition, between 1965 and 1981 the average prison term increased from 18 to 35 months.

The increased use of imprisonment has produced a severe shortage of available facilities. While 150 new prisons have been built in the last decade, with more presently under construction, the increase in the prison population still exceeds capacity. The result is antiquated, overcrowded, filthy, and violent institutions which on several dramatic occasions have errupted in riots—e.g., Attica in 1971 and Santa Fe in 1980. In addition, these institutions have become "factories for crime," turning many men and women into habitual criminals. There are two policy-related implications of the situation. First, federal courts have found that the conditions in more than two dozen state prisons constitute cruel and unusual punishment, prohibited by the Eighth Amendment, and ordered that they be changed. And, second, the public has been asked to pay the tab—at about $70,000 per new cell. The President's Task Force on Violent Crime recommended that the federal government spend $2 billion over 4 years for state correctional facilities, and officials in several states have asked voter approval for bonds to raise money for correctional facilities. The problem is that while people want more incarceration they do not seem willing to pay for more prisons. President Reagan, who endorsed most of the provisions of his task force report, failed to support the $2 billion recommendation. Similarly, voters in Oregon, Michigan, Ohio, and Rhode Island recently have turned down bond issues for prison construction. Short of a major decline in crime, either the taxpayers are going to have to agree to pay the bill, or the courts and prisons will have to release criminals.

Unfortunately, if we look to other nations for guidance, we find remedies which people in the United States have rejected—at least for the time being. As we have seen above, the trend in most other countries is to rely less and less on incarceration, except for the most serious crimes. Prison sentences in Japan, Switzerland, Sweden, Denmark, Norway, the Netherlands, and West Germany are not only less likely to be imposed, but when they are it is for shorter periods. In fact, "No other country in the world imprisons as great a proportion of the population as we do, and the length of sentence for an offender in the American criminal justice system is several times longer than that of his counterpart anywhere else in the world."[68]

Beyond the "depenalization" that has characterized criminal justice policy in the countries mentioned above, there are profound differences between many of them and the United States with regard to conditions in, and policies dealing with, penal institutions. First, prisons in most of these countries are considerably smaller than in the United States; they rarely have more than 300 to 400 inmates, compared to the 1,500 to 2,500 inmates typically held in U.S. prisons. Furthermore, many prisons in Europe have occupancy rates of only 60 to 80 percent, whereas most state prisons in the United States hold more inmates than they were designed to accommodate—in some cases twice as many. Smaller prisons allow for greater humanism and less depersonalization among prisoners.

In addition to their smaller size, the prisons of other countries differ dramatically from U.S. prisons in respect to the physical surroundings and prison life. Switzerland, Sweden, and Norway, in particular, have adopted approaches which they believe inhibit the development of criminal sub-cultures in prison and difficulties in readjusting to the outside world. Many prisons in these countries are "open"; inmates live not in cells but in private rooms or cottages with no bars, armed guards, or prison walls. While there are locks on the doors, the prisoners have the keys. Private visits from family, especially spouses, and girlfriends or boyfriends are permitted, as are furloughs and weekend home leaves. In Sweden, where this approach has gone the furthest, inmates are called "clients"; they are paid to either work or study; they have access to recreational facilities; they enjoy conjugal visits in their own private rooms, as well as home visits; and they are able to voice complaints and criticisms to Inmate Advisory Councils on which they are represented.[69] The result of these and similar practices in Norway and Switzerland is that, in contrast to the United States, there is virtually no prison violence in these countries.

American detractors of this approach point out that the recidivism rates in countries like Sweden, Norway, the Netherlands, and Switzerland are comparable to those of the United States. However, defenders contend that only proven, habitual criminals are imprisoned in these countries, while lesser criminals receive fines or probation. In general, Western European prisons are not the "factories of crimes" which virtually everyone acknowl-edges is the case with U.S. prisons.

But in the final analysis we return to the issue of exportability, and at this point there appears to be little effort toward or support of depenalization and more humane treatment of prisoners. In addition, there is the reality, mentioned in Chapter 1, that the United States is not Sweden. One obviously laudatory and envious comparison of the Swedish and California state penal systems realistically concluded:

> Compared to California prisons, Swedish prisons are smaller, more personal, more manageable, more heavily staffed, and more generously financed . . . Swedish prisoners are, ethnically, more homogeneous; are less prone to violent crime than California prisoners; and they are serving markedly shorter sentences. In short, Swedish prisons, like Swedish society, is very much unlike American prisons and American society.[70]

Prisons, and penal policy, like other social institutions and policy, reflect the values and history of a nation. It is possible for U.S. policy makers to emulate the practices of these other countries, and some prisons have experimented with such European practices as conjugal visits, furloughs, private rooms rather than cells, and the like, but these have been limited in number. The United States may move in this direction in the long run but not in the immediate future.

Eliminate the Causes   In a sense the discussion thus far has been on the conservatives' "home court." As we noted in the beginning of the chapter, conservative criminal justice policy proposals emphasize the manifestations of crime and what can be done about them. Hence, the concern with reforming the *criminal justice system.* Liberals, while not denying that the system needs reform, nevertheless emphasize the *social* causes rather than the manifestations of crime. Lyndon Johnson articulated the liberal approach to the growing national and political concern with crime in an address to the nation on July 27, 1967. In that speech Johnson argued that the solutions to the crime problem lay in "attacking the conditions that breed despair and violence. All of us know what those conditions are: ignorance, discrimination, slums, poverty, disease, not enough jobs." In a very real sense Johnson's "war on poverty" could be viewed as a "war on crime"; victory in the former would guarantee success in the latter.

Similarly, Charles Silberman underscores the relationship between poverty and crime:

> Why are violent criminals drawn so heavily from the ranks of the poor? The answer lies not in the genes, but in the nature of the lives poor people lead and of the communities in which they reside. The close association of violent crime with urban lower-class life is a direct result of the opportunities that are *not* available.[71]

Because of their emphasis on the causes of crime, liberals argue that no matter how well conceived criminal justice reforms might be, they cannot be successful as long as the reasons that force people to commit crimes are left untouched. Although liberals recognize that middle-class people commit crime—witness the rise in white-collar crime in the country—it is clear that those people without jobs, or who drop out of school, or who live in slums, are much more likely to commit crimes than those who are not victims of poverty. Harsher laws, longer prison sentences, more restrictive bail procedures, more prisons, and less sentencing discretion cannot eliminate or even significantly reduce crime as long as the causes are ignored. Better educational and job opportunities, better housing and living environments, and better nutrition and health care may not eliminate crime but most certainly will reduce it.

Furthermore, liberals argue that the proof, or at least partial proof, of their argument can be found outside the United States. We have seen that, compared to the democratic nations of Western Europe and Japan, the United States has the highest level of crime—and the highest number of impoverished people. One compelling liberal explanation for the lower levels of crime in these countries is not only that there are far fewer poor persons, but that governments in these countries play a more supportive role in ensuring that the housing, health care, educational, and job needs of all people are met. Yes, there are some who still commit crimes in the Scandinavian countries, but no one can contest the fact that the level and seriousness of crime is lower in these countries. Liberals suggest that a major reason for this is that the breeding grounds of crime—poverty, ignorance, slums, and too few jobs—have been virtually eliminated.

As we noted earlier, the political implications of the liberal position are profound. An assault on the cradles of crime requires an extraordinary assertion of material resources and of government commitment. Such an extraordinary war began under Lyndon Johnson during his "war on poverty." That effort, however, was aborted, or at least inadequately financed, because of the "other war" which Johnson decided to fight. Liberals do not see the "war on poverty" as a failure. It was an incomplete success which must be renewed if crime, of which the poor themselves are often the victims, is to be reduced.

Conservatives do not accept the argument that poverty and crime are highly correlated. James Q. Wilson and Ronald Reagan, for example, reject the assertion. President Reagan, in his 1981 speech to the International Association of Chiefs of Police, said:

> Many of the social thinkers of the 1950's and 60's who discussed crime only in the context of disadvantaged childhoods and poverty stricken neighborhoods were the same people who thought that massive government spending would wipe away our social ills. . . . The solution to the crime problem will not be found in the social worker's files, the psychiatrist's notes, or the bureaucrat's budget; it's a problem of the human heart, and it's there we must look for the answer.[72]

As we have seen before, a main conservative contention is that the individual, not society or social conditions, is responsible for crime. And the individual must be held accountable for his or her actions. Effective public policy must be directed toward that goal.

James Q. Wilson also questions the liberal thesis that poverty (and racism) "cause" crime. Wilson asks, for example, if poverty causes crime, why did crime increase at a time (the 1960s) when poverty declined, and why is it that most poor people do not commit crime?

> There is more crime in most poor neighborhoods than in most well-off ones, but even in poor communities most people do not steal. Furthermore, crime rose the fastest in this country at a time when the number of persons living in poverty or squalor was declining.[73]

Liberals, of course, would respond that while there may have been increased prosperity, it was not shared equally by all. In addition, this prosperity did nothing to undermine racism in the country. Finally, while it is true that not all poor people commit crimes, it is clear that poor people commit a disproportionate number of crimes.

As we have noted above, Wilson believes that the most effective response to crime is to concentrate on that small number of repeat offenders who commit a significant number of crimes, and to raise the "costs" of crime in general. It should be pointed out, however, that Wilson is not unmindful of a relationship between poverty and crime. The following quote from Wilson is important because it summarizes a major difference between the liberal and conservative positions on this policy issue.

> To a degree, anticrime policies may be frustrated by the failure of employment policies, but it would be equally correct to say that so long as the criminal justice system does not impede crime, efforts to reduce unemployment will not work. If legitimate opportunities for work are unavailable, many young persons will turn to crime; but if criminal opportunities are profitable, many young persons will not take those legitimate jobs that exist. The benefits of work and the costs of crime must be increased simultaneously. . . .[74]

In effect, Wilson acknowledges that unemployment is a factor in crime, but he notes that reducing unemployment without increasing the costs of crime will not reduce crime. Liberals, however, contend that poverty, including unemployment, slum living, etc., is *the* main reason why people commit crimes. Hence, primary, but not exclusive, emphasis should be put on ending poverty. The difference here is one of policy emphasis and sequence. It is a substantial difference.

SUMMARY

Crime has become one of the most compelling political issues of our time. People are frightened. They believe crime is increasing and is increasingly threatening their lives and lifestyles. In this chapter we have examined crime rates in this country and abroad, as well as some of the difficulties in assessing what those rates mean. We have examined some of the causes of crime and actual or proposed policy responses to crime in the United States and elsewhere. Liberal and conservative policy differences remain substantial in this area. Lyndon Johnson articulated the liberal responses to the growing national and political concern when he argued that the solutions to the crime problem lay in "attacking the conditions that breed despair and violence. All of us know what those conditions are: ignorance, discrimination, slums, poverty, disease, not enough jobs."

Whether that response was politically or materially inadequate, prematurely aborted, or just plain wrong, it did not work—or at least, it did not appear to work. Liberal optimism about the malleability of people and the ability of social institutions and policies to effect fundamental change has given way to the conservative belief, articulated by Ronald Reagan, "that men are basically good but prone to evil; and society has a right to be protected from them." Crime and criminals are to be punished and punished harshly. While this philosophy and its policy implications are contrary to the situation in many other industrialized and democratic nations, we cannot say they are wrong or right. People in the United States today are frightened and frustrated. And the conservative policy approach—effective or ineffective as it may prove to be—best expresses the fears and satisfies the frustrations of the country. Liberals do not deny the need to reform the criminal justice system. They do argue, however, that such reforms will not work as long as the causes of crime remain unchanged.

NOTES

1 *New York Times,* Sept. 29, 1981.
2 *Time,* Mar. 23, 1981.
3 *Cong. Rec.,* Mar. 31, 1981, p. H1222.
4 *Cong. Rec.,* Aug. 19, 1981, p. H4016.
5 *Cong. Rec.,* May 20, 1981, p. S5247.
6 See, for example, Ramsey Clark, *Crime in America* (New York: Simon and Schuster, 1970), Chapter 3; Charles E. Silberman, *Criminal Violence, Criminal Justice* (New York: Vintage Books, 1978), Appendix; Michael E. Milakovich and Kurt Weis, "Politics and Measure of Success in the War on Crime," *Crime and Delinquency,* 21 (Jan. 1975), 1–10; and Michael D. Maltz, "Crime Statistics: A Historical Perspective," *Crime and Delinquency,* 23 (Jan. 1977), 32–40.
7 Clark, p. 45.
8 Wesley G. Skogan, "Dimensions of the Dark Figure of Unreported Crime," *Crime and Delinquency,* 23 (Jan. 1977), 40–55.
9 Eugene Doleschal, "Crime: Some Popular Beliefs," *National Council on Crime and Delinquency,* 25 (Jan. 1979), 2.
10 Clark, pp. 49–50.
11 National Violence Commission, "U.S. National Commission on the Causes and Prevention of Violence," *Crime and Justice: The Criminal in Society,* ed. Leon Radzinowicz and Marvin E. Wolfgang (New York: Basic Books, 1971), p. 256.
12 Doleschal, "Crime: Some Popular Beliefs," p. 1.
13 Milakovich and Weis, p. 2.
14 *New York Times,* Feb. 2, 1981.
15 U.S. Department of Commerce, U.S. Bureau of the Census, *Social Indicators III* (1981), p. 237; and *Newsweek,* Mar. 23, 1981, p. 47.
16 Ted R. Gurr, "Historical Trends in Violent Crime: A Critical Review of the Evidence," in *Crime and Justice: An Annual Review of Research,* ed. Norval Lowry and Michael Morris (New York: Basic Books, 1981), p. 324.
17 *New York Times,* Feb. 2, 1982.
18 Quoted in Silberman, p. 28.
19 Roger Lane, "Criminal Violence in America. The First Hundred Years," *Annals*

   of the American Academy of Political and Social Sciences, 423 (Jan. 1967), 1–13.
20 Gurr, "Historical Trends in Violent Crime," p. 325.
21 See Lane, pp. 6–9.
22 Fredric Weitham, quoted in Congressional Quarterly Service, *Crime and Justice in America,* 2d ed. (Washington, D.C.: Congressional Quarterly, Dec., 1968), p. 7.
23 Gurr, "Historical Trends in Violent Crime," p. 339.
24 Silberman, p. 44.
25 Leon Radzinowicz and Joan King, *The Growth of Crime* (New York: Basic Books, 1977), p. 17.
26 Norman Ryder quoted in James Q. Wilson, *Thinking about Crime* (New York: Vintage Books, 1975), pp. 13–14.
27 Gurr, "Historical Trends in Violent Crime," p. 344.
28 Walter A. Lunden, "Violent Crimes in Japan in War and Peace, 1934–74," *International Journal of Criminology and Penology,* 4 (Nov. 1976), 354.
29 Dane Archer and Rosemary Gartner, "Violent Acts and Violent Times: A Comparative Approach to Postwar Homicide Rates," *American Sociological Review,* 41 (Dec. 1976), pp. 937–963.
30 R. J. Lifton quoted in Ibid., p. 943.
31 Ibid., p. 961.
32 Speech before the International Association of Chiefs of Police reported in *New York Times,* Sept. 29, 1981.
33 Ibid.
34 William A. Luksetich and Michael D. White, *Crime and Public Policy: An Economic Approach* (Boston: Little, Brown, 1982), p. 136.
35 Wilson, *Thinking about Crime,* p. 227.
36 Clark, p. 57.
37 See Edwin H. Sutherland and Donald R. Cressey, *Principles of Criminology,* 7th ed. (Philadelphia: J.B. Lippincott, 1966), pp. 74–81.
38 Robert K. Merton, "Social Structure and Anomie," *American Sociological Review,* 3 (Oct. 1938), 672–682.
39 Gurr, "Historical Trends in Violent Crime," pp. 328–330.
40 Quoted in James O. Finckenauer, "Crime as a National Political Issue: 1964–76," *Crime and Delinquency,* 24 (1978), 23; and Clark, p. 117.
41 *Crime and Justice in America,* p. 33.
42 Thomas E. Cronin, Tania E. Cronin, and Michael E. Milakovich, *U.S. Crime in the Streets* (Bloomington, Indiana: Indiana Univ. Press, 1981).
43 Ibid., p. ix.
44 This section draws heavily upon Sheldon Goldman, "Criminal Justice in the Federal Courts," *Current History,* 70 (June 1976), 241–260.
45 George L. Kelling et al., "The Kansas City Preventive Patrol Equipment: A Summary Report" (Washington, D.C.: Police Foundation, 1974), p. 16.
46 See, for example, James Q. Wilson and Barbara Boland, "The Effect of the Police on Crime," *Law and Society,* 12 (Spring 1978).
47 Silberman, p. 271.
48 Ibid., p. 275.

49 Quoted in *U.S. News and World Report,* May 10, 1976.

50 Clark, p. 157.

51 Wilson, *Thinking about Crime,* p. 125.

52 David H. Bayley, "Learning about Crime—The Japanese Experience," *Public Interest,* No. 44 (Summer 1976), 58.

53 Sir Eric Johnston, "The British Experience," *International Journal of Comparative Criminal Justice,* 1 (Spring 1977), 13.

54 Steven Schlesinger, *Exclusionary Injustice: The Problem of Illegally Obtained Evidence* (New York: Marcel Dekker, 1977), cited in Yale Kamisar, "Are Comparisons with Other Countries Meaningful?" *Judicature,* 62 (Feb. 1979), 348.

55 James Q. Wilson, "Crime and Punishment in England," *Public Interest,* No. 44 (Spring 1976), 13–14. The following material is based upon David Bayley, *Forces of Order* (Berkeley: Univ. of California Press, 1976); and Bayley, "Learning about Crime."

56 Bayley, "Learning about Crime," p. 68, emphasis added.

57 Ibid.

58 Marshal B. Clinard, *Cities with Little Crime* (Cambridge: Cambridge Univ. Press, 1978), p. 114.

59 Silberman, p. 377.

60 Ibid., p. 379.

61 John H. Langbein and Lloyd L. Weinreb, "Continental Criminal Procedure: 'Myth' and Reality," *The Yale Law Journal,* 87, No. 8 (July 1978), 1562.

62 Ted R. Gurr, *Rogues, Rebels and Reformers,* (Beverly Hills: Sage Publications, 1976), p. 147.

63 Bayley, *Forces of Order,* p. 141.

64 Clinard, p. 116.

65 Andrew Von Hersch, "The Aims of Imprisonment," *Current History,* 71, No. 418 (July–Aug. 1976), 3–4; Lee Bowker, "Crime and the Use of Prisons in the United States: A Time Series Analysis," *Crime and Delinquency,* 27 (Apr. 1981), 206–212; and Silberman, pp. 245–267.

66 Wilson, *Thinking about Crime,* p. 224.

67 See Von Hersch; and Lynn Curtis, "The Conservative New Criminology," *Society* (Mar.–Apr. 1977), 8, continued.

68 Eugene Doleschal, "Rates and Length of Imprisonment," *Crime and Delinquency,* 23 (Jan. 1977), 52.

69 See Harvey Siegel, "Criminal Justice—Swedish Style," *Offender Rehabilitation,* 3 (Spring 1976).

70 John Snortum, "Sweden's 'Special' Prisons," *Criminal Justice and Behavior,* 3 (Jan. 1976), 166.

71 Silberman, pp. 117–118, emphasis supplied.

72 Speech before the International Association of Chiefs of Police reported in *New York Times,* Sept. 29, 1981.

73 Wilson, *Thinking about Crime,* pp. xii–xiv.

74 Ibid., p. 227.

CHAPTER 7

EDUCATION: THE SEARCH FOR QUALITY AND EQUALITY

People in the United States always have placed extraordinary faith in education. The folks in the Massachusetts Bay Colony, who in 1647 adopted the first significant education law in the New World, viewed education as a major weapon in the battle against "that old deluder, Satan." They insisted, therefore, "that every township in this jurisdiction, after the Lord hath increased them to the number of fifty householders, shall then forthwith appoint one within their own town to teach all such children as shall resort to him to write and read." Thomas Jefferson, who was more concerned with preserving America's newly acquired liberty than with defeating the "old deluder," wrote to George Washington in 1786, "It is an axiom of my mind that our liberty can never be safe but in the hands of the people themselves, and that too of the people with a certain degree of instruction."[1]

Dwight Eisenhower occupied the White House over 300 years after the Massachusetts Bay Colony education law, but he too viewed education as critical in the battle against an "old deluder." In this case, however, it was international communism that posed the threat. In signing the National Defense Education Act (1958), which he sponsored in the wake of the national trauma associated with the Soviet launching of Sputnik in 1957, Eisenhower said that the act would "do much to strengthen our American system of education so that it can meet the broad and increasing demands imposed upon it by considerations of basic national security."

However, it was Lyndon Johnson, a former schoolteacher himself, who most succinctly articulated, and overstated, this extraordinary American faith in education. "The answer for all our national problems comes down to one single word: education."[2]

Johnson's unbounded confidence in education represents and reflects both the high point and turning point in recent attitudes toward education in the United States. While people in the United States have never "lost the faith"—80 percent of the people in a 1982 national Gallup poll felt that education was extremely important to one's future success[3]—they have become increasingly skeptical and critical of its quality. Since 1974 an annual Gallup poll on popular attitudes toward public education has included a question asking people to "grade" the public schools in their community. In 1974, 48 percent of those polled gave the schools "good" grades, that is, A or B, while 32 percent gave them poor grades, that is, C, D, or F (the remaining 20 percent "did not know"). In 1982, however, the numbers were just about reversed: 37 percent gave A or B grades, while 52 percent gave C through F grades. As in health care, poverty, and crime, the term "crisis" was being used to describe public education in the United States. In this chapter we will examine the indictment of U.S. public education.

The chapter begins by setting the jurisdictional parameters of education policy making. We will see that while the states and localities historically have dominated policy making in this area, the decade of the 1960s witnessed a surge in the role of the federal government. Next we examine the specific problems of education in the United States: "Why Can't Johnny Read?" and "Why Public Schools Fail."[4] Our first concern then is with the alleged decline in the quality of public education in the United States. Included in this discussion are comparisons with the quality of education in other countries.

The chapter then switches from a focus on quality to equality. Here we discuss the issue of equalizing the educational opportunities of all students regardless of race, social class, ethnic background, or physical impediments. Particular attention is focused on desegregation and busing, compensatory education for the poor, bilingual and bicultural education, and education for handicapped children.

FEDERALISM AND EDUCATION POLICY

Local Control

Education in the United States always has been a primarily local and state concern. While the Constitution is silent on the issue, the implicit assumption from the beginning of the Republic was that local and state governments were to take the lead in education policy. While state governments formally have ultimate control in education policy making, typically they have delegated considerable responsibility to local school authorities. "Local control" is, in fact, one of the most fiercely defended and distinguishing features of the U.S. education system. In general, local school districts determine the specific curriculum of the schools within their jurisdiction, formulate and adopt budgets, establish extracurricular activity programs, and define some facets of faculty hiring, retention, and promotion practices.

Beyond these general responsibilities it is necessary to emphasize that some of the most compelling and volatile issues of our time—school prayers, evolution versus creationism, book banning, segregation, bilingualism, etc.—involve local education and education authorities. It is at the local school district level that both the conflicts and the authority and will to resolve these conflicts ultimately reside. Throughout our history the local school has been both the battleground and mirror of our most basic conflicts. Although the focus of much of this chapter is on the increased federal involvement in education, it is critical for the reader to remember that ultimately it is in the neighborhood school that the problems of busing, bilingualism, special education, and declining educational achievement will be handled.

State Role

In general, state legislatures set the broad education policy guidelines within which the local authorities operate. These guidelines are then administered by state departments or boards of education. State authority includes control over minimum curricular standards, length of compulsory education, and certification of teachers. In addition, state education authorities collect statewide education statistics, distribute and administer state and federal funds to local school districts, and approve teacher-education programs.

A significant recent development in education has been the increase in influence of state governments over local school authorities. One author identified four reasons for this trend.[5] The first is the nationwide concern with the decline in the quality of education. While we examine this issue in detail later on, it is sufficient to note here that one result has been public pressure on state authorities to improve the quality of education, especially in the area of basic skills.

A second explanation for increased state control involves the financing of education. Simply stated, states have been called upon to help subsidize local education costs and remedy inequities between school districts. The latter problem derives from the fact that education is financed mainly through local property taxes.[6] Since there is considerable variation in property values between districts, there is considerable variation in how much money is available to spend on education. Because of this discrepancy state governments increasingly have been asked to remedy these inequalities.

The result is reflected in the reversed roles of state and local education financing. In the 1957–1958 school year the states were paying a smaller proportion of the nation's elementary and secondary school bill (30.4 percent) than the localities (53.5 percent). By the 1980–1981 school year, however, the states were paying a *larger* proportion than the localities: 48.5 percent compared to 44.6 percent.

A third factor contributing to greater state involvement is recent federal education legislation which requires state administration or oversight. The specific legislation, which we examine below, often has required state agencies either to administer or monitor federal programs or funds. This tendency was accelerated under the Reagan administration, which favored providing education "block grants" to the states rather than directly to the localities.

Finally, education interest groups increasingly have turned, because of the above trends, to state governments rather than the local authorities to make their demands concerning salaries, teaching conditions, and so on. In short, while local school districts and authorities continue to dominate education policy making in the United States, the last few decades have witnessed a centralizing tendency, with greater control being assumed by state education authorities.

Federal Involvement

From the beginning of the Republic the federal government has played a secondary role in education policy making. The modesty of this role is illustrated by federal spending on education. As late as the 1963–1964 school year federal expenditures accounted for only 4 percent of all money spent on elementary and secondary education in the United States. Furthermore, this money was used not to subsidize local education, but rather for specific programs such as school lunches.

Beginning in the 1950s and accelerating in the 1960s, the federal government became more active in education policy making. The first manifestation of this concerned the federal judiciary. Starting with the 1954 Supreme Court desegregation case (*Brown v. the Board of Education, Topeka, Kansas*) and followed in subsequent years by cases involving school prayers, financing, and special education, the federal government began having a greater impact on local education. Later on in this chapter we will examine some of the specific areas in which this impact was especially pronounced.

In 1965 this involvement took a new direction. The centerpiece of this effort was the Johnson-sponsored Elementary and Secondary Education Act (ESEA) aimed at improving educational programs and services for disadvantaged students (i.e., poor, handicapped, bilingual). The act, which is discussed below, had the effect of establishing a conspicuous federal role in education. In essence, the federal government enlisted—some say conscripted—local education in the national war on poverty and racial discrimination. For Lyndon Johnson, as we noted above, education was the key to unlocking the chains of poverty and discrimination.

Thus, beginning in the mid-1960s the federal role in education expanded. In terms of direct investment, federal expenditures for all elementary and secondary education increased from $1 billion (4 percent of total amount spent) in 1963–1964, to $10.1 billion (8.7 percent) in 1980–1981. It should be stressed that the ESEA specifically prohibited federal interference in curriculum, programs of instruction, textbook selection, and similar issues. The importance of ESEA, and subsequent federal legislation, lies less in the intimacy with which the federal government became involved in public education than in the assertion of the principle that the federal government has an important financial and agenda-setting role and responsibility in the area.

The symbolic and substantive capstone of this expanded role was the creation in 1980 of the cabinet-level Department of Education (ED). Some background on the creation of this department is necessary because of its place in the liberal-conservative debate over the federal role in education.

Although historically there were occasional calls for a separate, cabinet-level education department, responsibility in this area has always rested with a subcabinet agency—e.g., the Office of Education in the Department of Health, Education, and Welfare. However, with the expanded federal role in education, demands for such a department increased. The major proponent of a separate education department was the influential National Education Association (NEA). The NEA argued that with over 150 education programs scattered among more than 40 federal agencies, rational, effective policy implementation and direction were impossible.

A breakthrough in the NEA-led effort came in 1976 when presidential candidate Jimmy Carter endorsed the idea of an education department. In return, NEA, for the first time in its 120-year history, endorsed a presidential candidate—Jimmy Carter. That endorsement and campaign effort helped elect Carter President. According to Carter's campaign director, Hamilton Jordan, "The massive support from teachers was critical to our winning this very close election. All over the nation, we turned to the NEA for assistance. We asked for help and they delivered."[7]

In April 1978, President Carter also delivered; he introduced a bill to establish the Department of Education. We will not detail the 17-month legislative battle over the formation of ED. Suffice it to note that following a vigorous lobbying effort by President Carter, Congress approved the bill on September 27, 1979.

The Department of Education immediately became a lightning rod for conservative opposition. Conservatives opposed the ED because it represented further federal interference in local education affairs. Among the conservative opponents was candidate, and later President, Ronald Reagan. He promised that if elected he would reduce federal involvement in education and dismantle the bureaucratic symbol of that involvement, the ED. In 1982 President Reagan proposed replacing the ED with a subcabinet agency, the Foundation for Education Assistance. The foundation would perform some ED functions—but employ 1,400 fewer people—while other functions would be transferred to various federal agencies. At issue here is not simply a symbolic bureaucratic name-change, but rather a measure of the federal role and commitment in education. The demotion of the ED and the attendant diminution of federal resources, guidelines, and attention would reduce substantially the federal role in education. Liberals believe this would be a mistake because the resources and prestige of the federal government are needed to help accomplish the social goals which they favor. Conservatives believe that dismantling the ED would return education policy making to where it belongs, namely, to the states and localities.

Summing-Up

Education remains the primary responsibility of local and state governments. The term "local control" describes the reality and philosophical bias of U.S. education. While much of the impetus for change and controversy in education over the last few decades has come from the federal government, it is still at the local school level that the major policy battles have been fought and will ultimately be resolved. Despite the long tradition and continued reality of local control, two centralizing tendencies have occurred in U.S. education in recent decades. The first has been a shift toward greater financial responsibility and administrative oversight by state education agencies. The second has been the expanded role of the federal government. Beginning in the 1960s this expansion took the form of a larger financial obligation and, more critically, defining the goals and responsibilities of local education. The creation of the Department of Education reflected this expanded role.

ISSUES IN EDUCATION POLICY

According to Francis Keppel, former U.S. Commissioner of Education, there have been, thus far, two revolutions in U.S. education. The first was a revolution in *quantity*. "Everyone was to be provided the chance for an education of some sort. That revolution is almost won in the schools, and is on its way in higher education." The second revolution involves *equality* of educational opportunity, and that revolution continues today. Keppel predicted, in 1966, that a third revolution, concerned with *quality* in education, would soon begin.[8] That revolution, it would appear, is underway.

In recent years, the policy debate over education in the United States has focused on quality and equality in education. The third of Keppel's revolutions touches upon how well the schools are providing students with the skills necessary to perform successfully in society. The issue here is summarized and popularized in the question, "Why can't Johnny read?" The second issue, that of equality of opportunity, has been on the policy agenda since the 1954 Supreme Court decision, *Brown v. the Board of Education, Topeka, Kansas,* which declared that segregated education was inherently unequal. The concern with equalizing educational opportunities, initially based on race, has been extended to include students from backgrounds of poverty, those with limited English-speaking ability, and those with mental and physical handicaps. In the remainder of this chapter we examine these two most recent revolutions in U.S. education.

Why Johnny Can't Read: The Problem of Quality

The year 1982 *may* have marked a milestone in the public concern over education in the United States. In September of that year the College Entrance Examination Board announced that for the first time since 1963 Scholastic Aptitude Test (SAT) scores had risen. (See Figure 7-1.) The increase was not dramatic: two points on the verbal test (424 to 426) and one point on the mathematics test (466 to 467). However, for parents and educators who had been conditioned to bad news about the schools, this increase was warmly received. College Entrance Board President George Hanford said at the time, "This year's rise, however slight, combined with last year's holding steady, is a welcome sign for educators, parents and students that serious efforts by the nation's schools and their students to improve the quality of education are taking effect."[9]

Not everyone connected with education saw this "surge" as the dawn of a new era. William J. Bennett, chairman of the National Endowment for the Humanities, said one and two point gains were hardly "a cause for trumpets."[10] It will take, in fact, much more significant and sustained improvements in SAT scores and other indicators of education performance to convince a skeptical public that the schools are not failing.

The evidence of this failure is often highly subjective and anecdotal. For example, there is the case of "Dorothy Tillman, whose son Jimmy marched off to kindergarten in Chicago already reading at second-grade level, and after seven years, now reads at fourth-grade level."[11] Or ask any college professor who has taught for any length of time to compare current and past students. The response, we are confident, will be that today's college students do not write, or generally perform, as well as their predecessors.

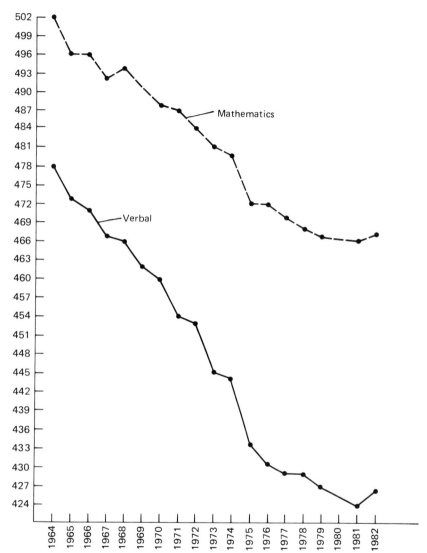

FIGURE 7-1
Scholastic aptitude test scores (SAT), 1964–1980.

The objective evidence seems to support popular impressions. Not only SAT scores, which have recorded a 52-point decline in verbal scores and a 35-point decline in quantitative scores since 1963, but other measures also reflect this decline in educational achievement. Since 1969 the National Assessment of Educational Progress (NAEP), which assesses educational achievement in ten learning areas for various age groups (9-, 13-, 17-year-olds), has recorded consistent declines in most areas. Following a decade of surveys NAEP found (1) a decline in math scores for all three groups, (2) no change in the writing ability of 9-year-olds but a decline for 13- and 17-year-olds, and (3) a decline in social studies achievement for 13- and 17-year-olds, with again no change for 9-year-olds. The most recent NAEP national survey (1980) showed a somewhat brighter picture for reading skills—at least among the 9-year-old age group. This age group showed improved reading skills over their cohorts of 1971 and 1974–1975. The skills of 13-year-olds remained stable over the previous survey but that of 17-year-olds showed a decline.[12]

An even more dramatic measure of the apparent failure of U.S. education is the fact that between the 1950s and 1980s the United States dropped from eighteenth to forty-ninth place among nations in terms of literacy. Today there are an estimated 60 million people in the United States who are functionally illiterate; that is, they cannot read or write well enough to fill out an application for a driver's license or read the directions on a medicine bottle. It is no wonder then people are convinced that the schools are failing.

It must be recognized, of course, that not all of the recent decline in educational achievement can be attributed to the educational system. Perhaps as much as two-thirds of the decline in SAT scores during the 1960s was attributed to changes in the test-taking population. "An increasingly diverse group of students began heading for college, including larger numbers of women (who average lower scores in math) and economically disadvantaged students (who average lower scores in all areas)."[13]

However, by the mid-1970s, when these new groups had become an integral part of the testing universe, the continuing decline could no longer be attributed to this change. Attention then shifted to other noneducational factors to explain declining achievement. Among the explanations offered were (1) diminished respect for all institutional authority growing out of the turmoil of the Vietnam and Watergate years; (2) changes in the U.S. family, and especially increases in the number of divorces, single-parent homes (which account for one-fifth of all the homes of students today), and working mothers. These changes weakened the traditional school-supporting role of the family; and (3) the deleterious influence of increased television viewing and the attendant decline in leisure time reading among school-age children.

Although these explanations account for *some* of the decline in achievement, the most consistent and convenient target continues to be the schools and educators. The indictment against U.S. public education is broadly defined. The alleged factors contributing to the decline in achievement include (1) the schools' failure to enforce discipline, (2) poor teacher training, (3) the movement in the 1960s to embrace and emphasize "relevant" courses of study at the expense of teaching basic skills, (4) teacher "burnout," and (5) the fact that teaching now attracts the least talented college students—in 1980 the SAT scores of high school seniors who indicated they would major in education were thirty-five points below the national average on the verbal test and forty-eight points below on the math test.

We will not examine each of these charges. As in the case of the noneducational factors listed above there is some truth to these allegations. The point that must be underscored is that the public and public policy makers believe them to be true. It may be that the schools are simply a more convenient target. It is certainly easier to legislate change in school curriculum than in family structure or television viewing habits. While there have been several policy proposals to remedy the problem, we will focus on three of these: (1) return to emphasizing basic skills, (2) competency testing of teachers, and (3) public support of private education.

Basics and Competency   Conservative critics maintain that U.S. education has strayed from a necessary and appropriate emphasis on teaching basic skills: reading, writing, and mathematics. The declining SAT scores, and other measures of skills competency, are eloquent testimony to this fact. These critics attribute this neglect to "humanistic educators," who gained influence in the 1960s. While the term "humanism" covers a broad range of perspectives on education, there are some identifiable common features ascribed to by most humanists. "These commonalities include an emphasis on the individual child's development and on the freedom for each child to set his or her own goals, free of the restrictions of preset, societally determined objectives."[14] This concern with tailoring education to individual student needs, as well as teaching "relevant" material, diverted attention from basic competency skills. The results of this inattention have been declining SAT scores and ill-prepared, non-college-bound high school graduates.

Defenders of the humanistic approach—and there is considerable overlap between educational humanists and political liberals—concede the need to address the problem of a skills deficiency among schoolchildren. They argue, however, that there is more to education than simply mastering basic skills. Society requires inculcating social responsibilities and sensitivities, which are not easily measured by test scores or typically included in basic skills curricula.

The public, however, was clearly concerned with permissive curriculum standards and a retreat from basics. Beginning in the 1970s, when the decline in SAT scores was made public, parents demanded a return to more traditional educational concerns. The policy response to these demands has taken two forms. The first has been to scrap many of the "fluff and miscellany" (to use the words of the *Wall Street Journal*) curriculum requirements and return to a more "solid" curriculum. In addition, many local school districts adopted back-to-basics programs or set up alternative schools devoted to teaching basic skills. However, by far the most common response was the establishment, in nearly forty states, of minimum competency tests as a requirement for high school graduation.

While the back-to-basics and minimum competency movements have had strong popular support, they have not been without their critics and problems. A case involving a 1976 Florida minimum competency test highlights some of the major theoretical and practical difficulties. In 1976 Florida enacted a two-part statewide Student Assessment Test. The first part was designed to measure basic English and math skills, while the second part was a functional literacy test. Under the law, students had to pass both parts as a requirement for a regular high school diploma. If they failed, they received a "certificate of completion," not a regular diploma. However, students could retake the test every 6 months until they passed. The test was first administered in October 1977, at which time 11,593 of the 41,724 students, a disproportionate number of whom were black, failed the math portion. Ten black students filed a class action suit in October 1978, claiming that the test violated their due process and equal protection rights. The case (*Debra P. v. Turlington*) was heard in a U.S. District Court in July 1979. The federal district judge upheld the validity of the principle of the test and ruled that this particular test was not racially or culturally discriminatory. However, he ruled that since most of the black students taking the test in the school year 1978–1979 had attended segregated and inferior schools—Florida schools were segregated until 1967—in their first 3 years of education, they were being punished for past discriminatory practices. The judge ordered that the implementation of the test be postponed until school year 1982–1983, when the remaining effects of segregated education disappeared from the background of black students.

The case was appealed by the state of Florida to the United States Fifth Circuit Court of Appeals. In May 1981, the court upheld the lower court decision on the right of the state to require such an examination and the delay to remedy previous discrimination in education. However, the court also declared that the state of Florida—and by legal extension all other states—had to prove that the test was "fair." The appeals court held, in effect, that Florida had not demonstrated that the test measured what actually was taught in Florida schools.

The implications of the case are clear. Most narrowly, some states, mainly in the south, will have to demonstrate that there are no residual effects of discriminatory education practices which might affect minority students' chances of success on competency tests. A longer-range consequence is that states using competency tests will have to prove that *every* student has had an adequate and fair opportunity to learn the skills necessary to pass the tests.

Beyond these legal problems remains the question of whether competency and functional literacy tests and back-to-basics curricula are pedagogically sound. Critics are concerned that schools will "teach to the tests," with the result that education will become narrow in content and fail to produce students with the full range of skills needed by modern society.

Teacher Competency   The 1970s brought not only a demand that students demonstrate their competency but that teachers and prospective teachers do so as well. The assumption here is that if the schools are failing to meet their responsibilities, at least some of the blame must be shared by the teachers. This essentially intuitive assessment received empirical support in 1980 when Florida gave an 8th-grade-level math test to 1,200 education majors, one-third of whom failed it. Similarly, in 1982 one-third of the 6,900 aspiring California teachers who took a required three-R's test failed it. Today approximately forty states require some form of competency testing for teachers or prospective teachers.

Vouchers, Tax Credits, and Private Education   As support for and faith in *public* schools decline, popular support for *private* schools appears to be on the rise. A 1982 Gallup poll found that nearly 50 percent of parents with children in school would opt for sending their children to private schools if both public and private schools were tuition-free. Parents apparently believe that private schools are safer and more stimulating and do a better job in teaching, building character, and preparing students for college. However, the nature of the qualifier—if private schools were free—clearly inflated this hypothetical support. Nevertheless, the magnitude of the favorable response rate, coupled with the increasingly low assessment of the public schools, suggests that many parents, given adequate incentives, might opt for private rather than public schools. And adequate incentives are precisely what policy makers have been proposing. Two specific and interrelated proposals of largely, but not exclusively, conservative origin have been forwarded: tuition tax credits and a voucher system.

We begin with tuition tax credits, the more modest of the two proposals. In August 1982, President Reagan submitted to Congress a bill which would have given a 50 percent federal income tax credit, not to exceed $500, to parents sending their children to private or parochial elementary and secondary schools. In other words, if parents spend $600 a year on their child's private school, they could, once the program is in full effect, deduct $300 from the amount they owe in federal income tax. The ostensible rationale behind the proposal is the issue of fairness. Parents who send their children to private schools pay twice for that education: once in the form of taxes for public schools and again in the form of fees for the private school.

The Reagan proposal was by no means new. In 1978, the Senate, after intense opposition from President Carter and the National Education Association, defeated a similar proposal. In addition, two states, Rhode Island and Minnesota, have enacted tuition state tax credit laws. The Rhode Island law was ruled unconstitutional because 94 percent of the students who were eligible attended parochial schools. The U.S. court of appeals, which ruled against the law, felt this effectively constituted state sponsorship of religion. The Minnesota law is almost identical to its Rhode Island counterpart—and almost all the schools benefiting from the law are parochial. This law was upheld, however, by a U.S. circuit court, and in 1983 the Supreme Court upheld the Minnesota law as well (*Mueller v. Allen*).

Basically, liberals oppose tax credits and conservatives favor them. Liberal opposition is based upon the following arguments. First, the proposal favors the rich; poor people, even with tax credits, will be unable to afford private schools, which have an annual average tuition of almost $800. Second, it will undermine public education by encouraging wealthier, and typically nonminority, parents to send their children to private schools. The public schools, which are already heavily populated by minority students, will become even more disproportionate. The quality of public education, therefore, will suffer. Third, the bill will encourage all-white, segregated private schools, setting back the cause of integrating U.S. society. Fourth, because 85 percent of the nation's private schools are church-related, tuition tax credits constitute state support of religious institutions, which is prohibited by the First Amendment.

Conservative support of tuition tax credits is based upon the following arguments. First, these credits do not constitute a danger to public education. Today almost 90 percent of all schoolchildren attend public schools. In fact, enrollment in private schools has declined to the point where their existence is threatened. Second, anything that contributes to competition and freedom of choice benefits all concerned. Tuition tax credits will encourage the public schools to improve in order to compete with private schools. Third, contrary to liberal criticism, tax credits will help poor and minority students. Thomas Sowell, a distinguished conservative, black economist, argues that right now blacks are "trapped in educationally deteriorating and physically dangerous public schools."[15] Tuition tax credits would allow the parents of ghetto children to choose an alternative to public education. Sowell believes that parochial education is already benefiting black students. "One of the great untold success stories of contemporary American education is the extent to which Catholic schools, left behind in ghettos by the departure of their original white clientele, are successfully educating black youngsters there at low cost."[16]

Tuition *vouchers* are a more ambitious version of the tax credit program. The idea was first suggested by Milton Friedman and is intended to allow parents to choose the schools to which they send their children. Under the plan parents would be given a voucher by the government redeemable for a certain sum of money to pay for the education of their children—perhaps $2,000, which is about the national per capita average expenditure on education. The voucher could be used in any accredited elementary or secondary public or private school.

There is no need to discuss the arguments for and against the voucher system—they are the same as those dealing with tuition tax credits. While the idea has generated considerable interest, it has not traveled nearly as far along the path of popular acceptance or policy discussion as have tax credits. It should be emphasized here that a voucher system too would be subject to scrutiny by the courts.

Comparing the Quality of Education in the United States and Abroad   Before comparing the quality of education in the United States and other industrial nations, it is necessary first to examine some critical differences between the U.S. system of education and Western European and Japanese systems of education. This is necessary not only to familiarize the reader with these latter systems, but also to explain why, in at least some areas, U.S. students do not perform as well as students of other countries on standardized international tests.

The first major difference is that, historically, schools in Western Europe and Japan have evaluated the academic promise of elementary school children and assigned them to different secondary schools based upon that evaluation. Thus, between the ages of 10 and 12, Japanese, German, Swedish, British, and students in other Western European countries took an examination, and based upon the results of the examination they then entered one of three types of secondary schools: college preparatory schools, vocational-technical schools, or general education-track schools leading to a terminal high school degree. In general, college preparatory schools contained students from the middle and upper classes, while the other schools consisted primarily of lower- and working-class students. The European and Japanese school systems then both reflected and perpetuated a rigid social class structure. Lower- and working-class students were condemned, at relatively young ages, to an educational "track" or "stream" that was unlikely to lead to upward social mobility.

Following World War II, egalitarian impulses led most Western European nations and Japan to introduce "comprehensive" schools, or schools which all students would attend regardless of academic ability or socioeconomic background. This is, of course, the approach to secondary education which has prevailed in the United States since the mid-nineteenth century. In nineteenth-century America these were called "common schools." The post-World War II development of comprehensive schools has proceeded unevenly in Western Europe and Japan. In the case of Japan, for example, a comprehensive system was set up almost immediately after the war, and now all Japanese students attend such schools. Similarly, in Sweden, since 1971, all students attend comprehensive schools. In West Germany, by way of contrast, only 16 percent of the secondary school students in 1981 were attending comprehensive schools, while the remainder were enrolled in the traditional three-track system. Finally, France, Denmark, and Norway represent yet a third model in the development of a comprehensive school system. In these countries differentiation between students does not occur until after the age of 14—more or less equivalent to our junior high school students. After age 14, students are placed in specialized senior secondary schools.

The first major difference, then, between U.S. and Western European and Japanese education systems is the longer tradition of common or comprehensive schooling in our country. While other industrial, democratic nations have moved toward the U.S. model in the last few decades, significant vestiges of the multitrack system remain.

The second difference between U.S. and other education systems is the significantly higher proportion of U.S. students who are retained through the final year of secondary school. Approximately 75 to 80 percent of those children in the United States starting elementary school in 1972 will still be in school through their senior year in 1984. Comparable approximate figures for other countries are Sweden, 70 percent; Australia, 35 percent; England, 30 percent; New Zealand, 25 percent; and West Germany, 15 percent. Only Japan, where 90 percent of all children graduate from 12th grade, exceeds the United States in school retention. In most of Western Europe the majority of students leave school when they are 15 or 16 years old and enter the labor market. Thus European senior high school students are an academically more select group than their U.S. and Japanese counterparts.

The final difference we wish to emphasize is that with some exceptions (e.g., Australia, Switzerland) in most other countries the national government plays a greater role in education policy making than in our country. The extent of that role varies, however, among countries. In France, Sweden, and Japan the national government plays a major role in financing education, establishing a uniform curriculum for all schools in the country, choosing textbooks, certifying teachers, and designing uniform national examinations. In Great Britain and West Germany, on the other hand, issues dealing with curriculum content, pedagogy, and day-to-day administration are left to

local authorities, although major education decisions such as comprehensivization and minimum school-leaving age are made by the central
government.

While there are many implications of a centralized educational system,
one in particular stands out. It is far easier in centralized systems to achieve
desired policy goals—such as improving quality or equality in education—
than in a decentralized system. If, for example, it appears that the nation
faces a serious shortage of science and mathematics teachers—as the
United States does in the 1980s—this can be remedied in a centralized
system by the education ministry increasing curriculum emphasis on these
subjects in schools and teacher training programs. This, by the way, is
precisely what the Japanese have done. In the United States, however,
such a decision must be taken, not by one central education ministry, but
by fifty state education departments and implemented by thousands of
colleges (in the case of teacher training) and about 16,000 school districts.
With this background in hand, we can now look at the issue of the quality
of education in other countries.

There has been, to our knowledge, only one systematic, multinational,
comparative study of educational achievement. This study was conducted
by the Stockholm-based International Association for the Evaluation of
Educational Achievement (IEA). It was conducted in the early 1970s,
involving nearly 260,000 children in twenty-two nations and covering six
subject areas: reading, literature, mathematics, science, civic education,
and a foreign language. Although the data are somewhat dated—in 1982
the IEA began preparing another survey, the results of which will not be
published for a few years—they still provide some interesting insights. The
first of these relates to the consequences of the higher retention rates of
U.S. schools. The study found that in certain key subject areas—e.g.,
mathematics, science, and social studies—U.S. high school seniors placed
at or near the bottom compared to their peers in the other nations. Part of
the explanation for this poor performance is that while in the United States
approximately 75 percent of the senior class age group will graduate, in
other countries the proportion is significantly lower. The high school senior
classes in West Germany, France, New Zealand, and Sweden represent
only the best students while the U.S. class reflects a cross-section of
achievement.

While this explains some of the achievement difference, it cannot explain
all of it. Japan, for example, retains a larger proportion of the school-age
group through the senior year. Yet the Japanese place at or near the top in
science and mathematics. Here the explanation seems to be in the greater
emphasis placed upon these subjects in Japan than in other countries, and
especially the United States. Clearly the U.S. system of mass education
and emphasis on high retention has its price in terms of apparently poor

performance in international competition. Many would argue, however, that "this is crucial to any effort to keep society fluid and to allow rich and poor, workers' and professional peoples' children, long-term Americans and recent immigrants to rise to the top."[17]

Because of the differences in retention, the IEA study also compared the performance of 14-year-olds, since in most advanced countries almost all students of this age group are in school. This group of U.S. students compared more favorably than the older group, placing near (but never at) the top on the reading, literature, and science tests and in the middle on the civic education test.

For those readers who are interested in whether we "won" or "lost" in the IEA study there is no simple answer. Clearly, total U.S. performance relative to other nations suffers from our more egalitarian approach to education. However, comparisons between more selected groups—e.g., all 14-year-olds or the top 5 percent of high school seniors in each country— reveal that U.S. students perform near the top but never at the top of the survey group.

It would be useful at this point to focus more closely on the one country which, at least in mathematics and science, was a "winner" in the IEA study, namely Japan. The Japanese system is of interest for two reasons. First, it is similar to our own in that it retains more than 80 percent of its senior class. And second, "In the 1980s the Japanese educational system is much better equipped than its U.S. counterpart to produce workers with the high levels of skill in math, science, and engineering that the economy of the future will require."[18] How have the Japanese accomplished this success?

To begin, Japanese students spend more days in school each year than their U.S. counterparts: about 225 to, typically, 180. As a result of the amount of time they spend in, and the societal emphasis placed on, education, the school plays a more central part in the lives of Japanese students than U.S. students.[19] Second, Japanese students are required to take more math, science, and social studies: 2 years of math and science and 3 of social studies, compared to 1 year of math and science and 2 years of social studies in most U.S. schools. Third, Japanese students take a wider variety of more advanced courses and go into greater depth than U.S. students. Fourth, "Japanese high schools offer only a fraction of the nonacademic electives that clutter the U.S. curriculum."[20] Finally, it must be remembered that the Japanese education system is highly centralized with a nationwide, uniform curriculum. Thus all Japanese students are exposed to the same demanding education. This contrasts sharply with the U.S. system, in which there is enormous range in the quality and content of education across the nation.

The Japanese success in educational achievement, however, has been bought at a high social price. The main problem derives from the enormous pressure placed upon students to succeed in school. "A major concern of the Japanese Ministry of Education is that academic competition is so intense that Japanese children are neglecting other aspects of their development. . . . Intense academic pressure also produces negative by-products, such as non-achievers who lose all sense of meaning in their lives and turn to truancy, gangs, and even suicide, partly because nonacademic vocations command little prestige."[21]

We conclude this section by noting that some of the education policy issues which are currently being debated or have recently been implemented in the United States have long been a part of the education systems of other advanced nations. Most countries of Western Europe, Japan, New Zealand, and Australia have competency examinations as a basis for graduation and admission to college. In addition, in all of these countries there is some provision for public aid to private schools. In fact, until recently Australia had a system of tuition tax credits. These were replaced, however, by a system of direct transfer payments by the federal and state governments to private schools. Whatever the particular mechanism, in all of these countries the government subsidizes private, including church-related, education.

Summary: The Problem of Quality   In recent years there has been an erosion in the faith long placed in public schools in the United States. People believe that the schools are failing in their most fundamental responsibility of providing a quality education. There is also evidence that U.S. students are not doing as well as students in other countries. There is concern, as there was following the Soviet launching of Sputnik in 1957, that we are falling behind other nations (e.g., the Soviet Union and Japan) in the critical areas of mathematics and science.

The policy response has been to reemphasize basic skills, to require that students demonstrate minimum competency in certain subject areas, and to require that schoolteachers, or those who would be schoolteachers, demonstrate *their* competency.

At the same time that there has been pressure on the public schools to improve their performance, there have been demands for policies that would facilitate parents sending children to private schools. Parents, in the words of Milton Friedman, should be "free to choose" the kind of education they want for their children without paying twice. The main policy proposals offered in this regard have been tuition tax credits and vouchers. Finally, we have seen that public financial assistance and incentives for private schools, as well as competency testing, are common features of educational systems in other industrialized democracies. We looked at one of these countries, Japan, in some detail because of its apparent success in education, as well as the fact that it has become, in effect, the "Joneses" with whom people in the United States are forever trying to keep up. It is clear that Japanese education is more demanding than U.S. education in terms of time, variety, depth of study, and social pressures.

We will now move on to the second major concern of this chapter, namely, equality of educational opportunity. The reader should be aware, and will be reminded, that the two issues, quality and equality, often intersect.

Equality of Educational Opportunity

While the issue of educational quality and achievement has generated an enthusiastic and serious national debate, it clearly has been overshadowed by the more traumatic battle over equal educational opportunity. This issue first manifested itself in the national debate over school desegregation and the right of blacks to equal access, along with the white majority, to quality education. Later on the policy debate was expanded to include claims of others who, because of mental or physical handicaps, material deprivation, linguistic and cultural background, or gender also were alleged to have been denied such access.

Because ours is a pluralistic society, the debate over equal educational opportunity was bound to be divisive. It was made even more so, however, because the policy agenda, in most instances, was set by the federal government and imposed upon the states and localities. Local school districts and state education agencies were given a mandate to solve some of our nation's most intractable problems. Thus, superimposed upon racial, ethnic, class, and gender conflicts were the perennially thorny issues of states' rights, federalism, and the growth of the federal government. It is difficult to conceive of a less propitious set of political conditions than that which attended the national policy debate over integration, busing, and bilingual education.

The Desegregation of U.S. Education   No dimension of the concern with equal educational opportunity has been more protracted or traumatic than the desegregation of U.S. schools. The starting point was the 1954 Supreme Court case of *Brown v. the Board of Education, Topeka, Kansas* (374 U.S. 493). In that decision Chief Justice Earl Warren, speaking for a unanimous court, reiterated the U.S. faith in education:

> Today, education is perhaps the most important function of state and local governments. It is required in the performance of our basic public responsibilities, even service in the armed forces. It is the very foundation of good citizenship. Today it is a principal instrument in awakening the child to cultural values, in preparing him for later professional training, and in helping him to adjust normally to his environment. In these days, it is doubtful that any child may reasonably

be expected to succeed in life if he is denied the opportunity of an education. Such an opportunity, where the state has undertaken to provide it, is a right which must be made available to all on equal terms.

The court went on to rule that separating schoolchildren solely on the basis of race deprives them of equal educational opportunities and, therefore, was unacceptable under the Fourteenth Amendment guarantee of the "equal protection of the law." From that day in May 1954 until the present, U.S. school systems have grappled with implementing (or avoiding) the Supreme Court desegregation mandate.

At first the issue seemed unambiguous. Southern states were told by the Court, in 1955, to end the dual system of education (i.e., one black and one white) and to do so "with all deliberate speed." This phrase proved, in retrospect, to be a seriously inappropriate guide to compliance. Most southern school districts chose to place the emphasis on "deliberate" rather than "speed." Rather than facilitating an orderly adjustment to the revolutionary mandate to desegregate, it led to the adoption of dilatory, disruptive, and racially divisive tactics. In some instances parents simply withdrew students from the public schools, at times closing them completely, and set up alternative private schools—leaving the public schools all black and virtually impoverished. Massive resistance by whites, occasionally accompanied by violence, effectively nullified the Court's mandate and exacerbated racial tensions in the south.

Fifteen years passed and still only 20 percent of black students in the south attended integrated schools. In some instances this delay was abetted by the federal government itself. This was specifically the case in 1969 when the Nixon White House ordered the Justice Department to support a request for more time made by several Mississippi school districts. Earlier, in October 1968, the Court had lost its patience and in *Alexander v. Holmes County Board of Education* (396 U.S. 19), it ordered the end of segregation "at once." With this unambiguous directive the possibility of *de jure* (of the law) segregation disappeared. The *Alexander* case and others produced the intended effect: by 1972, 44 percent of the black students in the eleven southern states were attending integrated schools. And by 1975, most rural districts and small-to-medium urban districts in the southern and border states were desegregated.

Ironically, the integration of U.S. schools progressed more rapidly and completely in the south (but especially in the rural areas of the region) than in the rest of the country. The problem outside of the south and in large urban areas in the south was not the result of de jure segregation but of *de facto* (of the fact) segregation. It was not the case of overt laws supporting segregation, but more subtle practices such as gerrymandering school districts or locating new schools in a way which guaranteed racial homogeneity.

In 1971 the Court began addressing the issue of de facto segregation. In the case *Swann v. the Charlotte-Mecklenburg Board of Education* (402 U.S. 1) the Court addressed the issue of busing as a means of desegregating schools. In this instance, however, the court was dealing with a district (in North Carolina) in which vestiges and consequences of a dual educational system remained. Thus the *Swann* decision, that busing is one tool which may be required to end segregation, primarily had its impact on southern states. In 1974, however, the Court began looking at the situation of de facto segregation in non-southern states. Over the next several years in cases involving Detroit, Denver, Dayton, Columbus, Pasadena, Milwaukee, Memphis, Norfolk, and Dallas, the federal courts articulated a policy which in essence said that if local school authorities intentionally contributed to or perpetuated segregation through new school building construction, pupil and teacher assignments, manipulating school boundaries, or other nefarious practices, the federal courts could order desegregation. And this is precisely what they have done in cities such as Denver, Boston, Columbus, and Dayton.[22]

Since 1971, literally scores of school districts from coast to coast have been ordered to bus schoolchildren to desegregate schools. Many of these efforts have been accompanied by violence. But even in the absence of overt violence, it is clear that few policy decisions have caused so much rancor in U.S. society. It would be useful at this point to sort out the arguments over desegregation and busing.

To begin, racism has played a part in public attitudes toward desegregation and busing. We feel it is accurate to say that it was more prevalent in the 1950s than in the 1980s, but it is still a factor governing public attitudes and policy responses. It would be unfair and inaccurate, however, to suggest that all people who oppose the federal government's policies in this area are racists. Responsible conservatives have been opposed to federal policy from the outset for a variety of reasons. No responsible conservative with whom we are familiar defends school *segregation*. Conservatives argue, however, that the remedy for this, and other social ills, rests not with the courts but with elected officials in the legislative and executive branches of government—and preferably at the state and local levels. William F. Buckley, Jr., for example, argues that the *Brown* decision was "bad law" because it was judicial legislation. Furthermore, Buckley does not buy the argument that the Court had to act because neither the state governments nor the U.S. Congress would. Buckley argues, in his own inimicable fashion, "If our legislative procedures are constipated (and I think they are) we should flush them out, rather than encourage the Supreme Court to proceed as a standing constitutional convention."[23]

Second, conservatives argue that by going beyond desegregating schools and ordering their integration, the Court is doing precisely what it denounced in *Brown,* namely, assigning children to schools on the basis of race.

Third, it is argued that integration will not improve the quality of education for blacks by providing them with equal educational opportunities. In 1975 conservatives received support on this point from a surprising source, James S. Coleman. Nearly a decade earlier Coleman had directed a study which examined educational opportunities among disadvantaged groups. Among the findings of the *Coleman Report* was that children from disadvantaged backgrounds including, but not exclusively, blacks did better in schools that were predominantly middle-class (and white) than in schools of largely lower-class children. The *Coleman Report,* and those who used it, urged, therefore, that school systems adopt compulsory integration plans, including busing, to improve the quality of education for disadvantaged children. Thus, it came as a considerable surprise to conservative critics of compulsory integration when in 1975, based upon new research, Coleman reported that rather than improving educational opportunities, mandatory integration was having the reverse effect: it was causing middle-class whites to flee to the suburbs, leaving behind increasingly impoverished and segregated or resegregated public schools. Furthermore, in what must have been music to conservative ears, Coleman said the courts are "the worst of all possible instruments for carrying out a very sensitive activity like integrating schools."[24]

Another conservative criticism of forced integration is that it has poisoned the social and educational environment of virtually all the communities it has touched, setting the cause of social and racial harmony, as well as the quality of education, back many years. On this point conservatives appear to have the public behind them. Busing is extremely unpopular. Public opinion polls in recent years consistently have shown that around 80 percent of those surveyed oppose busing. Furthermore, the proportion of blacks who support busing has declined over the years to where now a majority of them oppose it. In September 1982, William Reynolds, then head of the Justice Department's Civil Rights Division, announced that the Justice Department might support legal challenges to court-ordered busing. In an interview at the time, Mr. Reynolds summarized the case against busing. "For the first time in 10 or 15 years, you've got a Justice Department that is willing to stand up and say that if you have a decree that is tearing apart the community, that is eroding the tax base, impeding public school education and causing resegregation rather than desegregation, we are not going to sit by and blink at the result simply because somebody, at some point, said that busing is supposed to be a good thing."[25]

The liberal view on desegregation and integration prevailed for most of the first 25 years after *Brown.* This view reflected the following values and concerns. First, segregation was morally, as well as legally, wrong. Second, segregation, as the *Brown* decision noted, had a deleterious effect on the education of *both* black and white students. Third, because state governments and the legislative and executive branches of the federal government were derelict in dealing with segregation, the federal courts had to take responsibility. Fourth, not only desegregation, but integration, is necessary for the true realization of equal educational opportunity and quality education. Fifth, given the reality of residential living patterns, the sanctity of the neighborhood school, and, therefore, the tenacity of de facto segregation, busing is the only means to achieve integration in large urban areas. Liberals have not been unmindful of the costs of mandated integration. Nevertheless, they believe that the ultimate benefits, in the form of more equal educational and, therefore, economic, social, and political opportunities for all U.S. citizens, are worth the price.

Is the liberal dream of a more equitable, moral, and effective educational environment closer to reality now than it was in 1954? Or is the conservative view of a resegregated, racially divisive, and educationally ineffective environment closer to reality? As in so many policy debates the "truth" is hard to find. Take, for example, the issue of "white flight." Supreme Court Justice Lewis Powell thinks, "In all too many cities well-intentioned court decrees have had the primary effect of stimulating resegregation."[26] James S. Coleman shares this view in his 1975 report, as does sociologist Professor David J. Armor. In 1981 testimony before a Senate Judiciary subcommittee Professor Armor said:

> At this point in history, however, more complete evidence shows us that mandatory busing has failed as a feasible remedy for school segregation. It has failed, first, because opposition and white flight have been so extensive as to increase, rather than decrease, racial isolation in many cities.[27]

However, Professors Thomas Pettigrew of Harvard and Robert Green of Michigan State disagree. In a lengthy refutation of Coleman's "white flight" thesis in the *Harvard Educational Review* they present their own data, as well as that of other scholars, and reach the conclusion that *"desegregation had no discernible effect on the general trend of decline in white enrollment in the nation's truly largest urban school districts."*[28] What Pettigrew and Green show is that middle-income families have been fleeing to the suburbs since the end of World War II, and busing has not accelerated this process.

Well then, has desegregation resulted in improved educational achievement for blacks? Robert Crain and Rita Mahard of the Rand Corporation reviewed seventy-three studies of desegregation cases and found that black children generally do better in predominantly white schools than in black ones. However, Bradley and Bradley, reviewing many of the same studies as Crain and Mahard, concluded that "massive transfers of students within our school systems may not be the best means for improving black student achievement."[29]

Has desegregation led to greater racial harmony, tolerance, or interaction? Or has it increased racial tensions? A decade ago William F. Buckley, Jr., wrote: "A spot-check survey first completed by the Office of Education failed to find a single integrated high school—anywhere—that was free from racial conflict. In such urban centers as New York City and Chicago, racial animosity in high schools is so intense that only the presence of large numbers of police can assure even a precarious order. Needless to say, such an atmosphere is not conducive to learning."[30] And yet there is other evidence. Three years after writing the above statement, Mr. Buckley "wandered" around the state of Mississippi and found "a pleasant surprise." "In the past four years, Mississippi has achieved a racial integration unthought of in the North, the state is prospering, and relations between white and black are, for the most part, altogether relaxed."[31] In addition, it should be noted that at the height of the racial disorders in Boston the U.S Civil Rights Commission found that there was serious conflict in only four of the eighty Boston schools which were desegregated.[32]

The 30 years since *Brown* have been among the most revolutionary in the history of U.S. education. In 1968, 68 percent of all black children in the eleven southern states were attending all-black schools. By 1970 this had declined to 14.4 percent and by 1972, to 8.7 percent. Integration outside the south has not progressed as fast. The proportion of black children attending schools with less than 50 percent minority students barely increased from 1968 to 1972 in the north and west, from 27.6 percent to 28.3 percent.

Nevertheless, overall progress in black educational achievement has been substantial. Black illiteracy declined from 7.5 percent of all blacks in 1959 to 1.6 percent in 1979. In 1950 the median number of school years for whites 25 years old or over was 9.3 years and for blacks 25 years old or over it was 6.8 years. By 1980 there was virtually no difference between the races on school years completed: 12.5 years for whites and 12.0 years for blacks.

The cataclysm that many predicted, especially in the south, never occurred. Nevertheless, the system has been and is strained. Whether whites are fleeing the cities because of forced integration, increased crime, changes in job opportunities, decaying transportation systems, or just to escape the pressure and tensions of the city, they are leaving and in doing so are taking away a large portion of the school-supporting tax base of these cities. And, in their wake, they are leaving black schools. Thus, it is becoming increasingly difficult, if not impossible, to integrate school systems with only 8 percent white students (Atlanta) or 9 percent (Newark) or even 24 percent (Memphis). One way around this dilemma is through consolidation of urban and suburban school districts. In a 1974 case involving Detroit (*Milliken v. Bradley,* 418 U.S. 717), the Supreme Court ruled that separate school districts could be consolidated in order to achieve racial balance *if* it could be proved that all the districts involved had practiced deliberate segregation policies. Under the *Milliken* guidelines, Louisville, Kentucky, Wilmington, Delaware, and St. Louis, Missouri, have been ordered to consolidate with neighboring suburbs to achieve racial balance. It is impossible to predict whether other communities might be ordered to consolidate, but clearly this approach has major implications for the equal education controversy.[33]

Equal Educational Opportunities for the Poor   Lyndon Johnson called the Elementary and Secondary Education Act of 1965 (ESEA) "the greatest breakthrough in the advance of education since the Constitution was written." While one has to make allowance for typically Johnsonian hyperbole, there is little doubt that ESEA is among the most important pieces of education legislation in our nation's history.

The Elementary and Secondary Education Act, "an Act to strengthen and improve educational quality and educational opportunities in the Nation's elementary and secondary schools," is noteworthy for several reasons. First, it was the first time in our history the federal government provided general aid to education. Prior to this two major stumbling blocks prevented general federal aid to education. The first was liberal opposition to federal aid for segregated schools, and the second was the issue of federal aid to parochial schools. In the latter case, federal aid was opposed because it undermined the separation of church and state.[34] Both obstacles were removed, however, in 1965. First, the 1964 Civil Rights Act prohibited the use of federal funds for segregated institutions for any purpose, including education. Second, the ESEA provided that federal aid would be given to *children,* not *schools*—hence one was not giving money to private schools. Furthermore, federal aid for children in private and parochial schools was tucked away in the less visible portions of the bill dealing with libraries, instructional material, and other supplementary educational services. This bit of legislative legerdemain was sufficient to defuse opposition. Thus, the way was cleared for direct federal aid to education.

The second noteworthy feature of the ESEA was that aid was not only direct but substantial. Federal funding for elementary and secondary education increased from $1 billion in 1963–1964 (4 percent of all expenditures for education) to $2.6 billion in 1967–1968 (7.2 percent), and $10.1 billion (8.7 percent) in 1980–1981.

The third point to note about the ESEA is that it was a central part of Lyndon Johnson's "war on poverty." "Poverty has many roots," Johnson said, "but the taproot is ignorance." Education would break the vicious cycle of poverty which condemned the children of the poor to a limited and inferior education and to low-paying jobs. The act was a monument to liberal optimism and philosophy.

The original act contained five titles. The heart of the act was Title I, which provided federal funds to local school districts. The funds were allocated on the basis of a formula which took into account the number of low-income families (defined at the time as those earning less than $2,000 a year or on public assistance). Based upon the formula, virtually all of the school districts in the nation were eligible for aid, although most of the funds went to inner-city and poor, rural school districts. The act specified that the money was for programs "designed to meet the special educational needs of educationally deprived children."[35] Briefly, the other titles in the original act were:

Title II—federal grants for library material, textbooks, and other printed material.

Title III—federal grants to encourage innovative educational programs including specialized equipment, new courses, and counseling and social services.

Title IV—federal aid for construction of educational research facilities.

Title V—federal grants to state educational agencies for purposes of improving state education planning, data collecting, and personnel training.

In the following 2 years, Congress added three other titles to the original act:

Title VI—federal funds to assist states in educating the mentally and physically handicapped.

Title VII—federal aid to help states educate children from non-English-speaking families (i.e., bilingual education).

Title VIII—federal grants to local schools to establish programs to prevent school dropouts.

We will not chronicle all of the reauthorizations and changes of ESEA over the past 15 years. Certain general themes, however, are evident.

First, ESEA funds, and the federal presence accompanying those funds, became a permanent part of the education policy-making landscape of the country. Local districts included ESEA funds as a regular part of their operating budgets. Virtually no school district in the country went untouched by the ESEA.

Second, "the Congressional committees with jurisdiction over the Act have shown a zeal for greatly expanded spending [on ESEA] that both the Executive Branch and the Congressional appropriations committees resisted, with success."[36] In virtually no year have actual appropriations for the

ESEA equaled the money that was authorized by congressional committees. This was true under Democrats (Johnson and Carter) and Republicans (Nixon and Ford).

A third theme has been Republican and conservative opposition to the way in which ESEA funds are allocated. In general, conservatives have favored block grants to state education departments rather than categorical grants directly to local school districts as the original act provided. President Nixon proposed education "revenue sharing," which was essentially a block grants approach. Congress defeated efforts by the Nixon and Ford administrations to gain approval for revenue sharing in education, although in 1974 and again in 1976 it did combine some categorical grants which gave the states more discretion over ESEA programs. With the advent of the Reagan administration, yet another assault was made on the categorical-grant approach.

The result of the Reagan initiative was the 1981 Education Consolidation and Improvement Act. The act was much less than President Reagan had wanted. Congress consolidated several small programs, which accounted for $589 million of the $6.6 billion in elementary and secondary school aid into a single block grant. Reagan's original proposal would have consolidated fifty education programs, including Title I, into just two block grants. Reagan had to settle for a relatively modest consolidation and a commitment for further, also modest, consolidations in 1983. However, President Reagan reduced federal expenditures on ESEA programs by 25 percent, as well as revoking scores of existing federal education regulations.

Before concluding this section it is necessary to ask the question, "Has the Elementary and Secondary Education Act achieved its goals of improving educational opportunities and achievement among disadvantaged students?" By now the reader is aware of the unsurpassed ability of social scientists to find evidence supporting (or rejecting) all sides of an argument. Evaluations of the effectiveness of ESEA programs are no exception. The ESEA has been analyzed ad nauseum. Robert Rossi summarized 11 years (1966–1977) of Title I evaluations and found, among other things, "little evidence at the national level that programs had any positive impact on the eligible and participating children."[37] Three other reports, by the General Accounting Office (1975), the Educational Testing Service (1976), and the Stanford Research Institute (1976), corroborated Rossi's conclusions.[38]

Other studies, however, have declared Title I a success. For example, a National Institute of Education study reported that 1st- and 3d-graders in Title I programs made significant and sustained achievements in math and reading. Similarly, a study by the System Development Corporation of California found above-average gains in reading and mathematics for children in compensatory education programs.[39]

The explanation for these conflicting assessments is not hard to find. In trying to determine how well Title I is working, Professor Richard Brandt concedes, "This is not an easy question to answer as there are many matters to consider: on which specific achievements or deficiencies does one focus? What measuring sticks are available? How long does remediation take place before results are likely? What is the nature of the remediation?"[40] Finally, there is one point upon which critics agree. The success or failure of these compensatory programs is heavily dependent upon individual school administrators and teachers. And, with 14,000 school districts and approximately 6 million students involved in Title I, there is considerable variation in skills and program performance.

Equal Educational Opportunities for the Handicapped   In 1975 Congress passed Public Law (PL) 94-142, the Education for All Handicapped Children Act. This act is an outgrowth of the legal arguments, public awareness, and political sensitivity generated by the *Brown* decision. As in *Brown,* a disadvantaged and discriminated group demanded equal educational opportunities to improve their chances of success in society.[41]

Prior to the passage of PL 94-142 progress in education for the handicapped proceeded, unevenly, on two fronts. First, Title VI of the ESEA provided federal funds to assist states in the education of the mentally and physically handicapped. The funds actually appropriated for this purpose were relatively modest: $31 million of the $1.4 billion appropriated for all of ESEA in 1969, and $37.5 million of the $1.9 billion in 1972. Furthermore, Title VI did not require that states provide programs of free, public education for all handicapped children, and, as a result, the program ultimately served only a fraction of the estimated 7 to 8 million handicapped children in the country. In 1970 Title VI was replaced with the Education of the Handicapped Act. This act extended the provisions of Title VI in terms of time, substance, and resource commitment. Thus, by 1970, the federal government had recognized the exceptional educational needs of handicapped children and was assisting the states and localities in meeting those needs.

The cause of improving and equalizing educational opportunities for the handicapped was pursued at the state level as well. During the 1960s and early 1970s the parents of handicapped children pushed state governments to integrate their children into the public schools. A number of states, including California, Connecticut, Illinois, and Massachusetts, responded with new laws and opportunities for the handicapped. Other states (e.g., Pennsylvania), however, needed prodding from the courts.

Furthermore, some states were far more generous with their funds, and attentive to the needs of the handicapped, than others. What was needed, parents and supporters of the handicapped argued, was to establish the rights of the handicapped, and to secure the money to provide for these rights, on a national basis. And this is where PL 94-142 comes into the picture. The parents of handicapped children argued that despite recent federal and state efforts, only about one-half of the nation's 7 to 8 million handicapped children were receiving an adequate education. According to the Office of Education, 2.5 million handicapped children were receiving an *inadequate* education and 1.75 million were receiving *no education at all.* Sentiment on behalf of the handicapped was, predictably, strong within Congress, and PL 94-142 was easily passed. Despite considerable reluctance and hints of a veto, President Ford signed the Education for All Handicapped Children Act on November 29, 1975. Before examining President Ford's objections, we will look at the act.

Public Law 94-142 is extraordinarily complex, and there is no need for us to examine it in detail. The major provisions of the act were:

1 Each state accepting federal funds had to provide, by September 1, 1978, "a free appropriate public education" to *all* handicapped children between 3 and 18 years old, and by September 1, 1980, for 18- to 21-year-olds, regardless of the severity of their handicap.

2 To "the maximum extent appropriate, handicapped children" should be "educated with children who are not handicapped," (i.e., mainstreaming).

3 Local education authorities must prepare, in writing, an "individualized education program" (IEP) for each handicapped student which includes present and desired educational achievements, programs, and services planned for the child, and procedures for evaluating the IEP of each child.[42]

To help the states in this awesome and expensive undertaking, Congress authorized federal grants to the states which would go from $100 million in 1976 (or 5 percent of the total cost of the program) to $3.5 billion by 1982 (or 40 percent of the total cost of the program). It should be noted, however, that most of the cost—60 percent by 1982—would be borne by the states. Educating the handicapped—and it is estimated that it costs nearly twice as much to educate a handicapped than a nonhandicapped child—was going to be an enormously expensive enterprise for both the federal government and local school authorities.

The cost of the program was, and continues to be, the focus of much of the criticism of PL 94-142. President Ford argued, a few days after signing the bill, "Unfortunately, this bill promises more than the federal government can deliver, and its good intentions could be thwarted by the many unwise provisions it contains. . . . Even the strongest supporters of the measure know as well as I that they are falsely raising the expectations of the groups affected by claiming authorization levels which are excessive and unrealistic."[43] Ford's prediction turned out to be correct. While the federal government did achieve the intended authorization goals in the first years of the program, since 1980 it has failed to support the program at the intended levels.

At the same time that the federal government was falling behind in the promised level of support, inflation, tax-limitation referenda, and voter rejection of school tax levies all across the nation were putting incredible strains on school authorities to live up to the letter and spirit of PL 94-142. This problem will remain for the foreseeable future.

President Ford raised another familiar conservative objection to PL 94-142. Ford criticized the bill's "vast array of detailed, complex and costly administrative requirements which would unnecessarily assert federal control over traditional state and local government functions."[44]

While even critics have admitted that PL 94-142 "has probably hastened and broadened the extent to which handicapped children are being educated at public expense,"[45] it is clear that neither the federal government nor the states and localities will be able or willing to fund the program at its initially intended levels. The cause of handicapped children is too important and sensitive for the national effort to be abandoned. However, it has been, and will continue to be, scaled down.

Equal Educational Opportunities for Children with Limited English-Speaking Ability The concern with equalizing the educational opportunities for children with "limited English-speaking ability" (LESA) also traces its legal and spiritual origins to *Brown* and its policy baptism to the Elementary and Secondary Education Act. The problem with LESA children is that, because of their difficulty in understanding English, they immediately, and often irreversibly, fall behind English-speaking students in school. Thus, they too were denied the opportunity of equal participation and success in education. The answer to this problem, professional educators and political activists from various ethnic groups argued, was to introduce bilingual education. Children who speak little English should be instructed in their own native language while they are becoming proficient in English. Once proficient they could switch to all English-language classes.

Congress first responded to the demands of ethnic interest groups in 1967 when it adopted Title VII of ESEA, also known as the Bilingual Education Act. That act recognized the "special education needs" of children of limited English-speaking ability, particularly those from poverty backgrounds.

The development of bilingual education policy was accelerated in 1974. In that year two important policy decisions were made. The first was a Supreme Court decision, *Lau v. Nichols* (414 U.S. 563), stemming from a California case in which 1,800 children of Chinese ancestry with limited English-speaking ability sued the San Francisco school district for not providing them with special programs to help them overcome their language deficiency. The Court ruled that since the inability to speak English denied the students an equal opportunity to "effectively participate" in school programs, the schools had to provide remedial programs.

The *Lau* decision put pressure on Congress to expand the funding, scope, and mandate of the Bilingual Education Act and, in 1974, it did so. Funding for bilingual education was increased from $58 to $135 million, and an Office of Bilingual Education was established in the Office of Education.

Of the various policies introduced during the 1960s and 1970s to equalize educational opportunities, bilingual education has been among the most criticized. In general, the confrontation has pitted liberals against conservatives. Central to the debate is the question, "What is the purpose of bilingual education?" The key words in this particular debate are "transition" vs. "maintenance." Conservatives and neo-conservatives, including Ronald Reagan, Professor Nathan Glazer, and *Harper's* editor Tom Bethell, argue that the original, and only defensible, purpose of bilingual education is to help limited English speakers make a transition from their native language to English. Thus, students begin their studies in Spanish or Vietnamese, for example, so they do not fall behind, while at the same time learning English. "Then, when they have a sufficient grasp of English, they could be removed from bilingual classes and instructed in the normal way."[46] This is basically an assimilationist or "melting pot" vision of integrating non-English speakers into U.S. society. Glazer, for one, argues that this assimilationist approach worked during the great periods of U.S. immigration and is central to this country's success in nation building.[47]

Conservative critics argue, however, that the program has not operated this way. Instead of using bilingual education programs as a *transition* to English education, one study found that many, perhaps a majority, of the students were staying in the bilingual classes after they had mastered English. The study, done by the American Institutes for Research on behalf of the U.S. Office of Education, provided additional ammunition for critics. The researchers found, for example, little difference in academic performance between students in bilingual classes and those in regular classes.

Liberal defenders of bilingual-bicultural education, including Senators Edward Kennedy and Alan Cranston (D., Calif.), believe these programs should help preserve or *maintain* the cultural integrity of ethnic groups. They argue that the transition approach undermines the access to and integrity and viability of minority languages and cultures since students are encouraged to stop thinking and speaking in their native language. Kennedy and others do not deny the need for learning English. They argue that *both* languages, English and the native tongue, should be maintained. Says one defender of bilingualism, "Bilingual education has a long history of helping minority language groups adjust to U.S. society without eradicating the linguistic foundation of their social and cultural heritage."[48] Bilingual education will continue to be controversial for some time to come. The *Lau* decision has firmly established the right to remedial language programs. It is unlikely, and politically unrealistic, that bilingual education will be abandoned. Nevertheless, the debate over the nature of that education—transition or maintenance—will certainly play a role in future policy deliberations. And so too will the issue of money. A 1978 study found that it cost on the average of $376 more per pupil per year to educate bilingual pupils than it cost to educate pupils in regular classes. By 1982, the federal bilingual education program cost $160 million, making it the largest categorical program in the Education Department's budget.[49]

Equal Educational Opportunities in Comparative Perspective   Every modern industrial nation has confronted the issue of equalizing educational opportunities between various socially or culturally disadvantaged groups and a dominant majority. The degree of political trauma associated with this issue varies among countries. And the range of policy responses reflects the diversity of the countries involved and the origins of inequality. Despite this diversity certain general policy trends and approaches are apparent.

The most generalized and geographically widespread assault on educational inequalities in Western Europe and Japan has taken the form of introducing comprehensive secondary schools. Remember that comprehensive schools educate children of all socioeconomic backgrounds and academic potential within the same school through their secondary education. Until quite recently European and Japanese children were educationally "tracked" at early ages. In virtually every country of Western Europe and in Japan, poor and working-class children typically ended up in vocational schools in preparation for low-prestige and salaried, blue-collar employment. Middle- and upper-class children were academically tracked and destined for more lucrative and prestigious positions. Following World War II, egalitarian sentiment in Western Europe and Japan led to demands for a single comprehensive school system, although progress in that direction has gone farther and faster in some countries than in others.

The comprehensivization movement is, in an important sense, analogous to the ESEA. Both efforts were directed toward reducing existing educational inequalities among social classes. The major difference between these policies was that the effort in the United States was aimed at the most marginal and disadvantaged segment of U.S. society, while the comprehensive school policy was directed at a broader category, the working class. Therefore, U.S. policy has been more compensatory in orientation than European comprehensivization and has included such noneducational features as health and nutrition programs, as well as remedial educational programs.

In one sense the policy of comprehensivization appears to offer little to the United States in the way of a policy model. After all, we have had comprehensive schools since the mid-nineteenth century. However, the Japanese and European experiences do offer some insights into the utility of equalizing educational opportunities as a means of equalizing occupational opportunity and social mobility. Has improved educational opportunity through comprehensivization improved the condition of the working class in Western Europe and Japan? By improvement we mean are they more likely to do better in school, have greater access to higher education, and get better-paying, more prestigious employment after their education is completed?

To begin, in some countries, especially West Germany, Austria, and France, the process simply has not gone far enough, or been in effect long enough, to allow for a valid assessment. However, in two countries, Japan and Sweden, the requirements of duration and extent of applicability have been met. And in both countries, it appears that the policy has been successful. Cummings, in his study "The Egalitarian Transformation of Postwar Japanese Education," notes that while prior to World War II Japan was highly inegalitarian and hierarchical, since the war it has moved steadily toward a more egalitarian society. In fact, in terms of income equality, "by the mid-seventies Japan's income distribution was among the most equal of *all* advanced industrial societies, whether capitalist or socialist."[50] In addition to greater income equality, one also finds in Japan greater equality in educational achievement, regardless of gender, place of residence, or parental background, than before World War II, *or* than exists in other countries. "What accounts for this egalitarian shift? While rapid economic growth and the stable international context are important facilitating factors, the most impressive covariant is the emergence of a new educational system which rapidly expanded in scale and has openly promoted more equal and democratic orientations."[51]

While the case of Sweden is not quite as dramatic or successful as the case of Japan, it too offers evidence in support of the efficacy of equalizing educational opportunities. Like the Japanese, the Swedes set out specifically "to equalize educational recruitment and dismantle social inequalities due to educational differentiation."[52] And, in certain key respects, this effort has been successful. First, it is generally accepted that "Sweden appears to have the most egalitarian educational system in Europe," although this was not always true.[53] Second, there has been a dramatic reduction in, although not complete elimination of, the difference between working-class and upper-class students in terms of obtaining higher education. "Sweden has been experiencing an impressive movement toward parity in utilization of post-secondary opportunities for education."[54] While it is clear that Sweden has not gone as far as Japan in equalizing educational opportunities, it should be noted it was only in 1971 that the Swedes merged their high schools to complete the process of comprehensivization.

The evidence on the effects of comprehensive schooling in the rest of Western Europe is more ambiguous. Henry Levin, a severe critic of capitalism, has looked at the process with regard to the "extent to which the schools have tended to equalize resources devoted to secondary education among children drawn from different social origins and the extent to which they have tended to equalize the completion of secondary school and access to postsecondary education among youngsters from different social backgrounds."[55] Levin finds that the policy has done both; that is, there is greater equality of resource allocations and more working-class students are gaining access to postsecondary education. It is at this point, however, that Levin drops the second shoe. He argues that what has happened is that the traditional inequalities between social classes, which were characteristic of secondary education, now have been relocated into the postsecondary school environment. Thus, working-class students are admitted to the less prestigious and poorer quality colleges and universities (comparable and, he argues, analogous to U.S. community colleges), enter the less prestigious fields of study, and are more likely to drop out of higher education. In addition, while he concedes that there has been "a universal trend towards increasing equality for virtually all countries . . . there seems little relation between the increasing equality of educational attainments (in nominal years of schooling) and the distribution of income."[56]

When we turn from the broader context of equal educational opportunities for all social classes to the more narrowly defined one of racial equality, there are few Western European countries with comparable experiences. The fact that race has played so much more prominent a role in U.S. educational policy than in European policy is in part a function of scale— the racial minority in the United States is many times larger than the racial minority in, say, Great Britain or France—and in part the greater degree of political organization and sophistication of U.S. blacks than the more recently arrived nonwhite minorities of Western Europe.

It is only in England that one finds a situation which, in both substance and policy response but not in scale, is similar to the United States.[57] Beginning at the end of World War II, but especially during the 1950s, tens of thousands of nonwhite immigrants from Britain's former colonial possessions began migrating to England. While even today the group comprises less than 3 percent of the population, most of these immigrants settled in a few urban areas like London, Bradford, Leicester, and Bristol. By the early 1960s, the children of these immigrants constituted as much as 30 to 60 percent of the enrollment in some schools. At this point the parents of white schoolchildren became concerned that such heavy concentrations of immigrant children, many of whom had limited English-speaking ability, would lower the quality of education in those schools. In addition, some educators claimed that the heavy concentration of immigrants was tantamount to segregation, which was both morally and pedagogically wrong. Finally, in some schools the problem was simply one of overcrowding.

Whatever the justification for the concern, the initial policy response will be familiar to people in the United States—busing. In 1963, in the Southall section of London, the Local Education Authority (LEA) decided the best way to handle the heavy concentration of immigrant children in its district was through "dispersal." The LEA decided that no school should have more than a 30 percent immigrant population. Beyond that point, immigrant children would be bused to other schools. The Southall dispersal plan, which became the model for other school districts, was justified in the name of helping immigrant children better learn the English language and culture and, therefore, more easily integrate into English society. It was clear, however, to most observers that less defensible motives (e.g., racial hostility) underlie the policy of dispersal.

While dispersal was initiated at the local level, the policy received national government support in a 1965 administrative circular from the Department of Education and Science. In a section of the circular entitled "Spreading the Children," it was noted that the concentration of immigrant children in certain schools posed a problem to their eventual integration into society. Hence:

> It is therefore desirable that the catchment areas of schools [i.e., districts] should, wherever possible be arranged to avoid undue concentrations of immigrant children. Where this proves impracticable simply because the school serves an area which is occupied largely by immigrants, every effort should be made to disperse the immigrant children round a greater number of schools and to meet such problems of transport as may arise.[58]

While this statement was not binding upon local school authorities, it did legitimize the policy of dispersal initiated in Southall.

Unlike in the United States, in England opposition to busing came not from white parents, but from the parents of immigrant children. They argued that dispersal was essentially racist in origin and that busing was needlessly tiring, endangering, and inconveniencing their children—arguments with which most people in the United States are familiar. Furthermore, busing children into schools outside their community caused antagonism among the racial groups, thereby defeating one of the alleged aims of the plan— i.e., to help immigrant children integrate into English society.

As a result of this opposition, by the early 1970s the national government began backing off its 1965 support of dispersal. In November 1975, the Race Relations Board—the equivalent of our Civil Rights Commission—

ruled that "bussing on the basis of racial or ethnic identity alone, whether to promote interethnic contact or to create an ethnic mix conducive to acculturation," was illegal.[59] While it is still possible to bus children in England to accomplish certain educational goals—e.g., to expose children with limited English-speaking ability to English speakers—it has clearly fallen out of favor.

In addition to social class (and to a much lesser extent race), ethnicity has emerged as a major source of demands for equal educational opportunities throughout the industrialized West. As in the United States, the most outstanding issue concerns the role of minority languages and cultures in the educational process. Should these languages be used as transitional tools in the process of cultural assimilation or should they be maintained and encouraged? In other words, should the "melting pot" or the "mosaic" be the goal of educational policy?

While it is difficult to generalize about so many countries, it appears that the mosaic rather than the melting pot—historically the dominant metaphor in U.S. educational policy—is most prevalent. In West Germany, for example, where there are approximately one-half million children of migrant laborers (or guest workers), the policy since the early 1970s has been to help these children learn German in special preparatory classes so as to ensure their success in school. However, the state (Lander) education ministers have agreed that "school children should also have the opportunity of attending instruction given in their native language. The aim of this instruction is to preserve the pupil's ties to the language and culture of their homeland."[60] And, one might add, to facilitate their ultimate return to that homeland. In Sweden too, the primary emphasis is on cultural maintenance rather than complete assimilation. The Swedish case differs from the German case, however, in that different categories of minority students are identified and, to a certain extent, treated differently. One group consists of the children of immigrants, primarily from other Nordic countries like Finland, Norway, and Denmark. If necessary, these students are first educated in their native tongue while they learn Swedish. Once literate in Swedish, they are encouraged to maintain a bilingual and bicultural orientation.

The second minority category consists of about 14,000 Lapps who have been in Sweden since antiquity. For centuries the Lapps pursued a traditional way of life centered around reindeer husbandry. In the course of the twentieth century more and more Lapp children abandoned their traditional homes and culture and assimilated into the dominant Swedish culture. Concern among the Lapps, as well as the Swedish government, for the survival of this culture led the government to encourage special schools for Lapp children who wish to attend them. This policy gives the Lapps a choice between assimilation or cultural maintenance, although in practice, the majority continue to choose the route of assimilation.

While most of the other countries of Western Europe (and Canada) have chosen the path of cultural maintenance in their educational policies, the British have not quite made up their minds. Indeed, there is agreement among students of British politics that England has been directionless or vacillating in the area of racial policy in general and education policy in particular.[61] Clearly the policy of dispersal, initiated at the local level and legitimized by the central government, was an assimilationist-oriented policy. One purpose of dispersal was to get non-English-speaking immigrant children into an English-speaking educational environment. The retreat from dispersal has not been followed by any definitive policy statement, by either local or national leaders, as to what directions British education should take. "What is lacking is a clearly stated objective of building a pluralistic society with unity and allegiance to a common core of beliefs, along with respect for cultural differences."[62] In some respects, British indecision on how best to equalize the educational opportunities of limited English-speaking students—assimilation or maintenance—is reminiscent of the current stage of policy development in the United States.

CONCLUSIONS

Since the time of the Enlightenment in the eighteenth century, Western societies have placed enormous faith in education as a vehicle for both collective and individual accomplishment. For the French *philosophes* education was the key to human freedom, equality, progress, and even, in the case of the Marquis de Condorcet, perfection. Beginning in the eighteenth century and continuing into the present, this faith has found expression in two historical trends. The first major trend was adoption of the notion that education, because of its critical role in nation building, is a state responsibility. Both in the authoritarian states of Prussia, Russia, and Austria, and in the more democratic states of France, the United States, and Great Britain, the notion of state responsibility spread, unevenly, throughout the nations of the world. Today, every nation in the world accepts education as a public responsibility.

The second major trend involved defining who in society was to share in the individual and collective dreams associated with education. The "enlightened despots" of eighteenth- and early nineteenth-century Europe, mindful of the dangers in educating the uncleansed masses, restricted their educational reforms to the middle class. The "American dream," on the other hand, was that all people—with the exception of slaves, of course— should be educated. In the course of the nineteenth and early twentieth centuries the concept and reality of universal education was gradually embraced in more and more countries.

In the twentieth century, with the commitment to universal public education effectively established, new issues arose. The most profound of these is the debate over equality of educational opportunities. Clearly everyone, even the most disadvantaged in U.S. society and elsewhere in the industrialized democratic world, has access to free education—up to a certain level. But it is just as clear that such access has not led to equalizing educational opportunities or posteducational prospects. There are few people, of whom we are aware, who would suggest that black and white children were receiving an equal education in Alabama, or for that matter in New York, in 1954. Or that poor children, or the handicapped or those with limited English-speaking ability, were receiving an education equal to that available to middle-class, white, physically and mentally healthy children.

It is, of course, one thing to admit that inequalities exist and quite another to agree on what should be done about them and by whom. In the course of this chapter we have examined the differences between liberals and conservatives on this issue. No responsible person has come out in favor of supporting racism in the schools, neglecting the handicapped, or ignoring the problems of the poor and those with English-language deficiencies. Where disagreement arises is over how far government, and especially the federal government, can and should go in remedying these problems. In addition, there are genuine policy disagreements over what will and will not work—and precious little convincing and definitive data to resolve these disagreements.

The other major issue discussed in this chapter was the alleged decline in the quality of U.S. education. This concern has produced such policy responses as competency testing and an emphasis on basic skills in education. In addition, we discussed the fact that concern with the quality of public education has led some parents and policy makers to consider public support of private education. It is well to remember that public concern over the quality of education has been a perennial one in the United States. "Why can't Johnny read?" is a question that has been asked time and time again in this country—and each generation that asks it thinks they are the first to do so. And each generation seems to have its own answer—phonetics in the 1950s and back-to-basics in the 1980s; the National Defense Education Act in the 1950s and tuition tax credits in the 1980s. In the final analysis it very well may be the case that no significant or fundamental changes in educational *quality* and achievement will occur until the problem of educational *equality* is solved.

NOTES

1 Quoted in Henry J. Parkinson, *The Imperfect Panacea: American Faith in Education, 1865–1965* (New York: Random House, 1968), p. 28.

2 Quoted in Parkinson, frontispiece.

3 George H. Gallup, "Gallup Poll of the Attitudes Toward the Public Schools," *Phi Delta Kappan,* 64 (Sept. 1982), 46.

4 "Why Can't Johnny Read?" and "Why Public Schools Fail," *Newsweek,* Apr. 20, 1981.

5 Leonard M. Cantor, "The Growing Role of the States in American Education," *Comparative Education,* 16 (Mar. 1980), 25–31.

6 The major court cases dealing with equalizing financial support of public schools are *Serrano v. Priest,* 96 Cal., Rptr. 601 (1971) and *Rodriguez v. San Antonio Independent School Board,* 411 U.S. 1 (1973).

7 Stanley M. Elam, "The National Education Association: Political Powerhouse or Paper Tiger?" *Phi Delta Kappan,* 63 (Nov. 1981), 170.

8 Francis Keppel, *The Necessary Revolution in American Education* (New York: Harper & Row, 1966), p. 1.

9 *New York Times,* Sept. 22, 1982.

10 Ibid.

11 *Newsweek,* Apr. 20, 1981.

12 "Readings-Skill Picture Bright at Age 9, Less So for Older Students: NAEP," *Phi Delta Kappan,* 62 (June 1981), 692.

13 Richard M. Brandt, *Public Education Under Scrutiny,* (Washington, D.C.: University Press of America, 1981), pp. 9–10.

14 T. C. Venable, "Declining SAT Scores: Some Unpopular Hypotheses," *Phi Delta Kappan,* 62 (Feb. 1981), 445.

15 Thomas Sowell, "Tuition Tax Credits: A Social Revolution," *Policy Review* (Spring 1978), p. 79.

16 Thomas Sowell quoted in Daniel Patrick Moynihan, "The Case for Tuition Tax Credits," *Phi Delta Kappan,* 60 (Dec. 1978), 275.

17 Grace Hechinger and Fred M. Hechinger, "Are Schools Better in Other Countries?" *American Education* (Jan.–Feb. 1974), pp. 6–8.

18 Michael W. Kirst, "Japanese Education: Its Implications for Economic Competition in the 1980s," *Phi Delta Kappan,* 62 (June 1981), 707.

19 William Cummings, "The Egalitarian Transformation of Postwar Japanese Education," *Comparative Education Review,* 26 (Feb. 1982), 21.

20 Kirst, p. 707.

21 Ibid., p. 708.

22 See *Keyes v. School District No. 1,* 413 U.S. 189 (1973); *Dayton Board of Education v. Brinkman,* 443 U.S. 449 (1979).

23 William F. Buckley, Jr., "Mississippi on My Mind," *National Review,* 25 (Jan. 5, 1973), 49.

24 *National Observer,* June 7, 1957.

25 *New York Times,* Sept. 9, 1982.

26 Quoted in *Wall Street Journal,* Aug. 20, 1982.

27 *Cong. Rec.,* Feb. 23, 1982, p. S964.

28 Thomas Pettigrew and Robert Green, "School Desegregation in Large Cities: A Critique of the Coleman 'White Flight' Thesis," *Harvard Educational Review,* 46 (Feb. 1976), 39. Emphasis in original.

29 Quoted in "Does Desegregation Affect Achievement? Researchers Find Mixed

Results," *Phi Delta Kappan,* 61 (Sept. 1979), 3.

30 William F. Buckley, Jr., "The Fruits of Integration," *National Review,* 22 (Feb. 10, 1970) 122.

31 Buckley, "Mississippi on My Mind," p. 49.

32 Reported in Amos Issac, "The Issue is Not Busing but the Fourteenth Amendment," *Education and Urban Society,* 9 (May 1977), 269.

33 For those interested in a more detailed discussion of this issue see Harrell Rodgers, Jr., and Charles Bullock, III, *Coercion to Compliance* (Lexington, Mass.: Lexington Books, 1976).

34 The Supreme Court has dealt with the issue of public and private schools on several occasions. See, for example, *Cochran v. Board of Education,* 281 U.S. 370 (1930); *Everson v. Board of Education,* 330 U.S. 1 (1947); and *Lemon v. Kurtzman,* 403 U.S. 602 (1971).

35 *Congress and the Nation,* vol. 2, 1965–1968, (Washington, D.C.: Congressional Quarterly Service, 1969), p. 710.

36 Ibid., p. 729.

37 Robert Rossi, "Summaries of Major Title I Evaluations, 1966–1977," prepared for the National Institute of Education, DHEW, July 1977; as cited in Karen Hill-Scott and J. Eugene Grigsby, "Some Policy Recommendations for Compensatory Education," *Phi Delta Kappan,* 60 (Feb. 1979), 444.

38 Hill-Scott and Grigsby, p. 444.

39 For a summary of various studies on the effectiveness of Title I see Brandt, pp. 36–40.

40 Brandt, p. 37.

41 The similarities between the desegregation and handicapped movements are noted by Lynda Katz-Garris and Raymond P. Garris, "Desegregation and Mainstreaming," *Phi Delta Kappan,* 63 (Dec. 1981), 278–279.

42 For a copy of PL 94-142 see Erwin Levine and Elizabeth Wexler, *PL 94-142: An Act of Congress* (New York: Macmillan, 1981), pp. 191–214. For an evaluation of the act also see John C. Pittenger and Peter Kuriloff, "Educating the Handicapped: Reforming a Radical Law," *Public Interest,* No. 66 (Winter 1982), pp. 72–96.

43 *Congress and the Nation,* vol. 4, 1973–1976, p. 389.

44 Ibid.

45 Pittenger and Kuriloff, pp. 92–93.

46 Tom Bethell, "Against Bilingual Education," *Harper's,* 258 (Feb. 1979), 32.

47 Nathan Glazer, "Ethnicity and Education: Some Hard Questions," *Phi Delta Kappan,* 62 (Jan. 1981), 386–389.

48 Charles R. Foster, "Defusing the Issues in Bilingualism and Bilingual Education," *Phi Delta Kappan,* 63 (Jan. 1982), 344.

49 Foster, p. 343.

50 Cummings, pp. 16–17. Emphasis in original.

51 Cummings, p. 17.

52 Arnold J. Heidenheimer, "Achieving Equality through Educational Expansion," *Comparative Political Studies,* 10 (Oct. 1977), 415.

53 Henry M. Levin, "Educational Opportunity and Social Inequality in Western

Europe," *Social Problems,* 24 (Dec. 1976), 159.

54 A. C. Anderson, "Sweden Examines Higher Education," *Higher Education* 4 (1975), 405, quoted in Heidenheimer, p. 431.

55 Henry M. Levin, "The Dilemma of Comprehensive Secondary School Reforms in Western Europe," *Comparative Education Review* (Oct. 1978), p. 442.

56 Levin, "Educational Opportunity," p. 160.

57 This section relies heavily upon Lewis M. Killian, "School Busing in Britain: Policies and Perceptions," *Harvard Educational Review,* 49 (May 1979), 185–206.

58 Department of Education and Science, Circular 7/65, pp. 4–5, quoted in Killian, p. 196.

59 Killian, p. 200.

60 Ingeborg Wilkie, "Schooling of Immigrant Children in West Germany, Sweden, England: The Educationally Disadvantaged," *International Review of Education,* 21 (1975) 362.

61 Douglas Ashford, *Policy and Politics in Britain* (Philadelphia: Temple Univ. Press, 1981), Chapter 7.

62 George Male, "Multicultural Education and Education Policy: The British Experience," *Comparative Education Review,* 16 (Oct. 1980), 301.

CHAPTER 8

TO HOUSE A NATION

By the standards of most of the world, people in the United States are well-housed. Over 60 percent of all U.S. families own their own homes, and the vast majority of all people in the United States live in decent housing. But despite these facts, the United States has serious housing problems. There are at least three problems that are often identified:

1 Millions of people in the United States live in poor-quality housing or decaying and disrupted neighborhoods. Citizens who live in these houses or neighborhoods often receive inadequate public services and little or no public assistance.

2 High inflation and high interest rates have increased the price of housing to the extent that most first-home buyers have been priced out of the market.

3 Housing in the United States tends to be segregated by both race and socioeconomic status.

Housing stock in the United States has greatly improved during the twentieth century. The Department of Housing and Urban Development classifies housing as substandard when it lacks hot running water, or a private bath or shower, or is grossly dilapidated. In 1940, 49 percent of all housing was judged to be substandard. By 1960 only 16 percent was so classified, and by 1978 only 7.8 percent.[1] However, for some groups housing problems are severe. Among families earning less than $10,000, 25 percent of all black families and 10.6 percent of all white families live in substandard housing. In rural areas 32 percent of all black families with incomes below $10,000 live in poor-quality housing. President Reagan's Commission on Housing estimated that 5.6 million households lived in deficient housing in 1977.[2]

Not only do millions of families live in poor-quality housing, they tend to pay a disproportionate percentage of their total income for shelter. In 1976, 61 percent of all renter households with yearly incomes below $10,000 spent more than 25 percent of their income on rent. And 19 percent spent more than half of their income for rent.[3] Kristof reported that of the families living in poverty pockets, between 25 and 33 percent could not afford to pay the cost of adequate housing.[4] Because public programs do not fill this gap, most of these families must pay to live in housing that is deteriorating and poorly maintained.

While much more difficult to quantify, millions of people in the United States live in undesirable neighborhoods. The nation's major cities all contain poverty pockets, some of which contain several hundred thousand people. Some of the worst of these communities are called ghettos and are characterized by squalid housing, severe crime, and many other problems. Some of these communities—the South Bronx, large sections of St. Louis, Detroit, and Cleveland—represent some of the most frightening ruins in the United States. These neighborhoods provide extremely unwholesome environments for residents. Not only are they plagued by crime and poor and abandoned housing, they are isolated from job markets, generally provide poor-quality schools, and usually are inadequately served by the city. Most would agree that families living in such environments are disadvantaged in dozens of ways.

The second major problem noted above is the increasing cost of buying and financing a home. By 1981 the average new home in the United States was selling for almost $70,000. Most people in the United States who are not already homeowners cannot afford to buy a house in this price range. The freezing out of first-time home buyers is a reversal of post-World War II trends and expectations in the United States. In the mid-1970s over 80 percent of all families earning more than $20,000 a year owned their own homes.[5] In fact, home ownership is the major investment for most people in the United States. Goodman reports that by 1979 U.S. citizens owned $1.6 trillion in housing equity (net of mortgage). This investment is larger than the value of all stocks and bonds listed on the New York Stock Exchange.[6] For many people in the United States, then, a home is not only a place to live, it is their chief asset, an asset they expect to grow and provide security in their retirement years.

But the dream of home ownership that people in the United States long could depend on is becoming more elusive. In 1981 new housing starts numbered 1.1 million, the lowest number since 1946. In 1978 there were

2.1 million new houses built. Only 336,000 new homes were sold in 1981, down from 872,000 in 1978. Historically, high interest rates have even made it difficult to sell existing housing. In 1981 only about 2 million houses a month were sold, compared to an average of about 4 million a month in 1978. The nation's housing slump created an 18 percent unemployment rate in the construction trades by early 1982, and forced thousands of construction firms and subcontractors to declare bankruptcy.[7]

The nation's housing problems are occurring just when the demand for housing is rapidly increasing. During the 1980s more than 40 million people in the United States will reach the age of 30, creating record demands for housing.[8] Some housing specialists think that by the mid-1980s housing will become a volatile political issue.[9]

The last major problem is residential segregation by race and socioeconomic status. Housing segregation is the result of past and present racial discrimination and economic problems. The United States only developed the laws and legal apparatus to attack housing discrimination in the late 1960s and early 1970s. It is widely conceded that less change has occurred in this area of civil rights than any other. Indeed, housing has been called the last frontier of the civil rights movement.[10] But while racial discrimination in housing continues to some extent, it is widely conceded that economic barriers are the most important obstacle to neighborhood integration. In this chapter we examine the economic policies that are being debated to make it easier for any citizen, regardless of race, to purchase a home.

We begin our analysis of housing problems by reviewing the nation's existing housing programs. Emphasis is placed on why the government developed specific housing programs and the major criticisms of these policies by both conservatives and liberals. We then examine European housing policies to determine if these nations are using any policies that might inform housing policies in the United States. Last we compare conservative and liberal proposals to deal with the nation's most pressing housing deficiencies.

HOUSING PROGRAMS IN THE UNITED STATES: ASSISTANCE TO LOW-INCOME AND POOR CITIZENS

Compared to the other western industrialized nations, the United States does not have a comprehensive policy on housing. This is a fact of which European scholars often make note. For example, Headey observes:

> As for the United States, it scarcely even makes sense to talk about policy objectives and priorities since policy formulation is essentially a process in which diverse groups agree to disagree about objectives, but sometimes manage to put together pork barrel, omnibus programmes which command just enough support to pass Congress.[11]

Headey's observations reflect the typical European shock at the inability of the fragmented power structure in the United States to develop comprehensive public policies. In a parliamentary system of government (which is the rule in Europe) the executive's party is in control of the legislative branch, and disciplined parties ensure support for the executive's policies. In the United States power is split between the executive and Congress, Congress is divided into two competing branches, and party membership does not indicate support for the party. The result is that a consensus rarely can be reached on major policy objectives. As Headey notes, public policy in the United States is often a short-term compromise between competing interest groups to meet only limited, and sometimes conflicting, goals.

Essentially the philosophy of the United States is that the market should determine the quality and quantity of housing. However, market forces often have not been adequate to produce enough good quality housing to meet the public's needs. The primary response of the federal government has been to pass policies that subsidize the private market. The major housing assistance policies of the United States are devoted to helping middle- and upper-income citizens purchase homes. A series of much less expensive and comprehensive programs are designed to allow some low-income citizens to live in better housing than their own purchasing power would permit.

Like most social programs in the United States, housing policies date back to the great depression. The nation's economic calamity caused millions of U.S. citizens to lose their homes and threatened to force millions of additional families to forfeit their mortgages. Millions of other U.S. citizens were simply ill-housed. The nation's public leaders were reluctant to intervene in the housing market, but as the depression and its consequences deepened, they began to fear the political consequences of failing to act. The result was a series of programs designed to provide decent housing for some low-income citizens and assistance programs to help homeowners maintain their mortgage payments, while insuring mortgage lenders against losses.

The more radical reformers of the 1930s hoped to convince Congress to build a great deal of publicly owned housing that would be available to a wide range of income groups. The home-building associations were intensely opposed to such a policy, however, because they believed that it would seriously undermine the private enterprise housing sector. The result was that the Congress decided to limit publicly owned housing to poverty-level families and let the states decide if they wanted to build the housing with federal subsidies. In the Wagner Housing Act of 1937 Congress established subsidies and regulations for local governments that wanted to build and run housing projects for low-income citizens. As these policies have evolved, the federal government pays up to 100 percent of the initial costs of building the project and continues to subsidize it if the local government follows federal guidelines.

The Wagner Housing Act created an approach that precluded a national public housing policy. Public housing is a local option program, based on federal funds and standards. There have been several obvious results of this approach. First, the amount of public housing varies considerably by city. Second, limiting public housing to the poor has meant that it is a policy with little public support and considerable social stigma. This has greatly limited the amount of public housing in the nation. By 1978 there were only 1.3 million units of public housing in the United States, composing about 1.5 percent of the nation's housing stock.[12] This is the smallest amount of public housing of any nation in the western industrialized world. Last, some critics argue that limiting public housing to the poor doomed the policy to failure. They argue that such a policy creates housing which is a collecting point for welfare-dependent, jobless, disrupted families. One, perhaps predictable, outcome has been a proliferation of crime and social disorder in many of these projects, leading in some cases to complete failure. To make matters worse, until the Supreme Court ruled the practice unconstitutional in 1967, most housing projects were located in central cities, often in ghettos.[13] This policy contributed to racial segregation.

The housing problems of millions of poor and low-income U.S. citizens were increased by the Housing Act of 1949. The act authorized the construction of 810,000 units of public housing over a 6-year period. This part of the act was never carried out because Congress did not authorize the necessary funds. However, this same act authorized an urban redevelopment plan that eventually would be known as "urban renewal." Under this plan the federal government allowed local authorities to use their powers of eminent domain to purchase and clear blighted areas of their cities. The areas cleared were often the homes of the city's poorest residents. The city, in turn, could sell the land to developers at a loss. The federal government agreed to provide the city with a grant equal to two-thirds of the loss. The city sold the land at a loss to make it economically attractive to private developers. The builders, in turn, were under no obligation to rebuild housing for the poor. In fact, a great deal more housing was destroyed than was built under the program.

The poor and their representatives complained vigorously about a program that cost them so many homes. In 1954 Congress made an attempt to modify the program but failed. The 1954 act attempted to encourage rehabilitation of existing structures, reserving demolition for only the most irredeemable structures. The distinction amounted to little, since in practice the emphasis was still on clearance. Even when units were rehabilitated they were generally too expensive for the former occupants. Still, urban renewal funds were made available until 1974 when the Community Development Block Grant program was passed.

In the 1960s Congress passed a number of acts designed to help low-income families either rent or purchase a home. The best known of these programs were amendments to the 1968 Housing Act. Section 236 was a rental housing assistance program. Under the program the Department of Housing and Urban Development (HUD) agreed to pay specified landlords the difference between a low-income renter's payment and the fair market value of the unit. The renter paid at least 25 percent of his or her income toward the rent. Any discrepancy was paid by HUD. This program reached a much larger number of low-income citizens than had earlier programs. In 1977 Section 236 was subsidizing 650,000 units to families with a median income of $6,361.[14]

Section 235 of the 1968 act was a home-ownership assistance program. Much like Section 236, qualifying families purchased a home on the open market and received subsidies to help pay for it. The purchasing family was required to pay 20 percent of its income toward the mortgage, insurance, and taxes, and the government took care of any unmet proportion of these bills. The program also reached a large number of low-income families. In 1977 some 290,000 homes were being subsidized by Section 235, with the median income of recipient families being $8,085.[15] Neither Section 235 nor 236 really reached the nation's poorest families. In fact, one study estimated that no more than 10 percent of the families eligible for housing assistance because of low income actually were receiving assistance under the programs.[16]

While the government was obligated to continue to finance the families and units with which they contracted under Sections 235 and 236, the Nixon administration obtained a moratorium on further commitments in 1973. Nixon argued that housing priorities needed to be reexamined. Like earlier programs, the Section 236 program was criticized for giving builders subsidies that were too generous, and it often was charged that the homes purchased under Section 235 were overpriced and poorly constructed. Housing experts also were beginning to argue that it would make more sense simply to give poor families a grant that they could use to obtain better housing in the existing market. Proponents argued that the nation did not have a housing shortage, it simply had a shortage of housing for low-income citizens. They also pointed out that it was much cheaper to subsidize rents than home purchases.[17]

In 1974 Congress passed the Housing and Community Development Act. Section 8 of this act replaced Section 236. Unlike Section 236, Section 8 is oriented toward very low income families. Qualified renters pay between 15 and 25 percent of their income in rent, and HUD pays the difference between this amount and what it considers adequate rent for the given family. This part of the program works like a housing allowance for selected families, but the grant is paid directly to the landlord. By 1978 almost 500,000 families were receiving rent assistance under the program, but this was only a small proportion of all the families who were income-qualified. The median income of the families receiving assistance was about $3,700.[18]

Section 8 also has rental programs for newly constructed or substantially rehabilitated housing. Much like earlier programs, HUD subsidizes the rent of low-income families in specific buildings. These subsidies represent grants to designated developers and landlords. In 1978, 92,000 families were being subsidized by this program. Their median income was almost identical to that of the families receiving subsidies in existing housing. The emphasis of the 1968 act on rental assistance was designed to tailor assistance to household need and, to some extent, to disperse the poor. In actuality, the fair-market rent rule deters most recipients from renting better-quality housing and concentrates recipients in low-income areas. Additionally, landlords have the option of refusing Section 8 renters and many do.

In 1976 HUD revised the Section 235 home-ownership assistance program. The subsidy was lowered and the required family income was raised. This change was designed to orient the program toward families able to meet the mortgage payments. Under the old program the default rate was extremely high. By 1978 about 7,500 families were receiving assistance under the revised program. These families had a median income of about $11,000 a year, well above the median under the original program.[19]

By 1982, 3.4 million low-income to poor families were receiving housing assistance under one of the federal government's housing programs. The recipients of assistance represent about 38 percent of the total of 9 million families that are income-qualified for assistance. Most of the families receiving aid were in public housing or one of the rent-supplement programs. The total cost of the various programs was about $5.3 billion in 1982. Of the 5.6 million families who qualify for assistance, but receive no aid, millions are on waiting lists for public housing. In New York City, for example, there is an 18-year wait for a vacancy in public housing. Most of the nation's large cities also have such a shortage of public housing that waiting periods of several years are not uncommon.[20]

One other set of federal programs should be noted. The Housing and Community Development Act of 1974 provided grants to local governments to take the place of categorical programs such as Urban Renewal and Neighborhood Development. Local communities now receive a single grant, to be spent at their discretion, to improve neighborhoods. The allotments under the 1974 act are almost as expensive as all the funds spent directly on housing for low-income and poor citizens. In 1980 Community Development spending totaled $4.5 billion. There are literally a dozen or so other programs, mostly quite small, which fund some type of housing program. For example, the 1982 budget included $13.5 million for the urban homesteading program and $75 million for loans and grants to repair rural housing.

HOUSING PROGRAMS IN THE UNITED STATES: ASSISTANCE TO UPPER- AND MIDDLE-INCOME CITIZENS

At least from a monetary point of view, U.S. housing policy is oriented more toward assistance to middle- and upper-income citizens than to low-income citizens. As noted above, the federal government's first significant forays into the housing field grew out of the impact of the great depression on middle-income citizens, not the poor. During the depression there was considerable concern about the number of working families who had lost their homes, or were in imminent danger of doing so. By 1931, 50 percent of all mortgages were in default and residential construction was in a severe slump.[21] The Hoover administration's response was the Federal Home Loan Act which made loans to the nation's distressed mortgage lenders. The act assisted the lending institutions but not the nation's jobless homeowners, who continued to lose their homes at record levels over the next few years. By 1933 foreclosures were running 1,000 a day.

To deal with the foreclosure problem President Roosevelt convinced Congress to pass the Home Owners' Loan Act. This act set up the Home Owners' Loan Corporation which refinanced mortgages at 5 percent interest. By 1936 one home owner in five had been rescued by this corporation, and the immediate crisis was over.

The Roosevelt administration also addressed the problem of saving the home construction industry. Thus in 1934 Congress established the Federal Housing Administration (FHA). The FHA insured mortgages so that lenders, in effect, could make risk-free loans. This program assisted mortgage lenders but not builders, who still did not believe that there was sufficient demand for new housing. Congress again responded by creating in 1938 the Federal National Mortgage Association (Fannie Mae), a government corporation which would buy some lender mortgages. Fannie Mae allowed lenders to sell mortgages so that they could invest in other more profitable ventures. Until the 1950s both the FHA and Fannie Mae served middle-income home buyers, but under the Eisenhower administration FHA protections were extended to groups such as the elderly and those displaced by urban renewal. Other middle-income programs included the Veterans Administration (VA) housing programs. These programs provided both mortgage insurance and below-market interest rates to veterans. FHA, Fannie Mae, and the VA program have made very significant contributions to home ownership in the United States.

The major method by which homeowners are subsidized by the federal government is through the tax code. Homeowners are allowed to deduct all mortgage interest and taxes paid on a home. These provisions considerably reduce the cost of home ownership. The common practice of mortgage lenders is to collect most of the interest incurred on a loan within 10 years. The result is that during the first decade of a loan almost the total monthly house payment is tax-deductible. Those homeowners who receive the largest subsidy are those who can afford to purchase the most expensive homes and those who are in the highest tax brackets. Thus in the United States the most heavily subsidized homeowners are millionaires who live in mansions. Under this program there is also no limit on the number of houses for which the deduction can be claimed. If a person owns one home or a dozen, the deductions can be claimed for each residence. This tax policy is so lucrative that it is a major tax shelter. It has become common practice for many people in the United States to constantly trade up to higher-priced homes in order to protect their income from taxes. The tax program is the most expensive housing policy in the United States. In fiscal 1982 the mortgage interest deduction will cost approximately $25.3 billion, while the property tax deduction will cost approximately $10.9 billion.[22] The combined costs ($36.2 billion) represent about six times the amount of housing assistance given to low-income and poor citizens.

LIBERAL AND CONSERVATIVE CRITIQUES OF U.S. HOUSING PROGRAMS

As with many public issues, conservatives and liberals share some concerns about housing problems in the United States. Both are concerned about the barriers that first-time home buyers and other home buyers and sellers increasingly face, and the slump in housing starts and the construction industry. Both conservatives and liberals tend to agree that the cause of these problems has been high interest rates. As noted above, there are many reasons why both liberals and conservatives are concerned about these problems, but one important reason is that housing is potentially a quite volatile issue. A fundamental part of the American dream is owning one's own home. Of course, it is also generally accepted by both philosophical groups that a slump in the construction industry is bad for the economy.

One other area of general agreement involves public housing. Neither liberals nor conservatives are vigorous advocates of traditional public housing. Both groups tend to believe that the type of public housing that concentrates large numbers of poor, often jobless, families in one large project is often doomed to failure. Liberals, however, do generally support public housing for elderly citizens, especially when it can be located away from the slum areas of cities. Liberals also believe that the government should help expand the supply of decent low-cost housing, but not in the form of inner-city public housing. There is currently no significant support in the United States for the European-style public housing designed for a broad range of income groups. Indeed, most people in the United States are probably not even aware that this is a popular housing option in Europe.

Beyond these basic points, the differences between liberals and conservatives are considerable. Conservatives do not support an extensive role for government in the housing area because they believe that the market can meet the housing needs of people in the United States. Of course, conservatives do support government programs such as FHA and Fannie Mae and tax policies which subsidize and protect the private market. Conservatives in recent years have supported housing programs for low-income and poor citizens, but they believe that these programs should be kept modest.

The philosophical concerns of liberals about housing are much broader. The liberal position is that good housing and healthy neighborhoods are critical elements in the promotion of specific social goals. Poor housing and undesirable neighborhoods promote social problems such as cynicism and alienation, public health dangers, poor quality schools, and crime. Good and productive citizenship is promoted (but not necessarily guaranteed) by a healthy living environment. Decent housing, a critical part of that environment, should be a public right. In a wealthy society, liberals believe, all citizens have a right to expect decent housing to be made available to them.

The philosophical and policy concerns of liberals cause them to be quite critical of current housing policies in the United States. First, they argue, the government provides too little assistance to low-income and poor citizens. Only 3.4 million low-income families receive any assistance, and the cost of that assistance is less than 1 percent of the total federal budget. Some 5.6 million families who qualify for assistance receive no aid. Second, the primary method that most conservatives support to deal with the housing needs of most low-income citizens is not practical. Conservatives traditionally maintain that the housing needs of most low-income citizens can be met through "filtering." Filtering is the process by which homeowners trade up for better housing as their incomes improve, leaving their old housing for lower-income groups. Liberals argue that by the time most housing filters down to low-income groups, it is either in bad repair or located in squalid neighborhoods.

Liberals also contend that it is wrong for federal housing policy to be biased toward middle- and upper-income groups. It is unfair for the tax system to provide assistance to middle- and upper-income groups at four to six times the rate that low-income groups are given housing assistance. Such policies are both unfair and highly dysfunctional. They redistribute wealth toward upper-income groups, while often making housing a tax haven rather than a home. And they stimulate inflation in the housing market, further pricing lower-income citizens out of the housing market. Liberals believe that the tax laws need to be changed to take housing out of the investment speculation market.

Liberals also argue that the past, and to some extent current, policies of the FHA, VA, and other government agencies have segregated housing by race and socioeconomic status, while contributing to white flight to the suburbs. The impact of white flight has been to rob central cities of their tax base while isolating those citizens in the city who are too poor to flee. The consequences of white flight for U.S. education are discussed in Chapter 7.

Evidence supporting these charges is compelling. Until about the mid-1960s both the FHA and VA made most of their loans to buyers of suburban housing, housing that was sold almost entirely to white families.[23] By the time the official policies were changed, segregated residential patterns were well established.[24] Of course, public housing and rent subsidy programs also played a substantial role in isolating and segregating minorities and the poor in the central city. Well into the 1970s, local authorities maintained separate waiting lists for housing applicants, not allowing housing integration. Other federal policies, such as the federal highway program, encouraged flight to the suburbs, while frequently destroying the homes of the poor. In 1974 the U.S. Commission on Civil Rights pointed out, "Urban freeways have cut through ghettos to facilitate white suburbanites' travel from suburban homes to central city jobs. And the new roads also have uprooted suburban minority communities, forcing minority suburbanites to relocate in the central city."[25]

Liberals point out that the problems caused by decentralization of authority have served to aggravate these problems. As Headey observes:

> The problems of federalism, of decentralization and local autonomy are every-where evident in the housing field. Many programs, including public housing and urban renewal, require local authority initiative before any action can be taken and, in cases in which private developers propose building for lower income groups, they can often be effectively blocked by regulations included in housing and building codes and by rigid enforcement of zoning laws. Blocking tactics have been used not only to prevent racial integration, which is now mandatory in public housing, but also to prevent economic integration.[26]

Liberals often argue that federal housing policy in the United States is unplanned and uncoordinated. The federal government has never adopted a philosophy about housing goals or land-use policy. Until 1965, with the creation of the Department of Housing and Urban Development, there was no agency in charge of federal housing programs. The FHA, VA, and Urban Renewal all operated independently and often in violation of the specific orders of presidents.[27] The result, liberals argue, has been a set of housing policies that better reflect the policy demands of specific special interests than a rational approach to the nation's housing needs. Another result is that public policies often have been ineffective in meeting public needs. As one critic says:

> In a sense U.S. housing policy is to have no policy and rely on private enterprise. Private enterprise has, however, been stimulated by the increased demand for owner-occupied housing resulting from the tax concessions and mortgage guarantees which the federal government makes available to home-owners. Compared with Sweden and Britain lower income groups have been neglected. However, Congress has enacted diverse unco-ordinated programmes (e.g., public housing and subsidized rental and mortgage interest programmes) intended to assist both these groups and also groups with special needs (e.g., the elderly, war veterans, students, the handicapped). The programs have been launched with great optimism but have failed to serve more than a small proportion of those who, on paper, are eligible.[28]

A second effect, liberals say, is that local communities have been allowed to benefit from federal housing policies without any community or land-use planning. The frequent result is that urban areas have developed by random sprawl rather than plan, creating numerous social problems. Housing is often not thoughtfully related to the job market; thus many urbanites must travel long distances to work. In addition, uncharted sprawl makes it extremely difficult for many communities to provide public services such as garbage collection, police protection, street maintenance, and public transportation.

Both conservatives and liberals, then, have some substantial housing policy concerns. Before the specific proposals of both groups are examined, European housing policies will be reviewed. The emphasis will be on the policy decisions of western nations, the impact of these policies, and the implications of their experiences for dealing with housing needs in the United States.

EUROPEAN HOUSING POLICIES

Government intervention in the housing market is much more extensive in the European nations than in the United States. There are several reasons why this is true. First, during the twentieth century Europe has been ravaged by two wars and a major depression. These upheavals either destroyed much of the housing stock or disrupted home building. The critical shortages caused by these events required massive catch-up efforts that were at least partially directed and financed by the government. Once the government became involved in housing, it stayed involved. Second, the European nations, unlike the United States, have viable left-wing political movements, generally represented by labor unions and social democratic parties. These left-wing groups have made housing an important policy priority, forcing governments to devote attention and resources to its promotion. These groups have attempted, with some success, to promote the idea that housing is a fundamental right and that government has an obligation to assist all citizens, regardless of wealth, in obtaining decent housing.[29]

There are at least two other significant reasons why housing is given a high priority in Europe. Most of the Western European nations, and even the Eastern European nations, believe that housing represents a valuable national resource since it is a durable good. In addition, it provides jobs for those who finance, build, and maintain housing. The Western European nations also consider good housing to be a critical component of family and social policy. Like the family allowances discussed in the chapter on poverty, housing subsidies are designed to promote social well-being and a higher standard of living. In addition to the promotion of healthy families, many Europeans believe that an increasingly technological society will require a more educated and sophisticated public. It is their belief that an elevated standard of living is necessary to produce the type of citizens society will need. Thus, as McGuire says, from this perspective improvement in housing is "not just an adjunct to economic growth but an integral part of it."[30]

There are three major differences between European and U.S. housing policies that provide interesting insights. Each of these policies is worthy of examination in some detail.

Universal Assistance

Direct housing assistance is much more universal in Europe than in the United States. Direct assistance takes a variety of forms including housing allowances, public housing, home purchase grants, rehabilitation loans, and building and savings subsidies. Housing allowances are a common social-welfare benefit in the European nations. In Sweden and West Germany, for example, over 40 percent of the population is eligible for housing grants. In France housing allowances also are extended to a significant proportion of the population. In most countries the allowance varies with family size and income. In some nations the allowances are designed to give special assistance to particular groups, such as single mothers and the elderly. Both socialist and conservative parties in Europe generally have supported housing allowances. The socialists tend to like the redistributive potential of the grants, while the conservatives are comforted by the fact that the grants support the private housing sector.[31]

Publicly owned housing is also more extensive in Europe than in the United States. In Britain about 20 percent of all families live in publicly owned housing. Public housing is not as extensive in any of the other western nations, but it is more common in all the European nations than in the United States. Both Sweden and France also have a significant amount of quasi-public housing, which is housing subsidized and financed by the government and run by quasi-public authorities. Public and quasi-public housing in Europe is never limited to low-income families. In France, Britain, and Sweden there is no means test for such housing, and, therefore, it is common for middle-income families to live in public or quasi-public housing.[32]

Another method by which the government promotes housing in Europe is through direct subsidies to builders and purchasers. In most of the European nations the government provides below-market loans to builders, and sometimes buyers, as a method of holding down the costs of housing. In France and Sweden a considerable proportion of all housing is built or purchased with this type of assistance. In Sweden, for example, over 90 percent of all housing construction is financed, at least in part, by the government. In France first-time home purchasers receive special grants, and the state-directed financial institutions finance home construction with a bias toward moderate and low-income housing.

One of the most interesting government subsidies in Europe is the savings bonus. In Britain, for example, there are special savings accounts for citizens who want to save for the down payment on a home. If the citizen saves every month for 5 years, the government awards the saver a tax-free bonus equal to 1-year's savings. If the bonus is not withdrawn from the account for 2 years, it is doubled. In West Germany there is a similar plan. Savers can earn a government bonus equal to as much as 25 to 35 percent of the sum saved.[33]

As in the United States, the governments of Europe also promote home ownership by allowing purchasers to treat interest and tax expenses as tax deductions. However, in most European nations there are monetary limitations on these deductions. The limitations are designed to allow about 80 percent of all families (all but those at the highest income levels) to deduct the total cost of yearly mortgage interest and property taxes. In many of the nations the interest and tax deductions are limited to the imputed rental income of the house, which is the value of the rent that could have been obtained in the market.[34] In some countries there is also a limit on the number of years in which the deductions can be taken. For example, in France the deduction can only be taken during the first 10 years of the loan. In West Germany the deduction can only be taken by first-home buyers. The reasons for the limitations on deductions are fairly obvious. The governments want to encourage home purchasing without stimulating inflation in the housing market or unduly subsidizing wealthy citizens.

The Nonprofit Housing Market

A major difference between the U.S. and European housing markets is that in Europe there is a very large nonprofit housing construction sector. The nonprofit sector has been promoted primarily by labor unions and encouraged and financed by national governments. The nonprofit sector consists of building societies, housing associations, and housing cooperatives. The first two organizations operate much like savings and loan associations except that they often directly develop, own, and operate housing and commercial property.[35] Housing cooperatives raise money through bond or equity markets and build housing for their members which is then managed on a joint-ownership basis.[36]

The nonprofit sector has a long history in Europe, and in most of the nations it accounts for a very significant percentage of all home construction. In Sweden, for example, 65 percent of all postwar housing has been built by housing or consumer cooperatives.[37] The Swedish government partly financed this housing, as it did most of the privately built housing.

Land and Development Planning

Unlike in the United States, urban planning is common in the European nations. Planning is designed to promote manageable, functional, socially desirable growth. Fainstein describes the variety of goals that planning is designed to accomplish:

> European national and regional planning involves restrictions on investment in developed regions, incentives to growth in designated development areas, direct governmental investment in housing and industry, and subsidization of labor costs. Many countries require planning permission of any new construction, and such permission accrues to land only when it conforms to national and regional master plans, which set developmental priorities and seek to contain urban sprawl.[38]

As an integral part of planning, governments often purchase development property in urban areas. This is a common practice in Sweden and the Netherlands and increasingly common in Britain. The government, usually at the local level, purchases development property to make certain that sites for home building will remain available, to limit land speculation, and to retain profits from built-up land for the public. In Sweden, the Netherlands, and Britain the government has used its financing and publicly owned land to develop new towns. New towns are intended to reduce development pressure on urban areas or on the periphery of major metropolitan areas.

This review raises a couple of questions. First, how successful have European housing policies been? This, of course, is a value judgment, one that would be easier to address on a country-by-country basis. But our concern here is more general. There are a number of points that most observers would accept. Certainly, after World War II the European nations managed to build a great deal of quality housing in a relatively short period of time. Some nations, such as West Germany, Sweden, the Netherlands, and Britain, made very impressive gains. In recent years France also has built a great deal of quality housing. Both public and quasi-public housing, often combined with housing allowances, have provided millions of citizens with decent housing at very low cost. Subsidies for both home builders and purchasers also have served to promote home ownership. The comprehensive policies of Sweden have created the highest ratio of dwelling units to population and the best housing amenities of any nation in the world.[39] It also should be noted that there are no slums in Sweden.

A major area in which the European nations lag behind the United States, however, is in home ownership. The figures below show the rate of home ownership in selected nations in 1978:[40]

United States	63%
Belgium	56%
Canada	60%
France	45%
West Germany	34%
Sweden	35%
Switzerland	28%
United Kingdom	48%

As the figures show, Sweden, West Germany, and Switzerland, particularly, have much lower rates of home ownership than the United States. Both Britain and France are also significantly behind the United States in making home ownership possible. The reasons why the rate of home ownership varies by nation are numerous, but a major one is that some of the nations have not emphasized this policy. In those nations with generous housing allowances renting simply has been the most advantageous policy for most families. In more recent years, Britain, France, and Sweden have developed policies that make home ownership a more desirable alternative. While home ownership is not as extensive in many nations as it is in the United States, housing costs often take a relatively modest proportion of family income in those nations which emphasize apartment living.

Most observers believe that urban and land-use planning have been valuable methods by which European countries have made growth more manageable and attractive. There is little doubt that most European cities are better designed to accommodate the delivery of public services (including transportation) than are U.S. cities. Most European cities also provide a better mix of industrial and residential neighborhoods and parks and recreational space than do U.S. cities. Additionally, a few nations have used planning as a method of integrating housing by socioeconomic status and age. Sweden has been particularly successful in integrating housing along these lines. Of course, this has been made easier by the virtual absence of racial division.

A second question raised by this review concerns the applicability of European housing techniques to housing problems in the United States. This again involves a value judgment, but at the least it can be said that the European nations have effectively dealt with some of the housing problems that continue to prevail in the United States. The European nations have used allowances to greatly improve the shelter of millions of their citizens. They also have used public and quasi-public housing to provide quality housing to a broad range of families. By making public housing available to both low-income and middle-income families, the European nations have avoided many of the problems that have plagued public housing in the United States. Europeans also have successfully used rather simple techniques, such as savings bonuses, to stimulate both savings and home ownership. The United States has a comparatively low rate of savings, and one reason clearly is that U.S. tax policies actually discourage savings.

The nonprofit housing sector has contributed greatly to improved housing in Europe. However, the organizations that have promoted this type of housing are not very powerful in the United States. The stigma associated with public housing would also make it difficult to implement this kind of policy. Land and urban planning also have worked quite well in Europe, promoting more orderly and publicly controlled growth.

HOUSING REFORM: CONSERVATIVE PROPOSALS

Conservatives, like liberals, are not entirely united when it comes to proposals to deal with the nation's housing problems. Some conservative proposals have found broader support within conservative ranks than others. We begin by examining the major proposals of the Reagan administration and then discuss a few proposals put forth by conservative members of Congress.

In late 1981 a commission appointed by President Reagan to study the nation's housing needs made its official report.[41] The commission's major conclusions and proposals were consistent with recent conservative positions on housing. The commission concluded that the nation's housing needs could, and should, be met by reliance on the private sector. The commission noted that the private sector would need some subsidies, but that it could meet the nation's housing needs without major intervention by the government. The commission also concluded that there is no shortage of good housing in the United States. The problem, as the commission saw it, was that many families in the United States do not have the funds necessary to acquire the serviceable housing that is available.

The commission's major policy recommendation was that low-income families receive a consumer assistance grant to be used to rent adequate housing. The grant would simply be a housing allowance that the recipient could use to pay for more expensive housing than his or her personal income would allow. The commission favored this proposal over the Section 8 program which pays a grant directly to landlords. The commission felt that the allowance would give recipients more freedom in the selection of housing, allowing low-income families to better integrate into the community. In addition, the allowance would stimulate home and apartment construction.

The commission recommended that the allowance not be an entitlement program open to all eligible families. In fact, it proposed that the program be kept quite small. Priority should be given to low-income families living in inadequate housing, families paying rent in excess of 50 percent of their income, or families suffering involuntary displacement. In effect, the commission recommended a first-come, first-serve program limited by funding. This, of course, is a much more modest proposal than the housing allowances common in Europe.

Some conservatives are uncomfortable with housing allowance programs because they fear that the recipients will not use the money to improve their housing. As with proposals to "cash out" the Food Stamp program, some conservatives are skeptical that the money would be used wisely. For this reason the allowance program is not as popular with many conservatives as the Section 8 program which provides subsidies directly to landlords. Interestingly, some liberals share this fear. In 1970, HUD launched an experimental housing allowance program. Over an 11-year period some 30,000 households in twelve states participated in the experiment.[42] Evaluations of the program varied, with some investigators concluding that the program was more effective and much less expensive than traditional housing programs.[43] However, some liberals and conservatives had doubts. They noted that only about half the families that could have qualified under the program even applied. Second, most of the recipients did not use the grants to obtain better housing. Rather, they stayed put and used the subsidy to reduce their contribution to housing. To meet federal standards many of the recipients did make modest improvements in their housing, but the repairs were too minor to substantially improve their situation.

Many conservatives and liberals found it difficult to label this type of program a success. They argued that a good program should improve the quality of the housing and neighborhood in which recipients live. Many observers also noted that when recipients stay put, the housing market is not stimulated to build homes or even to substantially renovate existing housing. Of course, a rental allowance program could require recipients to seek better housing, but one implication of the study was that the poor are often quite reluctant to move. They may be reluctant to move because they do not believe that they could obtain substantially better housing with the supplemental grant.

The commission recommended three other proposals: (1) that local communities be allowed to use Community Development Block Grants to build new housing, (2) that pension funds be allowed to expand their investment in mortgages, and (3) that owners of residential property be given a special tax credit for rehabilitating rental structures. The commission made no estimate of the impact of these changes on the housing market.[44]

President Reagan had no official reaction to the commission's recommendations. In his 1983 budget proposal he recommended (1) continuing funding for the Section 8 program, with assistance budgeted for about 600,000 households, (2) no funding for Sections 235 or 236 housing, and (3) modestly increasing the number of families eligible for FHA mortgages, constructing 70,000 additional units of public housing, easing regulation of mortgage revenue bonds, and allowing pension funds to expand housing investments. In response to critics who charged that his policies were too modest given the nation's housing problems, Reagan argued that his economic policies would turn the economy around, and, once it did so, the nation's housing problems would be solved by market forces.

The nation's worsening housing problems stimulated some Republican members of Congress to break with the President and back emergency legislation to give the industry some immediate help. In the late spring of 1982 Senator Richard Lugar (R., Ind.) sponsored a $5.1 billion mortgage subsidy plan designed to create 700,000 new jobs in housing-related fields. Under the Lugar plan families with incomes of up to $30,000 a year ($37,000 in high-cost areas) would be eligible for interest rate subsidies to help them buy new homes. The government would provide subsidies to cut the mortgage rates by as much as 4 percentage points, but not below 11 percent. Recipients of the grants would be expected to repay them when the house was sold or refinanced. In support of the bill, Senator Lugar argued that legislation was needed to stimulate the housing market. Lugar noted, "Housing has led us out of past recessions, and it can do so again."[45]

Lugar's plan was passed by both the House and Senate in June 1982, but was vetoed by President Reagan.

HOUSING REFORM: LIBERAL PROPOSALS

Within Congress, the Democratic and liberal housing proposals pending in 1982 did not differ radically from those supported by moderate and conservative members of Congress. Henry Gonzales (D., Tex.) was the author of the most comprehensive housing recovery proposal.[46] Gonzales' proposal called for new funding for the Section 235 programs that subsidize mortgages for low- and moderate-income home buyers. Gonzales' bill called for $1 billion in Section 235 mortgage subsidies to stimulate the construction of about 10,000 homes for low-income families. The bill would also have authorized $3.5 billion for the Section 235(q) program which would lower interest rates to 9.5 percent during the first 10 years of a mortgage. Recipients would be required to repay part of the subsidy when the house was sold. The bill also provided $760 million in loans to homeowners faced with mortgage foreclosure because of economic problems. Because of the nation's economic problems there seemed to be little chance that Gonzales' total bill would actually pass Congress, or even be given very serious consideration. Some observers believed that some provisions of the bill might attract attention if the housing crisis continued through 1983.

Other moderate Democratic members of the House were proposing that the government provide first-time home buyers with loans for down payments on homes. A bipartisan proposal circulating in the House would give new-home buyers a $5,400 tax credit. During a severe housing slump in 1975 a similar plan had given new-home buyers a $2,000 tax credit. Last, some Democratic members of the House were proposing that Fannie Mae be authorized to buy up additional mortgage loans to give lenders new funds to lend to home buyers.

The housing proposals being actively supported by liberal members of Congress in 1982 were quite moderate. They were certainly not as extensive as the policies commonly employed in Europe. The difference between U.S. liberal proposals and those of the left in Europe, of course, reflects the much weaker position of the left in the United States. In Europe the labor unions and the social democratic parties are much more powerful and can win support for more egalitarian proposals. Liberals in the United States and left-wing scholars have put forth more radical proposals to deal with the nation's housing problems, but at the current time they are not being seriously considered by policy makers. Below we will review some of the major proposals of liberal scholars.

There are at least six major housing proposals that are often supported by liberals: a national housing budget, tax and interest rate limitations, housing allowances, financing and savings proposals, urban and land-use planning, and housing for the aged.[47]

A National Housing Budget

Liberals often argue that the United States subsidizes wealthier home buyers more than moderate- and low-income home buyers because the subsidies that go to higher-income groups are hidden within the tax expenditure budget. They believe that if it became common knowledge that the tax deductions for mortgage interest and taxes actually subsidize wealthier groups at several times the rate at which other groups are subsidized, the public would force the government to alter its policies. Thus liberals recommend that a national housing budget should be published each year. This budget would show all government expenditures (including tax expenditures) by income class for housing during that budget year. Such a budget, it is argued, would scandalize the public and force an alteration in housing priorities. As Headey argues, even conservative politicians would be reluctant to say "that it should be an objective of public policy to redistribute resources in favor of the rich."[48] Liberals, of course, hope that a reduction in benefits for wealthier groups would result in increased assistance for moderate- to low-income families and a reduction in housing inflation.

Tax and Interest Rate Limitations

Liberals say that current laws which allow home purchasers to deduct all mortgage interest and real estate taxes not only discriminate in favor of the rich, but also create housing inflation. To deal with both problems, they propose limitations on such deductions. There are a number of proposals along these lines. One idea is to place a limit on the amount of taxes and interest that could be deducted each year. As proposed, most citizens would be allowed the full deduction, with limitations imposed on only the most expensive mortgages. There are some variations on this theme. Some argue that the tax and interest deductions should be replaced by a housing expense deduction that would vary with family income and size. Another option is to place a limit on the number of years in which tax and interest deductions could be taken. A common proposal, along the lines of the West German plan, is that the deductions only be allowed during the first 10 years of a loan. The rationale for this is that the deductions should help people purchase a home, but the subsidy should be limited so that government resources could be shifted to low-income and first-home buyers. Last, it is often proposed that subsidies be available only for one home.

This proposal is obviously designed to limit government assistance to wealthier citizens.

Housing Allowances

Another liberal proposal would involve government housing allowances to low- and moderate-income earners. These housing allowances would be made available to at least the nation's lowest 10 to 20 percent of all income earners. This proposal would create a housing allowance system similar to those available in many European nations, but it would not be as extensive. The allowances would be given only to families living in decent housing or families willing to relocate to better housing. The allowances would be in the form of grants to the families, rather than the landlords. The intent is for family grants to allow recipients a broader range of housing options, hopefully resulting in better neighborhood integration of low-income families and the eventual end of major slums in the United States. Liberals feel that slum neighborhoods have negative social impacts on residents, and eventually on the larger society. Thus housing allowances and other housing assistance programs should be designed to banish slums from the American scene.

Financing and Savings Proposals

Liberals also favor public policies designed to encourage home purchases and sales. This would require the government to take those actions necessary to hold down interest rates and make home-loan money available. When interest rates are high (as they were in 1981 and 1982), the government could subsidize loans to bring the interest rates down, with a recovery option when the house was sold or refinanced. The government should adopt the European technique of builder and lender subsidies to reduce the costs of housing.

Furthermore, there are a number of things that the government could do to help ensure availability of mortgage money. One option would be the incentive saving plans that are popular in Europe. Families or individuals investing in a savings plan designed to accumulate the funds necessary to finance a home purchase could receive matching grants and tax breaks. As noted in the economics chapter, liberals also believe that current laws discriminate against small savers, often making it unprofitable for them to save. Small savers could be given tax breaks to encourage saving rather than spending. Limits on tax deductions for consumer spending also would help to encourage citizens to save rather than spend. Thus, liberals favor a number of policies to give all people in the United States more incentives to save and accumulate capital for home mortgages and other investments.

Urban and Land-Use Planning

From the liberal perspective, it is utter folly for cities to fail to employ building and land-use planning. Lack of planning has created a crazy-quilt pattern of municipal development, leading to unsightly and wasteful urban spread. In addition to other problems, sprawl makes delivery of standard services such as education and garbage collection more difficult. Property owners frequently are confronted with drainage or even flooding problems caused by hasty housing construction in underdeveloped areas. Cities usually must bear the cost of water control systems. The failure of cities to control urban property has contributed significantly to inflation in building prices. True, some cities have better growth planning than others, but basically liberals believe that most cities have done a poor job in this area. Liberals accept the fact that most cities are too developed to be transformed by planning, but they suggest that the adoption of planning would promote more rational and manageable growth, contributing to better urban environments.

Housing for the Aged

Liberals often argue that the government should build creative communities for retired citizens. Three reasons are offered in support of this policy. First, citizens should have rational housing and community options when they retire. The aged should have the option of moving to smaller, yet decent housing located away from the more congested areas of large cities. This housing should provide the support services (e.g., medical care and recreation) that aged citizens need. If such housing were available, the aged would have more manageable, safer, stimulating, and companionable environments in which to live. Such communities would provide alternatives to the nursing homes and decaying central city neighborhoods in which the aged often end up in the United States. Liberals favor housing projects created specifically for the aged and located outside central cities.

Second, by providing housing for the aged, the nation's stock of family dwellings would be significantly increased. As the aged moved out of their family residences to retirement communities their homes would become available, thereby increasing the number of residences available for families still in the work force.

Last, retirement communities would be cost-effective, if residence in such a community was based on ability to pay. Nursing home care is extremely expensive, and many of the residents of such facilities are there only because they have nowhere else to go or because they cannot perform some basic services (such as grocery shopping) for themselves. In a supportive environment many of the aged would remain viable and independent much longer and be much happier.

CONCLUSIONS

This chapter has examined three of the nation's most pressing housing problems. Current housing policies have been critiqued from both liberal and conservative perspectives. Both liberal and conservative proposals for housing reform in the United States have been examined and compared to European housing policies. This review has made several things apparent. First, while the United States has been quite successful since the end of World War II in housing most of its citizens, current housing problems are substantial. Conservatives and liberals clearly have different priorities, but both groups are concerned about specific problems in the area of housing. One reason for the shared concern is that current housing problems affect a very large proportion of the total population. Even middle-income citizens are having difficulty in purchasing or selling homes, and the construction and related housing industries are in very substantial difficulty. Conservatives and liberals also share concern for the millions of U.S. citizens who are not well-housed. Both agree that the government should sponsor programs to help low-income citizens obtain better housing, but, of course, they disagree over the mechanics and magnitude of such programs.

In addition, both conservatives and liberals agree that the policies established and administered by the federal government since the New Deal have played a major role in increasing the quality and affordability of U.S. housing. They also have created public expectations of attractive and affordable housing that policy makers are reluctant to disappoint. For this reason the nation's current housing problems are considered serious enough to become a major issue in future elections. Our review of current housing reforms under consideration in Congress, however, suggests that neither liberals nor conservatives support policies that are very radical. Both groups admit that if the policies under consideration were adopted, they would have only a modest impact on the nation's housing problems. Even liberal members of Congress currently support rather modest housing reforms, in part because they seem to think that more comprehensive proposals would not win support during a period in which the nation's economy is in a slump. Of course, the modesty of liberal proposals in Congress reflects the weakness of left-wing political movements in the United States, which is itself a reflection of our historical suspicion of government.

The differences between the housing proposals being supported by liberal and conservative members of Congress, and conservative and liberal scholars, reflect the fundamental differences between these two schools of political thought. Liberals want the government to play a larger role, and they want the emphasis of government assistance to be shifted from aid to upper- and middle-income and wealthy citizens to moderate- and lower-income citizens. Liberals want the government to play a larger role because they have less faith than conservatives in the power of the market to provide equitably for the housing needs of all citizens.

Liberals are more inclined to believe that a wealthy society has an obligation to succor the less fortunate members of society. Thus they believe that all citizens have a right to decent housing. Conservatives do not totally reject an obligation for the housing needs of low-income citizens. They support more modest programs for the poor on the grounds that extensive programs constitute too large a financial drag on the economy, thus rendering economic forces less capable of meeting public needs.

Liberals tend to have a more global view of the role of housing in society. They believe that citizens who are ill-housed and isolated in squalid neighborhoods are less capable of realizing their full human potential, and thus less capable of being viable, productive members of society. Conse-quently, society ends up paying a great price for its deprived citizens, in crime, low productivity, welfare expenses, and many other ways. Good housing and other preventive social services are investments that yield social, moral, and economic profits.

The differences between conservatives and liberals on the issue of housing, then, are consistent with those reflected in debates between these two groups over the other issues examined in this volume. Conservatives are more trusting than liberals in the ability of the market to solve social problems. They believe that costly social programs often interfere with the ability of the market to meet public needs. Liberals believe that government is a better friend of most citizens than the market, and that historical evidence shows that the market has been unable to equitably or efficiently meet most public needs. They often point out that the government accepted the obligation of providing many public services only when the market failed to meet public needs.

Conservatives point out that liberal policies are redistributive and expen-sive, requiring all citizens to pay higher taxes and have less control over their lives. Liberals generally accept this charge. They simply argue that if public services are financed by progressive taxes, moderate- and low-income citizens will receive better services than their personal incomes would provide, and the more equal distribution of income produced by progressive taxes would produce a less class-structured and more egalitarian society.

NOTES

1 Congressional Budget Office, *Federal Housing Policy: Current Problems and Recurring Issues,* June 1978, Tables 1 and 8.
2 U.S. Bureau of the Census, *Census of the Population and Housing, 1950, 1960, 1970, and Annual Housing Survey: 1977,* Part E; and *Congressional Quarterly:*

Weekly Report, "For the Poor, A Wait for Better Housing," Dec. 4, 1982, p. 2949.

3 Congressional Budget Office, *Federal Housing Policy: Current Problems and Recurring Issues,* June 1978, Tables 3 and 4.

4 Frank S. Kristof, "Federal Housing Policies: Subsidized Production, Filtration and Objectives: Part II," *Land Economics,* May 1973, p. 171.

5 Adam Smith, *Paper Money* (New York: Dell Books, 1981), p. 105.

6 Ibid., p. 104.

7 *Congressional Quarterly: Weekly Report,* Apr. 17, 1982, p. 852.

8 Ibid., p. 848.

9 Ibid.

10 U.S. Commission on Civil Rights, *Equal Opportunity In Suburbia* (Washington, D.C.: GPO, 1974), p. 10.

11 Bruce Headey, *Housing Policy in the Developed Economy: The United Kingdom, Sweden, and the United States* (London: Croom Helm, 1978), p. 242.

12 U.S. Bureau of the Census, *Statistical Abstract of the United States: 1980,* 101st ed. (Washington, D.C.: GPOffice, 1981), p. 798.

13 *Hills v. Gautreaux,* 425 U.S. 284 (1967).

14 Congressional Budget Office, *Federal Housing Policy: Current Problems and Recurring Issues,* p. 14.

15 Ibid., p. 18.

16 Ibid., p. 12.

17 David B. Carlson and John D. Heinberg, *How Housing Allowances Work* (Washington, D.C.: The Urban Institute, 1978), pp. 46–47.

18 Congressional Budget Office, *Federal Housing Policy: Current Problems and Recurring Issues,* p. 14.

19 Ibid.

20 *Congressional Quarterly: Weekly Report,* Dec. 4, 1982, p. 2949; and *Congressional Quarterly: Weekly Report,* Aug. 15, 1981, p. 1471.

21 See Headey, pp. 201–207; James Heilbrum, *Urban Economics and Public Policy* (New York: St. Martin's Press, 1981), pp. 366–367; Susan S. Fainstein, "American Policy for Housing and Community Development: A Comparative Examination," in *Housing Policy for the 1980s,* eds. Roger Montgomery and Dale Rogers Marshall (Lexington, Mass.: Lexington Books, 1980), pp. 215–216.

22 Office of Management and Budget, *The United States Budget In Brief: Fiscal Year 1982* (Washington, D.C.: GPO, 1982), p. 60.

23 Michael N. Danielson, *The Politics of Exclusion* (New York: Columbia Univ. Press, 1976), p. 242; and U.S. Commission on Civil Rights, *The Federal Civil Rights Enforcement Effort: To Provide Fair Housing* (Washington, D.C.: GPO, 1975), p. 41.

24 U. S. Commission on Civil Rights, *The Federal Civil Rights Enforcement Effort: To Provide Fair Housing,* pp. 46–48.

25 Ibid., p. 45.

26 Headey, p. 177.

27 Ibid., p. 223.

28 Ibid., p. 175.

29 Chester C. McGuire, *International Housing Policies: A Comparative Analysis* (Lexington, Mass.: Lexington Books, 1981), p. 8.

30 Ibid., p. 18.

31 Arnold J. Heidenheimer, Hugh Heclo, and Carolyn Teich Adams, *Comparative Public Policy: The Politics of Social Choice in Europe and America* (New York: St. Martin's Press, 1975), p. 77.

32 Ibid., p. 92.

33 McGuire, pp. 134, 147.

34 Ibid., pp. 53, 173.

35 Fainstein, p. 226; Headey, p. 45; and McGuire, p. 23.

36 Headey, pp. 44–48.

37 Ibid., p. 45.

38 Fainstein, p. 221.

39 Headey, p. 47.

40 Caroll Melton, *Housing Finance and Homeownership* (Chicago: International Union of Building Societies and Savings Associations, 1978), p. 44.

41 *Congressional Quarterly: Weekly Report,* Nov. 7, 1981, p. 2190.

42 See Raymond J. Struyk, Marc Bendick, Jr., eds. *Housing Vouchers for the Poor: Lessons from a National Experiment* (Washington, D.C.: The Urban Institute, 1981).

43 See Ibid.; and Bernard J. Frieden, "Housing Allowances: An Experiment That Worked," *The Public Interest,* Spring 1980, pp. 15–35.

44 *Congressional Quarterly: Weekly Report,* Nov. 7, 1981, p. 2190.

45 *Congressional Quarterly: Weekly Report,* Apr. 17, 1982, p. 847.

46 Ibid., p. 850.

47 Headey, pp. 258–263; and Fainstein, pp. 220–226.

48 Headey, p. 254.

CHAPTER 9

THE LESSONS AND LIMITS OF A COMPARATIVE PERSPECTIVE

If you take the policy issues and associated problems discussed in this book seriously, you can end up feeling really dispirited. Health care costs are soaring and so are crime rates. Schools are failing and so is the economy. Women are treated inequitably and so are poor people. And to make matters worse, political leaders in this country cannot seem to agree on any solutions to these problems. Liberals want government to do more and conservatives want it to do less. Clearly, the average citizen knows what he or she wants—less crime and poverty, better health and a stronger economy, etc.—but probably is not certain how we as a society can best achieve these goals.

At the beginning of this book we promised we *would not* provide simple answers to the extraordinarily complex problems associated with poverty, health care, crime, housing, education, a faltering economy, and a search for gender equality. We think we have delivered on that promise. But aside from reiterating that there are no simple answers to these problems, what can we offer by way of conclusion and, perhaps, consolation? There are five general points we wish to make about the nature of the current problems facing the United States in the 1980s and the approaches to solving these problems.

TOO MUCH GOVERNMENT OR TOO LITTLE?

Over 125 years ago, the famous British historian Thomas Babington Macaulay underscored a timeless dilemma in the governing of nations:

I hardly know which is the greater pest to society, a paternal government . . . which intrudes itself into every part of human life, and which thinks it can do everything for everybody better than anybody can do anything for himself, or a careless, lounging government, which suffers grievances, such as it could at once remove, to grow and multiply, and which to all complaint and remonstrance has only one answer: "We must let things find their own level."[1]

Clearly, neither of the extremes articulated by Macaulay is acceptable now, nor were they acceptable in his time. The history of Western Europe and the United States over the last one and one-half centuries has been a search for a politically acceptable and efficacious position between the extremes of an omnipresent, intrusive government and "a careless, lounging government." The pendulum has swung back and forth between these extremes as people have searched for just the right combination of public and private activity to solve the problems of the times. There may be some yet undiscovered social scientific law which can explain the velocity, frequency, and direction of that pendulumlike political swing from left (more government) to right (more private action) in democratic polities. But until the time that such a law is revealed we will have to content ourselves with simply recognizing that the search for the appropriate mix does not represent a failure of democratic societies, but rather is part of the process by which these systems seek not only to solve problems but also to accommodate political diversity. The search for the "right" mix is a perennial one in democratic societies. Thus far in our own country, while liberalism and conservatism have prevailed at different times, neither has supplanted the other permanently—nor do we suspect they ever will.

Our first concluding point then is this. The reader should not feel frustrated by the apparent endless groping and grappling by liberals and conservatives as they search for the solution to our outstanding problems. Politics in democratic societies always have been this way and that is as it should be. Only totalitarian societies discover ultimate truths.

MEETING IN THE MIDDLE

The second point we would make derives from the first. Differences between U.S. conservatives and liberals, while still great, tend to be muted in and by our system. The arc of the U.S. political pendulum, in other words, is confined to a fairly moderate sweep. Indeed, political constraint and consensus—with some notable exceptions like the Civil War—have long been hallmarks of U.S. politics. This is not to suggest that more extreme views have never prevailed, but they are largely kept in check.

The tendency toward consensus and moderation has had the effect of muting conservative and liberal conflict and reducing policy differences to matters of degree and emphasis rather than dogmatic principle. Thus, as we noted in Chapter 2, both conservatives and liberals now agree that government has a responsibility toward the poor, although they differ over which level of government should take primary responsibility and what should be done. Similarly, most conservatives accept *some* role, for *some* level of government, in health care, housing, and education and in managing the economy.

It is important to note in this context that the differences between left and right in the United States tend to be less pronounced than the differences in Western Europe. It would take us too far afield to adequately account for this important difference, but two explanations stand out. The first, which we noted in Chapter 1, is the sharing and separation of powers between and within the different levels of government in the United States. Thus, for example, both liberal Democratic and conservative Republican presidents have found it necessary to make both substantive and philo- sophical compromises with Congress in order to win approval of their legislative programs. Just such a compromise was noted in Chapter 6 with regard to Lyndon Johnson and the LEAA. Similarly, Ronald Reagan found it necessary to compromise both his principles and policies when dealing with a Democratic-controlled House of Representatives. In addition, the federal structure of the U.S. government often forces substantive and ideological compromise between levels of government. National leaders in Congress and the executive branch have found it necessary to moderate their positions in order to win acceptance of their programs by state and local officials in "wars" on crime, poverty, and discrimination.

The U.S. system of federalism and a presidential form of government with a separation of powers is in stark contrast to the typically unitary, parliamentary governments of Western Europe. In these countries there is a fusion rather than a separation of powers between the legislative and executive branches, with the chief executive (e.g., the prime minister) chosen from the legislature (e.g., the parliament) by a majority party or a majority coalition. Thus, the prime minister usually can count upon a legislative majority to implement his or her policies. In addition, since power in these unitary systems is concentrated at the center, rather than dispersed as in our federal system, it is much easier for the national government to implement policies throughout a nation without recourse to substantive or philosophical compromises. In this regard we would remind the reader of the point made in Chapter 7 concerning the ability of countries like Japan and Sweden to implement nationwide educational reforms with far greater facility than is possible (or perhaps desirable) in the United States.

In addition to the political differences which lead to less pronounced divisions between right and left in the United States than in Western Europe, there is also an important structural difference. This was the virtual absence of a highly class-stratified society during the formative years of our nation. Alexis de Tocqueville, the nineteenth-century French writer and politician who visited the United States in 1832 and wrote one of the most astute accounts of U.S. society ever written, noted:

> Among the novel objects that attracted my attention during my stay in the United States nothing struck me more forcibly than the general equality of condition among the people. I readily discovered the prodigious influence that this primary fact exercises on the whole course of society; it gives a peculiar direction to public opinion and a peculiar tenor to the laws; it imparts new maxims to the governing authorities and peculiar habits to the governed. . . . The more I advanced in the study of American society, the more I perceived that this equality of condition is the fundamental fact from which all others seem to be derived and the central point at which all my observations constantly terminated.[2]

A number of contemporary political scientists, including Louis Hartz and Robert Dahl, have elaborated upon the implications of this essential equality.[3] From our perspective the most profound consequence was that politics and political parties in the United States did not develop along class-based lines and, therefore, did not produce the more divisive political conflicts characteristic of many European nations.

European society was, until quite recently, highly stratified along strict class lines. It will be recalled that the use of a multitrack educational system throughout Western Europe and Japan, until after World War II, both reflected and perpetuated the class basis of these societies. As a result, politics, political parties, *and* public policy tended to be and still are more polarized in Europe than in the United States. One finds more clearly defined and substantial policy differences between European social democrats and conservatives than between U.S. liberals and conservatives. Thus, when social democrats have been in power in Western Europe they have been able to fashion more dramatic policies of the left (e.g., economic planning, national health insurance, public housing) than their liberal counterparts in the United States. And this introduces the third general point we wish to make.

THE LIMITS OF COMPARISON

We noted at the beginning of the book that there was a danger in comparative policy analysis of engaging in illogical, invalid, or inappropriate comparisons. The applicability of many of the policy solutions found in Western Europe and Japan is limited, but not precluded, by the fact that the United States is different in so many significant ways than other democratic societies. In addition to the obvious differences in size, global military obligations, degree of pluralism, and historical idiosyncrasies we can now add the political difference of moderation and consensus.

Many of the policies which U.S. liberals find so attractive, such as macroeconomic planning or public housing or a less restrictive penal system, have not been adopted, *in part,* because, *in the context of American politics,* they represent nonincremental policy departures outside the current arc of acceptable policy alternatives. This is not to suggest that these policies cannot, will not, or should not be adopted but simply to indicate one of the reasons why they have not been adopted. This, of course, does not entirely explain the failure of, for example, national health insurance— or any other policy discussed here. One would have to take into account, in the case of national health insurance, such factors as the role of the American Medical Association, the strong U.S. attachment to free enterprise, and other factors. But it does suggest one important reason.

Why can't we be more like Sweden or Hong Kong? One answer, we believe, is because to do so we would have to expand, either left or right, the acceptable arc of the U.S. political pendulum. Of course, this has happened in the past with the Social Security Act, Medicare and Medicaid, and others programs, and will undoubtedly happen again.

THE MORE THINGS CHANGE, THE MORE THEY REMAIN THE SAME

The fourth point we wish to make concerns the durability—really intractability—of the problems and proposed policy solutions discussed in this book. Consider, for example, the following characterizations of the housing, crime, education, health care, and welfare problems in the United States:

> Money for home mortgage loans is vanishing across the nation. . . . Fear of a complete breakdown in new home building—smashing the dreams of potential buyers and threatening widespread unemployment among construction workers— was expressed at a meeting of building men here [Washington, D.C.] today.[4]

> [The] Director of the Federal Bureau of Investigation said tonight that crime reached a new high last year with youth again figuring prominently on the nation's police blotters.[5]

> Once again the nation's public schools are in serious plight. . . . Incompetent teachers, poorly equipped classrooms, inadequate buildings and poor supervision combine to cheat the hundreds of thousands of young people. . . .[6]

> Oscar R. Ewing, Federal Security Administrator, said last night that the only way to improve the health and life expectancy of the Negro people was through a program of national health insurance. The speaker said that Negroes had a shorter life expectancy than whites and that forty-seven Negro babies died for every thousand live births, while twenty-nine white babies died for that number of live births.[7]

> The problems of welfare have been intensified in the last generation not only by

the increasing number of aged and children, but also by many factors . . . such as the break-up of families, which means more aid to dependent children and child welfare, and by the lack of adequate housing.[8]

The above quotations summarize some of the problems discussed in this book—and each statement is at least 30 years old. The fact that the issues, and to a considerable extent the proposed policy solutions, discussed here have persisted for so long may simply increase the frustration and disillusionment of the reader. We certainly are not going to urge that you "be patient." Some of our problems cannot be excused. The fact that the life expectancy of black persons in 1952 was shorter than the life expectancy of whites, for example, and continues to be shorter in the 1980s, is unconscionable. But it should be emphasized that the problems discussed here have been the result of long-term historical, social, and political practices (e.g., gender and social inequality), or macroeconomic cyclical trends (e.g., inflation, recession), or simply are very difficult to solve given their nature and the realities of U.S. politics and culture. This is not to suggest that they are unsolvable or that we as citizens should be any more patient with policy makers. Certainly, to suggest patience to a handicapped child who wants a chance for a decent education, or to a black person who wants better access to the "American dream," would be callous. Nevertheless, it is necessary for us to understand that all that is wrong in the United States is not necessarily the result of the ineptitude or malevolence of public policy makers. Some problems, we suspect, will never be *completely* solved, and future generations will seek solutions for a long time to come. That is simply the reality of the situation.

WE HAVE COME A LONG WAY

The final point may be, for some of the readers, the most controversial. Stated most simply, despite the fact that in many of the policy areas discussed in this book we, as a nation, have a long way to go, it is clear that we have come a long way as well over the past several decades. For example, in 1940 nonwhites in this country could expect to live, on the average, 11.1 years *less* than whites (53.1 years compared to 64.2 years). In 1979 nonwhites could expect to live 4.5 years less than whites (69.9 years to 74.4 years). Similarly, in 1940 the infant mortality rate among nonwhites was 73.8 per 1,000 live births compared to 43.2 for whites. By 1978 it was 39.7 for nonwhites compared to 27.2 for whites. To the extent that the differences in longevity and infant mortality are a function of political, social, and economic factors, any difference should be deemed unacceptable by both whites and nonwhites. Nevertheless, progress has been made.

Similarly, progress has been made in other areas as well. As we noted in the chapter on education, blacks have virtually closed the gap with whites in terms of median school years completed: in 1940 whites completed 8.6 years compared to 5.7 years for blacks, while in 1980 whites completed 12.5 years compared to 12.0 years for blacks. In 1967 only 19.2 percent of all females 18 to 24 years old were enrolled in college compared to 33.1 percent of all males. In 1978 the difference between males and females had declined significantly: 27.1 percent of the males and 23.7 percent of the 18- to 24-year-old females were enrolled in college. Here too, any differences in educational attainment which are a function of discriminatory social and political practices are unacceptable. But progress has been made.

Another area of progress has been in home ownership. In 1940 only 23.6 percent of all minority persons owned the home which they occupied, compared to 46 percent of all whites. In 1979, however, minority home ownership had nearly doubled to 44.5 percent, compared to 68.4 percent for whites. This, of course, does not say anything about the differences in quality, location, or value of homes. Nevertheless, it does appear to be an improvement.

Finally, as we noted in Chapter 2, the number and percentage of people who fall below the official poverty level have declined from 39.5 million or 22.4 percent of the population in 1959, to 31.8 million or 14 percent of the population in 1981. In addition, while in 1959, 55.1 percent of all blacks fell below the official poverty level, in 1981, 34.2 percent did so. Again, we must emphasize that we are not applauding the fact that one-third of all blacks in the United States are impoverished. Nor do we think that one should ignore the point that progress has been made.

Clearly, there are some policy areas where it is difficult to be sanguine about what we have achieved as a nation. After one acknowledges all of the caveats about crime statistics and what they represent, it is still hard to avoid the conclusion that we in the United States today *are* less secure in our persons and property than our parents and grandparents were in their day. In addition, despite the undeniable advances which minorities have made in many areas, the ratio of minority to white unemployment has remained constant at approximately 2:1 over the last three decades. And the median income ratio between nonwhite and white families also has remained constant over the last few decades, with nonwhite families earning only between 50 to 60 percent of what white families earn.

For a nation that is committed to providing equal opportunities for all our citizens regardless of race, creed, or gender we have achieved a great deal relative to our own past. In terms of what we *should* achieve, and what other nations have achieved, we have a long way to go. For the student who wishes to gauge our progress along the way, we suggest as a rough rule of thumb that things will not be quite as bad as liberals argue, or quite as good as conservatives argue.

NOTES

1 Thomas Babington Macaulay, *Speeches* (London: Longman, Brown, Green and Longman's, 1854), pp. 436, 437, as quoted in Jack H. Schuster, "Out of the Frying Pan: The Politics of Education in a New Era," *Phi Delta Kappan,* 63 (May 1982), 583.

2 Alexis de Tocqueville, *Democracy in America, I* (New York: Vantage Books, 1955), p. 3.

3 Louis Hartz, *The Liberal Tradition in America* (New York: Harcourt, Brace and World, 1955); and Robert Dahl, *Pluralist Democracy in the United States: Conflict and Consent* (Chicago: Rand McNally, 1967).

4 *New York Times,* May 18, 1951.

5 *New York Times,* Apr. 12, 1950.

6 *New York Times,* Jan. 14, 1952.

7 *New York Times,* Jan. 17, 1952.

8 *New York Times,* Nov. 4, 1951.

INDEX